Handicap-Disability-Learning and Living Difficulties:
Policy and Practice in Different European Settings

EUROPEAN SOCIAL INCLUSION
SOZIALGEMEINSCHAFT EUROPA

EDITED BY WOLF BLOEMERS · FRITZ-HELMUT WISCH

VOL. 1

PETER LANG

Frankfurt am Main · Berlin · Bern · Bruxelles · New York · Oxford · Wien

WOLF BLOEMERS · FRITZ-HELMUT WISCH (EDS.)

HANDICAP – DISABILITY
LEARNING AND LIVING DIFFICULTIES:
POLICY AND PRACTICE IN DIFFERENT EUROPEAN SETTINGS

EUROPEAN MODULE
EU-SOCRATES PROGRAMME

PETER LANG
Europäischer Verlag der Wissenschaften

Die Deutsche Bibliothek - CIP-Einheitsaufnahme

Handicap disability learning and living difficulties : policy and practice in different European settings / Wolf Bloemers ; Fritz-Helmut Wisch (eds.). - Frankfurt am Main ; Berlin ; Bern ; Bruxelles ; New York ; Oxford ; Wien : Lang, 2000
 (European social inclusion ; Vol. 1)
 ISBN 3-631-35564-5

ISSN 1615-2506
ISBN 3-631-35564-5
US-ISBN 0-8204-4706-4

© Peter Lang GmbH
Europäischer Verlag der Wissenschaften
Frankfurt am Main 2000
All rights reserved.

All parts of this publication are protected by copyright. Any utilisation outside the strict limits of the copyright law, without the permission of the publisher, is forbidden and liable to prosecution. This applies in particular to reproductions, translations, microfilming, and storage and processing in electronic retrieval systems.

Printed in Germany 1 2 3 4 6 7

CONTENT

	EDITORS' PREFACE	9
0.	**STARTING POINTS**	**12**
0.1	RATIONALE - HOW THE MODULE BEGAN	13
0.2	CHRONICLE OF THE GROUP	13
0.3	AIMS	13
0.4	OVERVIEW OF THE CHAPTERS	14
0.5	STRUCTURES IN THE THREE PARTICIPATING COUNTRIES	14
0.6	TEACHING AND LEARNING APPROACHES	15
0.7	METHODS OF ASSESSMENT	15
0.8	WHAT STUDENTS CAN BRING TO THE EUROPEAN MODULE	16
0.9	LITERATURE AND KEY TEXTS	16
1.	**EUROPEAN IDENTITY ?** **Wolf Bloemers**	**19**
1.1	INTRODUCTION	19
1.1.1	OBJECTIVES	20
1.1.2	LEARNING OUTCOMES	21
1.2	WHAT IS EUROPE? WHO (WHAT) ARE EUROPEANS?	22
1.3	HOW AND WHY DOES IDENTITY EVOLVE?	27
1.4	HOW DO "EUROPEANS" VIEW EUROPE?	34
1.5	WHAT SHOULD EUROPE LOOK LIKE? HOW SHOULD IT DEVELOPE? IS THERE A "NEED FOR EUROPE"?	40
1.6	(HOW) CAN WE BECOME EUROPEANS?	45
1.7	TASKS TO BE UNDERTAKEN	55
1.8	BIBLIOGRAPHY	56
1.8.1	REFERENCES	56
1.8.2	ADDITIONAL READINGS	61
2.	**LOOKING BACK - HISTORY OF DISABLEMENT** **David Johnstone**	**62**
2.1	INTRODUCTION	62

2.1.1	OBJECTIVES	62
2.1.2	LEARNING OUTCOMES	63
2.2	A CHRONOLOGICAL HISTORY OF DISABLEMENT IN EUROPE	63
2.2.1	THE BEGINNINGS OF PROVISION FOR DISABLED PEOPLE	65
2.2.2	THE PURPOSE AND PHILOSOPHY OF EUGENICS	68
2.2.3	THE RELATIONSHIP OF EUGENICS THEORY TO DISABILITY	69
2.3	TASKS TO BE UNDERTAKEN	71
2.4	BIBLIOGRAPHY	72
2.4.1	REFERENCES	72
2.4.2	ADDITIONAL READINGS	73
3.	LOOKING AT TODAY	74
3.1	CONTEMPORARY PERCEPTIONS OF DISADVANTAGE David Johnstone	74
3.1.1	INTRODUCTION	74
3.1.2	OBJECTIVES	75
3.1.3	LEARNING OUTCOMES	76
3.1.4	THE INDIVIDUAL TRAGEDY OR MEDICAL MODEL	76
3.1.5	THE SOCIAL MODEL OF DISABILITY	77
3.1.6	DISABILITY AND QUALITY OF LIFE	79
3.1.7	QUALITY OF LIFE: AN ETERNAL PARADOX?	81
3.1.8	QUALITY OF LIFE AS AN ARRAY OF VARIABLES	82
3.1.9	THE CONNECTION BETWEEN DISABILITY AND SPECIAL EDUCATIONAL NEEDS	86
3.1.10	FROM INTEGRATION TO INCLUSION	92
3.1.11	TASKS TO BE UNDERTAKEN	93
3.1.12	BIBLIOGRAPHY	93
3.1.12.1	REFERENCES	93
3.1.12.2	ADDITIONAL READINGS	94
3.2	POLICY VERSUS PRACTICE Bengt Eriksson	95
3.2.1	INTRODUCTION	95
3.2.2	OBJECTIVES	97
3.2.3	LEARNING OUTCOMES	98

3.2.4	WHAT IS "SOCIAL POLICY"?	98
3.2.4.1	CONSENSUS - KEY CONCEPT IN THE DISCOURSE OF SOCIAL POLICY	100
3.2.4.2	SOCIAL POLICY IN GERMANY, ENGLAND AND SWEDEN	103
3.2.4.3	BASIC LEGISLATIVE SOCIAL POLICY DOCUMENTS AND SPECIFIC RULES AND REGULATIONS CONCERNING DISABLED PEOPLE IN THE THREE COUNTRIES	107
3.2.4.4	WHAT DOES REALITY LOOK LIKE?	109
3.2.4.5	POLICY VERSUS PRACTICE!	109
3.2.5	TASKS TO BE UNDERTAKEN	110
3.2.6	BIBLIOGRAPHY	111
3.2.6.1	REFERENCES	111
3.2.6.2	ADDITIONAL READINGS	111
3.3	POWER, POLITICS AND USER INVOLVEMENT Åse-Britt Falch	113
3.3.1	INTRODUCTION	113
3.3.2	OBJECTIVES	115
3.3.3	LEARNING OUTCOMES	115
3.3.4	ADVOCACY, GROUPWORK AND EMPOWERMENT	116
3.3.4.1	DIFFERENT CONCEPTIONS AND BACKGROUND OF ADVOCACY AND EMPOWERMENT	116
3.3.4.2	GROUPWORK, GROUPPROCESS, SELF-HELP-GROUPS AND SELF-DIRECTED GROUPWORK	119
3.3.4.3	PARTICIPATORY RESEARCH AND EMPOWERMENT	124
3.3.4.4	SOME EXAMPLES	125
3.3.5	TASKS TO BE UNDERTAKEN	127
3.3.6	BIBLIOGRAPHY	128
3.3.6.1	REFERENCES	128
3.3.6.2	ADDITIONAL READINGS	129
4.	LOOKING FORWARD - MANAGEMENT OF CHANGES Fritz-Helmut Wisch	130
4.1	INTRODUCTION	130
4.1.1	OBJECTIVES	130
4.1.2	LEARNING OUTCOMES	131

4.1.3	CULTURE OF ORGANISATIONAL STRUCTURES: ROLES OF INDIVIDUALS	131
4.1.3.1	THE HIERARCHICAL STEP MODEL	131
4.1.3.2	THE INTERACTIVE CIRCLE-MODEL	134
4.1.3.3	COMMUNICATION SKILLS	136
4.1.3.4	CLIENT-ORIENTATED COMMUNICATION	137
4.1.3.5	THE NEED OF CHANGE WITHIN AND BETWEEN INDIVIDUALS	138
4.1.3.6	INVESTIGATION AND ANALYSIS OF THE CHANGING STRUCTURE AND MANAGEMENT OF AN ORGANISATION OF/FOR DISABLED/DISADVANTAGED PEOPLE	141
4.1.3.7	VISIONARY CONSTRUCT FOR NEW PROVISIONS IN RELATION TO DISABLED/DISADVANTAGED PEOPLE	143
4.1.4	TASKS TO BE UNDERTAKEN	145
4.1.5	BIBLIOGRAPHY	145
4.1.5.1	REFERENCES	145
4.1.5.2	ADDITIONAL READINGS	147
5.	EUROPEAN IDENTITY !	148
	Wolf Bloemers	
5.1	SUMMARY AND PERSPECTIVES	148
5.2	TASKS TO BE UNDERTAKEN	151
5.3	BIBLIOGRAPHY	151
5.3.1	REFERENCES	151
5.3.2	ADDITIONAL READINGS	152
6.	**PORTFOLIO TASKS / PROPOSALS**	153
	INDEX	155
	ABOUT THE AUTHORS	158
	ADDRESSES OF THE UNIVERSITIES	159

EDITORS' PREFACE

This book has originally been designed by five authors as a handbook for students of remedial, special and social education for a "Euro-Module" that has been taught regularly since 1998/99 in the curricula of

- Edge Hill University College, Ormskirk (England)
- Karlstad Universitet, Karlstad (Sweden)
- University of Applied Sciences, Magdeburg (Germany).

This edition represents the first volume of altogether three modules of which each one is independent. However, they base on one another.

The modules represent separate study units, which are to be completed by an examination and graded by credit points. These credit points can be accumulated for the entirety of study units in a study programme of comparably and consecutively organised study courses (Bachelor/Master). Credit points are considered compatible by other universities. In order to obtain nationally and internationally comparable structures and grading systems of so far relatively different academic majors and degrees (e.g. Bachelor, Master, Diploma, State Examination, Licentiate etc.), it is advantageous and essential to modulate and introduce a system of credit points.

Euro-Modules are study units that are developed with the financial support of the European Union within the Socrates Programme by at least three European universities. Those universities agreed upon the implementation of the modules in their curricula. The modules contain a European dimension, that is they are characterised by a plurinational and/or supranational focus, which aims at a multiperspective thinking beyond national borders and, thereby, encourage a common "European" acting.

The chapters of this Euro Module are to be seen as *introductions* into different problems of past, current and future living conditions of disabled and disadvantaged people from three European perspectives, that is from ways of thinking that have been influenced by three different cultures.

This book is obligatory for all participating students and serves as a common basic text. It furthermore demonstrates problems in the European context and is a starting point for further consolidating self-studies. Additionally, it is a basis for discussions concerning an "active engagement" with regard to a term paper and a thereby involved diverse exchange of ideas with other students from the partner universities via e-mail, video tape, fax or other means of communication.

Hence, despite different approaches on the authors' behalf, all chapters have the same principle: introduction, aims, learning outcomes, text, tasks and references. The content approximately meets the level of second year students. The Module is taught and written in English as well as in the correspondent native language. Thus, this volume is published in English and in the editors' native language, respectively. Some language problems derive from difficulties that occurred during the translation, which partly was made by students. We are hereby asking you to be lenient regarding the "European English" in some of the chapters.

Besides these didactic intentions and construction features aiming at the students, the authors want to address others active in the educational, psychological and socio-political field and those interested in issues of disablement, discrimination and integration. Thereby, they want to sensitise them for Europe orientated attitudes in the work with and for disabled and disadvantaged people and for respective European co-operation beyond boundaries. The communicative and dialogue encouraging design of the articles as well as the suggestions in the tasks are to give the readers impetuses in order to think critically and to act innovatively towards a future European social area.

In order to enlarge this Europe dedicated extension of ideas and actions regarding pedagogical and disability policy issues, we are publishing two further Euro-Modules (volume 2 and 3).

Euro-Module 2 ("Quality of Life Research and Disabled People - Ways to Research in Different European Settings") focuses on research issues and future tasks with regard to improving the living conditions of disabled and disadvantaged people in different European settings. Furthermore, it wants to sensitise and qualify for responsible acting within the field of action research.

The concluding volume - Euro-Module 3 - (Voices of Europe - Comparative Studies of Disabled People) represents an exemplary "application product" of the two previous modules: It documents reflection and research proceedings conducted by disabled people, students and professors as well as research results. Furthermore, it provides a "European Forum" for disabled people coming from three different countries so they will have the opportunity to present their personal stories and, additionally, facilitates an international and public exchange of experience as well as a communication process. Besides that, this volume is an encouragement, an action pattern and a learning aid (tool box) for participatory, practical research.

Magdeburg, January 2000　　　　　　　　　　　　Wolf Bloemers
　　　　　　　　　　　　　　　　　　　　　　　　Fritz-Helmut Wisch

0. STARTING POINTS

0.1 RATIONALE - HOW THE MODULE BEGAN

The idea for the development of this module has emerged from the Socrates programme for European co-operation and the shared thinking of partners in three European countries. In 1995 the Department of Social and Health Services of the Fachhochschule, Magdeburg and the Centre for Public Health Research in Karlstad with the Värmland University College of Health and Caring Services were already engaged in collaborative European initiatives. Edge Hill University College was invited to join the group in 1996. The starting point for the idea came with the belief of these higher education institutions that the social structure of Europe is changing. This change is emerging as a result of political and economic ideas in the European Parliament, Brussels and Luxembourg and which are causing all new Europeans to consider the meaning of the concept "social justice". But, change is also arising from the greater chances for mobility that arise from the opening-up of national borders and the expansion of the limits of human imagination.

From the outset, the programme structure of the European Modules have been developed in two parts:

Module 1 "Handicap – Disability, Learning and Living Difficulties: Policy and Practice in different European Settings"

Module 2 "Scientific Research Methods in the Field of Disabled persons"

Both modules are intended to develop a "shared body of knowledge" that focuses upon the opportunities for change from national to a European way of thinking about issues of disability and disadvantage.

The modules are intended to be included in the teaching programmes of each partner university. They are not designed to be combined with student mobility, in the first instance. Rather they are to be considered as providing opportunities for the exchange of ideas, materials and teaching personnel. In effect the modules are an attempt to begin a study and work a programme that can be taught and assessed in common in our three universities.

The central co-ordination of the modules is undertaken by Prof. Dr. Wolf Bloemers, the Fachhochschule Magdeburg.

0.2 CHRONICLE OF THE GROUP

Module 1 has been constructed by individual university academics in three countries: Germany, Sweden, and the United Kingdom. All the contributors are involved in some aspect of working with individuals who have been either described as "handicapped", "disabled", or in some sense "disadvantaged". It has also been a feature of the research work in the three universities involved. However, no matter the strength of these individual commitments, none of this work could have been developed without the financial help and assistance of the funds from the SOCRATES programme.

During the development of module 1 there have been opportunities for the authors to work together in each of the partner countries. These workshop sessions have both been academically and professionally rewarding. They have also helped to cement personal friendships. Lecture/seminars have been conducted by the authors in Sweden and Germany with students on courses in Health and Social Care.

0.3 AIMS

The module sets out to consider a number of important aims:

- To develop and share a common awareness of a European identity;
- To challenge and overcome national perceptions of disadvantage;
- To develop improved understanding through a common body of knowledge;
- To contribute to the progressive development of vocational and professional opportunities in the "caring" services across Europe;
- To gain skills to critically analyse, reflect and develop new theoretical and practical insights.

0.4 OVERVIEW OF THE CHAPTERS

The five chapters that make up module 1 are deliberately intended to be interactive and to encourage students to engage with the writer and to critically consider the points of view expressed.

Chapter 1 - European Identity? asks students to consider what constitutes being European are there any shared visions? What are the personal values and beliefs about European identity? The question mark in the chapter title is deliberate and is intended to set you asking questions.

Chapter 2 - Looking Back – The History of Disability, explores some of the historical associations between, disability, disadvantage, and the marginalisation of disabled people in a European context.

Chapter 3 - Looking at Today, is written in three sections and forms the main focus of the module; section 3. i) Contemporary Perceptions of Disadvantage explores the present circumstances of people in Europe with learning and living difficulties; section 3. ii) Policy versus Practice examines the various forms of legislation and services that have been constructed to meet the social needs of disadvantaged people and section 3.iii) Power, Politics and User involvement is an exploration of advocacy and empowerment.

Chapter 4 - Looking Forward – Management of Changes, considers the management of changes in both communication and the possibilities for the future. The possible meaning of a culture of disability and disadvantage in a European context is also explored.

Chapter 5 - European Identity! Summarises many of the issues previously explored and rases new questions for you to consider. This concluding chapter invites students to reflect upon the consideration of what it means to be disadvantaged and marginalised in Europe.

All the chapters have been designed to encourage students to consider the future direction of services for disabled and disadvantaged people.

Hopefully your thinking will have been affected by studying the contents of this module!

0.5 STRUCTURES IN THE THREE PARTICIPATING COUNTRIES

The authors of the chapters of this module are all attached to university departments that are training students to work with disabled people. All the authors have both a theoretical and practical awareness of issues and have contributed their knowledge and expertise to the writing of these modules. It is considered that the level of study to be undertaken is comparable with that of a Bachelor degree in each of our countries.

The common language for writing and teaching the module is English. Although all countries have differences in their entry requirements, it is important to have at least a basic level qualification in English language. Students choosing to study the modules will be a minimum of 19 years of age, although in general most will be older. Students who are interested in knowing more about the prospectus and modular structure of courses in Karlstad, Magdeburg and Ormskirk are advised to seek out details from individual university prospectuses.

0.6   TEACHING AND LEARNING APPROACHES

The teaching approach suggested for studying the European module programme is one of "active engagement". Students are encouraged to recognise that study can draw upon a number of disciplines, in order to understand the historical and contemporary circumstances of disabled people.

At various points in each chapter students are expected to engage in some self-study tasks, in order to sharpen their thinking. There are also "formative" study tasks within each chapter and a range of final or summative assignments to be undertaken as a course requirement. These are described at the end of the book. Supporting literature and additional readings are provided to each chapter. Texts in German, Swedish and English provide students with a range of choices to encourage their reading.

0.7   METHODS OF ASSESSMENT

Students will be assessed using a variety of methods. Throughout the module students will be asked to carry out formative tasks either as individuals or in small groups. The final "summative" assignment is in the form of a portfolio. This offers students a range of approaches including video, essays and dramatic representations for the presentation of evidence. Students are required to achieve a minimum grade of 60% to achieve a passing grade.

The final student portfolio will be assessed against the following dimensions:

- Introduction   5%
- Literature review   20%
- Theoretical Links   25%
- Critical Analysis   30%
- Structure/presentation 5%
- Conclusion   15%

It is anticipated that the portfolio will be completed in a minimum of 25 hours. Students will be invited to evaluate the effectiveness of the modules, the teaching and the demands they have made, at the conclusion of the modules.

0.8 WHAT STUDENTS CAN BRING TO THE EUROPEAN MODULE

Students are asked to be actively involved in the study of this module. It is anticipated that the total length of study time will vary between 150 and 200 hours. This includes lecture, Seminar/workshops and private study time.

0.9 LITERATURE AND KEY TEXTS

It is difficult to identify any one book that can cover all the sections of this module. However, the following texts are provided in English and German as indicative reading. We consider them to be useful and informative.

English Texts

Journals
Shakespeare T. &
Watson N. (1997)   Defending the Social Model of Disability, *Disability and Society* 12, 2, 293-298

Books
Chapter 1
Daunt, P (1991)   *Meeting Disability – A European Response*, London Cassell

Chapter 2
Hevey, D. (1992) *The Creatures Time Forgot*, London, Routledge
Oliver, M. (1990) *The Politics of Disablement*, London, Macmillan

Chapter 3.i
Johnstone, D. (1998) *An Introduction to Disability Studies*, London, Fulton
McKnight, J. (1995) *The Careless Society*, New York, Basic Books

Chapter 3.ii
Swain, J. Finkelstein V., French, S. et al (1996) *Disabling Barriers – Enabling Environments*, London, Sage
Johnstone, D (1998) *An Introduction to Disability Studies*, London, Fulton
Coleridge, P. (1994) *Disability, Liberation and Development*, London, Oxfam

Chapter 3.iii
Campbell, J and Oliver, M. (1996) *Disability Politics: understanding our past changing our future*, London, Routledge
Gooding, C. (1994) *Disabling Laws, Enabling Acts*, London, Pluto

Chapter 4
Billis, D and Harris, M. (1996) *Challenges of Organisation and Management*, London, Macmillan
Mullins, L. (1996) *Management and Organisational Behaviour*, London, Pitman

Chapter 5
Christensen, C and Rizvi, R. (1996) *Disability and the Dilemmas of Education and Justice*, Buckingham, Open University Press

German Texts

Bauman, U. & Klesczewski, R. (Hrsg.), (1997) *Penser I` Europa – Europa denken*. Tübingen und Basel, France Verlag

Möckel, A. (1988) *Geschichte der Heilpädagogik*. Stuttgart, Klett-Cotta

Opp, G. &Peterander, F. (Hrsg.), (1996) *Focus Heilpädagogik – Projekt Zukunft*, München, E. Reinhardt

Bundesministerium für Arbeit und Sozialordnung (1997): *EURO – ATLAS; Soziale Sicherheit im Vergleich*, Bonn

Theunissen, G. & Plaute, W. (1996) *Empowerment und Heilpädagogik*, Freiburg im Breisgau, Lambertus

Belz, H. & Siegrist, M. (1997) *Kursbuch Schlüsselqualifikationen, Ein Trainingsprogramm*, Freiburg im Breisgau, Lambertus

Schleicher, K. & Bos, W. (Hrsg.), (1994) *Realisierung der Bildung in Europa*, Darmstadt, Wissenschaftliche Buchgesellschaft

1. EUROPEAN IDENTITY?

Wolf Bloemers

1.1 INTRODUCTION

This component deals with the problem of a European partnership at the social level.

Does such a partnership - often propagated, desired, evoked, doubted - actually exist? Is it a myth, a tradition, a fact, or a suggestion? Is it a necessity? If so, for what purpose? What influences might possible 'European' cultural traditions exert upon processes of socialization, and how might answers to these questions contribute to the future development of forms of living more suitable to man? How, specifically, can an internalized European awareness contribute to the emergence of public-spirited forms of cooperation?

In this chapter, we will attempt to present an in-depth investigation into aspects of history, politics, language, art, literature, religion, and everyday culture - in other words, into manifestations of human activity in Europe - and, in doing so, will attempt to look for answers to the question of 'European' identity.

The complexities; interdisciplinary nature; and diverse political, subjective , and national perspectives inherent to this topic must force us to limit this chapter - as regards the module - to an approach that focuses on selected aspects only yet to one that can pave the way to a more extensive, rational treatment.

In lieu of an exhaustive and systematic approach, we have chosen to concentrate on a didactic presentation of basic problems and facts, which - by means of a treatment of selected aspects, details, and areas - should help

- to increase knowledge,
- to harness reflective capability,
- to foster critical understanding and awareness

as regards the question of European identity.

The chapter will deal with:

- our image of Europe: *What is Europe? Who (what) are Europeans?*
- the sense of belonging: *How does identity arise and to what end?*
- national and supranational perceptions and attitudes: *How do 'Europeans' see Europe?*
- the need for Europe/ideas for the future: *What should Europe look like? How should it develop? Is there a 'need for Europe'?*
- processes of learning and conveying: *(How) Can we become Europeans?*

1.1.1 OBJECTIVES

Students shall:

- identify and critically assess dimensions of European culture and history
- consider identity of place, nation, neighbourhood, and community in the European context
- critically evaluate the role of language, belief systems, architecture, art, and literature
- critically consider the emergence of "new" belief systems (movements) explaining disadvantage in Europe
- perceive the development of elements in European awareness as an educational task

Work related to this component may be structured as follows:

- factual information in the form of literature (given here) and lectures
- independent study of recommended literature
- term papers containing an analysis of source material
- leading seminar sessions devoted to an examination of presented theses
- development of dossiers consisting of current (audio-visual) materials
- oral reports
- possible field trips to relevant institutions

- creation of wall collages
- conducting and evaluating interviews
- analysis of the language used in political texts

1.1.2 LEARNING OUTCOMES

At the end of the chapter students will have acquired:

- knowledge of the many different sources of European culture and European common understanding
- an overview of the processes of developing identity and of the controversies and challenges that arise from overlapping identities
- a critical awareness of the lack of social and communicative participation in the creation of a united European political body
- an awareness of the personal contribution required for the building of the concept of the "unity of Europe"

Internationalization, globalization, Europeanization - these international tendencies towards amalgamation and supranational cooperation are developments that can be seen worldwide. Increasingly, they have begun to transform the way we live together and our membership in traditional communities. They also have led to a greater feeling of insecurity. New ideas, ways of life, policies, means of communication, economic alliances, and means of transportation have started to threaten traditional structures and must thereby be approached in new ways. In no small way does this apply to fringe groups, which would include the so-called "handicapped" people.

How will these matters affect remedial education? Is it necessary, desirable, sensible to Europeanize this area as well? What would that mean and imply? Are there physically disabled, so called "handicapped" individuals who are 'European'? Does being disabled possess a European dimension? Is there such a thing as European remedial education? Should there be such a thing?

Before we can examine these more specific questions, we must discuss existing perceptions of 'Europe' basically. Existing opinions and definitions regarding this concept tend to be so varied, multifaceted, and controversial that this artifact called 'Europe' will remain diffuse and open to manipulation unless we endeavor to clarify the concept rationally in order to gain a common understanding and a common ground for communication.

1.2 WHAT IS EUROPE? WHO (WHAT) ARE EUROPEANS?

How do you view the following answers?

1) 'One becomes a European upon becoming a civis romanis' (Curtius 1969, 22)

2) 'The idea of the universal unity of man is the idea of European mankind. Europe owes its civilization to this idea; only for this idea does it exist.' (Dostojewsky)

3) 'Each European consists of a battleground of passions, wills, and characters. In each European, one will find his/her ancestors killing and raping one another.` (Coudenhove-Kalergi, 1949)

These are three views taken from a vast array of views that try to pinpoint that which is common to Europeans and typical for being a European. (Do you know of any pertinent definitions that are the same or perhaps different?)

To understand these views, it is necessary to realize that they are based upon fundamental attitudes and contexts (anthropological, political, national, etc.) as well as upon individual preconceptions.

By failing to link these quotations to their proper background, we risk keeping them within the nebulous realm of the rhetorical or treating them as intellectual dazzle.(For a better background understanding, consult a literary encyclopedia or the actual sources.)

Though different in origin and intellectual approach, our three quotations are united by their authors' awareness of belonging the same entity and system of values and thus of being part of a community that transcends national boundaries.

These quotations reflect an attempt to identify with an envisioned set of values that could form the basis of a social community. Similarly, they reveal an attempt to develop or envision the awareness of belonging to a larger community. (The motives and structures leading to attempts at self-definition, collective self-interpretation, and the formation of awareness will be examined in more detail in the next section.)

Major political changes occurring on the international scene and the attempts to consolidate economic, political, and social structures have contributed to an emerging awareness of new forms of community. Thus, as regards Europe, we are posed with the challenge of searching for traditions and values and examining their capability of contributing to a shared set of values-real or imagined-upon which future social communities can be built.

'Without an awareness of Europe as being a historically justified, politically meaningful, and morally legitimized community, a European parliament will merely reflect the continent's national power structures: its economic power, population, the political alliances among its nations, and - owing to the absence of a recognizable and recognized common good in Europe - the constant need to go to Europe's highest court to sue for additional administrative norms' (Hentig 1993, 73).

Recourse to common European aspects can be approached in various ways. Individuals, social groups, artists, researchers, and politicians tend to uncover and interpret such aspects-actual or felt-by delving into historical constellations, intellectual traditions, symbolic references, social structures, and other roots. They do so according to perspectives based on interests or socialization.

Here is a brief outline of a few examples:

- *Supranational Cultural Assets That Embrace Europe:*

    The culture of antiquity was disseminated by the Roman emperors. Christianity spread with the help of monasteries (religion). The rule of Charlemagne in Germany and France, for example, contributed to our understanding of the concept of a dynastic progenitor . Other aspects include the Hanseatic League, the Reformation and Counterreformation, the Crusades, military consolidation against the Turks, artists and scholars as Europeans, scientific thought and the universities, aesthetics, *Regnum, Sacerdotium, Studium* (see Schleicher 1993, 4 ff).

- *Philosophical Structures*

    European human rights
    rights of the individual
    emergence of democracy
    money economy
    rule of law
    enlightenment
    (consult Jaspers 1947, 9)

    capitalism
    universal science
    predictability
    right to freedom
    idea of humanity

- *Literary Traditions*

    'We need not remind ourselves that, as Europe is a whole (and still, in its progressive mutilation and disfigurement, the organism out of which any greater world harmony must develop), so European literature is a whole, the several numbers of which cannot flourish, if the same blood-stream does not circulate throughout the whole body' (Eliot, cited in Assmann 1993, 98).

- *The Latinate Base*

    'Latinate means more than a common linguistic identity, such as that found among the speakers of the romance languages. It is the most succinct designation for a European mode of behavior that the European way of thinking has tried to create for the last 2000 years - despite all setbacks and relapses' (Eberle 1966, 230).

- *Basis of Values*

    'When asked to list the modes of living and behavior as well as the set of values that could be viewed as being specifically . . . European and that have been embraced the most, those questioned in a 1990 survey listed, peace (47%), democracy (38%), culture (33%) and quality of life (28%) . . . . Similar findings are revealed in a summary of survey results from the year 1989. According to these findings, a respect for basic human rights is seen as the common heritage of European political traditions and ideals. 78% of Europeans believe democracy to be the best of all forms of government. 60% believe that the preservation of human rights is a matter worthy of risk and sacrifice' (Eurobarometer of June 1990, p. 3; November 1989, p. 4, 31 ff.).

European culture and identity are based to no small degree 'upon the development of a society founded upon a respect for human rights, upon democracy, upon freedom of speech and thought, upon pluralism, . . .upon an awareness of a common cultural heritage, upon the desire build the future together . . . ' This is the foundation upon which the various European cultures should seek reconciliation and endeavor cooperation (Mulcahy 1992, 46).

Non-Europeans as well have dealt with perceptions of what is typically European

- *'Typical Associations'*

    Individualism and collective security, humanist traditions, dynamic economies, isolationism with a concurrent limited global responsibility (see Schleicher 1993, 2).

- *American Perspectives*

    'If asked as an American to describe what Europe means to me, I would start with the concept of liberation-in other words of being liberated from that which passes as culture in America. Diversity, earnestness, standards, the density of European culture create an Archimedic point from which, in thought, I can make the world move' (Sontag 1988, 131 f.).

Divisive elements, however, tend to be a specific characteristic of Europe as much as unifying aspects are. With regard to this, we present a limited selection of facts, developments, and relevant interpretations. These will help to reveal the heavily centrifugal and divergent tendencies that currently mark social and cultural developments on the continent and that show a striking contrast to the present economic and political efforts aimed at fostering unification (see McLean 1993, 264).

Of note are the following:

- Increasing regionalism, such as in Spain or Belgium
- new national boundaries (Czechia/Slovakia)
- ethnic exclusion and violence/genocide (Serbia, Croatia)
- segregation based on religion (Christianity/Islam)
- split between politics and law (bio-ethical-convention)
- the widening gap between rich and poor (unemployment/repelling Baltic contacts)

All of this has led to a Euroscepticism which, in turn, has made a common European identity - often claimed as a 'given' by the European Union - appear invalid. Divisive trends such as those just listed demonstrate that an inherited burden of nationalism, chauvinism, racism, and xenophobia have begun to endanger the creation of a common identity (see Bürli 1997, 18). Such a burden has been kept alive by deep-seated fears of anything foreign and by the dark characteristics found in each of us. It has led to inner alienation and has proved capable of preventing the emergence of a feeling of common identity.

Thus, we may also regard European identity as being

"... the way in which we are situated, geographically, historically, internationally and environmentally . What we once viewed as being barriers-the Vistula and the Rhine, the Alps and the Pyrenees, the North Sea and the Adriatic-have now become links, travel destinations, areas for contact and exchange, but also dangerous focal points. Rivers carry toxic waste from country to country. Countries bordering on a large body of water share its pollution. The windward side of mountains catches the acid rain originating in an area hundreds of kilometers away. National boundaries do not stop radioactive clouds. War, a burden passed along to us through the centuries, the destruction of our common natural environment, migration of the poor from areas void of a future to areas void of space-all of these phenomena will force us to think in continental terms. They will necessitate agreement on a basic curriculum of European convictions, without which the people(s) of Europe will not make the sacrifices and compromises demanded by today's situation.
Day-to-day political activity in Europe has shown the continent to have limited sensitivity towards its own public welfare, towards the development of a set of principles that serve to distinguish and to unite: we need only to cite the transportation of nuclear waste from one country to another, the use of common laws to control imports, above all, the virtual detachment with which the countries of Europe have been watching the occurrence of genocide in Yugoslavia. I do not wish to pass judgment. I have no conclusive idea of what could have been done. I simply notice the lack of action" (Von Hentig, 1993, 79f).

What is Europe? Who (what) are Europeans? On having reflected upon the previous outlines, we can join Bürli in observing:

'What has been consistent in the historical development of European civilization, culture, and politics have been, according to Künzli (1992)et. al., inconsistency, ambivalence, and skepticism. Europe has always been unsure when attempting to determine its cultural identity. Europe even has refused to allow total identification, thus permitting unrest and uncertainty to continue. When threatened from the outside and conscious of its own cultural identity, Europe has tended to question the superiority of its own values, thereby initiating a process of permanent self-criticism. Until now, Europe's educational heritage has been unable to contribute to the emergence of a common European awareness. Consequently, European identity is still characterized by diversity rather than uniformity' (Bürli 1979, 15).

This, however, also means 'that Europe has lost neither the awareness of a common European culture, of mutual ties, and of the mutual dependencies that govern the fate of all European countries nor the awareness of the necessity to cooperate' (Gorbatschow 1987, 258). An ethical imperative for the development of a common perspective is, therefore, justified.

ADDITIONAL, IN-DEPTH ASSIGNMENTS:

- Identify three visual artists whose significance, dimension, and quality could be described as European. Give clear examples and locate the place of these examples within a system of values and awareness to justify your choice.
- Identify three authors whose significance, dimension, and quality could be described as European. Give clear examples and locate the place of these example within a system of values and awareness to justify your choice.
- Identify three composers whose significance, dimension, and quality could be described as European. Give clear examples and locate the place of these examples within a system of values and awareness to justify your choice.
- Identify two art historical styles of which the significance, dimension, and quality could be described as European. Give specific examples and locate the place of these examples within a system of values and awareness to justify your choice.
- Give additional examples of the plurality and diversification of reality in European reality.
- Give a critical evaluation of the quotations given above, and justify your opinions.

1.3 HOW AND WHY DOES IDENTITY EVOLVE?

Thus far, we have made frequent reference to the concept of identity

When we refer to identity, we envision an equality or consensus among several things, people, or that which they have in common. Identity, to our understanding, also refers to authenticity and of being one's self. It is necessary to differentiate on the basis of

- an ego identity, which refers to the inner quality of identity: that is, to "the way each individual perceives his/her own situation and his/her own continuity and individuality according to the various types of experience gained in society" (GOFFMAN 1967, 132). Ego identity is based upon subjective perception, upon an inner image of the self.
- and a social identity: that is, man's routine, standardized self-placement into social categories. Social identity refers to membership in such a category

(e.g., student, German, soldier, etc.) (see GOFFMANN ibid. 10) and specifies group affiliation, participation in a system of roles, being like others.

Other sociological theories of identity (KRAPPMANN, THIMM, FREY) emphasize the demands made by others (by external influences) upon social identity. In their words, they emphasize our need to submit to general expectations dictated externally, our need to be like others, our need to submit to external processes of categorization.

All theories of identity have shown identity to be a balancing act between a self-image (ego identity), the identity that we assume others to have, and the actual identity of others, between ego-identity and social identity. They have shown that individuals wish to retain their self-identity, once it has been established, and to resist change. A secured place in a network of social bonds is a factor of particular high value, thus giving special priority to continuity as a basis for the preservation of identity. According to findings in developmental and social psychology, fundamental forms of identity tend, for the most part, to be shaped via processes of deculturation and socialization, particularly in a regional context, during the primary and secondary stages of socialization (family and school). Such processes of identity are characterized

- more by time rather than by space (see SCHLEICHER, 1974, 113)
- by the use of adherence strategies to avoid change
- by the development of awareness and of a set of values during early childhood rather than during adulthood and via a long-term rather than a short-term process.
- by identity needs based upon relatively stable environmental, cultural, and communication influences.

These characteristics clearly illustrate that psychological conditions pose a considerable threat to the search for new transnational similarities, to the search for a (new) European identity (see Schleicher,1974, 7). Moreover, research data in the area of political socialization indicate that basic attitudes towards ethnic and national identitiy are formed before puberty (TORNEY-PURTA et. al., 1986) and that the phenomena of ethnic experience and shared awareness tend to be older than the awareness of belonging to a nation-state. These phenomena tend to exert a stronger influence on populations than do new European identities created by others. To the same extent, religious affiliations that have emerged over a long period tend to be more binding and more conducive to the creation of identity than are identies created and dictated politically.

Enclosed social environments such as local geographical and cultural regions are factors influencing identity. They tend to be so, more than anonymous European superstructures, which are perceived as posing a threat to identity. "The significance of such identity factors can be seen in a comparison of the various degrees to which Europeans are willing to identify with local, regional, national, and European structures. According to a 1991 survey, considerably more citizens (85%+) feel are closer link to local,. regional, and national structures than to the European Community or to Europe as a whole (47%+). (See EUROBAROMETER, Dec. 1991, p.66).

Apparently, only half as many citizens feel as closely tied to the European Community as they do to their country or region. A comparison of countries indicates that local and regional ties are the most pronounced in Greece, Portugal, and Spain (local 73%+, regional 69%+). Strong national ties can be found in Greece but in Denmark and Ireland (72%+) as well. Generally, ties to the European Community are lower. In Spain, Italy, and Luxembourg, they tend to be somewhat noticeable (16%+) (ibid., p. 66f)."

Illustration 1: Degrees of identification with local, regional, national entities and with Europe

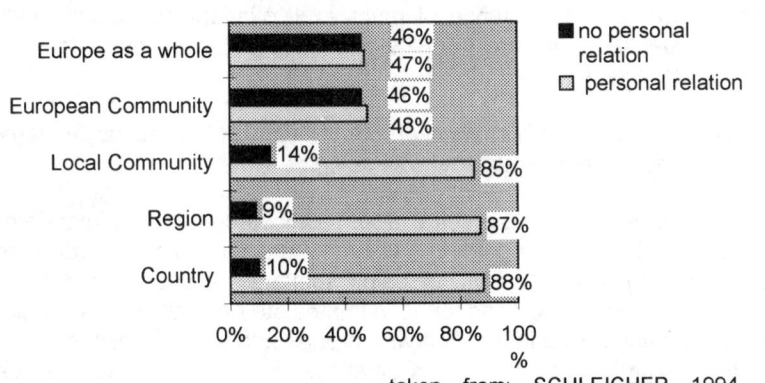

taken from: SCHLEICHER 1994, 108

Tab. 1: Degree of Attachment According to Country (given in percent)
(the 3 highest and lowest national values respectively)

Degree of Attachment	EG 12 ∅	highest						lowest
Community	54	GR 81	P 75	E 73	..	UK 42	F 40	NL 28
Region	55	GR 87	E 71	P 69	...	B 41	F 41	NL 34
Nation	53	GR 86	DK 84	IRL 72	...	D(Ost) 45	NL 40	B 30
EC	12	E 18	I 18	L 16	...	D(Ost) 8	UK 6	NL 4
Europe as a whole	12	I 19	E 18	GR 16	...	IRL 8	UK 8	NL 5

taken from: SCHLEICHER 1994, 108
Summarized according to Eurobarometer, Dec. 1991, A67.

These empirical findings convey the existence of a strong degree of attachment to local community structures situated within a small area. They also convey, however, the existance of multi-level, overlapping, double and particularistic identities that are non-static and characterized by dynamic processes and by variety.

The search for and maintenance of identity can be viewed as fundamental processes necessary to emotional well-being.

These processes regarding a self image, balanced between various demands made upon it externally, regarding a view of mankind and of the world, perpetrating a feeling of attachment, of being sheltered, and of being "at home" thrive best in a context of living found in immediate proximity to the self, in vital experience gained from interaction with groups and social constructions. This is particularly true when awareness develops in such a way that it serves to clarify identity through the pronounced self-participation and through varied processes of communication. Self-determined participation, active involvement in the creation of public-spirit convey a feeling of security in dealing with partners and peer groups, a feeling of validity and of having found the proper role in society.

With reference to Erikson, we can conclude by characterizing identity as a perceived agreement between the individual's self-image as a member of society, as a man or a woman, as a member of a vocational and a social group with the respective expectations imposed by society. This feeling of contentment on one's chosen path and the conviction of having done the right thing in the opinion of others affords us a feeling of security and satisfaction. It renders us reliable as a social partners, for we are acting within the framework set by our role in society-a role with which we can identify and which includes us in the general feeling of being part of a group identity (see SCHRAML 1976[6], 197).

In a pluralistic society -- above all, in one marked by fragile, rapid, and encompassing changes occuring in Europe today and in one making new demands and producing new groups, the search for identity has been made difficult. The validity of existing identity structures has been questioned. What has emerged in Europe is the all-too-well-known socio-emotioanl threat posed by a need to adhere to identitiy structures that confine and isolate, such as those offered by groups marked by rasicsm, fanatic religious views, or by other, similarly radical prejudiced views.

ADDITIONAL, IN-DEPTH TASKS:

- Identify several examples of current trends showing increased processes of ethnic identity and confinement. Try to explain these processes in a political and historical context.
- Identify several examples of current trends showing increased processes of identity and confinement based on region and on culture group. Try to explain these process in a political and historical context.
- Reflect upon your own identity or identities. List it/them as a noun/as nouns and try to explain whey/how this identitiy/these identities make you feel comfortable or not.
- Examine the interaction model showing FREY's concept of identity (taken from CLOERKES, G.: Sociology of the Handicapped 1997). discuss it with your classmates and try utilize it to find yourself, your own processes of identity. You can best accomplish this by giving concrete examples for the various headwords or by replacing the headwords with concrete examples. Illustration:
- One student describes his/her social status by saying "Professor X sees me as a student"
- He/she evaluates the indvidual: "Professor X views me as being intelligent and reserved/communicative"

- He/she has expectations regarding the individual: "Professor X expects me to do well on my exams."

Illustration 2: FREY'S model of interaction relating to the concept of identity
(taken from CLOERKES 1997, 163)

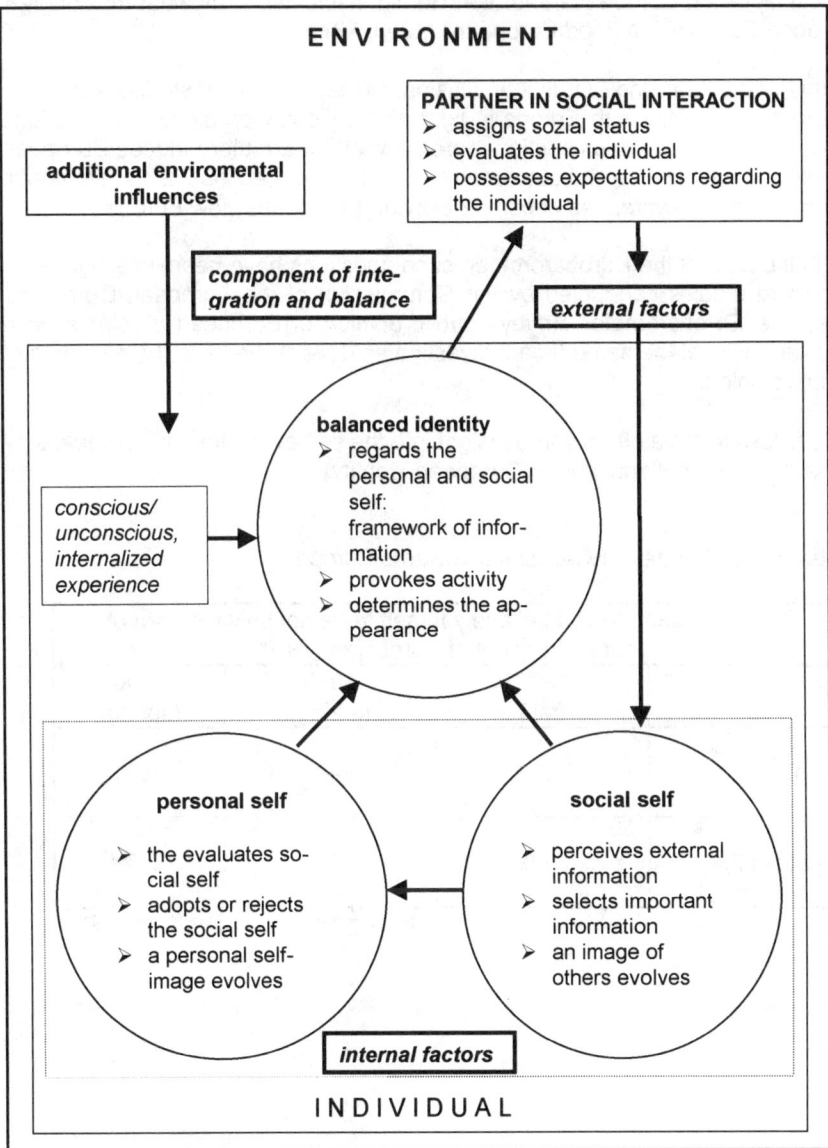

1.4 HOW DO "EUROPEANS" VIEW EUROPE?

In a chapter on Europe Hartmut von Hentig insinuates-somewhat mockingly?- "A good German is a good European" (1993, 73).

Is this wishful thinking? Or is it an illusion, perhaps even a distorted view? Are attempts to identify with Europe-in light of the identity problems and fixations described in the previous section-merely a wish, or are there indeed European identities that can be substantiated? How pronounced has a transnational, Euro-collective awareness become? How do Europeans view Europe?

With the help of the Eurobarometer, such questions have been investigated in empirical studies conducted by the Commission of the European Communities. The Eurobarometer surveys public opinion of European problems on a regular basis; at the same time it investigates developments in the evolution of public opinion.

The following table offers some insight into the self-evaluation of Europeans regarding their national and/or European identity.

Tab.2: The attitude of EC-Citizens Towards Europe

"To what extent do you believe yourself to be not only a citizen of your country but of Europe as well?"			
EC	1988 (fall)	1989 (spring)	1990 (spring)
often	16%	14%	15%
occationally	37%	34%	31%

taken from: SCHLEICHER 1994, 91

Tab. 3: Changes in Attitude within the EG (given in percent) (a ten-point scale, ranging from "very much" to " not at all," subdivided into 4 categories, two positives given)

	EC (10)								EC (12)			
	1975**		1985		1985		1989		1991			
	very much	some what	very much	somew hat	very much	somew hat	very much	somew hat	very much	somew hat		
overall satisfaction with life*	19	56	18	57	18	56	24	59	23	58		
positive attitude towards European unification	31	38	28	47	29	45	37	41	33	46		
			1986		1986							
Interest in political affairs of the EC	12	-	24	-	24	-	14	40	11	36		
Satisfaction with democratic processes	7	42	1985		1985							
	1977		8	42	10	42	10	47	7	43		
			1986		1986							
Significance of the European Parlament for the EC	10	27	13	40	11	38	15	44	13	43		
			1988		1988							
Affirmative attitude towards a unifiemarket	-	-	19	47	18	48	17	49	15	45		

*months of the survey: primarily October and November   **data are not availabble from all years
Eurobarometer 1974-91, S. 16ff., 34f., 74ff., 151ff., 178, 203f

Upon examination of table 2, we can notice that since 1988 there has been a drop in the willingness to identify with Europe. Table 2 conveys that there has been a constant decrease in attitudes oriented towards Europe since 1989. These negative trends have been caused by a variety of factors, not the least of which is the discrepancy between the-mainly positive-images and expectations that EC citizens have regarding Europe and the-largely negative-opinions that they harbor regarding the ability of politicians to realize political goals dealing with Europe.

The following 3 graphs show changes in the attitudes towards European and national identity. With the exception of Denmark, a more positive trend has emerged in general regarding the view that both identities-European and national-can be seen as being complementary.

Illustration 3: European and National Identity. Opposites or complementary?

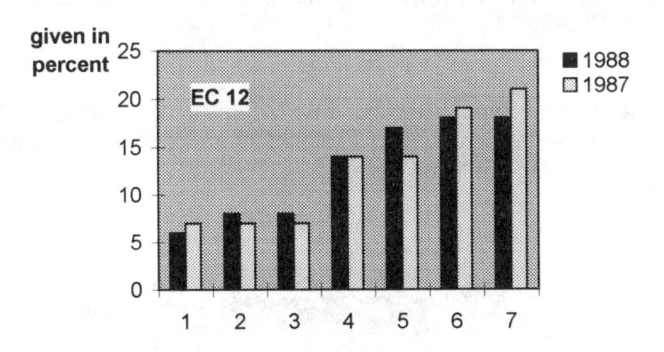

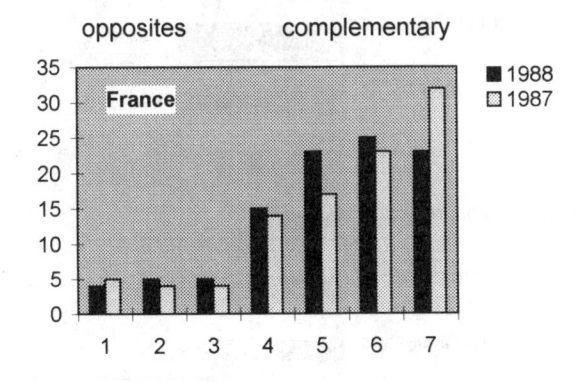

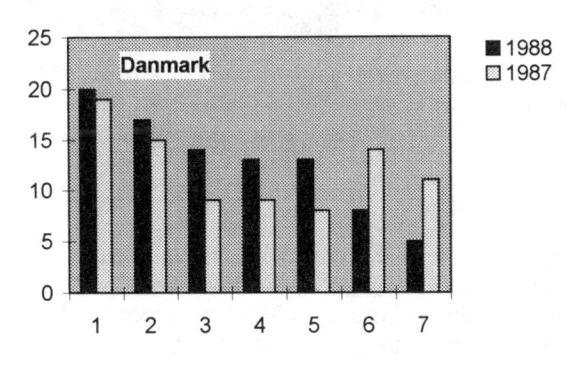

[Bar chart: EC 12, comparing 1988 and 1987, categories 1–7, y-axis "given in percent" 0–25]

[Bar chart: France, with "opposites" on left and "complementary" on right, comparing 1988 and 1987, categories 1–7, y-axis 0–35]

[Bar chart: Danmark, comparing 1988 and 1987, categories 1–7, y-axis 0–25]

taken from: SCHLEICHER 1994, 104

With regard to the level (national/supranational) on which political decisions should be made, the next illustration (4) may prove instructive (Eurobarometer, June 1993, p. 42, A26).

Illustration 4: Where Should Decisions Be Made: At the National or Supra national Level. (10 of a total of 20 areas of political decision-making are listed here.)

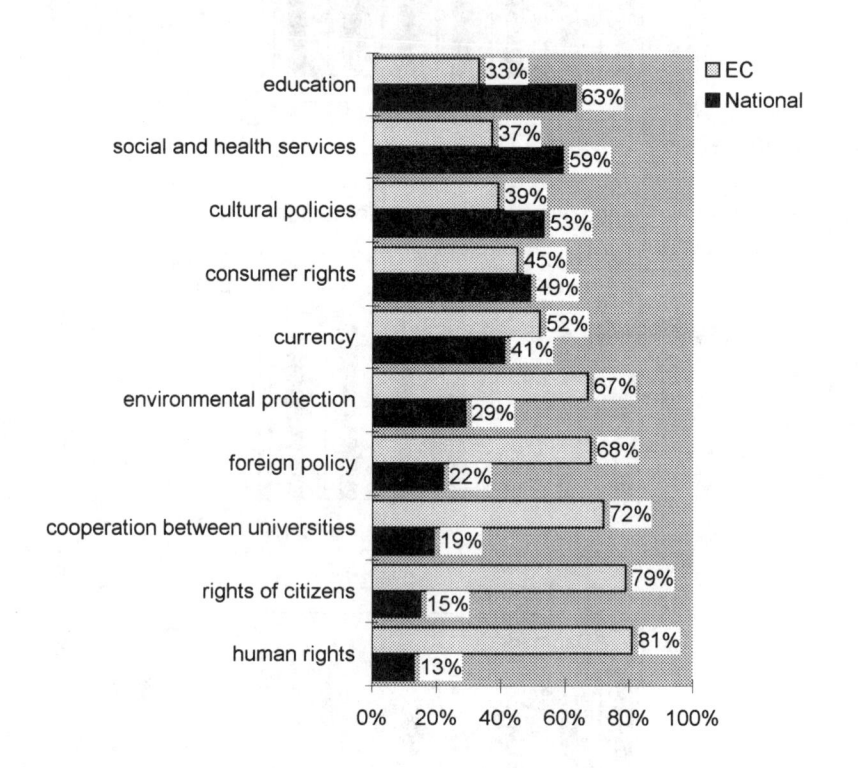

Area	EC	National
education	33%	63%
social and health services	37%	59%
cultural policies	39%	53%
consumer rights	45%	49%
currency	52%	41%
environmental protection	67%	29%
foreign policy	68%	22%
cooperation between universities	72%	19%
rights of citizens	79%	15%
human rights	81%	13%

Questions pertaining to human rights, the rights of citizens, cooperative efforts between universities, foreign policy, environmental protection, and money are seen mainly as tasks to be dealt with at a European level. In contrast, consumer rights, cultural policies, social and health services, as well as education are seen as belonging to the sphere of national responsibility. A 1991 survey conveyed similar findings regarding analogous areas of decision-making (illustration 5).

Illustration 5: Should the following areas be treated at a European or at a national level?

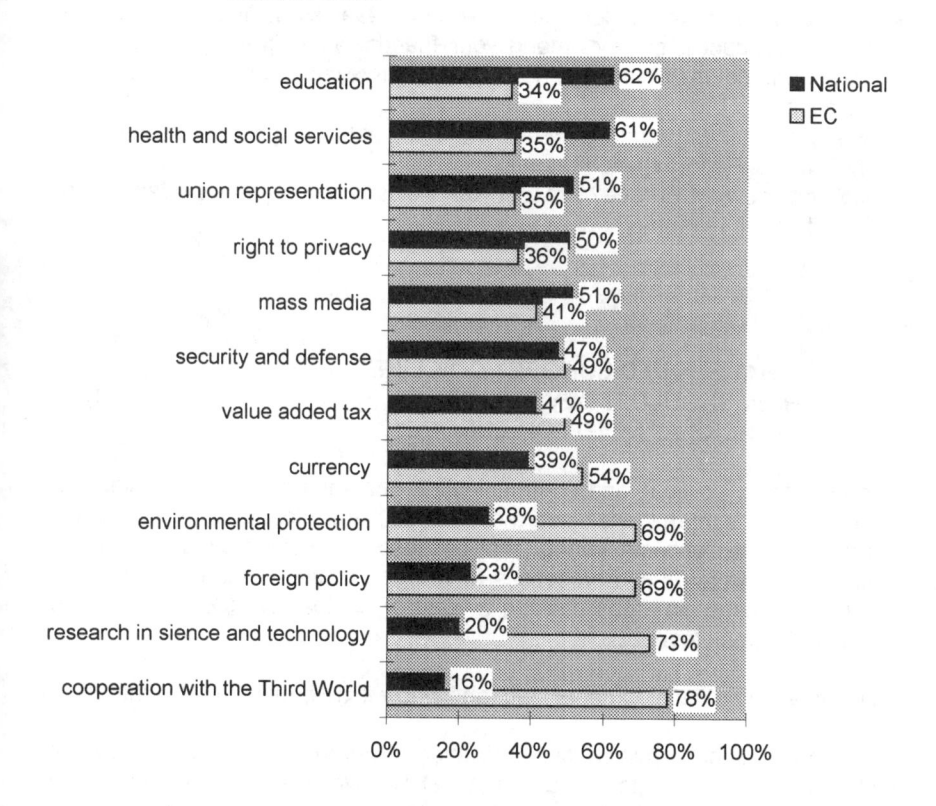

Area	National	EC
education	62%	34%
health and social services	61%	35%
union representation	51%	35%
right to privacy	50%	36%
mass media	51%	41%
security and defense	47%	49%
value added tax	41%	49%
currency	39%	54%
environmental protection	28%	69%
foreign policy	23%	69%
research in sience and technology	20%	73%
cooperation with the Third World	16%	78%

taken from: SCHLEICHER 1993,15

Source: Commission of the European Communities: Eurobarometer, No. 36. Brussels, Dec. 1991, p. 30. Illustration 5

In sum, we can maintain that "European" attitudes towards Europe vary throughout. They vary according to topic, nationality (we are reminded here of Denmarks initial rejection the Masstricht accord in a referendum held in that country), age (youths/older citizens), and social status.

ADDITIONAL, IN-DEPTH TASKS:

- Try to find the reasons for the drop, shown in table 2 and 3 (p. 28 and 29), in positive attitudes towards Europe. Make hypotheses, and test them against the sources given (e.g. SCHLEICHER (ed.) Realizing a European Educational Policy: European Awareness despite Cultural Identity? 1994, 91-136).
- On the basis of the problems surveyed in the tables and illustrations shown above, conduct a survey among your friends, acquaintances, and classmates and compare findings. Each group surveyed should comprise about 20 people.
- Ask your friends, acquaintances, and classmates to give the reasons for their views. Record these reasons.
- How do you view Europe? Present your views and how you experience your identity. Give reasons.

1.5 WHAT SHOULD EUROPE LOOK LIKE? HOW SHOULD IT DEVELOP? IS THERE A "NEED FOR EUROPE"?

The economic, political, and communication demands mentioned earlier and their national, supranational, supra-continental, and global dimensions have led to processes of restructuring that possess dimensions equally as great. Until now, however, these processes have been limited primarily to administrative and economic areas, leaving a want of comparable processes at the social and human level.

To what will such developments lead, and who will determine their course?

The economic and administrative unification of Europe is growing markedly at a steady pace; yet competition and a tendency towards separation have led to an ever increasing lack of an awareness capable of transcending national boundaries. The preservation of advantages existing at the national level (financial rebates, the policies towards asylum-seekers etc.) and the helplessness indeed, the failure-marking international crises (Bosnia/Albania/Kurd refugees) have shown how far Europe is still away to embrace an effective common identity on the level of international solidarity and loyalty.

Although Europe has become an economic and administrative unit, can it become a social unit?

Spatial units often remind us of rooms, which, in turn, form a house. In 1987, during Perestroika, Michael Gorbatschow, who at that time was President of the Soviet Union, offered us the image of a 'common European house'. In doing so, he pointed out that this image was not a illusion but rather the product of a careful analysis of the situation existing in Europe (1987, 254). This house, described about a decade ago, was seen as one in which each family had its own apartment and as one which even possessed various entrances: nonetheless, it offered common safeguards against fire and other catastrophic events. Only with the help of a common effort could this house be kept safe and sound (see 1987, 253). This implies a moral imperative, based upon the concept of common, mutual *responsibility*.

A few years later, though, in 1993, SCHLEICHER found that a blueprint was all that really existed of this "European House," which was still in need of real tenants (1993, 303). Let us use the house metaphor to raise the question as to why this problem exists. Is there a problem

a) in the constructional design of the house (i.e. in the goals)

b) with the builders, their training, their instructions, and their work methods (i.e. the methods of construction and of making the house livable)?

In this section, we will attempt to answer question a and will wait until the following chapter before dealing with answers to question b.

The previous section illustrated quite clearly that the majority of Europeans favors transnational goals and decision-making processes. Is there a viable set of values upon which all multicultural and multinational groups can really agree and with which they can truly identify?

Only the existence of what SMOLICZ (1985) refers to as *core values* - in other words, commonly recognized fundamental values embedded in an overarching system or framework of values binding two or more cultures - can ensure that a multicultural and multinational society is capable of functioning as a community that offers all of its members true and equal participation and access based on partnership. ANWEILER and KUEBART (1987) have related the significance of having a common set of basic values and ideological orientation markers to the ethnically pluralistic state of country of Canada. Integration based on the concept of 'Canadian citizenship' is the foundation for the awareness on the part of all Canadians of belonging to a common society. The threat of destabilization will tend to increase when there is a lack of common values serving to bind a multinational community with a common identity. The tragic fate of former Yugoslavia, a community that had been held together by force, demonstrates this point rather painfully.

How does all of this relate to our question regarding Europe's goals, regarding an end to interethnic strife and an ensuing creation of a humane European union - of a European community uniting all of its citizens with an inner awareness of being European?

What basic, fundamental values can be regarded as being *European* values that bind all European nationalities and the ethnic minorities living among them? The characteristic *language*, usually given high regard as an ethnic hallmark, cannot serve our purposes on account of the political recognition given to Europe's multilingual status. Thus, what can we use instead? Will the Euro as a common currency and mercantile symbol help fill the void? That is doubtful and is, actually, counterproductive as an answer to our question.

The question pertaining to Europe's goals, profile, and scale is the focus of various programs supported by the EC-Commission. Dealing primarily with education, these programs, such as ERASMUS, KOMMETT, FORCE, LINGUA, TEMPUS, SOKRATES and many others are designed to promote exchange, integration, and cooperation. They have helped plant the seeds of hope from which a new European identity can germinate. In some cases, though, germination has been stifled by tense animosities and irrational outbreaks of violence in some parts of Europe.

Sociological research has shown internal orientation and the development of identity to be subject to historical change, thus giving such development the characteristic of an ongoing process (see LEONTJEW, 1982). We refer here to the so-called culture of migrants, normally shared by two social spheres (see STRAUBE, 1987). Sociological research has also shown the emergence of identity to be a historical process of individuation and to be determined by current living conditions (see DECS/EGT, 1986,. 41). We can use these findings to assert that the core values of an emerging European identity are capable of being developed as contemporary attempts to interpret the nature of mutual bonds and as a common search for a common meaning.

What should Europe be like? How should Europe develop? Which fundamental core values - in the sense of "synchronic elements of awareness" (SCHMIDT 1987, 116) and of an overarching European set of values-can we derive from, for example, the problems related to the Italian state under the rule of law, the British welfare state, the Irish religious state, and the French agrarian state (see SCHLEICHER 1993, 302).

We could derive the following, all of equal importance:

- the protection of the biosphere
- the elimination of poverty
- the common monitoring of social developments and social property
- unity not as uniformity but rather as a tolerated, accepted variety of various identities and identity needs
- making identities complement federal structures
- making educational systems interchangeable
- the acceptance of cultural pluralism: preserving, affirming, and respecting things foreign
- multiculturalism: seeing migrants and minorities as an enhancement and advantage to society

These common, interconnected goals and tasks can be approached from a variety of different world views, cultural, traditions, and forms of living.

They would constitute the pillars, the walls and roof of the "common European house." The foundation would be of an ethical nature. It would consist of an "ethic of responsibility" (WEBER 1985), a "principle of responsibility" (JONAS, 1984), a "common responsibility found in mutual respect" (KÜNG 1991, 61), and a "moral code of foresight with empathy" (MITSCHERLICH, 1977).

From this perspective, we can direct our attention away from Europe's quantitative increase and expansion, which has consisted until now of the removal of frontiers, to the qualitative emergence of human qualities, to the search for and expansion of the inner boundaries and experience of individual and social awareness. We can direct our attention to intensifying and utilizing human resources- the human potential. We can concentrate on discovering, renewing, and using mankind's inner wealth and on taking recourse to the epistemological view of man that emphasizes the potential for rationality, for reflection, for autonomy, and for communication (SCHLEE 1992).

The basic idea expressed here is that of the paradigm pertaining to subjective, social awareness on a humanistic level (see HARMAN 1978, 57). Its essence was described in 1981 by the president of the Club of Rome AURELIO

PECCEI, who maintained that the problems with which we are dealing on an individual, European, and global level are not caused by external conditions but are found instead within each of us (1981, 153).

How should Europe develop?

Psychosocial uncertainty, structural change, and the dissolution of traditonal values have shown that there is a "need" for Europe. The crisis of confidence, feeling of alienation, and serious gaps in educational policy marking current developments in Europe have given these uncertainties and changes the ability to help us search for new goals-above all, goals leading to a reorientation and to new meaning on a social and humane level.

In this spirit, ideas for a "new Europe" are being created. These ideas
"are based on democratic principles derived from human rights and basic freedoms. They are based on prosperity produced by a free market, on social equality, and on an equal measure of security for all nations" (COUNCIL OF EUROPE, 1990).

The Treaty of Maastricht illustrates that unity based on these factors is not viewed as uniformity:

"The Community will strive to emphasize the cultural heritage common to all of ist members while, at the same time, contributing to the development of the individual cultural identity of each member state through the preservation of the community's multi-national and multi-regional diversity" (EUROPEAN COMMUNITY/ EUROPEAN UNION, 1992)".

There is a "need" for Europe, yet how far has our "ability" to be European (SCHLEICHER 1993, 306) developed? This question is being posed not only by "the Europeans" themselves but by non-European nations as well. The world wished to know, for example, what Europe's policy-or, at least, what the European Union's policy was with respect to the Gulf War and to the war-like, genocidal conflict in former Yugoslavia. In other words, the world seems to expect a common European policy and responsibility in the power play of world politics, politically, economically, and in humane-social affairs (see PINGEL 1994, 168f.).

ADDITIONAL, IN-DEPTH ASSIGNMENTS:

- Make a list of European political institutions and committees, and render a brief description of their tasks.
- Provide a brief description of European educational programs, and summarize their goals, target groups, and work methods.
- Together with your classmates, create a collage on the topic "Our View of What Europe Should Be Like!"
- Together with your classmates, compile a wall sheet consisting of current print media (newspapers, magazines, brochures) on the topic "This Is What Europe Should Be Like?
- Read the sections of the Maastricht Treaty that deal with educational and social policy, and, after a critical examination, draw up a table showing their strengths and weaknesses.

1.6 (HOW) CAN WE BECOME EUROPEANS?

In sum, our explanations have illustrated the following until now: On the one hand, there seems to be a general acceptance among Europeans of the need for Europe to grow together, for a development of European identity. There also seems to be an acceptance (albeit varying, depending on national differences) of the changes brought about by these new developments. On the other hand, the emergence of Euroscepticism, Eurorejection, Eurofear, and in some areas, "Euroaggression" has become just as apparent.

The discrepancy, contradiction, and ambivalence inherent in the concurrency of acceptance and rejection should provoke us into asking two questions:

1.) What are the reasons for this discrepancy?
And
2.) How could/should this discrepancy be overcome? That is, how is Europe to continue?

Let us begin by concentrating on finding answers to the first question.

There are two causes for these contradictory trends, both causes being mutually dependent:

a.) psychosocial conditions found in exisiting or emerging social groups and groups of citizens,

b.) political-administrative directives of organizations and political bodies.

As regards a), there is fear owing to the dissolution of and changes in the communities and forms of living that, until now, have offered the protection, security, and sense of belonging comprising traditional identities but that are now being penetrated by things considered "foreign," "different," "alien." This phenomenon can best be seen in the various forms of interethnic strife.

Migrant laborers, asylum-seekers, refugees, immigrants from eastern Europe, indigenous minorities in all European countries, immigration, and the vast search for living space on the part of individuals and groups that feel threatened have led to large-scale change. The mobility endorsed politically in Europe, the freedom to work and live where one pleases, will probably lead to a considerable increase in the ethnic and cultural mix. The problem, however, does not exist in actual occurence but rather in the awareness, on the part of all concerned, of this occurence. This awareness is determined by several factors, consisting of the function of immigrants, their distribution, their dynamics, their outward appearance, the strength of their ethnic, cultural, religious, political identity and the respective identity of the host country (see HENTIG 1993, 82).

A determining factor is the system of values found in a society. Other important factors are the mutual value judgments and feelings that ignite, cause unsecurity, and evoke alienation when traditional, culturally acquired, patterns of perception are forcibly confronted with elements that are different. In his 1987 essay on racism, the Tunisian-born sociologist MEMMI found that "the perception of something different is a disquieting element. The perceived difference consists of the unknown. The unknown is perceived as harboring danger. Something perceived as being different even has the ability to cause discomfort in those rare cases when it possesses a seductive quality" (1987, 35). The feeling of exposure to threat can lead to reactions in the form of xenophobia and nationalistic obstinacy. It can lead to fundamentalism, occultism, autonomous chaotic behavior, political terror, or even to total apolitical attitudes. All of these occurences can be seen as the irrational expression of relevant fears, of mental, economic, political, intellectual, and existential distress used to construct new barriers by means of physical, emotional, economic, and structural force. They serve to illustrate the feelings of helplessness, of anger, and of being a victim of lies. Feelings that emerge in times of strain.

These are not the best preconditions for European unity. This is especially true if frontiers are removed to facilitate economic and individual mobility but if, at the same time, the unleashing of economies helps unleash, irrational, uncontrolled emotional behavior that is allowed to transcend the laws of humans rights and human dignity. The war in the Balkan states, terrorist attacks by the ETA, the IRA and the RAF, ruthless egocentric attitudes, and a disregard for public well-being reflect in an ugly manner, our inner limitations, contradictions. According to modern psychoanalysis, we tend to repress the evil, darks aspects of such phenomena, project these aspects onto our own external concepts of an enemy, and attempt to resist fear by forcibly violating the boundaries separating us from the "other."

Differences cause feelings of discomfort; change and upheavals cause fear. Individuals as well as groups tend to resist and repress the knowledge needed to overcome this problem. Modern psychoanalysis refers here to neurotics who attempt to ward off those aspects of self-knowledge and human relationships ,that they threating to their inner security but who do so with such extremity that they suffer a nervous breakdown once environmental tolerance has been exhausted. According to HARMAN (see 1978, 25) there might be an analogy in the form of a "social nervous breakdown," caused by uncontrollable feelings of insecurity in the face of possible alientation and isolation, of a fragmentation of identity, of a feeling of hopelessness for an ever increasing number of unemployed, homeless, and otherwise disenfranchised individuals. A breakdown of this order, however, is not perceived as being yet another reason for lamentation fueled by cultural pessimism. Rather, it is seen as a great opportunity and challenge to go beyond the false solutions arrived at to date, beyond all failures and concealments, to find ultimate causes and to make important, basic decisions leading to constructive, transitional solutions; for deep down we know that the current situation is intolerable and that the current disruption and destruction is the "psychosocial price" (HURRELMANN) exacted by our present way of living.

In sociology and in the humanities, we can find explanations, interpretations, and research findings as regards the complex cause relationships and the problems of the pschological-social realities that influence the adversity of social majorities towards social minorities and that mark the lack of social awareness in multiethnic and multicultural societies involved in the transformational processes leading to a united Europe. Relevant and quite new areas of research worthy of mention here are the areas of "multicultural education," "migration research," "ethnic heritage studies," and comparative "educational research." Their contexts of meaning differ respectively.

The following table, based on an overview by HEITMEYER (1993) and dealing with the multi-layered problem of interethnic strife in Europe, may prove useful towards understanding the types of confrontation with foreign cultures and the experiences of foreigness. Such understanding is a preconditons for overcoming interethnic strife.

Tab. 4: Problem of interethnic in Europe

syndrome	core argument	dominant emotional base
racism (anti-semitism)	degradation of others on account of biological differences, alleged superiority/inferiority	belief
ethnocentrism	self aggrandizement by claiming a higher cultural and economic achievement	pride/overbearing behavior
xenophobia	competition with foreigners and with foreign culture	fear
heterophobia	rejection of others within one's own ethnic group(homosexuals, physically challenged)	fear
established rights	priority for those groups who "were here first" (this includes resident aliens rejecting new immigrants)	egoism, self-assertiveness

Common to all of these attitudes are the various ideologies and deceptive visions of inequality that are used to legitimize violence. As can be seen, the various attitudes and forms of behavor given in this general overview are in need of different pedagogic treatment. The deciding factor can be seen in the fact that differences are judged negatively from varous interest perspectives.

Research findings in the social sciences have brought one very important aspect into focus: differences in attitude and behavior are compounded by differences of social structures in that marginalization and minority status are brought about by social disenfranchisement in education, employment, and housing. In other words, social structures and the social realities of poor living conditions are the actual causes of the social and socially induced emotional state of minorities (see GRIESE 1980 and 1984). According to GALTUNG socioeconomic discrimination can also be referred to as structural violence

(1975). All of us participate in this violence "by engaging in activities that increase the wealth of the northern hemisphere and poverty of the southern hemisphere. The neutral term usually employed here is "terms of trade," the law of world economy. Since all of us are responsible-albeit in varying degrees-for maintaining this disproportion, our interest in effecting an appropriate change is minimal" (GAMM 1993, 56).

We are thus confronted with a "circulus vitiosus" (vicious circle), which consists of different forms of violence and which perpetuates disastrous processes in education. Human inequality is perceived as being natural rather than a product of historical social processes. It leads to attempts at securing hegemony. Differences thus unjustly determined to be of an ethnic quality appear as social differences and contradict interpretations of conflict that are influenced by culturalistic elements.

To underline the above-described syndrome of "ethnocentrism" and to differentiate between the various patterns of interpretation, we shall refer briefly to ADORNO'S findings. In his "Studies on Authority and Prejudice," he describes ethnocentrism as being a relatively constant, rigid mental structure from which debasing reactions directed against anything foreign originate. By referring to the theory of psychoanalysis, he conveys how we deny those aspects of the self which upbringing has taught us to view negatively and how we then project those aspects onto members of foreign cultures. The weakness of so-called ego-functions leads to a tendency on the part of an ethnocentrist to identify solely with his/her own group. An ethnocentrist is incapable of individual experience (see ADORNO, 1968).

The various causes outlined above illustrate that interethnic strife is largely a product of socially predetermined conditions and structures and of individual pschologicalsocial attitudes shaped by social upbringing. However, as social realities are determined by society, they are capable of being changed.

The undeniable increase of "structural violence" and mutual exclusion has led us to the conclusion that the above-mentioned findings in the fields of social science have hardly affected political processes.

We now turn to b.):
Nearly all critical analyses of official European policies to date convey unanimously that the development of European policy has occured at the government and organizational level with disregard to grassroots needs and participation of the citizens and of their social groups. A top down policy of this nature has neglected, forgotten, or (for fear of conveying unpleasant truths and

thus forfeiting reelection chances), may even have served to suppress public opinion as an essential instrument of democratic social identity. It has thus supported-even intensified-the mechanisms of fear that are aimed against foreign cultures and has programmed European citizens to accept Europe without affording these citizens the necessary preparation and leadership.

The following table, which appeared in the Eurobarometer of June 1993, substantiates the low level of knowledge among Europeans as regards European institutions. According to research conducted in the area of political socialization, the degree of public knowledge reflects the degree to which European citizens deal with European structures and thus the level at which they tend to maintain interest in and identify with such structures.

Tab. 5: Knowledge of National and European Institutions

Index* National Knowledge	EC	B	DK	D (W)	GR	E	F	IRL	I	L	NL	P	GB**
very high	13	16	12	8	14	13	11	26	13	6	17	16	23
high	65	66	57	63	64	61	70	62	72	48	67	77	57
limited	19	15	22	25	21	26	18	12	13	43	14	5	17
extremely limited	3	0	5	4	1	1	1	1	2	3	2	2	3
Index* EC-Knowledge													
very high	2	2	3	2	2	2	4	2	0	1	1	1	1
high	36	49	58	30	47	32	55	39	29	58	34	40	30
limited	49	45	37	55	34	49	36	46	58	36	57	40	52
extremely limited	4	3	13	15	18	18	6	13	14	5	9	19	18

* Index=the differing number of national and European questions have been grouped into four catagories, depending on the number of correct answers. For the sake of clarity, these categories have been labeled "very high" to "extremely limited."
**GB does not include Northern Ireland

Source: Eurobarometer, June 1993 A36, Tab. 41a, taken from: SCHLEICHER 1994, 99

Many Eurocratic policies and regulations-such as those governing the length and curvature of bananas to be sold in Europe-are seen by many EU citizens as being alien and non-responsive to the actual needs and problems of Europeans. Considered a characteristic of forced unity mandated from "above," such policies have created feelings of apathy or resentment towards Europe.

The "emotional preconditions for a selective perception of Europe on a rational basis" (SCHEICHER 1994, 95) have not been afforded enough consideration. A public agreement on common European goals has not been allowed to emerge.... "How can Europe's citizens develop a sense of being responsible Europeans and how can a European sense of public mindedness arise, if these citizens are denied the possibility of participating in the creation of a united European body politic ?" (SCHLEICHER 1994, 79).
We must point out that, in addition to the top-down-policy perceived as being undemocratic, there has been a fundamental lack of programs designed towards educating the public on the creation of European unity. Such a lack must be viewed as an example of political failure-especially if we remember that this lack has contributed towards the new psycho-social fears and processes of exclusion that have marked the attitudes of established social groups towards a new Europe.

After having offered some answers to queston 1, we will now attempt to treat the second question ("How can an awareness of Europe be developed on a scale that is adjusted to citizens' needs and that can be accepted and experienced by the majority of citizens?"). In doing so, we will try to find constructive solutions for future perspectives.

Critical analyses of Europe that have been made from various perspectives have all come to an vital conclusion.

- This conclusion is that the core values, described in section 1.5 as consisting of visionary but realizable transformational goals, great ideas and thoughts, inner images leading to the emergence of a new awareness of social responsibility and a new respect for multicultural diversity can be achieved only by means of vast processes of reeducation. Only such processes can help us to overcome the social segregation, exclusion and fear described in this section.

Such processes must involve all aspects of educational policy. Though recognized in 1988 as forming the "heart of European integration" (EC-COMMISSION 1988), they have not been the concern of the professional field actually responsible for encouraging the growth of a European awareness and for the creation of a truly united Europe. The educational system will thus become a primary factor in social and economic progress and in the preservation of peace (see BÜRLI 1997, 189). Educational policies must be developed with a view towards expanding knowledge of Europe, overcoming the limitations of nationally determined forms of perception, encouraging intercultural communication, mobilizing the grass roots, and adopting measures to alleviate alienation.

- What we are referring to basically are developments and concepts of activity that will involve the entire population and all social strata in the planning and realization of society's tasks on a continual basis and that will hence contribute to the emergence of learning processes.

- **What is needed** is a "bottom up policy ex post": the political participation of Europeans for the purpose of making up time lost politically. "42 years have passed since the Montan Agreement and 36 years since the Treaty of Rome. Yet to date no one in Strasbourg or in Brussels has given much thought to how an encompassing awareness of "being European" can be created in the societies of European countries" (LENZEN 1994, 31).

- **What is needed** are public forums and events, such as the 1998 "Week of Europe," to be held in Saxony-Anhalt. An event of this kind serves to invite public participation in Europe. The Ministry of Economics, Technology, and European Affairs has distributed a letter containing the following: "As in the last few years, this year's Week of Europe" plans to offer local citizens various possibilities for learning about topics and political activities relevant to Europe and occuring in Saxony-Anhalt. In addition, the "Week of Europe" aims to acquaint vast portions of the local public with various aspects of European integration and with the unification of all of Europe"(BEHRENDT 1997).

SCHLEICHER (see 1994, 120) has determined European identity to be understandable to the extent to which citizens are able to develop an interest and a feeling of being able to participate in the making of European policy. Events such as the "Week of Europe" have shown this to be true.

- **We need** to teach about Europe, its cultural diversity, history, politics, economy, and peoples. This is essential for overcoming the public's general lack of knowledge about Europe.

- **We need** a rational and clear treatment of various culture-specific perceptions, forms of interpretation, and interests. This demands the implementation of learning materials based on multidisciplinary, multiperspective, multinational, problem, situation, and activity-oriented approaches.

- **What is mostly needed** are concrete form of learning through experience with the help of supranational, intercultural exchange programs (between pupils, teachers, students, families, trainees, etc.). We need continuing support, common supranational projects and learning programs, each based on double systems of national perceptions and perspectives.

- **What is needed** are diverse forms of intercultural cooperation on a small scale, such as between families, religious organizations, and athletic clubs. Neighborhood festivals can be held to include migrant families, the socially disadvantaged, the socalled handicapped/disabled, and other marginalized groups.

- **We need** intensified foreign-language learning, international social services, an exchange of company employees, internships abroad, supranatinal environmental project, and medical assistance projects.

What is needed is the advancement of academic mobility, the development of European educational and training programs, common European degrees and transferable credits, and the expansion of European studies. (Note: In the 14th century, student mobility at the University of Ferrara reached 10 percent, a level now envisioned but re-attainable only by means of considerable effort.)

All of these listed aims are measures and forms of learning that are an essential part of social education and of psychogical-social change. They can thus lead to an improvement in mutual understanding and to the emergence of a common, binding awareness of Europe. Above all, these suggested measures are to be part of common learning processes that can be realized and that have indeed been realized in part in various definite projects.

Nevertheless, to preserve a certain degree of emotional hygiene, it is necessary to point out that such projects and measures cannot be realized overnight. With a view towards the realities of European history, we must not forget that contributions to changes in attitude effected by education, upbringing, and teaching can occur on a step-by-step basis only, extending over a long period of time.

Taking these factors into account should, however, encourage us to intensify the measures and goals suggested above and to support a European community of learning that would be gradual but continuous and that would recognize the frailty and complexity of human and social relationships.

(How) Can We Become Europeans ?

We can do so by attempting to meet the needs and goals described above.

Nonetheless, there is the question as to who will assure the responsibility for implementing, organizing, monitoring, and evaluating appropriate measures.

In this regard, those EU programs dealing with educational policy deserve mention: COMETT / ERASMUS / SOKRATES (which also provides support for the development of this module on Europe). LINGUS / TEMPUS / PETRA / EUROTECNET and many others. There are the Council of Europe, UNESCO, European Networks (teachers' and parents' organizations), the Euopean Conference of University and College Presidents and many others. There are publishing firms, business associations, and, of course, institutes of higher education, which-historically-have been Europe's social institutions par excellence-a role which they continue-or should continue-to play. College and universities are able to implement teaching and research in the clarification of complex, supranational relationships. They are capable of offering critical clarification of the ubiquitous socio-cultural structures consisting of individual needs, economic and political conditions and social structures and process. They can encourage social innovation, especially from an anthropocentric perspective.

(How) can we become Europeans? This means taking the individual citizens into account, the indivdual in the community. Becoming "European" means being mobile internationally and contributing personally towards interaction and integration in other countries.

(How) can we become Europeans? We can become so by taking the long road balanced between visions and dreams:

"If we want our dreams to become reality, we must not waiver when our dreams sometimes appear impossible to realize. Without a dream of a better Europe, we will be unable to create a better Europe" (HAVEL, cited by STOBART 1994, 43) and:

We can become Europeans by taking the long road balanced between effort and ability:

"Considerable amounts of work, caution, and knowledge are necessary to advance successfully on the road" (SCHAUMANN 1994, 20).

Let us conclude this chapter by introducing the last tasks. In doing so, let us pose the question as to whether our everyday language contains terms that have, over time, conditioned us to see things foreign as things strange, far removed, and excluded from our own cultural sphere and if, thus, these everyday terms are in need of careful revision. In other words, what do we Europeans mean when we use the term 'foreigner'-the meanings of which have strongly been influenced by history?

By dealing with these meanings and their changes, we may be able to increase our ability to perceive the term and to reflect on what it means. Expanding and altering our self perception and our perception of others and thus our perception of the restrictive linguistic categories of the world (see BONO 1991, 156) could serve as a first clear personal step towards a public spirited and humane creation of a common European home and as a further step towards becoming European.

1.7 TASKS TO BE UNDERTAKEN

- Collect newspaper and magazine articles for a portfolio treating the problem of xenophobia. Decide how to classify your documents, and support your decision. Offer theses on possible solutions.

- Provide a critical analysis of statements and attitudes that claim, for example, that "cheap foreign labourers from Eastern Europe are depriving German of jobs and housing." Support your views. Refer to the HEITMEYER's table, given earlier.

- In a group discuss the quotation given by GAMM in this section and offer theses on possible solutions.

- Interview 5 foreign employees from various countries and ask them whether or not they feel integrated where they live and work in Germany. List possible contributions that you could make towards changing or influencing these attitudes.

- Give 3 basic suggestions on how a public education policy conducive to European integration could be initiated in Magdeburg.

- Decide how you can make a personal contribution towards European integration. Provide a detailed description on how you would achieve this. Share your thoughts with your classmates. If you are not able to do so, please explain clearly.

1.8 BIBLIOGRAPHY

1.8.1 REFERENCES

ADORNO, T.:	Erziehung nach Auschwitz. In: Erziehung zur Mündigkeit. Frankfurt o.J., S. 88-104.
ANWEILER, O./KUEBART, E.:	"International 'ne vospitanie" und "multicultural education" - Aspekte eines Vergleichs zweier politisch-pädagogischer Konzepte. In: Erz.i.d. multikulturellen Gesellschaft. VE-Info. Nr. 17, 1987, S. 128 ff.
ASSMANN, A.:	Arbeit am nationalen Gedächtnis. Eine kurze Geschichte der deutschen Bildungsidee. Frankfurt/New York 1993.
BACHMANN, W. / MESTERH'AZI, Z. (Hrsg.):	Trends und Perspektiven der gegenwärtigen ungarischen Heilpädagogik. Giessen 1990.
BACHMANN, W../ECKERT, U./POZNANSKI, K. (Hrsg.):	Tradition und Trends der polnischen Sonderpädagogik. Giessen 1991.
BACHMANN, W.:	Das unselige Erbe des Christentums: die Wechselbälge. Giessen: 1985.
BACHMANN, W.:	Bausteine zu einer europäischen Geschichte der Heilpädagogik. In: Heilpädagogik 1992 (5), 290-298.

BEHRENDT, R.: Europawoche 1998. Verfügung des Ministeriums für Wirtschaft, Technologie und Europaangelegenheiten des Landes Sachsen-Anhalt. 1997, 02.12.
BONO, E.:de: I am right - you are wrong. London, Penguin Book 1991.
BONO, E.: de: Der Klügere gibt nach. Düsseldorf, Wien, NewYork 1991.
BÜRLI, A.: Sonderpädagogik international. Luzern 1997.
CLOERKES, G.: Soziologie der Behinderten. Heidelberg 1997.
COUDENHOVE-KALERGI, R.: Ein Leben für Europa. Kampf um Europa. Aus meinem Leben. Zürich 1948.
CURTIUS, E.R.: Europäische Literatur und lateinisches Mittelalter. Bern 1969.
DECS/EGT, Directorate for Education, Culture and Sport: The education and cultural development of migrants. Project No. 7. Final report of the project group. Council of Europe. Strasbourg 1986.
DEUTSCHE GESELLSCHAFT FÜR ERZIEHUNGSWISSENSCHAFT: Bildung und Erziehung in Europa. Weinheim und Basel 1994.
EBERLE, I.: Lateinische Nächte. Essays über die lateinische Welt. Stuttgart 1966.
EG-KOMMISSION der Europäischen Gemeinschaften: Bildungspolitik - ein Herzstück der europäischen Integration. In: Perspektive '92 der Kommission 1 (1988).
ERIKSON, E.H.: Kindheit und Gesellschaft. Stuttgart 1982^8.
EUROBAROMETER: Public Opinion in the European Community . Commission of the European Communities, Brussels, 1987-1994.
EUROPÄISCHE GEMEINSCHAFT: Die Vertragstexte von Maastricht. Bonn 1992.
EUROPARAT/COUNCIL OF EUROPE: Recommendation No. R(90/5).
FERNAU, J.: Wie es euch gefällt. Eine lächelnde Stilkunde. Donauwörth 1969.

FREY, H.P.:	Stigma und Identität. Eine empirische Untersuchung zur Genese und Änderung krimineller Identität bei Jugendlichen. Weinheim/Basel 1983.
GAMM, H.J.:	Fremdenfeindlichkeit und Erziehung. In: Pädagogik 10/1993, 55-57.
GALTUNG, J.:	Strukturelle Gewalt. Reinbek 1975.
GOFFMAN, E.:	Stigma. Über Techniken der Bewältigung beschädigter Identität. Frankfurt/Main 1967.
GORBATSCHOW, M.:	Perestroika. Die zweite russische Revolution. München 1987.
GRIESE, H.M.:	Wider die Pädagogisierung der Ausländerrpobleme. In: Materialien zum Projektbereich "Ausländische Arbeiter". 1980, Nr. 30.; S. 41 ff.
GRIESE, H.M.:	Kritisch-exemplarische Überlegungen zur Situation und Funktion der Ausländerforschung und einer verstehenden Ausländerpolitik. In: ders. (Hrsg.): Der gläserne Fremde. Opladen 1984.
HARMAN, W.W.:	Gangbare Wege in die Zukunft? Darmstadt 1978.
HEITMEYER, W.:	Pädagogik und Fremdenfeindlichkeit. In: Landesinstitut für Schule und Weiterbildung (Hrsg.): Aktuelle Gewaltentwicklung in der Gesellschaft. SOEST 1993, 33-41.
HENTIG, H. von:	Die Schule neu denken. Eine Übung in praktischer Vernunft. München, Wien 1993.
HURRELMANN, K.:	Aggression und Gewalt in der Schule. In: Ursachen, Erscheinungsformen und Gegenmaßnahmen. In: Pädagogisches Forum 2/1992, 65-74.
JASPERS, K.:	Vom europäischen Geist. München 1947.
JONAS, H.:	Das Prinzip Verantwortung. Versuch einer Ethik für die technologische Zivilisation. Frankfurt/Main 1984.
KLAUER, K.J./MITTER, W. (Hrsg.):	Vergleichende Sonderpädagogik. Berlin, Marhold 1987.

KOCH, W.:	Kleine Stilkunde der Baukunst. Gütersloh 1970.
KÜNG, H.:	Projekt Weltethos. München, Zürich 1991.
KÜNZLI, R.:	Herkunft und Zukunft oder inwiefern Europa ein vernünftiger Bezugspunkt für Bildungsprozesse sein kann. In: Bund-Länder-Kommission für Bildungsplanung (Hrsg.): Lernen für Europa. Köllen Verlag 1992, 8-20.
LENZEN, D.:	Bildung und Erziehung für Europa? In: DGFE (Hrsg.): Bildung und Erziehung in Europa. Weinheim und Basel 1994, 31-48.
LEONTJEW, A.N.:	Tätigkeit, Bewußtsein, Persönlichkeit. Köln 1982.
LISSNER, I.:	Wir sind das Abendland. Gütersloh 1966.
McLEAN, M.:	Das europäische Curriculum. In: Schleicher (Hrsg.) 1993, S. 261-276.
MEMMI, A.:	Rassismus. Frankfurt/Main 1987.
MITSCHERLICH, A.u.M.:	Die Unfähigkeit zu trauern. München 1977.
MULCAHY, D.G.:	Auf der Suche nach der Europäischen Dimension im Bildungswesen. In: Pädagogik und Schule in Ost und West 1 (1992), S. 43 ff.
MÜLLER, K.E.:	Der Krüppel. Ethnologia passionis humanae. München 1996.
PECCEI, A.:	Die Zukunft in unserer Hand. Gedanken und Reflexionen des Präsidenten des Club of Rome. Wien 1981.
PINGEL, F.:	Europa - Nation - Region: Historisch-politische Bildung in europäischen Schulbüchern. In: Schleicher/Bos (Hrsg.) 1194, 153-170.
SCHAUMANN, F.:	Grußwort. In: DGFE (Hrsg.), Weinheim und Basel 1994, S. 20-22.

SCHLEE, J.:	Förderung und Unterstützung von Reflexivität. In: Schulamt für die Stadt Aachen (Hrsg.): Beiträge zur Bedeutung des Forschungsprogramms "Subjektive Theorien" für Schule und Lehrerbildung. Aachen 1992.
SCHLEICHER, K. (Hrsg.):	Zukunft der Bildung in Europa. Darmstadt 1993.
SCHLEICHER, K./ BOS, W.: (Hrsg.)	Realisierung der Bildung in Europa. Darmstadt 1994.
SCHMIDT, U.:	Interkulturelle Kommunikation und interkulturelles Lernen. In: Jahrbuch "Pädagogik: Dritte Welt" 1986. Kulturelle Identität und Universalität. Frankfurt/Main 1987.
SCHRAML, W.J.:	Einführung in die Tiefenpsychologie für Pädagogen und Sozialpädagogen. Stuttgart 1976^6.
SMOLICZ, J.J.:	Multiculturalism and an overarching framework of values: Educational responses to assimilation, interaction and separatism in ethically plural societies. In: Bildung und Erziehung, Beiheft 2, Mitter/Swift 1985.
SONTAG, S.:	Noch eine Elegie. In: Literaturmagazin 22.Sonderband. Ein Traum von Europa. Reinbek b. Hamburg 1988, S. 131-136.
STOBART, M.:	Der Europarat und die Bildungsanforderungen im "Neuen Europa". In: Schleicher/Bos, 1994, 1945.
STRAUBE, H.:	Türkisches Leben in der Bundesrepublik. Frankfurt, New York 1987.
TORNEY-PURTA, J./ SCHWILLE, J.:	Civic Values Learned in School: Policy and Practice in Industrialized Countries. In: Comparative Education/Review 1 (1986).
WEBER, M.:	Politik als Beruf. In: Gesammelte politische Schriften. Tübingen 1958, S. 505-560.

1.8.2 ADDITIONAL READINGS

DAUN, Å.:	Den europeiska identiteten: Sverige och Italien, EU och framtiden
FJORDBO, M.:	En europeisk coctail. 1993
KNUDSEN, A.:	Kulturelle världar: kultur och kulturkonflikter i Europa.1997
VIKLUND, D.:	Att första EU: Sverige och Europa
WEBER, M.:	Politik als Beruf. In: Gesammelte politische Schriften. Tübingen 1958, S. 505-560.

2. LOOKING BACK – HISTORY OF DISABLEMENT

David Johnstone

2.1. INTRODUCTION

This chapter explores the historical background to disability and the development of special education in Europe It presupposes no in depth understandings or prior knowledge. However, students who have some direct, or indirect experience of disability, impairment or handicap, will have much to contribute.

The chapter encourages students to engage in a critical examination of the concepts of disability and ability in their own country. Whilst we do not presuppose any prior knowledge of disability issues, students are expected to have an interest in some of the current debates that involve the management of provision for and by disabled people. The module takes the view that the concept of disability is not fixed or absolute. It has been and continues to be, re-defined in a variety of ways throughout our history. The course sets out to address some of these views and to challenge the range of misconceptions and stereotypes that have emerged.

2.1.1 OBJECTIVES

Students shall:

- critically evaluate the history of disability as "pathology" or individual deficit;
- compare and contrast the social constructions of disability at two different points in history;
- critically assess the purpose and philosophy of the eugenics movement at the beginning of the 20th Century;
- critically identify and describe the role of religious bodies in the development of provision for disabled people

Work related to these objectives should be related as fully as possible to learning outcomes.

2.1.2 LEARNING OUTCOMES

By the end of this section students will have acquired:

- a critical awareness of the historical explanations for the oppression and "invisibility" of disabled people
- knowledge of the historical base for some of the controversies and challenges that disabled people in Britain and Europe continue to face.

The history of disabled people and their lives can be traced using three broad and overlapping phases. All of them are associated with different stages of political, historical and economic development across Europe. None of the stages are distinct and there are traces of all of them still to be seen. However they can be traced in an historical linear progression as follows:

Medical Care   -   Segregation/Isolation   -   Rights and Social Justice

2.2   A CHRONOLOGICAL HISTORY OF DISABLEMENT IN EUROPE

Year	Person	Event	Category
597	St Augustine		General Care
1260	Louis IX (France)	Hospice Nationale of Quinze-Vingts	blind
1570	Pedro Ponce (Spain)	Lip reading	deaf
1601	Poor Law Act (UK)	beginning of secular responsibility for the poor and needy in each parish, through local taxes	

Year	Person/Place	Contribution	Disability
1620	Juan Paulo Bonet (Spain)	one handed signing	deaf
1624	Sweden	Laws for hospitals/special provision for disabled people	
1651	Dr Harsdorffer (Germany)	wax tablets	blind
1745	London (UK)	Founding Hospital for the physically handicapped	physical handicap
1766	Thomas Braidwood (UK)	Academy for the Deaf and Dumb	deaf
1778	Pestalozzi (Switzerland)	home for mentally retarded and mental handicap	mental handicap
1778	Samuel Heinicke Leipzig (Germany)	oral methods	deaf
1785	(UK)	Sunday Schools	disadvantage
1799	Itard (France) Edouard Seguin	The Wild Boy of Aveyron	mental handicap (autistic)
1829	Louis Braille (France)	first introduces his system of signing	blind
1832	Munich (Germany)	Kurtz Foundation	physical handicap
1841	Guggenbühl Abendburg (Germany)	Institution for Cretins,	mental handicap
1842	(Sweden)	Compulsory schooling for all	
1850	Christiania, Göteborg (Sweden)	Industrial Schools	physical handicap
1865	J.D. Georgens & M. Deinhardt (Baden/Vienna)	Heilpflege- und Erziehungsanstalt "Levana"	mental handicap

1866	John L. Down (England)	research and systematic/ Training of trisomie 21/ Downsyndrome	mental handicap
1867	Dresden (Germany)	day auxiliary schools	mental handicap
1904	Kerr and Eichholz Charlottenburg (Germany)	first open air school	delicate
1908	Camberwell, London (UK)	first special provision	partial sight

2.2.1 THE BEGINNINGS OF PROVISION FOR DISABLED PEOPLE

The beginnings of the provision for disabled people in general is shrouded in some mystery. It is hidden in official records, religious superstition and the accounts of charitable organisations. Before the eighteenth century discussions were linked to health treatments and Christian principles of care. Paracelsus, a Swiss physician of the early sixteenth century proposed a fundamental Christian argument in the care and management of people with mental handicaps:

"his (man's) wisdom is nothing before God, but rather that all of us in our wisdom are like the fools ... Therefore the fools, our brethren, stand before us ... And he who redeemed the intelligent one also redeemed the fool, as the fool, thus the intelligent one."

Paracelsus went as far as to state that fools were not only equal to other people in God's eyes but even superior, being nearer to God, "Because the animal body they inhabit has been marred ... the wisdom that is also in fools, like in a fog, can shine through more clearly."

The ideas that mentally handicapped people do not suffer from as many worldly corruptions as others and are nearer somehow to some truer or more basic conception of human nature persists into the present day. On the other hand, the idea that disabled people are a consequence of the evils of mankind is also a recurrent theme of early history. St Augustine states clearly that fools are a punishment for the fall of Adam. And the belief in disabled children as changelings, taken by the devil in exchange for a child in more human form was most forcefully articulated by Martin Luther "The devil sits in such change lings where the soul should have been." The idea of handicapped children being a punishment for the sins of individual parents, rather than those of mankind in general, is clearly seen in Luther. Abnormal children were the result of sexual intercourse between a woman and the devil and for a long time giving birth to a disabled child was grounds, in Europe, for considering a woman to be a witch. The associations between sensuality, immorality and the animal nature of disabled people also linked blame to mothers. here are instances of blaming women who become mothers of disabled children recurring throughout the nineteenth and well into the twentieth century.

Thus it can be seen that, from the outset, the history of state provision for disabled people moved from the exploration of private and individual circumstances towards a debate of wider public concern. Since the early nineteenth century the concern for disabled people has involved the relationship between the demands of the labour market and the social costs of providing services. It is above all else, a history of political groups working to further their economic interests under the guise of philanthropy. The history of education for disabled people is no exception:

"... for too long education in all sectors has colluded with the demands of the labour market to keep disabled people out of the workforce. Most disabled children leave school thinking they are unemployable and immediately have this reinforced by social education centres and colleges of further education with their offers of 'further on' courses and 'independence training'* (Oliver, 1992 p.6)

The relationship between disabled people and the economy is seen in the original 'philanthropic' ideals that lay behind the development of a structured system of the institutions and "colonies" that were built in both Europe and the United States in the nineteenth century. In some areas they continued to form the basis for residential care until the present shift in policy towards "Care in the Community." Some semi-formal education and vocational training for people with disabilities and learning difficulties had been an established feature of the asylums of the nineteenth century. The Edinburgh Review of 1865 gives an interesting and from an equal opportunities perspective, somewhat voyeuristic and patronising insight into the activities in the Earlswood Asylum, situated then just outside London. There, young men and women with learning difficulties and psychiatric disorders were given training in carpentry, needlework and horticulture as well as basic literacy and numeracy instruction.

"...It was in furthering the many schemes for the improvement of idiots, a most important object to enable those capable of reaping the highest advantages, to become adept in some useful branch of industry, and to make their work remunerative, exchanging their solitary and idle habits for social, industrious and productive occupation." Edinburgh Review 1865 (p.56)

This enlightened, if paternalistic, approach was soon to be replaced by the harsher, more custodial activities associated with asylums as arenas for the protection of society, rather than as places of refuge for disabled people. In the "Moral Panic" that grew up around eugenics the populist demand grew for the asylums to become places of custody. This meant a shift in emphasis; from training individuals in order to protect them from the threats and exploitation from the rest of society, to the protection of society from the supposed debilitating effects of physically, intellectually (any by association morally) inadequate people. The guiding model of care imposed was fundamentally akin to the age-old model of medical treatment where a powerful professional, in the guise of a doctor conducts a diagnosis of the 'problem', prescribes a treatment and as a result of this expertise the patient is cured. In the case of diagnosing or assessing disability such ultimate judgements were still firmly in the hands of the medical profession.

Disability in these circumstances was considered to be a personal affair and a tragedy for the person concerned. This in turn had a profound effect on the kinds of education and training provision made and also on the manner in which it was implemented. Even today, if a person has a disability, the medical model of causation implies that to all intents and purposes, "It's your own fault!" As Oliver (1990) has pointed out this pervasive influence from medicine is a major factor in the individualisation of "care" issues. Brisenden (1986), writing as a disabled person, has put the medical model even more dramatically in perspective:

"... the problem from our point of view, is that medical people tend to see all difficulties solely from the perspective of proposed treatments for a "patient", without recognising that the individual has to weight up whether this treatment fits into the overall economy of their lives. In the past especially, doctors have been too willing to suggest medical treatment and hospitalisation, even when this would not necessarily improve the quality of life for the person concerned. Indeed, questions about the quality of life have sometimes been portrayed as something of an intrusion upon the purely medical equation. This has occurred due to a failure of imagination, the result of the medical profession's participation in the construction of a definition of disability which is partial and limited. This definition has portrayed disability as almost entirely a medical problem and it has led to a situation where doctors and others are trapped in their responses by a definition of their own making." (Brisenden 1986 P.8)

It is not difficult to see how, from the beginnings, the discourse around disability has tended to be dominated by this medically defined construct. For students with learning difficulties and disabilities, who have come through a school system that continues to pay great heed to the interpretations and wishes of the medical services, there is a tacit acceptance that medical interventions and interpretations of difference are part of their way of life. As Oliver (1986) has suggested their education may have been disrupted by the inputs of a variety of pseudo, or para-medical professions eg physiotherapy, speech-therapy and the like. If children have left school and become adults believing through a range of medical and para-medical interventions that they are ill, then it is no real surprise if they accept the passive role of being sick and dependent; receivers of care and expected to be grateful for it.

Evidence that disabled people are denied the full rights to citizenship as a result of the demands of the labour market is overwhelming. It seems evident that despite political rhetoric to the contrary "social disadvantage" has become associated with disability and learning difficulties and that young people with disabilities are still cases to be treated rather than individuals with rights.

The development of psychology from the discipline of medicine, at the beginning of the 20th century, introduced the belief that disability was a measurable construct and that disabled people could be considered in the same way as patients in hospital. The belief in disability as illness is still very powerful today. Whilst human behaviour may not depend on heredity alone, the system of biological needs and functions carried by the genotype are passed on at conception and relate us in some way to all other living creatures. How much of an individual's intellectual ability is determined by environmental factors and how much is already decided by a person's genetic makeup is one of the oldest debates in the area of disability studies. Heredity may set the limit that one may reach in intellectual capacity, but the environment determines how close one comes to achieving the potential within us all. The relationship of genetics to the circumstances of people with disabilities, brings us to a consideration of the capricious workings of the laws of mutation and the principles of inheritance, dominance and recessive genes.

2.2.2   THE PURPOSE AND PHILOSOPHY OF EUGENICS

The late nineteenth century saw the emergence of the consideration of eugenics as a science, but the construct has a longer history. As we approach the end of the twentieth century, the issue of eugenics has moved from the narrowly defined definition of heredity and moved more towards issues related to pregnancy, abortion, euthanasia and genetic engineering. The aim of this chapter is to expand the debate away from the perception of genetics as a dangerous science and to focus instead on gene technology as a dimension of effective therapeutic strategies and personal choice.

In more recent times this theme of enforced sterilisation has been resurrected. For example, the racist claims that blacks are intellectually inferior to whites, as a result of inherited characteristics has been raised by Hernstein and Murray (1994) in their provocative account of the dispersion of IQ. At the time of writing, the Nordic policy of forced sterilisation on people with developmental disabilities as practised in Scandinavia between 1934 and 1976 has been exposed (*The Guardian,* Sept. 3rd 1997 p. 13). It is a reminder that delusions of racial purity lurk just beneath the surface of the collective human psyche.

2.2.3 THE RELATIONSHIP OF EUGENICS THEORY TO DISABILITY

Historically, eugenics has certainly existed as a deliberate response to control unwanted impairments since the Greeks and their mythology. Artistic portrayals of procreation between the gods and earthly mortals in a union of bodily perfection, practical accomplishment and intellectual agility are exhibited in art galleries and literature. The Greek civilisations, obsessed with bodily perfection, also served to justify the practice of abandonment and death, through the exposure of newborn babies considered to be imperfect. This ultimate form of subordination of disabled people continues today in a variety of more diluted forms of prejudice.

Barker, (1983) has provided a well argued analysis of the belief systems that underlie eugenics theory. In summary, he indicates the three assumptions upon which the proposition is built:

- human characteristics could be determined by inheritance according to laws that are knowable;
- it was possible to identify "desirable" and "undesirable" human characteristics;
- social policy should encourage the increased fertility of those with "desirable" characteristics

Desirability, as bodily wholeness, has historically remained in an image of masculinity and male dominance. The physically strong, lean and active male body is contrasted with the traditional an stereotypically passive female body. The female is doll-like, acted upon, dressed and undressed. Feminists suggest that this desire to manipulate the body is reflected in the institutional motives of the fashion, health, and pornography industries (Marris 1996; Wilson 1985 p.3). Biological determinism continues today in the life histories of thousands of disabled people who have lived through the brutal realities of institutional conformity and prejudice. The renewed threats to the "right to life" of disabled people has also reemerged as the implications of the Human Genome Project come to be more widely considered and understood. Some commentators see this project as a breakthrough in gene therapy whilst others in the community of disabled people fear that it "has given massive impetus and renewed rhetorical weight to the claims of biological determinism" (Shakespeare 1995 p. 23).

The practical reality beyond any discourse about the right to life (and the right to die) is the very deliberate killing of people at either the beginning or the end of their lives. Disabled people and their parents are at the centre of this. Proponents of this killing claim it to be justified on the grounds that disabled people are surplus to the requirements of society. The debate has become more urgent as scientific knowledge begins to move more rapidly in advance of both our moral interpretations of the findings and the legislative processes that frame their resolution. Furthermore, the term "New" eugenics highlights some of the ethical dilemmas that face us all in relation to the sort of global society that we are becoming.

The oppression of disabled people occurs across different cultural groups and manifests itself in different ways. Racism is the most obvious example of stereotyping and discrimination based on and shaped by, prejudice. The pseudo-scientific ideology of racism that has been used as a justification for institutional oppression of Black people has it parallels in the power and prejudice of eugenics as a justification for the covert exploitation experiences by people with disabilities. The attempts to construct a science of measurement formed around the genetic basis for intelligence and human potential has shaped much of the history of disabled people in the twentieth century. The relationship between statistical science and eugenics, links the statistician, Sir Francis Galton, with his cousin Charles Darwin – whose notion of the evolutionary advantage of the fittest forms the basis for eugenics. The possibilities for a scientific explanation of intelligence, rather than divine intervention, caused an explosion of interest in attempts to measure differences. Francis Galton, seriously believed that "the heredity-chances of becoming famous are twenty four times greater for a child with a famous father." (quoted in Malson and Itard 1972 p.16) He also believed that it was possible to determine a gene for intelligence and that "survival of the fittest" required the elimination of "defective stock" in society.

The rejection of disabled people in its most extreme form has been dramatically advocated in the ideology of fascism. The fascist glorification of the "perfect" human being resulted, under Hitler, in a deliberate effort to exterminate disabled people as "imperfections which contaminate the genetic stream." (Coleridge 1993 p.45) The Nazi euthanasia programme attempted to justify the elimination of disabled people on the grounds that they made no contribution to society and were a drain on resources; they were perceived as "unless eaters" of resources without capital to contribute to the human lot. The Nazis and eugenicists may belong to history, but the emergence of newer forms of Social Darwinism continue the assumptions that only the fit and fully functional have a right to real life, (see Levine 1985).

The false logic of eugenicists who attempt to link the deterioration of social orders in society with the size of families and unchecked reproductive practices has been ruthlessly exposed, (eg Gould 1996). However, renewed interest in biological determinism is evident in the reactionary responses of the new right and "back-to-basics" biology, encouraged by the mass media and spurious academic research studies such as that by Hernstein and Murray (1994) linking IQ with class, race and genetic causation.

2.3   TASKS TO BE UNDERTAKEN

Disability in the Ancient World

Students are expected to:

- consider the foundations of western civilisation, e.g. the Greeks and Romans and the Greco-Romanic attitude towards disabled people
- reflect upon the pursuit of physical and intellectual fitness that was the Greek obsession with the body. Critically consider if this attitude is continued in your own country today
- think of times when you have felt less able than others. Try to describe these emotions
- consider the assumptions that are made about the nature of the lives of disabled people in your own country

Disability and the Christian Tradition

- explore the references in the New Testament to the circumstances of disabled people and the references to the consequences of wrong doing as a consequence of impairment
- contrast of the Jewish/Christian religion and Islamic faith in its representation of "caring" for the "sick" and the "less fortunate"
- consider the economic circumstances of Christianity, as the religion of the underprivileged and its association with charity and disability
- critically consider the exercise of power through fear of the Devil and the link between impairment, impurity and sin
- explore the subjugation of women and depictions of disabled people in theatre, children's literature and popular culture, (eg Luther, Shakespeare, Ibsen, Witchcraft)
- consider the links between religion, disability and property rights in European culture
- trace the connections between, disablement, religion, care and charity. Present you results as a poster.
- explore the clash between science and superstition with regard to the issue of disability

2.4 BIBLIOGRAPHY

2.4.1 REFERENCES

Abberley P (1993)	Disabled People and Normality, in Swain J et al (eds) *Disabling Barriers – Enabling Environments*, London, Sage
Begum N (1994)	*Reflections*, IPPR, London
Brechin A & Walmsley J (1990)	*Making Connections,* Hodder and Stoughton, London
Casling D (1993)	Cobblers and Songbirds: the language and imagery of disability, *Disability and Society,* 8,2, 203-210

Davis L (1995)	*Enforcing Normalcy – Disability, Deafness and the Body,* London, Verso
Foucault M (1977)	*Discipline and Punish,* Harmondsworth, Allen Lane
Gould SJ (1981)	*The Mismeasue of Man,* New York, W.W. Norton
Haffter C (1968)	The Changeling: History and Psycholdynamics of Attitudes to Handicapped Children in European Folklore, *Journal of the History of Behavioural Sciences,* 4, 55-61
Hevey D (1992)	*Creatures Time Forgot,* Routledge, London
Hooks B (1990)	*Yearning: Race, Gender and/cultural* Politics, South End Press New York
MacFarlene I (1979)	*The Origins of English Individualism,* Oxford, Basil Blackwell
Oliver M (1991)	*The Politics of Disablement,* Macmillan, London
Ryan J & Thonas F (1987)	*The Politics of Mental Handicap (revised edition)* London, Free Association Books
Soder M (1990)	Prejudice or ambivalence? Attitudes towards persons with disabilities, *Disability, Handicap and Society* 5, 3, (227-241)
Stone D (1984)	*The Disabled State,* London, Macmillan
Swain, J Finkelstein V et al (1993)	*Disabling Barriers – Enabling Environments,* Sage, London

2.4.2 ADDITIONAL READINGS

BACHMANN, W.:	Das unselige Erbe des Christentums: Die Wechselbälge. Giessen 1985
MÜLLER, K.E. :	Der Krüppel. Ethnologia passionis humanae. München 1996
MÖCKEL, A.:	Geschichte der Heilpädagogik. Stuttgart 1988
HOLGERSSON, L.:	Socialtjänst, Lagtexter med kommentarer i historisk beslysning . Stockholm 1995
HOLGERSSON, L.:	Socialpolitik och socialt arbete. Stockholm 1997
LAGERHJELM, B.:	Att utvecklas med handikapp. Stockholm 1988
STATENS HANDIKAPPRAD:	Handikapp vad är det? 9 uppl. Stockholm 1966

3. LOOKING AT TODAY

3.1 CONTEMPORARY PERCEPTIONS OF DISADVANTAGE

David Johnstone

3.1.1 INTRODUCTION

Explanations of disability as personal tragedy for the person concerned have emerged from a long history. Rioux, (1996) and Johnstone (1995) have indicated some of the sociological and psychological adaptations that tend to be made by non-disabled people in their adjustments towards disabled people in society. The medical model projects a dualism which tends to categorise the able-bodied as somehow "better" or superior to people with disabilities. It shares much in common with the earlier taxonomy established by Kurtz (1964), with particular reference to people with learning difficulties. The image of disabled people is identified with pity, fear and charity and it is these considerations that contribute the explanatory power of such a hypothesis. The theoretical explanation of the model relies on its legitimation of the primitive fears associated with disability rather than any attempts at objective rigour):

Ablebodied	v	Disabled
Normal		Abnormal
Good		Bad
Clean		Unclean
Fit		Unfit
Able		Unable
Independent		Dependent

Such descriptions have been used to justify the assumptions that it is legitimate to do things *to* people with disabilities rather than attempt to do things with them. Such explanations served as the rationale for large asylums and coercive control of disabled people in the guise of philanthropy that denied the right of reproduction to disabled people at the beginning of the twentieth century.

Yet, as has already been indicated, disabled people do not readily conform to a particular type. The creation of a taxonomy of categories does little to adequately represent the sheer diversity and range that makes up the population of people with disabilities. As Oliver (1990 p.4) says, about the medical model: "It conserves the notion of impairment as abnormality in function, disability as not being able to perform an activity considered normal for a human being and handicap as the inability to perform a normal social role."

Rioux (1996) has argued that such explanation of disability as a taxonomy of medical/biological problems has now grown and matured to encompass characteristics of disability as a service or social problem:

"Using this formulation, the hypothesis is that the deficit lies within the individual, but the concept of treatment is broadened to include both ameliorating the condition and developing ways to enable people to develop the potential they have. From this perspective there has been no attempt to reframe the notion that the problems experienced by people with disabilities are a result of their individual impairments." (Rioux 1996 p.124)

3.1.2 OBJECTIVES

Students shall:

critically explore "disadvantages" as a measurable, "fixed" or relative concept

a) psychologically
b) economically
c) legally
d) medically
e) sociologically
f) educationally

3.1.3 LEARNING OUTCOMES

By the end of this section students will be expected to have:

- developed a chronological time line for the development of inclusive education in the 20th Century
- explored the beginnings of scientific rationality in relation to disabled people
- develop their understanding of the underlying theories of eugenics and its Utopian ideals in the 20th Century
- compared the humanitarianism and the repressions, represented by education in an industrial, economic society
- developed an understanding between a marxist and a libertarian model of explanation for disablement in society

3.1.4 THE INDIVIDUAL TRAGEDY OR MEDICAL MODEL

What has come to be described as the "medical" model, emerged from the tendency of most of us to see medical services as the epitome of a powerful professional group. Doctors carry with them an aura of God like responsibility over life and death. This reification in turn had a profound effect on the kinds of professional services received, the education and training provision made and also the manner in which these were implemented. This powerful influence suggests that, if a person has a disability, the medical model of causation implies that to all intents and purposes, "It's your own fault!" As Oliver (1990) and Johnstone (1995) have pointed out, this pervasive influence from medicine is a major factor in the individualisation of "care" issues.

It is not difficult to see how, from their beginnings, service-providers have defined the "problem" of disablement as somehow the responsibility of disabled people themselves. For example the traditional function of the medical profession is to assess patient need, prescribe an intervention and to facilitate a cure. It is as close as any of us get to playing the almighty. Disabled people have tended to collude with and to be dominated by, this medically defined construct as much as anyone who is "under the doctor." The "medical model" is deceptively simple. Nevertheless, when it is used as an explanation for society's response to impairment and disablement it can be seen to be problematic. The medical model is grounded firmly in the principles of normalisation, the return to 'wholeness' which is impossible to achieve (and may not be desired). The three elements of medical cure outlined in the model share many of the characteristics provided by other professional services:-

- **Medical condition (symptoms)**
- **Diagnosis/Prescription**
- **Cure or treatment**

The model has an immediate appeal for the return of a bodily or sensori "wholeness." However, it is disengenous when applied to disabled people who have, perhaps, been impaired since birth. It also emphasises the patient status and thereby carries assumptions of a required passivity from disabled people. The result is an emphasis on what disabled people cannot do and what disabled people will need if their lives are to function adequately with a particular medical condition. "An assumption is made that disabled people function at a lower rate than an able-bodied person and that, in fact, a disabled person is inadequate." (Gillespie-Sells and Campbell 1991 p.15) This in turn reinforces the cycle of prejudice and discrimination that so often accompanies the "difficult" patient who fails to respond to treatment from the caring professional:

- **Failure (label)**
- **Blame (low self esteem and/or dependency on services)**
- **Repeat presentation of symptoms to another specialist**

The understanding of this concept of disability is premised on a shared understanding of normality. It clearly emphasises a power relationship in favour of the professionals and reinforces the personal tragedy theory of disablement. The subtle message of the medical model is that people with impairments and disabilities should be grateful for their treatment and that if there is a problem it is, in effect, the fault and responsibility of the patient for failing to follow the recommended intervention.

3.1.5 THE SOCIAL MODEL OF DISABILITY

The medical model encourages the simplistic view that disability is a personal tragedy for the individuals concerned. It is disabled people who are seen to have, and may come to see themselves as having, "needs." The challenge and the strength of the social model of disability lies in its ability to reverse the emphasis of causation away from the individual and personal towards shared and collective responsibility. It is a theory founded on the premise that it is society that perpetuates the oppression and exclusion of people with disabilities. Thus the onus of responsibility is shifted from the individual with an impairment or disability to the restrictions imposed by the construction of the environment and the attitudes of institutions and organisations.

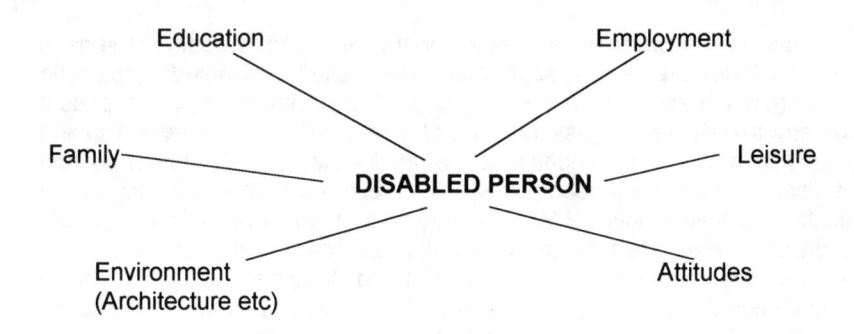

```
        Education                        Employment
                \                       /
                 \                     /
   Family ─────────────               ───────── Leisure
                    DISABLED PERSON
                 /                     \
                /                       \
        Environment                      Attitudes
        (Architecture etc)
```

The essential difference between the medical and the social model of disability revolves around the shift in the explanatory power. The social model, unlike the medical, acknowledges the structural and personal barriers created by society. It also recognises the need for the participation of disabled people in decision making and the limitations of professional expertise. The elements of the model can be summarised as follows:

THE SOCIAL MODEL

- Recognises the interaction of structural and attitudinal variables that create disability in society
- Recognises the voice/opinion of the disabled person
- Acknowledges the political processes that oppress and deny civil rights to disabled people
- Begins to put power/information within the control of disabled people and their organisations

Criticisms of the social model of disability have begun to emerge since the beginnings of the 1990s. The social model has been accused for being atheoretical, with no firm foundation of established scientific "truth" against which it can be measured and tested. There are also the concerns raised by disabled people who have drawn attention to the reality that some impairments involve chronic and enduring pain and discomfort that can be relieved through medical interventions (Crow 1996). These criticisms are important, but unfortunately tend to undermine what has been a useful and accessible explanation for shifting both collective and individual thinking about disability issues. It is also rather presumptuous to believe that any one model can ever fully account for the social actions of human behaviour. By its nature, the social model has emerged from the lived experiences of disabled people in order to generate its illustrative power. As an explanation it must somehow begin to incorporate, rather than stand in opposition to, the medical/deficit model of disablement.In other words the bureaucracy and limitations indicated by the medical model can be seen to form part of the institutional limitations that are fundamental to the social model of disability.

Some people may be affected by more than one form of impairment, but may only feel themselves to be disabled by one of these. Thus, for example a person with asthma, hearing loss and arthritis may find that their asthma can be controlled by medication, and that the provision of a hearing aid may give them sufficiently adequate hearing to cope with most situations, but if they cannot walk up steps and stairs they are disabled by the interaction of arthritis and the built environment. Generalising about disability is further complicated by the range and variety in the severity of the effects of forms of impairment. Throughout the research literature on disability it is apparent that for some people their level of disability has increased and is likely to continue to do so, whilst for others there is no pattern of deterioration. In many cases people have 'good days and bad days' and they live their lives accordingly.

The social model, nevertheless, appears to be grounded in liberal rather than radical conceptions of equal opportunities. It thereby suffers from some of the weaknesses associated with this paradigm (eg excess bureaucratisation at the point of decision making and an emphasis on fairness being perceived as individual rather than collective justice). A more radical conception of social justice within disability politics has come to be associated with the emergence of legislation, rights and "quality of life."

3.1.6 DISABILITY AND QUALITY OF LIFE

The Social model of disability recognises disability as a socially determined phenomenon. In a world created by and designed for non-disabled people the positions of power have not been occupied by disabled people. Nor have the institutions and political organisations that shape our lives been determined with the lives of disabled people in mind.The historical debates about the rights and entitlements of disabled people form the context in which the key issues of quality of life can be explored:

Tab.6: Objective assessment of life conditions
Subjective Assessment of Personal Satisfaction

physical Well-being	material Well-being	social Well-being	Development & Activity	emotional Well-being
• Health • personal Safety • Fitness • Activity • Mobility • Housework	• Finance& Income • Housing Quality • Privacy • Neighbourhood • Possession • Meals or food • Transport • Security and Tenure	• Personal Relationships • Household life • Family & Relatives • Friends & Sozial Life • Community Involvement • Activities • Acceptance& Support	• Competence • Independence • Choice & Control • Production & Activity • Job • Homelife & Housework • Leisure & Hobbies	• Positive Affect • Fulfilment – stress • Mental Health • Self – esteem • Status & Respect • Faith & Belief • Sexuality
Personal Values Quality of Life					

taken from: Felce D. und Perry J., 1996

Many of the markers of "quality of life" are clearly subjective and personalised perceptions of one's place in the environment and the responses that one receives from others. Brown et at (1992) reporting on research conducted in Canada, have addressed the complexity of the term, indicating that quality of life is not simply about happiness and satisfaction, but also about striving and dissatisfaction (Brown et al 1992). A similar attempt to measure quality of life indicators has been attempted in Europe, (Moniga & Vianello 1995). The range of discourses suggest that there are fundamental implications for both service providers, carers and the opinions of disabled people. Research suggests that "quality of life" is a complex concept represented not only by balances between satisfaction and dissatisfaction; primarily it is about gaining a positive self-image and a sense of empowerment and control over the mechanisms that regulate one's environment.

3.1.7 QUALITY OF LIFE: AN ETERNAL PARADOX?

Johnstone (1995) has indicated, with reference to the United Kingdom, and Banfelvy (1996) in a wider European context, that there is a looming crisis of confidence around the concept of quality of life in general. There are those who claim that welfare has eroded the work ethic and the moral fibre of a nation's workforce (Hernstein and Murray 1994). As we approach the end of the century new conditions are being imposed on benefits and touch law and order measures introduced in order to control anti-social behaviour. This millenial tension is being echoed in the search for moral guidance in our leaders and our public services. The apparent failure of human relations has also disadvantaged many people who are perceived to be socially as well as sensorily, cognitively, or physically disabled. Disabled people lead lives in which they will have been treated ambivalently. This often manifests itself in a kind of social inappropriateness, where disabled people perceive themselves not only as different, but also as unprepared, or unwilling to adjust to a range of social situations. This can result in the repression of effective relationships in the home, community and the workplace.

The ability to fulfil the expectations of those around you, or the hopes of significant others, is a large burden and reactions can take the form of withdrawal and depression. At the same time there is often a disappointing lack of contact between disabled people themselves. There are few opportunities to establish and maintain intimate and mutually respectful friendships in settings that are constantly supervised. In such circumstances and with such fragile relationships, many disabled people do really need more contact with trusted companions who are capable of forming a social "umbrella" of support to encourage them to form wider social networks and friendships. Such a network can cross the boundaries of generations, social status and gender.

Finance, or the lack of it, has already been indicated as a source of real hardship to all people without qualifications The wage earned in low paid open employment is little different from the amount paid to people on training programmes or receiving social security payments. For many people with disabilities, some of whom may be entitled to higher allowances due to disability, their welfare entitlements can far exceed their realistic earning potential. A failure of citizenship on the part of the whole society forces many disabled people to remain financially disadvantaged by a range of circumstances. Independence for them becomes an illusion. Either they remain living at home with their families, or they become economically dependent upon others; perhaps in the form of a spouse, partner or the state. If disabled people try to live alone or to joint groups they can rapidly run into financial difficulties and confrontations with bureaucratic regulations. In such circumstances, where the bureaucratic procedures of an independent adult status are only beginning to be understood, it is important to be able to turn to somebody for knowledgeable advice.

Those who are unfamiliar with handling the requirements of increasing bureaucracy may try to avoid contact with official authority, be it an institution or an agency. Quality of life may begin with the need for help in getting hold of such things as birth certificates, identity cards, passports, registration certificates etc. There may be need for advice on how to obtain insurances and how to cancel the same if they are inadequate or too expensive. There may be need for technical support in dealing with public correspondence; for example in response to notices or demands or how to appeal against procedural decisions that may affect their lives. The ability to respond effectively can be a key factor in raising an individual's level of self-confidence and feelings of self-esteem.

3.1.8 QUALITY OF LIFE AS AN ARRAY OF VARIABLES

The model of quality of life indicated in 4.1 has tended to be founded on the lifestyles of non-disabled people and the normal social rhythms and circumstances that are so frequently considered as fundamental. As such it is an atheoretical, simple rights-based model similar to the work of O'Brien's "Five Accomplishments." Research studies in the UK and Europe (eg Moniga & Vianello 1995; Berrington et al 1996) investigating quality of life measures identified by disabled people suggest that the concept can be considered as a product of a number of interconnected variables. Thus, the construct of "quality of life" can be organised by both subjective and objective criteria

- **material well being**

This is a potentially sensitive area. As well as income levels it might include observations and judgements about eg the quality of housing, lifetime changes in relation to residence, financial circumstances, transport availability;

- **physical well being**

This includes any additional impairments, the need to use adaptations or prosthetic equipment. It might involve understanding of specialist services eg speech therapy, chiropody, dieticians. Certainly it will incorporate an awareness of the importance of health and fitness, exercise and safety;

- **social well-being**

This suggests community involvement as well as personal relationships. It will involve an understanding of the sources of support, aspects of everyday living and sources of help and advice in the community;

- **development and activity**

While linked to objective measures of employment this variable is also to do with subjectively perceived levels of independence and the opportunities for choice and control in people's lives. It may refer to opportunities for education and training, including the uses made of day centres;

- **emotional well being**

This is tied to feelings of self-worth; the levels of status and respect accorded to and subjectively assumed by people. It is also linked with the sense of fulfilment that people attach to their lives.

- **mobility**

In order to properly develop quality of life, the mobility of disabled people has to be addressed and promoted. The awareness and removal of a number of architectural barriers (stairs and entrances to houses, toilets and public buildings) has improved across the United Kingdom and throughout Europe as a result of legislation. These considerations, together with adaptations to the means of transport (buses, trains, aeroplanes, taxis etc) and improvement in signage and the provision of information (eg sonorous traffic lights; tactile signs) are fundamental considerations for any adequate measure of effective quality of life.

- **housing/dwelling place**

There are many different considerations that must be taken into account when the housing needs of disabled people are considered. On one side of the argument there are all the difficulties related to the level of autonomy of the person; on the other there are the real practical considerations of people with physical and sensory impairments. We have also to distinguish between the perceived needs of those who continue to live in an institution from those in a group home, or those who share a house or apartment and those who live and dwell independently.

- **leisure time**

Quality of life is not only determined by the health and employment prospects of an individual, but also by opportunities that come together during leisure time. Holiday resorts, holiday houses, camping, recreational and sporting facilities must all be considered and made suitably accessible and available. There is a tendency for marked differentiations in this area. For example, in sport, where, on the one hand, there are some activities designated only for disabled athletes and disabled sports people, while alternatively, it is considered by others that sport and recreation is an ideal medium for promoting inclusion in community settings.

- **vocational training**

Many people with disabilities are invisible to the general public following years of segregated educational provision. The majority of disabled school-leavers, it is argued, do not have the pre-requisite skills for employment and this identifies them as having special training needs, regardless of whether this was evident whilst they were at school. These notions echo Freeman (1988) who has argued that disabled and "delinquent" young people leaving school have been crudely redefined as not only unskilled but also as socially incompetent and in need of categorical programmes of vocational training and further training in social skills.

A great variety of vocational programmes for disabled people have been established across Europe. They are based on the principles of developing successful and satisfying placements in both the work place and wider society. The programmes tend towards specific skills training, but also teach the social behaviours and habits that are usually considered desirable in a work setting. Education and training in basic skills is also maintained; with an emphasis on concepts such as self-advocacy, independence, self-determination and citizenship. It is evident that vocational training is emerging as an extension of the inclusive educational principles that are in favour in schools. It follows that vocational training which favours self-determination and independence also stresses the importance of changing attitudes towards disabled people. Perhaps this requires a re-negotiation of the relationships between young people, their parents, teachers and social workers.

- **access to work/employment**

The criticisms applied to education are equally applicable to other forms of service provision for disabled people. Employment provision is dominated by the notion that disabled people are in need of care. Professionals tend to deal in 'needs' and 'care'. Thus, it can be argued that disabled people provide employment for (in the main, non-disabled) carers. Disabled people often prefer to talk about 'personal assistance', rejecting the association between care and dependency. The comfortable certainties and routines of childhood are intended to serve as a preliminary to the often more informal and haphazard aspects of life as an adult. One of the most inclusive and until the 1990's, ordinary things about adult life is employment. It is therefore no surprise that many of our formative childhood and "pretend" experiences are related to jobs. In similar fashion, education and training have been expected to accommodate the expectations of employers in preparing young people for the job market; by developing personal and social skills, craft skills and qualifications as prerequisites for securing employment.

Some of the benefits of paid employment are obvious. As has been pointed out, people have defined themselves by their work throughout this century:-

"They were miners, engineers, printers, draymen, tanners. And they were predominantly male. But as the manufacturing industries collapsed, more jobs were taken by women and millions of badly education men could no longer define themselves. 'I'm a printer' could be said with pride; 'I'm on benefit' is a mark of exclusion." (Hugill The Observer 1997 p.29)

The combination of social interaction and feelings of self-worth that employment and the process of task completion can provide apply equally to people with disabilities. Some of the benefits of a job can be usefully summarised as follows:-

i) A job provides economic independence and a better standard of living;

ii) A job can empower people, by enabling them to become self-determining rather than living their lives as others dictate;
iii) A job provides status that influences positive attitudes towards disabled people and public visibility;

iv) Workplaces in integrated settings provide opportunities for social interaction and friendships;

v) A job is one of the ways in which the majority of people continue to learn and develop skills, competences and intellectual abilities;

vi) Work gives our lives a routine and structure. Successful employment and job satisfaction gives people a sense of fulfillment, achievement, confidence and dignity;

In traditional, industrial-society terms, the theory of a person's value within the workplace has been argued something like this: employment potential is determined by an employee's efficiency and productivity and those people who are not capable of benefiting from training are not likely to be either economically efficient or profitable. Bu definition, it is argued, disabled people are less capable and more dependent than non-disabled people; therefore they are both at a disadvantage and more expensive. These attitudinal barriers are deeply rooted and whilst special training initiatives have expanded for all young people they have also helped to provide a new justification for the subtle perpetuation of prejudices that limit the social and economic position of an increasing number of disillusioned and alienated young people. At the same time, work opportunities for disabled people are in danger of being redefined in order to include a growing population of those described as the underclass – people who are socially and economically deprived rather than disadvantaged through impairments. As jobs have disappeared and special services have been redefined in order to incorporate this underclass, we are beginning to see the expansion of special provision for those deemed as failures economically and vocationally.

3.1.9 THE CONNECTION BETWEEN DISABILITY AND SPECIAL EDUCATIONAL NEEDS

The concept of "educational need" had first emerged in Europe following the 1939-1945 War. The need to re-build economies placed an emphasis on getting the best from national education systems. In the United Kingdom regulations led to the establishment of services and schools that acted on behalf of, rather than in consultation with disabled people. This, in turn has led until recently, to a kind of passive citizenship on the part of disabled people within a fundamentally needs-based provision determined by professionals. The legal framework of the UK has consistently portrayed disabled people as a cost to the exchequer rather than as individuals entitled to participate in the exercise of citizenship. Far from becoming involved in legislation that establishes the rights of disabled people, enabling them to determine their own needs, we have created a system that continues to exclude.

A feature of the 1944 Act was the creation of categories of handicap reflecting society's needs rather than individual considerations. Regulations in Pamphlet 5 following the Act, actually stated that some pupils may require special educational "treatment", borrowing heavily from the medical model already referred to. For young people with handicaps and disabilities leaving school meant a probable future in sheltered or closed employment. Even in 1968 it was estimated that there were approximately 70,000 severely mentally handicapped adults in England and Wales, approximately 24,500 of whom attended Adult Training Centres. (Whelan & Speake 1977). The need to re-establish employment for returning members of the armed forces following the Second World War had the effect of excluding disabled individuals from open employment, even though some of them had fulfilled important work during the war years.

The much more specific definition of learning difficulties within the concept 'Special Educational Needs' formed part of the legal framework of the 1981 Education Act and followed from the recommendations put forward by the Warnock Committee of Enquiry (1978). The suggestions it lay down in relation to students with special needs in further education are embedded in the notion of progression and 'transition to adulthood' in Chapter Ten of the Report. Very little was included in the way of guidelines for either differentiating the college from the school curriculum or for distinguishing in law the status of a student, a young person, or a child with special needs. For the purposes of definition a child was described as somebody who remained in school until their nineteenth birthday, but no indications were given for the status of an individual who may leave at sixteen and go to college or on to a training scheme. Thus, in terms of developing the rights and entitlements to adult status implied in the phrase 'transition to adulthood', the Warnock principles left a good deal to be desired. Other confusions still have not been fully resolved around the very definitions of special educational need and learning difficulty which was at the heart of the Committee's Report and has subsequently formed the basis for legislation in the 1981 and 1993 Education Acts.

As Booth (1992) has argued the implications of the definitions are that children and students are to be measured using both "within the individual" measures eg standard tests of intelligence or ability (which in themselves, suggest measuring the incompetence or failure of a person is the basis of learning difficulties) and secondly, "environmental judgements" of the adequacy or otherwise of the resources available to facilitate and support teaching and learning. The whole concept of "need" is problematic and confusing. For children in schools it has led to an increase in services established for the purpose of meeting individual need and providing support. It is only recently that some commentators have begun to question if the very services set up to help establish better learning may not instead, be helping to create the problems they were designed to resolve (Booth, 1992. Corbett and Barton 1992).

The fundamentally child-centres ideas of the Warnock Report, attempted to establish a concept of citizenship by building on the notion of need, determined by the collaboration of ' experts' and through the wider integration of children from segregated educational provision into the mainstream. It has in fact, failed to alter many of the old prejudices. Had the recommendations made been adequately resourced in the first place, then the demands for change might not have become so strident now. The move towards inclusive education, (described more fully in chapter 5) is itself a recognition that full integration is an ideal that may not ultimately be achievable or even desired by everyone. More than anything else, however, the concept of special educational needs failed to face up to the fundamental issue of ensuring that basic educational rights are part of every children's entitlement. As Booth points out Special Educational Need has become such an abused and misunderstood term that it has diminished two perfectly honourable and worthwhile concepts: "Care" and "Need" which have fundamentally influenced the use of the term in the first place. The system of meeting a child or student's "needs" has continued to perpetuate some of the worst abuses of the old models of medical care through the imposition of bureaucratic assessment procedures on young people and their families and the perpetuation of segregated educational and residential facilities which deny the right for some people to live where they choose. This in turn has denied them from any feelings of "normality." In short the concept of "Special Educational Needs" has continued to label young people who experience learning difficulties or disabilities as a problem, in the same fashion as the old categories of handicap, which the construct had been intended to replace (Fulcher 1989).

3.1.10 FROM INTEGRATION TO INCLUSION

During the late 1970s and early 1980s an increasing challenge to the separateness of special education began to be posed by a combination of factors emerging in a number of countries across the western world. These factors came together under the broad banner of inclusive education and community amongst special education services which were beginning to reinterpret the concepts of equal opportunites. Ironically, some of the very organisations that had first helped to legitimate the need and recognition for a separate educational entitlement for young people with disabilities and learning difficulties were amongst the most vociferous voices fighting to dismantle the systems that had been the products of their early successes.

The inability to meet the needs of increasing numbers of young people, who were being excluded on grounds of failure to learn, or to maintain disciplinary codes, led to the emergence of specialist provision in terms of both place (either special class or special school) and curricular support (adapted materials, specialist equipment or additional teacher support procedures). To abandon these carefully considered practices and to sacrifice them on the alter of inclusion is for many teachers like suggesting that those involved in special education have been deluding themselves; and perhaps they have. The simulated practice environments in the special school classrooms, plastic money and cardboard cut-out supermarkets that were a feature of the infant classroom to be a part of the learning environment for many disabled people. These situations contribute nothing to the concept of "education for adulthood", but do a lot to confirm separateness and preparation for the long years in the day centre.

One of the fundamental purposes of education for students with learning difficulties and/or disabilities is essentially linked to the negotiation of adult services rather than a perpetuation of child-oriented and protected provision. The development of inclusive education, as distinct from integration has been built on the notion of equity and rights for marginalised groups who have traditionally been excluded from educational and community services. Put at its simplest the concept celebrates the value of an individual for those qualities which he/she brings to a situation or human encounter, rather than attempting to place conditions upon their acceptance. Thus, whereas integration is in many ways an ultimate goal where all people are accepted equally, inclusion is a step along the way in which people with disabilities are accepted and accorded recognition on their contribution to any human transaction, precisely because of their differences.

It is almost certainly the case that the majority of people who are employed in the education system, at whatever level, are attempting to improve people's lives. This underlying philosophy is certainly apparent amongst those people who work in what is broadly termed as special education. For this reason, if no other, the enthusiasms for integration amongst some teachers, parents and administrators is difficult to interpret and evaluate. The initial and fundamental "gut" reaction would be to agree with any cause that professes to have at its heart improved access to social and educational opportunity. It is nevertheless a matter of some confusion for those who work in settings especially designed and equipped to serve people with learning difficulties and disabilities to find their efforts being criticised on the basis that they are continually creating services that segregate people and exclude them from being full participants in social activities. For teachers who have worked in segregated special education systems for a number of years it can only come as a shock to realise that they are considered by their critics to be perpetuating a kind of educational apartheid. That despite their best endeavours to serve they have, in fact, been preparing children and students for segregated lives in the future. In other words the experiences that the education system has created for children and young people with learning difficulties has "systematically disengaged them from natural connections, and from the mainstream of life in their communities" (Tyne 1993).

The popular movement towards Inclusive Education has grown out of debates on the effectiveness of mainstreaming and questions about the validity of special classes. When the concept of integration was gaining momentum in the early 1980s it was met with mixed reactions. It had few complete supporters. What has happened in the years since then has been a reflection of the growing awareness of normalisation principles that were first developed in Scandinavia and Canada by Wolfensberger. The rapid increase in enthusiasm for inclusive education in recent years, in the rest of Europe, on the other hand, has coincided with the growth of the rhetoric of citizen rights. This is understandable and inevitable, for supporters of inclusive principles have argued that education is the most appropriate vehicle for the movement's fullest realisation. Advocates of inclusive education and community living have also maintained that if education is to be part of an education for "emerging adulthood", it surely has to involve all students in the fullest participation in both realistic and mainstream activities (Whittaker 1989).

Like the arguments in favour of integration advocated in the 1970's, there is a strong moral imperative that persuades in favour of inclusion and yet behind the "rightness" of the case there appears to be little hard evidence that it will always prove the most appropriate educational, or even social outcome for the young people concerned. Ultimately, the central issue at the heart of inclusion is similar to that which lies at the heart of other causes that are strong on rhetoric, but less solid on practical reality. It is a question of empowerment and the lifting of restriction on people's lives; it is about the power to choose.

Special education, as we have seen, emerged as an alternative system in response to the failure of mainstream education. The latter had either failed to meet the needs of a particular group of pupils, or it excluded children on the ground of bureaucratic and administrative convenience. As supporters of inclusion have explained, in attempting to describe the ways in which educational and welfare services for disabled people continue to systematically exclude:

"By 'exclusion' I am not talking of articulate people making a clear choice of a 'disabled culture' nor of groups of disabled and non-disabled people choosing to share a somewhat separate life in a purposefully formed idealistic community. Nor by 'systematic' do I mean that anyone necessarily intends people to be excluded. I am though, talking of a system which offers few or no options to disabled children, and whose inevitable consequence is that children grow into an adult life of exclusion" (Tyne 1994 p.151).

Thus, discussions about Inclusion and Exclusion is not really concerned with the failure of Special Education, but with the visible instrument of exclusion – the Special School. However, by aiming at a target that is itself a product of the failure of the mainstream education system the critics of exclusion reduce a complex analysis of wider social, economic and political considerations to a somewhat simplistic debate: ordinary schools are good – special schools are bad.

On the basis of this argument the concept of inclusion, as a celebration of difference, begins to emerge as a more problematic construct. The initial response to a movement that seems to be promoting ideals associated with integration and equality of opportunity is a positive one; inclusion is a process that most people would find it hard to disagree with. However, the reality of experience suggests that this initial enthusiasm is not universal. The movement reflects the value systems of different teachers or educational sectors through whom its meaning will be interpreted. Inclusion cannot be a static entity, achieved by simply following established rules and procedures.

The shape of special education across Europe faces a number of challenges as each country attempts to interpret the aspiration of the Salamanca Statement (1994) that we should all be moving towards the goal of inclusive education. The closure of special schools in favour of placing youngsters into regular classes suggests that appropriate support mechanisms are already in place. However, this is not always the case:

"Special schools in many countries (across Europe) represent a major investment in staff and expertise, in buildings and equipment, in software and other materials – the whole gamut of things that regular schools lack where pupils who have difficulty in learning are concerned" (Hegarty 1995 p 35).

In order to retain some of the best qualities of special school provision learning support in mainstream forces all concerned to take a fresh look at the function and purpose of learning as we move towards the 21st Century.

3.1.11   TASKS TO BE UNDERTAKEN

- Critically consider what sociology contributes to the understanding of the civil rights of disabled people.

- Develop a chronological time line for the progress of inclusive education in the 20th Century.

- Critically consider the statement that disability is more an economic than a medical issue.

- Develop a portfolio of evidence that represents the concept "quality of life" in relation to disabled people.

- Consider the competing explanations for the oppression and "invisibility" of disabled people outlined in this section.

- Develop a portfolio of evidence that demonstrates a social model of disablement.

- Explore the legislation that operates in relation to disabled people in 2 European countries.

3.1.12 BIBLIOGRAPHY

3.1.12.1 REFERENCES

Alcock P (1993)	*Understanding Poverty,* Macmillan, London
Barnes C (1994)	*Disabled People in Britain and Discrimination,* Hurst, London
Barton L (1993)	The Struggle for Citizenship: the case for disabled people, *Disability, Handicap and Society,* 8,3, (235-248)
Booth T (1992)	*Making Connections,* Milton Keynes, Open University Press
Brechin A & Walmsley J (1990)	*Making Connections,* Hodder and Stoughton, London
Brisenden A (1986)	Independent Living and the Medical Model, *Disability, Handicap and Society,* 1,2, 173-178
Corbett J & Barton L (1992)	*The Struggle for Choice,* London, Routledge
Gould S J (1981)	*The Mismeasure of Man,* W W Norton, New York
Hernstein R & Murray C (1994)	*The Bell Curve: Intelligence and Class Structure in American Live,* London, The Free Press
Hevey D (1992)	*The Creatures Time Forgot,* Routledge, London
Hernstein R & Murray C (1994)	*The Bell Curve: Intelligence and Class Structure in American Life,* The Free Press, London
Hugill, B. (1997)	Britain's expansion zone, The Observer, 13th April, 29
Johnstone D (1995)	*Further Opportunities: Learning Difficulties and Disabilities in FE,* Cassell, London
Johnstone D (1998)	*An Introduction to Disability Studies,* London, Fulton
Morris J (1989)	*Able Lives,* Women's Press, London
Morris J (1991)	*Pride Against Prejudice: transforming attitudes towards disability,* The Women's Press, London
Oliver, M (1986)	Social Policy and Disability: Some Theoretical Issues, *Disability, Handicap and Society* 1, 1

Oliver M (1991)	*The Politics of Disablement*, Macmillan, London
Pritchard D (1960)	*Education and the Handicapped 1760-1960*, London, Routledge
Porter G & Richler D (1991)	*Changing Canadian Schools*, Roher Institute, Toronto
Riesser R & Mason M (1991)	*Disability in the Classroon*, ILEA, London
Ryan J & Thomas F (1980)	*The politics of Mental Handicap*, Penguin, London
Swain J. Finkelstein V et al (1993)	*Disabling Barriers – Enabling Environments*, Sage, London
Warnock M (Chair) (1978)	*Report of the Committee of Enquiry into the Education of Handicapped Children and Young People*, London, HMSO

3.1.12.2 ADDITIONAL READINGS

Antor,G:/Bleidick, U.:	*Recht auf Leben - Recht auf Bildung*. Heidelberg 1995
Opp,G./ Peterander F. (Hrsg):	*Focus Heilpädagogik. Projekt Zukunft*. München/Basel 1996
Seligman, M.:	*Erlernte Hilflosigkeit*. Weinheim 1992
Theunissen,G.:	*Empowerment und Heilpädagogik*. Freiburg im Breisgana 1995
Wolfensberger, W.:	*Der neue Genozid an den Benachteiligten, Alten und Behinderten*. Gütersloh 1996

http://bidok.uibk.ac.at/links/index.html
http://behinderung.org/all-info.htm
http://www.bbv.umweltdata.de/zeitung/zeitung.htm
http://selbsthilfe.seiten.de/laediert/

3.2 POLICY VERSUS PRACTICE

Bengt Eriksson

3.2.1 INTRODUCTION

A vast majority of European countries do - more or less - regard themselves as "welfare states." One could say that there is an awareness of what has been called "the social dimension." In most countries (all) arrangements are undertaken to support and sustain the weakest and to overcome shorter or longer breaks in welfare, at least regarding basic materialistic issues. However, the means intended to achieve the desired goals differs. Some countries rely heavily on the state, addressing themselves to the idea of "the strong society," or "the welfare state." In others, a more or less explicit co-operation has been formed between the state, the most influential trade unions and the employers sometimes called "a social contract." There are also countries that to a large extent rely on voluntary work committed by organisations, such as churches or unions, or on individuals, for instance relatives or neighbours. In spite of differences in actual settings, it appears that in all countries in question there is a mix of contributions from the state, the labour-market parties and voluntary forces forming the "face of welfare."

Nevertheless, welfare arrangements are often criticised and welfare institutions are often under heavy pressure. The criticism points out shortcomings regarding the amount of welfare resources available, and how these resources are allocated among the needy. There is also criticism regarding the organisation and the funding of welfare.

Irrespective of differences in system and coverage of welfare arrangements in relation to the needs, there seems to be a gap between ideology and practice. There are individuals and groups, at times large groups, who do not benefit from the welfare system to the extent they are entitled to. This is a problematic fact which can be considered from different standpoints: as a problem of trustworthiness of the democratic system, as a question of inequality of power, as a problem of justice, as a methodological shortcoming concerning social care and social work, or as a personal problem for those who suffer.

This course focuses on disabled people, their living conditions and how these conditions can be improved by means of social care/social work. Differing approaches in the European countries are of special interest. However, to grasp this issue, it might be necessary to widen the perspective for a while, to the field of social policy on the whole. Social care, social work for the disabled and other efforts that might be undertaken to improve their conditions, is one part among others in the field of social policy. To understand this part it might be helpful to reflect a little upon the emergence and present state of social policy in different European countries: What are the basic roots of social policy, what differences and similarities can be revealed by studying the history of social policy in some European countries? And what about the present laws and regulations controlling the field of social policy - in general and concerning the disabled specifically? And, finally, what are the relations between the rules and regulations and the factual conditions for the disabled? Between what is said and what is actually achieved?

"What is social policy?" Social policy is considered to be a "fuzzy" concept, denoting various meanings in different settings. Some definitions are given and the need for limitations is discussed.

When studying social policy in the European post-war democracies, the concept of consensus seems to be of special interest. Structural analyses of social policy are often centred round the presence or absence of consensus. Therefore, the concept of consensus will be highlighted and discussed.

Further on the focus lies on the historical development of social policy in the three partner countries, mainly during the post-war period. In all three countries there has been an evident growth in the welfare sector, even though they differ in many ways: The German way is to place a great deal of responsibility on employers and canalize the welfare arrangements through the labour market. Trade unions and voluntary organisations, for instance churches, are also important providers of social welfare. England is characterised by, to some extent, consensus between the state, unions and employers, on the need of a welfare sector. However, this consensus has been put under heavy stress during periods of right-wing government. In England as well, the voluntary sector plays an important role. In comparison, Sweden has shown the strongest form of consensus concerning the need of a comprehensive welfare sector run by the state. This consensus has also proved to be relatively resistant through times of economic strain. From this study of historical facts up to our days the focus will shift.
The next perspective is a study of documents defining present ambitions concerning social welfare in the three countries. These documents consist of basic legislative documents (laws and regulations) and legislative documents specifying welfare conditions for the disabled. This study has two aspects:

Firstly, to define the officially promised level of welfare for disabled people, as a preparation for comparing with the level they actually achieve. Secondly, to compare the political/ideological level of ambition between the three countries.

Next part is to compare the political/ideological level with the factual. By means of different sources the political documents will be carefully scrutinised in the light of facts describing the situation for different groups of disabled. These sources will basically consist of available statistics concerning "welfare consumption," but also research reports and articles from scientific journals and popular press. Data might also be collected by interviews.

This part of the course will end with an attempt to answer the basic question of Policy versus Practice: Are there differences between policy and practice? If so, which are the gaps that can be found between what is said and what is actually done and achieved? What about disabled people as regarded as one needy group among others? Are there any patterns of inequality within the group of disabled? Can differences between countries be identified (and explained)?

Work that is related to this component might be structured as follows:

- attending lectures
- study of advised, recommended textbooks as well as free choice of literature
- search for statistics and other sources describing the present situation concerning disabled people
- group work comparing policy and practice. Papers from such comparisons will also serve as examinations on this part of the course.
- taking active part in seminars discussing the findings and problemizing the gaps found between policy and practice

3.2.2 OBJECTIVES

Students shall:

- compare Policy documents related to disabled people in 3 European countries
- evaluate and understand the gaps between legislation and practice relating to disabled people in Sweden, Great Britain and Germany

- communicate directly with colleagues in partner countries to develop a portfolio of evidence of policy for comparison and contrast

3.2.3 LEARNING OUTCOMES

By the end of this part students will be able to

- understand and see the politics of social policy and its effects for disabled people and professionals in different countries

- be aware of laws and policy documents concerning disabled people in different countries

3.2.4 WHAT IS "SOCIAL POLICY"?

This part of the course deals with the question of (social) "policy" versus "practice." It might, therefore, be adequate to start reflecting on the concept of social policy. It is a broad concept, used in a large number of settings and with many different meanings. Titmuss (1974) carefully examines this concept, starting by discussing the words "policy" and "social." Policy implies that one expects some kind of change - unwanted conditions can and will be changed in the desired direction by means of planned action. We do not have, Titmuss says, a policy concerning the weather, because we do not try to change it according to our wishes. The word social is used (misused?) in a lot of connections and with different denotations. Titmuss argues that they all "in short, emphasise that man is a social being; that he is not solely an Economic Man; and that society cannot be considered in terms of mechanistic-organic models or physiological models?" (ibid. page 24)

Furthermore, the term social policy inevitably has value implications. There is no value-free social policy. In most cases, social policy is thought of as a way of furthering the interests of the weaker parties; for instance the unemployed, the poor, the disabled. Even so, there are usually a lot of justified needs, while the resources definitely are limited. The issue of judging between different needs is in the end value-based. From this follows that it is a basic demand to declare ones values, when discussing social policy.

There are a number of definitions of social policy, ranging from the very narrow and restricted to the broad and extensive. An example of the former might be Hagenbuch's definition, that says "the mainspring of social policy may be said to be the desire to ensure every member of the community certain minimum standards and certain opportunities" (from Titmuss 1974). The opposite, a broad definition, is offered by Macbeath. "Social policies are concerned with the right ordering of the network of relationships between men and women who live together in societies, or with the principles which should govern the activities of individuals and groups so far as they affect the lives and interests of other people" (from Titmuss 1974). Finally, a third example from the same source, a more restricted and practical definition provided by Marshall. His opinion is that the concept social policy does not have an exact meaning, but "is taken to refer to the policy of governments with regard to action having a direct impact on the welfare of the citizens, by providing them with services or income. The central core consists, therefore, of insurance, public (or national) assistance, the health and welfare services, housing policy" (ibid. page 30).

After scrutinising a number of definitions, Titmuss concludes that there seem to be three different basic perspectives on social policy. The first and most restricted perspective he names "The Residual Welfare Model of Social policy." According to this model, the welfare of the individual will normally be provided by the family (the private sphere) or by the commercial market. Only when these two sources fail, welfare policy run by the state should be available. Even in these cases only to a very limited extent and totally without ambitions of structural changes, such as levelling living conditions for large groups.

The second model is "The Industrial Achievement-Performance Model of Social Policy." In this model, the labour market plays a significant role. What you can receive in terms of welfare is to a large extent related to what you have put in, mainly during your working life. People outside the labour market not being able to take part of a great deal of the welfare benefits might be considered a major disadvantage connected to this model.

Thirdly, there is "The Institutional Redistributive Model of Social Policy." In this case, welfare arrangements, in a broad meaning, plays an important, not to say major, role in many senses. Social policy is not only to be relied on when everything else fails, rather is it normal to benefit from social welfare on many occasions, from birth to death. Social policy is also one way of redistributing resources, from the rich to the poor and so it extends the influence of social policy to the field of equality and allocation of resources.

Even though this classification into three models was made some twenty-five years ago, it is still up to date. Later authors (see for instance Nygren 1994, Salonen 1994, Socialstyrelsen 1997) follow Titmuss but reduce his scheme to two models: The marginal model and the institutional model, corresponding to the Residual Welfare Model, and the Institutional Redistributive Model. In reality, most countries have combinations of all three models.

Within the European Union there is a discussion about what has been called "the social dimension". In turn, the social dimension consists of two parts, the social dialogue and the Community Charter of Fundamental Social Rights of Workers. However, these concepts are only in a very limited sense connected to what is normally meant by social policy. The social dimension in the EC is about workers' conditions and working conditions, not about social welfare in general. It deals with certain rights for the workers, such as the right to establish and run unions, to collectively negotiate about wages and other conditions, to obtain information and be able to influence when major changes take place in the enterprise where you are employed and so on (Trost 1991).

FOR THE STUDENTS TO DISCUSS:

- Consider the classification provided by Titmuss. Are there more appropriate ways of classifying models of social policy?

- Which model is predominant in your country? Is it a combination of models?

- Give practical and concrete examples highlighting predominant patterns of social policy in your own country.

3.2.4.1 CONSENSUS - A KEY CONCEPT IN THE DISCOURSE OF SOCIAL POLICY

Why do countries become welfare states? This is a basic issue of great interest that mainly lies beyond the range of this course. Apparently, it originally has to do with the nature of human being and the fundamental destiny of men and women to become social creatures. Strictly spoken, we have an unconditioned responsibility to take care of each other. One cannot survive without the other. Developed countries are, among other things, characterised by their complexity, division of labour and need for special societal arrangements to meet basic needs. In most cases, typical fields for such societal arrangements are communications, education, medical health and social welfare (besides, of course, jurisdiction, the police force and the defence) which make these issues important political questions. One way of examining the development of social policy is to use the concepts of conflict and consensus.

Inevitably, some kind of general agreement has characterised, for shorter or longer periods, the social policy debate and the decisions made in this field, in many western countries. This has often been referred to as consensus. Sullivan (1992) defines consensus as "substantial agreement at the level of principle about the need for government intervention to ensure economic growth, full employment and the provision of more or less comprehensive welfare services. (ibid. page 1)

The point is, that if the state (the legislative power), the employers organisations and the trade unions set up a (more or less formal) agreement to support each others interests, they can all gain from it. The employers will achieve economic growth and political stability, the workers will take advantage of increasing wages and other work-related improvements and the politicians will be able to realise social reforms to better peoples/their voters conditions (and thereby increase their opportunities to remain in power).

Sweden is often regarded to be one of the most evident examples of successful consensus policy. The co-operation between the government, unions and employers has lasted for a long period, from the end of the inter-war period, to (with some exceptions) the midst of the 1970's. (Especially the formalised co-operation between employers and unions has got a specific label; "the spirit of Saltsjöbaden," referring to the place where this agreement was set up.) The necessary prerequisite was the long-lasting period of social democratic ruling and the close connection between the political power and the unions, often referred to as two branches of the same tree. However, since about ten, fifteen years, the idea of the strong society is very strained, in Sweden as in other western countries. According to Mishra (1990) the decision made by Swedish politicians is to keep as much as possible of the welfare state, which Mishra calls a policy of maintenance. He regards this as a measure of the strength of the welfare state.

In England, during the inter-war period, an opinion was formed by a minority of politicians in the parliament, that some kind of "settlement between capital and labour" (Sullivan 1992 page 7) was desirable. The establishment of such ideas was facilitated by the emergence of the Keynesian theory, that the state ought to interfere to level the ups and downs in the trade cycle. From the social aspect, the Beveridge report nourished the same kind of thinking. According to this report, the society bears a responsibility towards its members, to ensure them reasonably good living conditions. At the end of the war, this opinion had grown among a majority of influential politicians as well as among the people, resulting in what has been named "the 1945 settlement." In brief, this was an agreement between employers and unions, among capital and labour. On the whole, however, the consensus established in England was not as strong as its equivalent in Sweden. And it was definitely challenged when Mrs Thatcher came into power.

In Germany (what is said below describes the situation in former West Germany) the development of social policy is rooted in traditions going back to Bismarck. In the end of the nineteenth century he founded laws concerning health care insurance, accident care insurance and insurance concerning care for the elderly and handicapped. The social welfare system of today's Germany is the result of a gradual societal development on this basis (Socialstyrelsen 1991).

One basic feature of the German system is that the family is the core unit, not the individual, as for instance in Sweden. The reciprocal responsibility for each member of the family to take care of the others is marked much stronger. Children are, to a large extent, responsible for the welfare of their parents. The responsibility of the society emerges when the family no longer is capable of fulfilling its obligations, an arrangement that has been called the principle of subsidiary.

Another basic feature is the insurance-model of welfare arrangements. Strictly spoken, you get back what you have paid in advance. The benefits are based on individual fees and contributions from the employer. Both compulsory and voluntary connections to the insurance are used. The labour market parties handle the social welfare insurance in collaboration, according to the law of 1949. The state (the different "länder") influences and governs through legislation and supervision.

Obviously, some kind of consensus exists in Germany as well with regards to the social welfare sector. Historically this "agreement" has not been established through struggles between different social classes, "labour and capital" in the way one can see in Sweden and especially in England. The family is the base of social welfare responsibility. Different voluntary organisations, often tied to churches or unions, play an important role.

3.2.4.2 SOCIAL POLICY AND SOCIAL WELFARE IN GERMANY, ENGLAND AND SWEDEN

As already mentioned, there are fundamentally three different ways of providing welfare, from a structural point of view. It can - firstly - be done by means of systems regulated, guaranteed and run by the state. Secondly, the issues of providing welfare can be entrusted to the market, meaning that you have to be a "consumer" of welfare. This implies, that arrangements of welfare will be available when there is both an evident need and people are rich enough to pay for what they want. The third way is to handle the issue of social welfare through the family, voluntary organisations and informal social networks, which sometimes has been called the "civil society."

In reality, all societies show a mixture of all three structural models, a compromise between the informal sector, the state and the market, although they vary with regards to their main emphasis. Figure 1 shows the three different systems of social welfare and also where the three countries in question might be placed in relation to them.

Illustration 9: Overview of social welfare models in regard to three European countries.

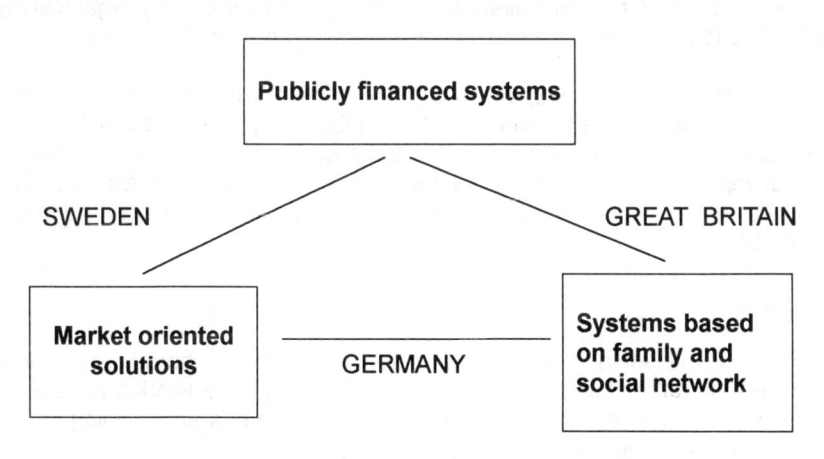

```
                    ┌─────────────────────────────┐
                    │  Publicly financed systems  │
                    └─────────────────────────────┘
                           /              \
          SWEDEN          /                \     GREAT BRITAIN
                         /                  \
   ┌──────────────────┐                        ┌──────────────────┐
   │ Market oriented  │        GERMANY         │  Systems based   │
   │    solutions     │  ────────────────────  │  on family and   │
   │                  │                        │  social network  │
   └──────────────────┘                        └──────────────────┘
```

taken from Socialstyrelsen 1991, p. 10

In the following section each country will be briefly described with regards to their social welfare system.

Germany

The reciprocal responsibility between individuals and family members is the basic principle. This is especially emphasised concerning the care of the children, the elderly and the disabled. Health services, pensions and unemployment benefits rest on insurance systems, separated from the state even thought they are regulated through state legislation. Approximately 90% of the population are voluntary or compulsory connected to these three basic insurance systems. About one of four completes it with a private insurance. The coverage of the insurance systems is generally good.

The various insurances are financed by means of fees, mainly from the employee and the employer, half the sum each. In some cases the state also contributes. People may be covered by the insurance even though they have not been employed and able to pay any fee.

Concerning the care for the elderly and the disabled the principal of reciprocal responsibility between family members comes in the first place. Old people's homes and home help are available, normally run by voluntary organisations, often tied to churches or unions, but supervised by the municipalities.

As a result of growing needs and a strained economy, the questions of care for the elderly and disabled is under debate in Germany. The tradition of trusting the family is considered to be a barrier for large groups of women to enter the labour market. The integration between the former East- and West-Germany is still a major issue, because of the strain it is causing, in the first hand economically.

England

In England the social welfare systems are built upon a shared responsibility between the authorities on the one hand and the social network and voluntary organisations (the informal sector) on the other. There is an on-going change towards market-oriented solutions (see below).

Two separate insurance systems are fundamental parts of the social welfare system. Both are regulated, financed and mainly governed by the state. First there is the National Health Service (NHS), concerning health care and dental care. NHS includes a comprehensive system of General Practitioners, taking care of the basic needs of health care. It also includes hospitals and nursing homes.

Second, there is an insurance system covering pensions, unemployment benefits and so on. Even though the state provides capital for most of these systems there are also fees paid by the individual and by the employer.

Concerning the elderly and the disabled it is an overarching goal to enhance their possibilities to remain at home. Thus, the help and care available is centred round this ambition. The municipalities are responsible for these kind of services. However, a major part of the work is done by voluntary organisations, which have a long-lasting tradition in the British society. There are close to 170 000 different voluntary organisations, partly financed by the municipalities, partly by voluntary contributions.

Members of the family, relatives and others included in the social network are expected to contribute in care giving, together with the municipality and voluntary organisations. For severely handicapped and very frail people there are institutions available. About 5% of the elderly live in such institutions.

Sweden

The Swedish model of social welfare policy rests on an out-spoken consensus between capital, labour and politics. As a result, there have been considerable resources available for social welfare within the public sector. Aside of this, there is also a (growing) part of the welfare arrangements run by market oriented agencies. The welfare sector in Sweden is, to a large extent, decentralised and run by the municipalities.

The systems of health care, dental care, pensions and so on cover the whole population. The levels of compensation are generally high, even though they have decreased in many cases during the last decade, due to cut-downs in the insurance systems.

Like in England, the main goal concerning help and care for the elderly and disabled is to facilitate their staying at home to the largest extent and as long as possible. Therefore, welfare arrangements, such as home help, transportation service, meals on wheels are well built out and managed by the municipalities. Nevertheless, relatives and other members of the social network make a very substantial contribution, at least to the same amount as the authorities. The role of voluntary organisations is increasing as well.

Trends for the future

The models of social policy in all three countries are in transition. In Germany, there is a change towards greater influence from the political arena, the state is taking more responsibility. In the long run, this might relieve the responsibility from the family. Great Britain is moving towards market orientation and decentralisation. The movement towards market orientation can also be identified in Sweden. In the Swedish case, the process of decentralisation has been going on for many years. The changes integrated into figure 1 (shown earlier) can be illustrated like this.

Illustration 10: Overview of social welfare models in regard to three European countries.

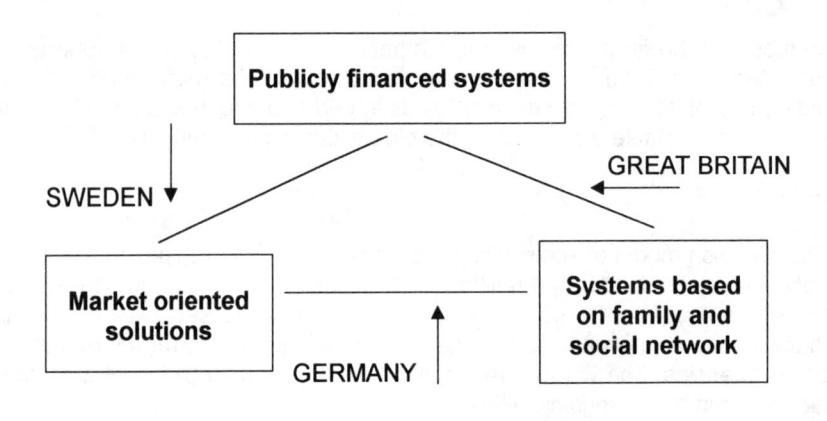

```
                    ┌─────────────────────────┐
                    │ Publicly financed systems│
                    └─────────────────────────┘
                          ╱           ╲
                         ╱             ╲    GREAT BRITAIN
              SWEDEN ▼  ╱               ╲   ◄─────
                       ╱                 ╲
         ┌──────────────────┐      ┌──────────────────┐
         │  Market oriented │──────│  Systems based   │
         │    solutions     │   ▲  │  on family and   │
         │                  │   │  │  social network  │
         └──────────────────┘      └──────────────────┘
                             GERMANY
```

taken from Socialstyrelsen 1991, p. 10

Obviously, all three basic models of social welfare policy are under stress. In some respects, they are converging, in others they are keeping their main features, due to cultural and historical differences. Even so, the direction of travel during the post-war era has mainly been the same: One long period of building up and expansion followed by stagnation, cut-downs and revaluation (Lindberg 1998). The threats are coming from the outside and from the inside of social policy systems.

FOR THE STUDENTS TO DISCUSS:

- What is the impact of historical and cultural conditions on the way social policy systems develop?

- The level of benefit and the degree of coverage are two important aspects of social welfare arrangements, differing within and between the countries. Give examples and discuss these differences.

- Are the social welfare systems in the three countries converging? If so, how does it show?

- The European co-operation is developing. What impact will it have on the social policy systems?

3.2.4.3 BASIC LEGISLATIVE SOCIAL POLICY DOCUMENTS AND SPECIFIC RULES AND REGULATIONS CONCERNING DISABLED PEOPLE IN THE THREE COUNTRIES

Germany

In Germany, there are four laws in particular that govern the social welfare policy.

1. Most significant is the Article 3 in the constitutional law (Grundgesetz), saying that it is not allowed to discriminate anyone because of handicap and disablement.

2. The Bundes-Sozial-Hilfe-Gesetz (BSGH) contains paragraphs about different kinds of welfare benefits in various situations in life.

3. The Betreungsgesetz is a law about care for the disabled and the handicapped, entitling them to personal assistance when there is a need for it.

4. In the Kinder-Jugend-Hilfe-Gesetz there are paragraphs covering the rights for children and young people to get protection and different kinds of support, from agencies run by authorities as well as by other organisations.

England

In England, the following four sources mainly govern the social welfare policy.

1. The Disability Discrimination Act (1995). The first section refers to definitions of disability, the second section to Employment and the third section, which is about Goods and Services.

2. The Chronically Sick and Disabled Person´s Act (1970).

3. The Education Act (1998)

4. The Tomlinson Report, from 1946.

Sweden

In Sweden, there are mainly three laws of importance in this field.

1. The Social Services Act (1982). It contains the fundamental rights for people to get the help they need and the unconditional responsibility for the state to deliver help, care and assistance.

2. The Health and Medical Service Act (1981) regulates the health care system, run by county councils and municipalities.

3. The Act concerning Support and Service for persons with certain Functional Impairments (1994) is a law ensuring handicapped and disabled people special benefits.

Aside of these national laws from Germany, Great Britain and Sweden, it is essential to keep in mind the global statements from the World Health Organisation, concerning human rights in general and for handicapped and disabled people in particular. The Salamanca Statement from UNESCO is also a basic source concerning human rights especially for these groups.

3.2.4.4 WHAT DOES REALITY LOOK LIKE?

All three countries have well-established social welfare systems. However - and unfortunately - this doesn't mean that all people actually can enjoy all the help and support they need to live their life in the best way possible.

It is not enough to study the policy-level. It must be combined with empirical studies of the factual situation concerning welfare and its distribution. Each group of students in the three countries is therefore expected to collect and organise data concerning living conditions for people and groups of needy persons.

This could be carried out through:

1. Studies of statistics concerning welfare and the distribution of welfare benefits in the population

2. Studies of research reports about different aspects of welfare or bad conditions for specific groups.

3. Studies of articles in the popular press

4. Interviews with representatives for client organisations or individuals belonging to identified needy groups (for instance drug addicts, disabled, poor pensioners, families in strained situations.

Each group of students decides which way(s) they will use to collect information and how they will organise the data they have collected.

3.2.4.5 POLICY VERSUS PRACTICE!

This is the part of comparison. What is said in the official documents will be compared to what the students have found about reality. Difficulties to find adequate sources of information will be discussed here.

FOR THE STUDENTS TO DISCUSS:

- Is the collected material covering and truly mirroring the situation for people in need of help and care?

- How well or bad does policy correspond to practice in the compared respects?

- Considering the different social policy models: What can be said about differences in their possibilities to fulfil needs?

3.2.5 TASKS TO BE UNDERTAKEN

- Deepen your knowledge of different structural models of social policy, tarting from this section's text,

- Study your own country's social policy system in general and, in some chosen areas, more in detail.

- Collect empirical data concerning reality for some chosen groups of people in need of help from the welfare system.

- Critically compare social policy versus the factual situation for these groups.

- Consider the consequences -positive and negative - of different social policy models, when it comes to their ability to meet and fulfil needs.

- Develop a portfolio of evidence showing the result of your comparison

The work done by students from the three part-taking universities will be communicated, to enable cross-country comparisons and learning from each other, concerning different social policy models and gaps between policy and practice.

3.2.6 BIBLIOGRAPHY

3.2.6.1 REFERENCES

Lindberg, I. (1998)	Vägval i välfärdspolitik. LO Debatt
Mishra, R. (1990)	The Welfare State in Capitalist Society. London: Harvester Wheatsheaf
Nygren, L. (1994)	Trygghet under omprövning. Stockholm: Publica
Salonen, T. (1994)	Välfärdens marginaler. Stockholm: Publica Social laws, from Germany, England and Sweden
Socialstyrelsen (1991)	Vård och omsorg i sex europeiska länder. Rapport 1991:37. Stockholm: Allmänna förlaget.
Socialstyrelsen (1997)	Social Rapport 1997. SoS-rapport 1997:14. Stockholm: Fritzes
Sullivan, M. (1992)	The Politics of Social Policy. London: Harvester Wheatsheaf
Titmuss, M. (1974)	Social policy - an introduction. London: George Allen & Unwin Ltd.
Trost, H. (1991)	Sverige, EG-ismen och socialpolitiken. Stockholm: Verdandi Förlag

3.2.6.2 ADDITIONAL READINGS

Kaurmann, F.-X. (1997)	Herausforderungen des Sozialstaats. Frankfurt/Main, edition Suhrkamp 2053.
Schmidt, M. G. (1988)	Sozialpolitik. Historische und internationale Entwicklung im Vergleich. Opladen, Leske & Budrich
Schmid, J. (1996)	Wohlfahrtsstaaten im Vergleich. Soziale Sicherungssysteme in Europa: Organisation, Finanzierung, Leistungen und Probleme. Opladen, Leske & Budrich.

Hughes B. and
Patterson K. (1997)   The Social Model of Disability and the Disappearing Body; towards a sociology of impairment, *Disability and Society*, Vol 12,3,325-240

Shakespeare,T. and
Watson, N. (1997)   Defending the Social Model of Disability, *Disability and Society*, 12,2,293

3.3 POWER, POLITICS AND USER INVOLVEMENT

Åse -Britt Falch

3.3.1 INTRODUCTION

This part of chapter three deals with the questions of advocacy, user involvement and empowerment. During the last years there has been a change in how you look at people with disabilities. From the vision that it is a group that professionals should take care of, in some respects disabled people have been seen as a group that are unable to take responsibility for their own life, to be seen as a group of individuals that have their own force.

If you regard people with disabilities as individuals with their own force, this view changes social care and social work. For professionals it is important to learn how to provide socially, mentally or physically handicapped individuals and groups with help to self-help. Too see the role and functions of groups/organisations "of" disabled people versus groups "for" disabled people. Social work and social care of today also concern reinforcing and implementing models of user-profile.

It is to see this group of disabled people as individuals and experts on their own lives. When you meet people with a handicap it is important to open your mind and see that it is an individual with their own capacity. Life quality and power are important issues to deal with when you meet people with disabilities. Each individual has the right to have, as defined by professor emeritus in social work Harald Swedner, "A good voyage towards life" (Swedner, 1983).

Even if you regard disabled people as individuals you must also realise the power of a group. The idea that people with the same problems could get organised and add power and force to their demands and take place in arenas where they as individuals would have had difficulties entering into. People with similar problems can help and support each other in special ways through sharing and participating in other ways than professionals can. Self-help groups have been started all over the world from the experience of sharing the same problems. Parents of children with disabilities, drug addicts, people that were abused in childhood, people with Celebes Pares are some examples of groups that have come together to support each other and more forcefully demand their rights.

Support has also been given to disabled people in charity organisations, often connected with different religious backgrounds. Organisations have been started with good aims to help groups with handicaps. Today the opinion that if you are disabled you should not ask for charity is voiced. The society should be obliged to provide legal rights which means to be able to live in equal conditions with or without a handicap to all its members. The demand for equal rights has lead to the start of new organisations not for but by disabled people.

There are models to start group processes of groups that are disadvantaged with the goal to reinforce and give them power to grow stronger and find solutions in their own way. An important area of practice has been to assist the development of self-help groups. Workers have supported groups of clients sharing the same problems to come together in order to support one another. New responses to and ideas about appropriate services often arise from these groups. The groups either create them themselves, or pressure agencies to change their practice. Different expressions have been used for these phenomena; self-directed group work, self-helps groups and participatory action, are some of the expressions that have been used. There is a special branch of research that is called participatory research.

In social work you also have long traditions of working in two different models; one towards individuals and one towards groups. These two models have their roots in the work of two of the pioneers in social work; Mary Richmond and Jane Addams, who lived in America in the beginning of this century. Mary Richmond provided a model of "Friendly visitors" and an introduction to social casework "Social diagnosis". Jane Addams started the Settlement movement. She worked directly in society to give power to oppressed groups and she considered the social problems she saw to be effects of the organisation of society (Soydan, 1994).

Even today you have discussions about how to help people with special needs. To help and reinforce individuals or groups is an issue of today's social care and social work. This is illustrated in models of community work and in psychosocial models of social work. In community work today you often have the ambition to work in the society, close to the clients and to reinforce groups to seize power over their own lives.

When helping individuals and groups it is common to talk about empowerment and advocacy in social care and social work. Malcolm Payne (1997, page 266) defines empowerment and advocacy:

"Empowerment seeks to help clients gain power of decision and action over their own lives by reducing the effect of social or personal blocks to exercising

existing power, by increasing capacity and self-confidence to use power by transferring power from the environment to clients. Advocacy seeks to represent the interest of powerless clients to powerful individuals and social structures."

Payne's definition is a very good introduction to this part chapter 3 about power, politics and user involvement.

3.3.2 OBJECTIVES

Students shall:

- identify different forms of advocacy in relation to "disability, learning and living difficulties" and disadvantage
- critically evaluate concepts of "power" and "empowerment" in relation to disability and disadvantage
- undertake a critical exploration of the role and functions of groups/organisations "of" disabled people versus groups "for" disabled people

Work related to this component might be structured in the following way:
- Factual information from of literature (provided here) and lectures
- Independent study of recommended literature
- Field studies, visits to user organisations and interviews with individuals
- Seminars of the field studies with a theoretical connection to the literature

3.3.3 LEARNING OUTCOMES

By the end of the chapter students will have acquired:

- The understanding of advocacy and empowerment and the importance of these questions for disadvantaged groups.
- How to start and organise self-helps groups on a level of community work.

3.3.4 ADVOCACY, GROUP WORK AND EMPOWERMENT

3.3.4.1 DIFFERENT CONCEPTIONS OF AND THE BACKGROUND OF ADVOCACY AND EMPOWERMENT

The idea of empowerment was introduced in the USA around 1970 and was of interest in local development and the mobilisation of disadvantaged groups. It was also a strategy in social work to change the way of working with disadvantaged groups. Earlier there had been what you can call a top-down strategy and a wanted strategy working from bottom to top was desired. This means that the groups were given more influence and it became important to have a user profile in social work (Forsberg, Starrin, 1997).

In the beginning, talking about empowerment was a radical political streak was. Today this radical and political touch is more or less gone. Empowerment is something that has many different meanings, but it has an essence of something positive that has to do with enforcing people with special needs because of disadvantages. It can be groups with different handicaps; economical, legal, medical, or sociological reasons. What they have in common is the need to be reinforced with a strategy working from the bottom to the top. This strategy is often called that you give empowerment to groups.

You can regard empowerment as a movement in society to return the right of decision to disabled people. During, at least the last fifty years, professionals and the society have taken over more and more of what was before the responsibility of the individuals and the families. In many ways you can say that it was a negative effect of the social reforms during this period. Empowerment can, in certain ways, be seen as a movement against the social planning that has been provided by the society during the last period of social reforms.

Social reforms and strong social strategies is a good thing but it can also take away the power from the citizens. The state's actions and the outlook on the state can be apprehended as a form of paternalism; taking care of you, but at the same time restricting you. You could feel and also be treated as a child by professionals that are educated and employed in social work and social care. Thus, disabled people can experience a loss of self-confidence and have difficulties seeing their own strength. This is one of the reasons that empowerment is so popular in 1998.

Empowerment is also something that you connect with local community work and local development. It is also connected with help to self-help. You can also use the expression of empowerment to start and enforce local autonomy and self-government in strategies of prevention and intervention.

Barbara Solomon (1976) and Stephanie Riger (1981) were among the first to publish material about and describe empowerment. Solomon described the mobilisation of the black people and Riger described the emancipation of women. One article often referred to is Rappaport (1981). The article criticises the classical model of prevention and tries to give alternatives to this model. Later on Swift and Lewin (1987) published an article about empowerment and mental health (Forsberg, Starrin 1997).

Today you can say that empowerment is, what you can call a "catchword", that is used in many different contexts and with different meanings. It is an expression that is very popular to use and it is difficult to define it, but there is a mutual sense that empowerment is something good and worth striving for. In American encyclopaedias you find that empower has two meanings:

1, To give power to or authorisation to
2, To give possibilities to or permission to

The origin of the word empowerment is Latin "potere", which means that you are able to. You can also see that the word is active and has nothing to do with asking for something. It contains the meaning of seizing the power. It is easier to say what empower is not than to say what it is. It is absolutely not alienation, helplessness, hopelessness and powerlessness. It rather stands for social support, self-reliance, competence, autonomy, self-control, citizenship and pride (Forsberg, Starrin 1997).

Something in common when you talk about empowerment is that you question the role of the professionals. Professionals can give the impression that they have the monopoly on knowledge and competence to help disabled people in their daily lives. When you talk about empowerment it concerns giving the power back people with disabilities. To understand that they are the experts of their own lives, disabled or not.

Discussions about professionals taking over the planning of the lives of disabled people are often raised. As a disabled person you can get the feeling that you have no power over your own life. Many disabled people have mouthed this and have also declared that the result of this is that they don't have a good life and they feel dependent.

When you are active in an organisation and you work there is based on the ideas of empowerment you take exception to hierarchies in your organisation. You believe in equal rights and you see the force of working together side by side. You see a mutual goal of a fight to have human rights and respect for yourself and the groups you are involved with. You don't believe in authority, guardianship and professional influence, you have a perspective of working from the bottom to the top. You believe in the possibilities to mobilise the force to gain what you are authorised to have as a citizen, whether you are disabled or not (Forsberg, Starrin 1997).

To be successful in social actions and in mobilising the force of groups for disabled people you have to create a feeling of common identification and pride. Many disabled people have a feeling of stigmatisation and also a feeling of shame, which could result in the fact that you hide yourself. In empowerment you can see that this stigmatisation and the feeling of shame go away. You get the force to stand up openly in society. Clients have power, which they do not use if they are not aware of their own force. Oppressed groups can bee very strong if they successfully increase the total amount of power in the group. Another effect could be groups taking steps of social actions that are illegal to achieve their rights. Loyalty and solidarity towards the group is stronger than towards legislation.

Advocacy can be seen as an aspect of empowerment since it can be used to fight for resources for oppressed groups. Historically it has been seen as an aspect of welfare rights work. Advocacy has evolved strongly as part of the movement to discharge many people from long-stay institutions in which they would previously have been cared for, and as part of welfare rights work (Payne, 1997).

Professionals, social workers and advocates have, on behalf of clients within their own agencies or arguing on their behalf with other agencies, helped disadvantaged groups to obtain their social and legal rights. Critical voices have been raised towards this way of work, because some believe that oppressed groups themselves, through self- or peer-advocacy can only practise it. However, as well as taking the traditional professional role of working on behalf of clients, workers can act as formal advocates, by following clients instruction (Payne, 1997).

Power given by a worker leaves the power with the worker. Clients must seize power, and it is the role of social work to organise the institutional response, which makes this, possible and accept it when it occurs. Ideas such as normalisation and self-advocacy have often become associated with civil liberty perspectives that focus on the need to free clients oppressed by assumptions about their dependency on care (Payne, 1997).

In university education of social care-workers or social workers, you often use the expression that you are educated to become "The advocate of the poor". That means that you have to have a good education in legislation and in the social welfare system to be able to help oppressed groups to obtain their legal rights. To work with an advocacy-profile should be a normal way of working for a social care-worker or social worker of today.

Another important point of view is that you are educated to focus on the client, to have a client perspective and work with user involvement. This question is very important today when finances are getting worse and professionals can be asked to save money for the authorities in the organisations of social care. Thus, disabled people can have difficulties to obtain their legal rights to have the opportunity to have a normal life society. It will probably be necessary for professionals to work more with advocacy in the future to help disabled people obtain their legal rights.

3.3.4.2 GROUPWORK, GROUP PROCESS, SELF-HELP-GROUPS AND SELF-DIRECTED GROUPWORK

An important area of practice in social work and social care has been to assist and start different groups of and for disadvantaged people. As a community worker, you are expected to support groups of clients sharing the same problems to come together to support one another. New responses and ideas about appropriate services often arise from these groups. The groups either create themselves, or pressure agencies to change their practice (Payne, 1997).

Groupwork can be described in different ways and be initialised for different reasons. Groupwork is a common method in all pedagogic arenas. It is well known that it is a good method to change the way people think, to feel social community, to obtain new understanding and facilitate learning. It can also be started as a political movement to create pressure to produce changes in society. Self-help groups are also an advanced way of goupworking. In self-help groups you can add a social aspect to the groupwork.

What happens in a group? When you put people together you start a process. You can call this a group process. It is a bit difficult to describe what a group process is. It is a feeling that everybody is aware of if they have had the opportunity to work in a group. You can say that the group process is what happens in the group including different kinds of relationships between the members of the group. The group process is co-operation, different meanings and aspects, new knowledge, support, identifications, feelings, community and a feeling of sharing. To create a positive group process is sometimes not the easiest thing to do. The result of groupwork can also be negative. The members' conflicts and the work in the group can give bad and unsatisfied feelings. It is important to be aware of this negative side of groupwork and the group process. An important thing when this happens is that you can get supervision to be able to leave this problem and enter a positive group process.

When we talk about groups and group processes for oppressed groups you automatically think of self-helps groups. Often you also talk about self-directed groupwork. In self-help groups the groupwork is summarised into six aspects:

1. To leave isolation.
2. To promote social adaptation.
3. To prepare for changes in life, or for a crises in life.
4. To solve personal problems or family problems.
5. To solve or survey problems in the environment.
6. To gain insight, understanding and knowledge.
(Heap, 1987)

When a self-help group starts it is important to be aware of techniques to ensure a good start of the group process. Good communication and group processes in the group demand few members. A group with 6-10 members is the optimal. You can say that a self-help group should not be directed towards results (Heap, 1987). The important things are the activity in the group, that the members give each other support and the feeling of chairing. Because of that it is best if the group members deal with the same problems. For disabled people the discussion of stigmatisation and shame can be of importance. The group could help you with the special feeling of sharing the same problems, which makes the individuals stronger to come out and seize power in the society. Groups of parents of disabled children can get much help in self-helps groups to deal with the special problems you have has as a parent of a disabled child.

When you join a self-help group you should be motivated to join the group. In the start of self-help groups, professionals, with their experience, can help the group to come to work and show ways to support the process. It is important that the professionals in these groups have a role as a supervisor and do not interfere to much in the group.

Mullender and Wards (199) provide a clear view of empowerment theory, focused on groupwork settings and processes) in their book "Self-directed Groupwork: Users take action for empowerment". They also offer it (p.2) as a basis for wider forms of social action. They argue that empowering action must be "self-directed" (that is, by service users) but also oppose oppression. Such a definition implies that empowering work must confront the nature of power. Many ideas from feminist and anti-racist work are relevant to self-directed work. In the acknowledgement of their book they write that: " This book has grown directly out of the efforts of many groupworkers and group members to find a way of working together that is rooted in anti-oppressive principals."

Mullender and Wards say that the work to give empowerment to oppressed people is better done in groups. Because in individual and family work, individualisation of private troubles is too powerful to promote shared, social responses. Groups allow people to share resourses and initiative and experiment with action jointly. They also show on a model of practice in empowerment that has five stages:

1. *Pre-planning*: find a compatible co-working team, consultancy support and agree on empowering principles.
2. *Taking off*: engage with users as partners and plan the group jointly through open planning.
3. *Group-preparation for action*: help the group explore what issues are to be tackled, why these issues exist and how we can produce change.
4. *Taking action*: group members carry out agreed actions.
5. *Taking over*: workers begin to withdraw, and the group reviews what it has achieved, seeing connection between what, why and how. It then identifies new issues, sees links between the issues and again decides what actions to take. This process then continues throughout the group's life. (Payne 1997,p.281)

Mullenders and Wards (1991) also talk about five important empowering practice principles:

1. All people have skills, understanding and ability. We must recognise these rather than negative labels.
2. People have rights - especially to be heard, to control their own lives, to choose. To participate or not and to define issues and take action.

3. Peoples' problems always reflect issues of oppression, policy, economy and power as well as personal inadequacies.
4. People acting collectively can be powerful, and practice should build on this.
5. Practising what you preach involves facilitation, not "leading" and challenging oppression.
(Payne, 1997,p.281)

Common for self-help groups and self-directed groups is that both talk of user-involvement and that power and force is created when people work together sharing the same experiences. The difference is that self-help groups work to strengthen the individuals to cope with their personal life. Self-directed groups are action groups working towards political oppression, to reinforce groups to get more power in society, to be empowered to social actions.

If you look at empowerment as a movement to fight the oppression of disability and disadvantaged groups you also understand the importance of groupwork, group process, self-help groups and self-directed groups. As a professional it is necessary to have respect and give oppressed groups the opportunity to take the responsibility for his or her own life and understand the importance of that to receive a good quality of life.

ROISIN MULDOON

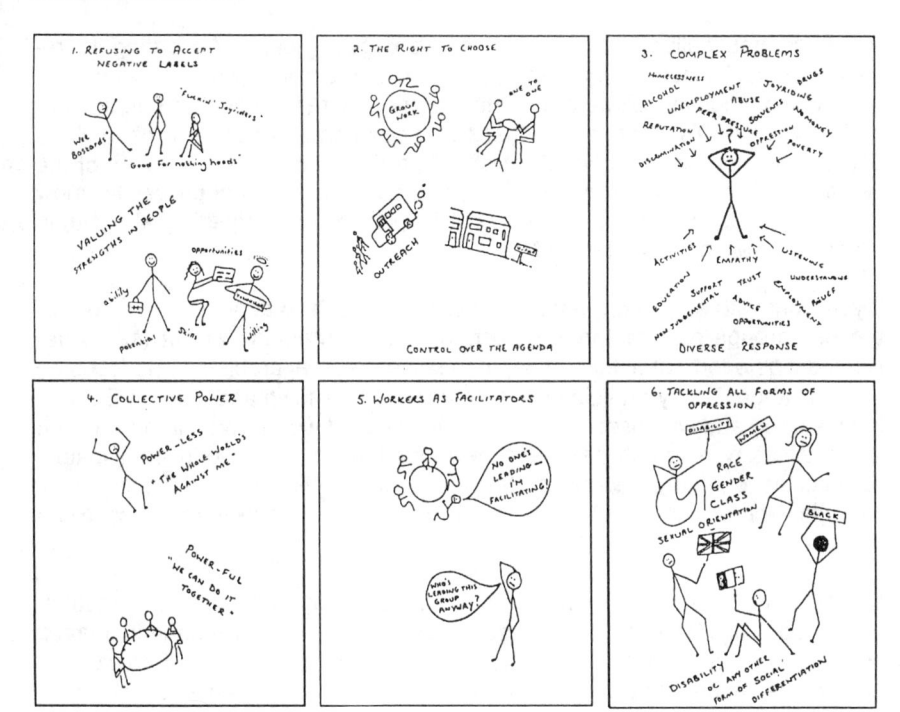

SOCIAL ACTION; Volume Two, Number Three 1994/95

3.3.4.3 PARTICIPATORY RESEARCH AND EMPOWERMENT

Research has called attention to disadvantaged groups. According to researchers social deprivation is a result from the fact that the disadvantaged, the shortcomings in welfare are related to unequal resources and unequal opportunities. WHO's standpoint is that better co-operation between researchers and practitioners is essential. How often are those who are the object of the research informed about the results? How often do the groups get to know anything about the research that could help them do something about their situation (Svensson, Starrin, 1992).

If you work with empowerment and different methods to achieve power for oppressed groups participatory research is a useful method. Lewin (1946) described it as a form of action research to solve practical problems and focus on social change. Today participatory research is well known and used in Europe, but it started and was used as a method in the third world. Even if the tradition of participatory research has been developed in the third world participatory research is primarily geared to the needs of people whose existence is a struggle, who are oppressed, that kind of people you find in Europe as well as in Africa.

Participatory research can be seen as a research, education and action-oriented activity. One of the key assumptions in participatory research is that it will lead to change, by and for those who carry out the research. Participatory research is, in the first place, a project for those whose existence is a struggle, who are oppressed and who live in poverty. The aim of participatory research is to find strategies and paths for empowerment. Conventional research has criticised participatory research projects saying that the collection and analysis of data is not sufficiently systematic. But we must also remember that the scientific society can easily become irrelevant to ordinary people (Svensson, Starrin, 1992).

Users of participatory research have developed some basic principles in their work. They are meant to be used as conceptual and practical tools, but it should be stressed that there is no absolute model for participatory research. The principles on which to be generally agreed have been formulated by Hall (1984) as follows:

1. Research should involve people in the entire process beginning with identification of the issues, through discussions of how to get information, to analysis and use of results within the context of action.

2. Research should result in some direct and positive benefits of those communities and people involved.
3. Research is a process of systematic creation of knowledge, which may or not involve people who have been professionally trained as researchers.
4. Knowledge is depended, enriched, and made more socially usable when it is produced collectively.
5. Research involves a combination of methods designed to facilitate social, co-operative, or collective production of knowledge.
6. Research, learning, and knowledge production are often aspects of the same intellectual process in the context of action (Hall, 1984, pp291-292).

When you see the principles of Hall you can understand the connection between participatory research and empowerment. It is a strategy working from the bottom to the top to evaluate concepts of power to oppressed groups and both have a user-profile.

3.3.4.4 SOME EXAMPLES

You can easily find examples in dissertations, articles and books that are written about power, politics and user involvement. It is a field that has become more and more popular with scientists, social workers and user organisations.

In Disability, Handicap and Society (1989) you can read an article by Brown and Ringma "New disability services: the critical role of staff in a consumer-directed empowerment model for service for physically disabled people." This paper reports and evaluates a non-institutional service model of community living for physically disabled people, that seek to achieve consumer empowerment.

Brown and Ringma (1989) describe a project in Brisbane Catholic Social Welfare Secretariat, a non-government and voluntary welfare agency, in conjunction with four previously institutionalised, severely physically disabled adults in one domesticscale residence. The consumers were aged 18 to 42. The purpose was to facilitate the process of deinstitutionalisation, to develop a community living model with consumer control, consumer development of new living skills, and achieve community integration.

The form of this praxis was that the four consumers were involved in all aspects of management. They became responsible for the running of the house and also of the employment of the staff. Through the project you can see that empowerment was used in all stages to have user involvement. You can see the same thoughts in America and Europe with the start of different "Independent living groups". In these groups disabled people take responsibility for their lives and see themselves as employees of the staff they need to lead a normal life in the society.

Sweden had a new law in 1994, "The act concerning Support and Services for persons with certain functional Impairments (LSS). by this law people with severe functional disabilities with physical or mental disorders are given the possibility to employ their own personal assistants. This law has been constructed out of strong demands from different organisations of disabled people. You can say that LSS is a result of empowerment and user involvement. Pressure groups where organised and worked with the construction of the law and with carrying it through (Allmänna råd, Socialstyrelsen 1994:1).

Projects have been started all over the world on the concept of Community Based Rehabilitation (CBR). CBR involves rehabilitative measures taken at community level, which use and build on the resources of the community, including the impaired, disabled and handicapped people themselves, their families and their neighbourhood. Handicap is seen as a social phenomenon occurring when an individual with impairment or a disability cannot fulfil his/her role in a given society. At this stage attitude, psychological or physical barriers are the decisive factors. A disabled person may be handicapped in one environment but not in another.

CBR-projects are started with a strong user profile and by groups with disabilities. The role of the professionals is to stay in the background to start the processes and not to be too much involved with the actions that are performed. The project works with empowerment, often with a model of participatory research, to mobilise power correspondent to equalisation of opportunities and full participation in the society.

In Sweden two CBR based projects have been started in Värmland 1994. One is directed towards individual service planning (ISP) where you build a network in consultation with parents of children with impairments. The parents and not the professionals have the initiative and make the decision of whom are going to be in the network and what kind of support the families wants. The other CBR-project works to enforce parents with disabled children in a thinly populated area with the help of a participatory research model. The aim of the project is to change the perspective from the professional organisations towards the children and parents and to get a local attachment. The group also has a function of self-support and self-help (Svensson, Starrin 1997).

Participation research has been started for and by people with learning difficulties in different countries. Berith Cech (1997) has started groups and the empowering process has been strong in these groups. Disabled people with a mental handicap are a group that has had difficulties obtaining power. Their lives have been organised by professionals and parents and few have asked for their opinions. Research shows that participatory research can be a model to reach empowerment in these groups.

3.3.5 TASKS TO BE UNDERTAKEN

1. Describe different forms of empowerment and advocacy in relation to disability, learning and living difficulties and disadvantages in your country.
2. User involvement? Does it exist today?
3. What are the differences of the role and functions of groups/organisation "of" disabled people versus groups "for" disabled people?
4. Give examples from your own experience of groupwork and group processes.
5. Give examples how disabled people can be empowered.
6. Have experts and professionals had too much influence in the daily life of disabled people?
7. Is there any danger with empowerment and social actions? Can it be used as an excuse for the politicians not to give resources to educate and employ professionals too?

3.3.6 BIBLIOGRAPHY

3.3.6.1 REFERENCES

Brown, C & Ringma C. (1989) *New Disability Services: the critical role of staff in a consumer-directed empowerment model of service for physically disabled persons.* Disability Handicap & Society. Vol, NO 3.

Cech, B. (1997) *Vardagsverklighet och livskvalitet för per soner med utvecklingsstörning.* Vårdhögskolan i Göteborg, Institutionen för social omsorg.

Forsberg, E & Starrin, B. (1997) *Frigörande kraft, empowerment som mod ell i skola, omsorg och arbetsliv.* Göteborg.

Hall, B. (1984) *Research, commitment and action: The role of participatory research.* International Review of Education, 30.

Heap, K. (1987) *Gruppmetod för socialarbetare och per sonal inom hälso och sjukvård.* Helsingborg.

Levin, K. (1946) *Action research and minority problems.* Journal of Social Problems, 2.

LSS. (1994) *Socialstyrelsens Almänna Råd 1994:4*

Muldoon, R. (1994/95) *The demystfication of social action group work principles.* Volume Two, Number Three 1994/95

SOCIAL ACTION,
Mullender, A & Ward, D. (1991) *Self-directed Groupwork: Users Take Ac tion for Empowerment.* London.

Payne, M. (1997) *Modern social work theory.* London.

Rappaport, J. (1981) *In Praise of Paradox: a social policy of Empowerment over Prevention.* American Journal of Community Psychology.

Riger, S. (1981) *Towards A Community.* Psychology News letter

Solomon, B. (1976) *Black Empowerment: Social work in Op pressed communities.* New York.

Soydan, H. (1993) *Det sociala arbets idéhistoria.* Lund.
Svensson, P-G &

Starrin, B. (1992)   *Health Policy. Development for disadvan taged groups.* Kristinasand.
Swedner, H. (1983)   *Socialt arbete en tankeram.* Lund.
Swift, C. & Lewin G. (1987)   *Empowerment: An Emerging Mental Health Technology.* Journal of Primary Prevention.

3.3.6.2 ADDITIONAL READINGS

Theunissen, G. &
Plaute, W. (1996)   *Empowerment und Heilpädagogik.* Freiburg im Breisgau.

4. LOOKING FORWARD - MANAGEMENT OF CHANGES

Fritz-Helmut Wisch

4.1 INTRODUCTION

Forms of social living follow certain organisational structures. Families, groups, associations, companies, etc. are structured and organised following a set of agreed (traditional) rules. Today, we mainly differentiate between *authoritarian* and *democratic* forms of social living.

By means of a model organisation for disabled children, called EUROHAND, we will discuss different forms of social living. The discussion will show that authoritarian systems follow hierarchical principles, whereas democratic forms of social living are based upon interactive principles and are subject to mutual control and influence. We will present the tasks and objectives of democratically structured forms of social living and examine innovative management techniques which, in our point of view, primarily consist of skills of communication. A more detailed analysis will investigate the need of change within and between people (individuals) which will lead to developing a visionary construct for co-operation.

4.1.1 OBJECTIVES

Students shall

- explore the culture of organisational structures and the part that individuals play in them,
- develop skills of communication,
- critically reflect upon the need of change within and between individuals,
- critically investigate and analyse the changing structure and management of an organisation of/for disabled people,
- draft their collective visionary construct for new provisions in relation to disabled/disadvantaged people.

4.1.2 LEARNING OUTCOMES

When having completed this module, the students will be able to

- investigate the structures of an organisation of/for disabled / disadvantaged people,
- reflect upon the management of an organisation of/for disabled / disadvantaged people,
- communicate about visions in relation to disabled / disadvantaged people.

4.1.3 CULTURE OF ORGANISATIONAL STRUCTURES: ROLES OF INDIVIDUALS

4.1.3.1 THE HIERARCHICAL STEP MODEL

Lets take a closer look at the model home for disabled children and juveniles, which we will call **EUROHAND**. We will see groups which have structures similar to those of a family and which present themselves as *micro-systems* in the sense of *Bronfenbrenner*. Educators (carers) work shift; there is a head of group; there may be a head of department; there certainly is a board of managers. Additional (co-operative) experts work as therapists, such as practioners, psychologists, remedial and special educators, speech therapists, ergotherapists, etc. A caretaker, housekeeping staff, trainees (meso-system), etc. complement the staff and provide services to the benefit of the patients.

It goes without saying that the well-organised EUROHAND home is not autonomous. It is integrated in the municipal or *local* network of organisations managed by EUROHAND*LOC* which supports and advises EUROHAND with regard to specific disabilities, economic and organisational matters. EUROHAND*LOC* is not a local organisation but belongs to EUROHAND*REG* together with all the other EUROHAND*LOC* 's in the *region*. All EUROHAND*REG*'s are members of the *country organisation* or central organisation, called EUROHAND*COUNTRY*.

Conclusion: The EUROHAND model home is not isolated. It gets support, information, and instructions from many sides and is embedded in the hierarchical system of the EUROHAND organisation.

EUROHANDCOUNTRY
EUROHANDREG   EUROHANDREG
EUROHANDLOC EUROHANDLOC EUROHANDLOC EUROHANDLOC
EUROHAND EUROHAND EUROHAND EUROHAND EUROHAND EUROHAND

The micro-system of our EUROHAND model home is reflected in the macro-system of the EUROHAND organisation, where managers and staff at all levels pursue the
common goal to serve the well-being of the patients. The system is structured as follows:

Management
Therapists   Head of Departement
Caretaker Caretaker Caretaker Caretaker Caretaker   Housekeeping staff   Trainees
Patients Patients Patients Patients Patients Patients Patients Patients Patients Patients

---

HIERARCHICAL STEP MODEL

Obviously, there is a high potential of fear, conflict, and aggression - both in the hierarchical (micro-) system and in the corresponding macro-system. The *management style* of the present model is, for obvious reasons, based on *directives*. Attributes such as authoritarian and patriarchal are associated with the model of directive management (*Gregor-Rauschtenberger/Hansel,* 1993; *Denger,* 1997). This 'obsolete model' is familiar to us: the master craftsman manages his craftsman's business; the farmer manages his farm; at the beginning of industrialisation, the founder managed his firm. In the army, the leadership principle *of command and obedience* has never been questioned. Most of us have been educated in the light of these traditions.

At personal level, we were educated by our primary persons of reference (our parents). At school and during our vocational training, our teachers, trainers, and superiors followed these principles. Everybody within a clearly structured step model knows to what level he or she belongs:
to the bottom, to the middle, or to the top!

Let us come back to the EUROHAND model home:
Patients, which belong to the lowest level, experience each other as rivals and the carers as well as all others at higher levels as *superiors*. They can only vent their frustration upon those at the same level or upon weaker individuals at lower levels.
Carers experience each other and those at the same (i.e. low) level as rivals and all others at higher levels as superiors. They can only vent their frustration upon weaker individuals (patients).

Therapists/heads of department experience each other and all others at the same level as rivals. For them, only the managers are superiors. They can only vent their frustration upon weaker individuals (carers, housekeeping staff, ... patients)

The managers do not have superiors (within the home) and can only vent their frustration upon weaker individuals (therapists, heads of department, carers, ..., patients).

These few examples shall provide us with enough information to show the potential conflicts that exist at the EUROHAND model home and to demonstrate that any similar organisation is, to no small extent, a highly explosive construct. We deliberately neglect the role that parents and any other persons involved (exogenous system) play and will not analyse the system-related and professional conditions that apply to them.

There is a high potential of conflict. It is only obvious that preventive measures must be taken to prevent escalation and that existing conflicts must be constantly kept under control.

Fear is spreading. The members of staff hide their perceptions. They painstakingly watch out for any situation that might give rise to conflict, suppress any spark of creativity, and prevent any breath of fresh air from entering the home that might let smouldering conflicts break out. The EUROHAND model home presents itself as a typical, well-organised, and clearly structured organisation following traditional principles. Everybody knows what to think of each other; any activity is predetermined or even controlled and remains calculable. Nothing is left to chance; each member can always rely on the other members.

The organisational structure model should actually belong to the past, although it is still wide-spread. It should have been replaced by a modern operational management emphasising quality (of care). Unfortunately, we still find constructs, social communities, and homes for disabled people which are organised exactly according to the above negative structure and which follow the directive step model. We must re-emphasise the fact that, in this model, the *weak persons* are at the lowest level whereas the *strong persons* are at the top. The pecking order between these levels is fixed. The game of power can be repeated at random. Whoever wants to leave the order, does not obey the rules, or follows his/her own way, loses ground. If he/she is lucky, he/she will reach safe ground. If not, he/she will be harmed if he/she does not find the right way out. It goes without saying that those within the organisation find it hard to help an outsider who disturbs the order.

We have already mentioned that the presented step model of co-operation is built upon authority, discipline, and obedience; follows the principle of *law and order* known from military organisations, and gives rise to hypocrisy and its well-known negative impact. Therefore, the step model cannot form the basis of an organisational model for modern, future-oriented social communities. All attempts to conserve, restore, or even consolidate such a model must not only be rejected but be attacked. The step model belongs to the past. History has shown that blind obedience and absolute confidence in law and order results in tragedy, chaos, and war.

4.1.3.2 THE INTERACTIVE CIRCLE MODEL

On the threshold to the third millennium, on the way into the future, totally different models are taking on shape and will become standard, since social action, public-spirited co-operation, free and democratic principles have to be established; human rights have to be generally accepted and consolidated.

What does our future model of peaceful co-operation look like?

This future model is not based on hierarchical structures. The main emphasis is not placed on patients and carers. All patients and members of staff form a team. There are no superiors and inferiors. What counts is the 'team spirit'.

The objective of this future model is not limited to improving the situation of the patients, for example. We pursue a broader objective. We want to improve the overall situation of all members of the organisation and increase their wellbeing by living together in a democratic way. How can we achieve this goal? We envision a circle model without any points of attack, without superiors and inferiors and which is designed to foster a peaceful and democratic cooperation.

Circle diagram with labels around the circumference: Patients, Caretaker, Housekeeping, Staff, Trainees, Management, Therapists, Head of Department, Patients, Patients (reading around the circle)

INTERACTIVE CIRCLE MODEL

It is obvious that a *pacified* co-operation (Begemann, 1994) is much easier to realise in the present (circle) model than in a traditional, authority-oriented and hierarchical step model, which automatically includes superiors and inferiors. In the circle model, all team members are at the same level. Carers and patients form a social partnership in which *innovative requests for normalisation and integration in order to humanise the world of disabled people in a democratic society are no empty words (Jacobs, 1995).*

Although our Scandinavian neighbours have realised and internalised these democratic objectives of normalisation and integration for a couple of decades already (*Bank-Mikkelsen, DK/Nirje; SVE*), humanitarian ideologies and principles still have to be accepted at the European and international scene. It goes without saying that we can only approximate to these anthroposophical ideas if organisational structures are changing (can change) and if there is a willingness to adopt interactive (non directive) social manners.

It seems, however, that more and more organisations and social communities follow the democratic objectives of *normalisation and integration* in relation to living with disabled people. In the following, we will continue to call them patients. We remain optimistic that the *Principle of Hope (Bloch, 1959)* which has been expanded to include the *Principle of Responsibility (Jonas, 1987)* will not only support us on our way to more democratic co-operation but help develop ourselves in the future; that the *dialogical approach (Buber, 1979)* will enable us to come nearer to forms of living that require a public-spirited co-operation.

In the interactive circle model, there is also a form of management or direction which, however, does not stand out but functions differently. Decision-making and solution-finding processes are not pre-defined; they are worked out and defined interactively, i.e. in form of mutual influence. The integration of all parties concerned is not only desired but necessary. The result is that

- each individual is taken into consideration and supported;
- each individual increasingly identifies himself with his work and the objectives of the organisation;
- each individual has more freedom for action;
- decisions are clear (accepted);
- the team is motivated;
- the team is developing into a self-controlled group (self-coaching);
- management, staff, and patients co-operate.

Democratic co-operation requires innovative management techniques. In the future, the task of management will consist in co-ordinating the process of communication and decision-making, i.e. managers master the art of rhetoric or apply communication techniques and strategies, as we say today.

4.1.3.3 COMMUNICATION SKILLS

Interactive co-operation requires a respectful, accepting, and understanding approach towards each other. We have learnt from *Tausch und Tausch* that a person should follow three basic principles that can be identified by the interlocutor if a conversation is to be successful:

- *understanding* the other partner and making him feel that you understand him
- leading the conversation in a *respectful and warm* manner

- let you partner feel that the conversation is *authentic*

These basic dialogical attitudes or principles are valid for both individual or group discussions. They are "also" necessary and sufficient general prerequisites for any other human relationship and help develop one's personality. This is true for parents and children, life companions, practioners and patients, lecturers and students, company staff, carers and patients, etc. *(Tausch und Tausch, 1990, pp 300+).*

4.1.3.4 CLIENT-ORIENTATED COMMUNICATION

Let us come back to the EUROHAND model home:
Does the relationship between the managers, clients, and customers, between carers and patients, reflect the three basic principles of *understanding, respect/warmth*, and *authenticity*? If so, we can assume that there is a good climate of communication.

Against this background, we rather talk of *customer-orientated communication* than of client-oriented communication today. *Customer-orientated communication* wants to make things clear, both for the interlocutor or receiver and the sender.

- What does the customer expect from EUROHAND?
- What does EUROHAND offer?
- Are the customer's wishes restricted?
- How flexible are such restrictions?

If things are clear, we take our interlocutor seriously. The customer knows what he can expect; the sender gets to know the customer's wishes. Clarity in a discussion mainly relates to three aspects:

- *Relationship* between the communication partners
- Objectives and topics of the conversation.
- Procedure

A clearly structured procedure, which reveals the intentions of the communication partners, as well as clear objectives provide guidance and security for the customers, who might have a totally different background and come from totally different social environments:

- Persons in need requiring care (patients),
- Staff
- Case managers (practioners, relations, carers)
- Financing bodies (social welfare office, youth welfare office)
- Public (press, politics, friends, competitors)
- Committees (boards of management, work groups)

In general, *customer-orientated communication* relates to:

- Target-oriented communication
- Communication between equal and integrated partners
- Co-operative communication
- Responding to the personal situation of the interlocutor

As its name implies, customer-orientated communication responds to the requirements of the customer and takes his wishes and expectations into consideration. In times where money is short in supply it is getting more and more difficult to keep or even improve the standards reached in health and social care. The healthcare service sector in general and, what is important for our approach, the field of rehabilitation in particular are undergoing dramatic change and are confronted with economic and financial restrictions.

4.1.3.5 THE NEED OF CHANGE WITHIN AND BETWEEN INDIVIDUALS

During this period of restructuring and change intelligent solutions must be found quickly. On the one hand, existing quality standards must not be abandoned; on the other hand, we are confronted with the torturing question: 'How can these standards be kept or even improved in times where money is short in supply?'.

Developments based on market economy and business management can provide valuable assistance in this respect.

For a couple years, professional managers have taken over the management of rehabilitation organisations from the former directors, for example. Everywhere, honorary carers are supported (or replaced) by full-time staff who restructure (rehabilitation) organisations by implementing economic policies. The same applies to the EUROHAND model home.

Changes are taking place at two levels. On the one hand, the shift to general management affects the individuals (at managerial level). On the other hand, changes influence the relationships between individuals and the way they co-operate.

Why has the self-image of (honorary) carers changed? Everybody says that self-sacrificing 'honorary carers' are disappearing. In recent years, the reasons for the change at managerial level have been widely discussed under the catch phrases of 'helper syndrome' and 'burn-out syndrome', not only by those concerned. The honorary carers, who have felt called to be what they are due to personal experience and who recruited themselves from self-help groups, have found it very difficult to assess their highly-motivated work as being the work of 'helpless helpers' (*Schmidbauer, 1977*). Mainly *historical and content-related reasons* have to be put forward which illustrate the potential conflicts between honorary and professional carers.

First, we will briefly investigate the historical dimension:
Honorary carers have managed self-help groups until the latter have become so strong that professional support has proved to be necessary. The honorary carers (must) realise that they cannot cope with the situation as far as the time involved and the work are concerned. In organisations with self-help groups, another aspect must be taken into consideration. The founders (parents and friends) cannot give up control and still want *to be in charge*. They see themselves as having more experience than the professional carers.

As far as the *content-related* dimension is concerned, honorary carers are highly motivated due to the fact that they are personally involved. On the one hand, this involvement can positively influence the care provided. On the other hand, it may lead to extremely difficult relationships and much more potential conflicts. Both *conflicts between father and son* as well as the problem of *presence and distance* make life very hard for both sides. The founders could trust each other blindly. Uncontrolled presence gets dangerous only if emotions instead of rational thinking dominate at personal level.

Trust alone is not enough to guide staff and clients on a matter-of-fact basis; in other words with professional *distance*.

The ever growing professionalism yields, to no small extent, conflict and re-quires sensitive co-operation of all persons involved (team members) in rela-tion to customer-oriented communication. Traditional behaviour relying on state-funding is replaced by self-assured, market-oriented behaviour and re-sponds to the challenges and opportunities of economic developments. The trend towards a market economy and the efforts to implement new structures are reflected in a number of new terms and catch phrases that have recently been introduced into rehabilitation, health and social care. We will find terms, such as:

- Lean management
- Social management
- Quality management and assurance
- Personnel management
- Fund-raising
- Social sponsoring

These are new perceptions and strategies that have emerged under the pressure and need of (monetary) change in the social network, i.e. the structural change in the social service sector. The *social management of change (Holzamer, 1996)*, therefore, adapts economic and business strategies to find a competent approach to questions and problems that arise on the threshold to the next millennium.

Against this background, the EUROHAND model home will have to change dramatically. Following the principle of *lean management* (in the following the other management strategies will not be further investigated), the members of staff (managers, therapists, carers, housekeepers,...) will identify themselves with the objectives of the new management strategy, which include:

- Total customer orientation
- Higher quality care
- Avoiding errors
- Improving procedures and services
- Avoiding waste of money (cost management)
- Flexibility and quick reaction to change in circumstance
- Fast implementation
- Concentration on core activities
- Maintaining and safeguarding competitiveness

To achieve these goals the staff of EUROHAND will probably have to give up habits and customs they have grown fond of, since lean management has little respect for traditional behaviour, established working procedures, and authoritarian structures. High requirements are placed on the staff, since lean management is not a single (short) process, but must be seen as a long-term strategy. If a rehabilitation organisation, such as EUROHAND, accepts this innovative policy, it will gain a lot of advantages:

- Re-orientation instead of rigidity
- Flexibility instead of inflexibility
- Clarity instead of obscurity
- Interaction instead of hierarchy
- Dynamic instead of static organisation

If you adopt the strategy of lean management, you are responsible for a set of methods. In the beginning, these methods create fear in the persons involved because they are new. The staff must be convinced of their efficiency carefully. To motivate the staff and to create the desired working climate, an array of tools are available which require committed directors:

- Supervision
- Self-coaching
- Team building
- Training
- Specialist training
- Post qualification
- Exchange of specialists
- Open (team) discussions
- Responsibility and freedom of action

Motivation of staff seems to be difficult (not only because money is short in supply; a fact that affects, to no small extent, the social sector). Considering the above challenges, motivation, however, is a vital instrument for improving the working climate which, in turn, is the prerequisite for implementing a basic quality assurance policy and for improving standards of quality, for example.

4.1.3.6 INVESTIGATION AND ANALYSIS OF THE CHANGING STRUCTURE AND MANAGEMENT OF AN ORGANISATION OF/FOR DISABLED/DISADVANTAGED PEOPLE

Staff motivation is an important instrument - if not the most important one - to meet new and changing requirements relating to the work with disabled people. The future-oriented policies mentioned above, such as lean management, social management, quality management, quality assurance personnel management, fund-raising, and social sponsoring, reflect the many attempts made to find a suitable approach to changing market conditions.

We suppose that the EUROHAND model home has undergone structural change due to the consequent implementation of future-oriented policies, such as

- *customer-orientated communication*
- *lean management*

and has developed from a hierarchical into an interactive organisation.

How does the new EUROHAND organisation look like? Let us take a closer look at the EUROHAND TEAM:

Management — The new EUROHAND organisation also has a management. The management, however, does not decide on its own in an arbitrary manner (as in the hierarchical system), but continuously interacts with the members of staff. As all other staff, the managers give advice and are criticised. Since UROHAND is oriented towards its customers, the managers always seek to improve the care delivered to the patients (quality assurance). Basically, the behaviour of the managers is not in the slightest different to the behaviour of the members of staff.

Staff — All members of staff, sworn in to the same common objective, hink and act in the same direction. The common, customer-orientated objective is to maintain and increase the well-being of all patients (customers) at EUROHAND. All members of staff communicate with each other peacefully and democratically and try to improve the service delivered. As the managers, the carers, therapists as well as all other staff consider the patients as being equal partners. Weak points are identified at all levels, openly discussed and, if possible, eliminated quickly (avoiding errors).

Patients — The customers, actually being the most important persons at the EUROHAND model home, feel that they are taken seriously. Acceptance is not discussed but practised. The spirit of HUMANITAS reigns at the EUROHAND model home.

To summarise the change from hierarchical to interactive co-operation we can say that there has been a shift from management to responsibility, from domination to sharing.

This change or the implementation of new forms of social living is taking place in many fields of social care. Nevertheless, there are still organisations which have not yet been inspired by the WIND of CHANGE. Everywhere you will feel resistance to and fear of new developments. On the threshold to the next millennium, the *challenge* consists in overcoming these feelings. We have to face this challenge with determination if we do not want to become the laughing-stock of history.

4.1.3.7 VISIONARY CONSTRUCT FOR NEW PROVISIONS IN RELATION TO DISABLED/DISADVANTAGED PEOPLE

I HAVE A DREAM (M. Luther-King)
WE SHALL OVERCOME (P. Seager)
ICH BIN EIN BERLINER (J.F. Kennedy)

These are three views which, in the second half of the last century, touched, moved to tears and, at the same time, made young people, even many people in the whole world, set out to broaden their horizon.

Martin Luther King envisioned a united America without segregation. In the context of our perceptions, we recognise the hope for INTEGRATION.

In his unforgottable song, *Pete Seager* expressed his longing for PEACE and NORMALITY. Related to our vision (of co-operation between disabled and non disabled people), we are thinking of abolishing discrimination of oppressed, weak, and disabled people.

John F. Kennedy's unforgettable statement spoken in front of the Brandenburger Tor in Berlin burned in the ears of all those who suffered from the cruel division of Germany and who had not yet given up the yearning for a Germany UNITED in PEACE and FREEDOM. Furthermore, mankind experienced a glimpse of Beethoven's notion of ALLE MENSCHEN WERDEN BRÜDER (LET ALL PEOPLE BE UNITED); a perception which may be both start and finish for remedial and special educators. We seem to know that these statements convey something of the uniqueness which distinguishes man from all other beings: RELIGIO, namely the ability to interrelate with others, to approach and internalise the (Christian) commandment of charity.

What are today's visions of future remedial educators?

A survey among first-year students at the department of remedial education conducted at Fachhochschule Magdeburg in spring 1998 revealed, among others:

Visions of remedial education

- Remedial education is superfluous (remedial education is no longer necessary)
- People are not marginalised (integration is no longer necessary)
- Fulfilling the wishes of all disabled people (own apartment, etc.)
- Society is ready to accept disabled people
- No discrimination as regards access to culture, education, health care, ...
- International co-operation (multi-cultural coexistence)
- Change of emphasis as regard social and economic interests
- Change of values
- No supporters of utilitarism (Singer 1993)
- No compulsory sterilisation
- Free development of all people
- Practising charity

Most answers did not surprise and would presumably be the same in other regions of Germany or Europe. They express the Christian tradition of the Occident which Europeans are born into. They reflect the cultural heritage of Europe to which young Europeans feel obliged - whether they want or not.

In addition, the statements reflect the universal spirit which the youth of the world increasingly exemplifies in an impressive manner in their own way of life.

4.1.4 TASKS TO BE UNDERTAKEN

1. Visit an organisation of/for disabled people and identify its organisational structures.

2. Paint a picture or write a poem to visualise the structure of this organisation.

3. Write a play about client-orientated communication, find some actors, and perform the play.

4. Videotape the play about client-orientated communication.

5. Write down, paint, or play YOUR visionary construct for new provisions in relation to disabled / disadvantaged people.

4.1.5 BIBLIOGRAPHY

4.1.5.1 REFERENCES

Beck, M.(Hrsg.):	Handbuch Sozialmanagement. Stuttgart 1995
Begemann, E.:	Frieden als (ethisches) Ziel der (Sonderschul-)Erziehung. Anregungen zu einem Verständnis, das nicht mehr trennt zwischen Unterricht und Erziehung. In: *Schmetz, D./Wachtel, P. (Hrsg.):* Erschwerte Lebenssituationen: Erziehung und pädagogische Begleitung. Würzburg 1994
Belz, H./ Siegrist, M.:	Kursbuch Schlüsselqualifikationen. Freiburg i.Br. 1997
Bloch, E.:	Das Prinzip Hoffnung. Frankfurt 1959
Bronfenbrenner, U.:	Die Ökologie der menschlichen Entwicklung. Stuttgart 1981
Buber, M.(Hrsg.):	Das dialogische Prinzip. Frankfurt 1979

Bundesvereinigung Lebenshilfe
für Geistig Behinderte (Hrsg.): Normalisierung - eine Chance für Menschen mit geistiger Behinderung. Marburg/Lahn 1986

Decker, F.: Das große Handbuch; Management für soziale Institutionen. Landsberg/Lech 1997

Denger, J. (Hrsg.): Lebensformen in der sozialtherapeutischen Arbeit. Stuttgart 1995

Gehm, T.: Kommunikation im Beruf. Weinheim; Basel 1994

Gregor-Rauschtenberger, B./Hansel, J.: Innovative Projektführung. Berlin Heidelberg 1993

Holzamer, H.-H. (Hrsg.): Management des Wandels. München; Landsberg am Lech 1996

Jacobs, K.: Die Dorfgemeinschaft auf anthroposophischer Grundlage im Blickwinkel von Normalisierung und Integration. In: *Denger, J. (Hrsg.):* Lebensformen in der sozialtherapeutischen Arbeit. Stuttgart 1995

Jonas, H.: Technik, Medizin und Ethik. Zur Praxis des Prinzips Verantwortung. Frankfurt 1987

Maelicke, B. (Hrsg.): Handbuch Sozialmanagement 2000. Baden-Baden 1998

Owens, R.G.: Organizational Behaviour in Education. Boston, London, Toronto, Sydney, Tokyo, Singapore 1995

Rogers. C.: Therapeut und Klient. Frankfurt a.M. 1991

Schmetz, D./Wachtel, P. (Hrsg.): Erschwerte Lebenssituationen: Erziehung und pädagogische Begleitung. Würzburg 1994

Schmidbauer, W.: Die hilflosen Helfer. Über die seelische Problematik der helfenden Berufe. Reinbek 1977

Schulz von Thun, F.: Miteinander Reden. Bd.1 und 2. Reinbek 1989

Singer, P.: Practical Ethics. Cambridge University Press 1993

Speck, O.: System Heilpädagogik. Eine ökologisch reflexive Grundlegung. München, Basel 1991

Tausch, R./Tausch, A.-M.:   Gesprächs-Psychotherapie. 9. Aufl.;
Göttingen 1990
Ysseldyke, J./Algozzine, B.:   Critical Issues in Special and Remedial
Education. Boston 1992
Weiß, J. (Hrsg.).:   Selbstcoaching. Paderborn 1990

4.1.5.2 ADDITIONAL READINGS

Andersson, C.:   Organisationsteori. Lund 1994
Campbell, J. and Oliver, M.:   Disability Politics: understanding our past, changing our future. London, Routledge, 1996
Thylefors, I.:   Ledarskap i vard, omsorg och utbildning. Stockholm 1991

5. EUROPEAN IDENTITY !

Wolf Bloemers

5.1 SUMMARY AND PERSPECTIVES

At the end of this component, the exclamation mark behind the heading of this final module chapter is used for emphasis and serves as a signal:

a) On the one hand, the exclamation mark emphasises the significance of the preceding words. It refers to the question mark(s) set in the introduction and provides comprehensive answers to the questions and issues raised in the following modules.

b) On the other hand, the exclamation mark visualises the fact that this exclamation which is an outcry to the public entails a task and an obligation for the future and gives a professional order.

ad a)

The investigation into European history, society, social policies, and culture has shown that Europe is more than just an agglomeration of individual states and a congregation of different people. Europe is a network of similarities that has gradually developed over time and that has led to a supranational identity. The demand for the existence and efficiency of such similarities is becoming more and more obvious today, especially against the background of the current radical changes and challenges. This also includes the preservation of other small units of identity. The threads of the net spun from - both negative and positive - common sources and heritage of common culture, politics, and economy have created a common awareness and understanding that integrate many aspects to form a common denominator.

The social "knots", the fixed links that give strength to the overall network - if we continue to stick to the network metaphor - are particularly important; they are even an essential part of the European network of identity.

The fact that, today, we depend on each other owing to cross-border links of commercial, financial, and ecological lifelines and functional interrelation (see BIDDIS, 1997, 8) actually forces us to develop what MITTERAND once called "une théorie des ensembles"; to jointly devise a common set of social values to respond to the reality of social interdependence and to consequently take concrete, cross-border, and practical decisions, which means to tie the "knots". The module has shown that there are still not enough of these knots; the current network is still too wide-meshed to cater for fringe groups, disadvantaged people, and those individuals on the edge of society.

The exclamation mark behind "European Identity" is an ethical imperative for the development of transnational, social, and democratic "common knots"; it emphasises and underlines the decisive, humane and social topic of "accepting the other" (CACCIATORE, 1997, 93) and the basic democratic right of the other person for a new orientation, both theoretically and practically.

This includes all of us, and especially the fringe groups, disadvantaged and so-called handicapped individuals.

At the end, the module invites us to critically reflect upon the questions whether an emerging European identity (already) includes handicapped people and what challenges will professionals in the so-called fields of remedial education and social pedagogics be posed with in order to recognise and realise theoretical and practical changes within their profession. The exclamation mark points the way to drawing adequate conclusions; especially since the science of remedial education is based on action.

ad b)

To define and detail the professional orders and ideas resulting from this module and to lead over to b) let us give the floor to a philosopher who approaches the issue of "European identity" from the legal side of being different and comes close to LEVINAS' ideas on accepting the asymmetry of another person:

"Living together with others, living with what is different in other persons is a universal task which is valid both on a small and on a large scale. The way we learn to live with others during our adolescence or - as we say - when we enter into society is the same for other groups of individuals, peoples, and states. It is perhaps Europe's privilege that she could and had to learn to live with the difference to a larger extent than other countries" (GADAMER, 1989, 21f, quoted from CACCIATORE, 1997).

Privilege and obligation, chance and task; this is a second conclusion from/interpretation of the exclamation mark. In this respect, professional action is required!

If you have followed the ideas so far and if your thinking of and feeling for Europe and its people - especially those with learning difficulties and handicaps - has changed after having worked on the material presented and tasks defined in this module, you will now have the opportunity to stop, to recapitulate and put down sketchy notes describing the main characteristic changes in knowledge and feeling, and to write down concrete ideas, suggestions, wishes, etc. reflecting the conclusions you have drawn from this learning process.

The actions resulting from the above task can be manifold; you can define actions for yourself, for others or together with others, fix your thoughts, enter into discussions, and develop many other activities. What is important is that you should consider those individuals with disadvantages and handicaps, let them take part, integrate them, and let them act as well. Thus, they can contribute individually - as Europeans having equal rights -to the process of developing a European identity.

Europe is growing together at social level; and during the process of developing an identity Europe offers the great - even historical - chance for individuals with disadvantages and handicaps to be integrated, to be among the winners of a new humane and social feeling of unity, and to be part of a community that transcends existing - even internal - boundaries.

At the end of this module, the authors express their wish that, while working on the material presented, you have developed a feeling of sensitivity, curiosity and perhaps the willingness to commit yourself at the socio-political level in order to foster and initiate a deeper European understanding, to gradually implement normality, realise integration, and empowerment; according to the professional focus of and theoretical canon devised for remedial educators and social pedagogues, these are the most important values of a European identity for disadvantaged and handicapped citizens.

The module has shown that European identity has to be communicated to and learnt by all Europeans. A good means to this end is a common field of learning and action such as international co-operation within organisations, partnerships, and networks where common perspectives and programmes are developed; the process of development and the resulting products and applications can deliver concrete stimuli for a growing identity.

5.2 TASKS TO BE UNDERTAKEN

• Students will evaluate how their individual thinking about Europe has changed as a result of taking part in this module: e.g. students may videotape and/or audiotape a discussion or present a personal reflection.

5.3 BIBLIOGRAPHY

5.3.1 REFERENCES

BÜRLI, A.:	Sonderpädagogik international. Luzern 1997
BAUMANN, U.:/KLESZEWSKI, R.: (Hrsg.)	Penser l' Europe - Europa denken. Tübingen und Basel 1997
CLOERKES, G.:	Soziologie der Behinderten. Heidelberg 1997
COUDENHOVE-KALERGI, R.:	Ein Leben für Europa. Kampf um Europa. Aus meinem Leben. Zürich 1948
DEUTSCHE GESELLSCHAFT FÜR ERZIEHUNGSWISSENSCHAFT:	Bildung und Erziehung in Europa. Beiträge zum 14. Kongreß des DFG. Weinheim und Basel 1994
EUROPÄISCHE GEMEINSCHAFT:	Die Vertragstexte von Maastricht. Bonn 1992
FERNAU, J.:	Wie es euch gefällt. Eine lächelnde Stilkunde. Donauwörth 1969
JASPERS, K.:	Vom europäischen Geist. München 1947
KÜNG, H.:	Projekt Weltethos. München/Zürich 1991
LISSNER, I.:	Wir sind das Abendland. Gütersloh 1966
SCHLEICHER, K./BOS, W.: (Hrsg.):	Realisierung der Bildung in Europa. Darmstadt 1994
SCHLEICHER, K. (Hrsg.):	Zukunft der Bildung in Europa. Darmstadt 1993

5.3.2 ADDITIONAL READINGS

BAUMANN,U./
KLESZEWSKI, R.(Hrsg.)   Penser L´ Europe - Europa denken.
Tübingen/Basel 1997

6. PORTFOLIO TASKS / PROPOSALS

It is anticipated that the portfolio will be completed in a minimum of 25 hours.

- Follow the media, make interviews, fieldwork and see if there is a gap between legislation and practice in your country.

- Devise your own portfolio so you are able to describe what kind of laws, social documents and social policy you have in your country for disabled people.

- How do you view Europe? Present your views and how you experience your identity. Give reasons.

- Collect newspaper & magazine articles for a portfolio treating the problem of xenophobia. Decide how to clarify your documents and support your decision. Offer arguments on possible solutions.

- Decide how you can make a personal contribution towards European Integration. Provide a detailed description on how you would achieve this. Share your thoughts with your fellow students.

- Give three basis suggestions on how a public education policy, conducive to European Integration, could be initiated in your country.

- Identify three visual artists whose significance, dimension and quality could be described as European. Give clear examples and locate the place of these examples within a system of values and awareness of disability and disadvantage to justify your choice.

- Visit an organisation of/for disabled people and identify it's organisational structures.

- Paint a picture/write a poem to visualise the structure of this organisation.

- Develop a portfolio that assesses the issues involved in altering an aspect of the physical and/or social infra-structure of a particular environment.

This will include

> Proposals for change
> Funding implications
> Relevant legislation
> Mechanical consideration
> Environmental/architectural design
> Nature of the planning process
> Interviews with/access to people who use the environment

- Critically describe different forms of empowerment and advocacy in relation to disability, learning and living difficulties and disadvantage in your country.

INDEX

A
Ability 44 ff, 54 ff, 62, 68, 88, 110, 121
Acceptance 43 ff, 68, 80, 89, 142
Access to work 85
Action research 124
Activity 19, 26, 52 ff, 75, 80 ff, 120 ff, 133
Advocacy 85, 113 ff, 154, 172
Aid 11, 79
Awareness, critical 21, 63

B
Basic values 41
Bibliography 56, 72, 93, 111, 128, 145, 151
Bodily wholeness 69

C
Care 116 ff, 133 ff
Care for the elderly 102 ff
Categories of handicap / disability 87 ff
Community 89 ff, 99 ff, 114, 119 ff, 150
Community work 115, 117
Community worker 119
Concept of „educational need" 86 ff
Concept of citizenship 41, 88
Concept of identity 27 ff
Conflict 44, 49, 101, 120, 132 ff
Consensus 27, 96, 100 ff
Control 26, 69, 74 ff, 121 ff, 130 ff
Cooperation 19 ff, 42, 53
Core values 41 ff, 51
Crisis 44, 81

D
Diagnosis 67, 77 114
Disability 62 ff, 71 ff, 81 ff, 108 ff, 153

E
EC, European Community 29, 42 ff, 53
Efficiency 86, 141, 148
Ego identity 27 ff

Empowerment 81, 91, 113 ff, 150 ff
England 65, 87, 96, 101 ff
Environmental factors 68, 155
Eugenics 62 ff
Eurobarometer 24, 29 ff, 50
European common understanding / consciousness 21 ff
European culture 20 ff, 72
European Identity 19, 25 ff, 34, 42 ff, 148 ff
Euroscepticism 25, 45
Exclusion 25, 49 ff, 78 ff

F
Feelings of self-worth 83 ff
Finance 80 ff, 104 ff, 119
Force 19, 26, 42 ff, 66 ff, 81, 118 ff, 149
Foreign 25, 38, 43, 48 ff
Forms of social living 130, 143
Fund-raising 140 ff

G
Gene technology 69
Genetic engineering 68
Genetic makeup 68
Genetics 68 ff
Germany 23, 55, 102 ff, 143 ff
Great Britain 87, 96 ff, 101 ff

H
Health Services 12, 38, 104
Help to self-help 113, 117
Heredity 68 ff
Hierarchical principle 130
Home 64, 81 ff, 104 ff, 131 ff
Human Rights 23 ff, 38 ff, 108, 118, 134

I
Identity 31 ff, 40
Image 20, 27, 30 ff, 51, 69 ff
Impairment 62 ff, 108, 126

Inclusion 84 ff
Inclusive education 76, 85 ff
Informal Sector 103 ff
Insurance 82, 99, 102 ff, 155Interaction 30 ff, 54, 78 ff, 85 ff, 141
Interactive principle 130
Intervention 68 ff, 76 ff, 101, 117
Isolation 25, 47, 63, 120

L
Laws 26, 47, 64 ff, 96 ff, 153
Lean Management 140 ff
Learning Difficulties 66 ff, 87 ff, 127, 158
Leisure time 84
Lifestyle 82
Living difficulties 115, 127, 154

M
Market Orientation 106
Medical Care 63, 88
Medical Condition 77
Medicine 67 ff, 76
Meso-system 131
Micro-system 131 ff
Migrants 42 ff, 57
Mobility 46, 53, 80 ff
Models
- Hierarchical step model 131 ff
- Interaction model 31
- Interactive circle model 134 ff
- Medical model 67, 74 ff, 87
- Social model 77 ff, 92, 114

Module 9 ff, 131, 148 ff
Moral code 43
Movement 20, 62, 90, 99, 106, 116 ff

N
Need for Europe 20 ff, 40 ff
Network 28, 54, 81, 99, 103 ff, 140 ff
Normalisation 76, 90, 118, 135 ff

O
Oppression 63, 70, 78, 92 121 ff

P
Participation 21, 28 ff, 41, 49 ff, 78, 90, 126
Participatory research 114, 124 ff
Personnel management 140 ff
Physical well being 83
Portfolio 15 ff, 55, 92, 98, 110, 153
Post qualification 141Prejudices 86 ff
Prevention 117
Professionalism 136

Q
Quality assurance 141 ff
Quality management 140 ff
Quality of life 24, 67, 79 ff, 92, 122

R
Regulation, Rule 51, 82, 87 ff, 107, 130 ff
Rehabilitation 126, 138 ff
Remedial education 21, 144, 149
Right of decision 116

S
Self-confidence 82, 115 ff
Self-determination Self-esteem 82 ff
Self-help group 113 ff, 119 ff, 139
Self-image 28, 31, 81, 139
Similarities 28, 96, 148
Skill 84 ff, 121 ff, 130, 136
Social adaption 120
Social deprivation 124
Social identity 27 ff, 50
Social justice 63, 79
Social management 140 ff
Social policy 96 ff
Social sponsoring 140 ff
Social worker 85, 118 ff, 125
Special education 62, 86 ff
Specialist 77, 83, 89, 141
Staff motivation 141
Subordination 69
Sweden 64 ff, 97 ff, 126
System of values 22, 27, 46, 153

T
Theories of identity 28
Top-down strategy 116
Training, 41, 53, 65 ff, 81 ff, 133, 141
Treatment 48 ff, 65 ff, 75 ff
Trends for the future 106

U
User 113 ff, 121 ff
User involvement 113 ff, 119 ff

V
Violence 25, 42, 48 ff
Vision 48 ff, 120, 130 ff, 143 ff
Vocational training 68, 84 ff, 133
Voluntary, honorary 95 ff, 102 ff, 125, 138 ff

ABOUT THE AUTHORS

Prof. Dr. Wolf Bloemers, University of Applied Sciences Magdeburg, Germany
Dr. Bengt Eriksson, Karlstad University, Sweden
Åse-Britt Falch, MA, Karlstad University, Sweden
David Johnstone, B.Phil., M.Ed., M.Sc., Cert. Ed., Edge Hill University College, Ormskirk, United Kingdom
Prof. Dr. Fritz-Helmut Wisch, University of Applied Sciences Magdeburg, Germany

WOLF BLOEMERS
Professor for Remedial and Special Education at the University of Applied Sciences Magdeburg. He is coordinator of the study course "Remedial Education and Rehabilitation", the chairman of the board of foreign affairs of the University and the responsable coordinator for a EU-Socrates programme of developing European Modules. His main emphasis is in making studies international and in interdisciplinary thinking, researching and acting.

BENGT ERIKSSON
Ph D in social work, lecturer in social care, Department of Social Science, Karlstad University, Sweden. Vocational experience as social worker, followed by Ph D studies. Special research interests: Evaluation, assessment and quality improvement in social care/social work and research concerning conditions for the elderly and disabled.

ÅSE-BRITT FALCH
MA in social work, educated teacher in social care. Lecturer in social care, Department of Social Sciences, Karlstad University, Sweden. Started to be a teacher in social care 1990 after 10 years of social work as a welfare counsellor in different areas, the last years specialised towards people with mental handicap. She was involved in Research studies in the field of people with learning difficulties and in a study of a community-based project for parents with disabled people.

DAVID JOHNSTONE
Senior lecturer at Edge Hill University College, Ormskirk, Lancashire. United Kingdom. He is course leader to the modular degree in Disability and Community Studies. He has degrees from the University of Birmingham and the University of Virginia and is a former Head of Special Education for students with learning difficulties. Johnstone has written widely on post 16 education and training involving disabled people.

FRITZ-HELMUT WISCH
Professor for Remedial and Special Education at the University of Applied Sciences Magdeburg. Being a teacher for the deaf he was involved in Parent Guidance - Teacher Training - and Sign Language Interpreting Programs. Wisch is the Co-Author of the German Sign-Language Dictionary which is a documentation of 20.000 signs in four books. Main interests: Communication, Ethics, Integration of disabled people.

ADDRESSES OF THE UNIVERSITIES

EDGE HILL UNIVERSITY COLLEGE
St. Helens Road
Ormskirk/Lancashire L39 4QP
England

KARLSTAD UNIVERSITET
Universitätsgatan
S 650 09 Karlstad
Sweden

UNIVERSITY OF APPLIED SCIENCES, MAGDEBURG
FACHHOCHSCHULE MAGDEBURG
Breitscheidstr. 2
39114 Magdeburg
Germany

BEHINDERUNG BEEINTRÄCHTIGUNG LERN- UND LEBENS- SCHWIERIGKEITEN

POLITIK UND PRAXIS VOR DEM HINTERGRUND UNTERSCHIEDLICHER EUROPÄISCHER GEGEBENHEITEN

INHALTSVERZEICHNIS

	VORWORT DER HERAUSGEBER	167
0.	VORBEMERKUNGEN	170
0.1	DIE BEWEGGRÜNDE - ÜBER DIE ANFÄNGE DES MODULS	170
0.2	ZUR ENTSTEHUNG DES AUTORENTEAMS	171
0.3	ZIELSETZUNGEN	171
0.4	ÜBERBLICK ÜBER DIE KAPITEL	172
0.5	STRUKTUREN IN DEN DREI BETEILIGTEN LÄNDERN	173
0.6	LEHR- UND LERNANSÄTZE	174
0.7	BEWERTUNGSMASSSTÄBE	174
0.8.	WAS DIE STUDENTEN ZU DEM EUROPÄISCHEN MODUL BEITRAGEN KÖNNEN	175
0.9	LITERATUR UND SCHLÜSSELTEXTE	175

1.	EUROPÄISCHE IDENTITÄT?	178
	Wolf Bloemers	
1.1	EINFÜHRUNG	178
1.1.1	ZIELE	179
1.1.2.	LERNERGEBNISSE	180
1.2.	WAS IST EUROPA? WER (WAS) SIND EUROPÄER?	181
1.3	WIE UND WOZU ENTSTEHT IDENTITÄT?	186
1.4	WIE SEHEN DIE „EUROPÄER" EUROPA?	193
1.5	WIE SOLL EUROPA SEIN, WERDEN? GIBT ES „EUROPABEDARF"?	199
1.6	(WIE) WERDEN WIR EUROPÄER?	204
1.7	WEITERFÜHRENDE, VERTIEFENDE AUFGABEN	215
1.8	BIBLIOGRAPHIE	216
1.8.1	LITERATURHINWEISE	216
1.8.2	ZUSÄTZLICHE LITERATUR	219

2.	EIN BLICK ZURÜCK - GESCHICHTE DER „BEHINDERUNGEN" David Johnstone	220
2.1	EINLEITUNG	220
2.1.1	ZIELE	220
2.1.2	LERNERGEBNISSE	221
2.2	EIN CHRONOLOGISCHER ABRISS VON „BEHINDERUNG" IN EUROPA	222
2.2.1	ANFÄNGE DER HILFE FÜR BEHINDERTE MENSCHEN	223
2.2.2	DER SINN UND DIE PHILOSOPHIE DER EUGENIK	227
2.2.3	DIE BEZIEHUNG ZWISCHEN EUGENISCHER THEORIE UND BEHINDERUNG	228
2.3	AUFGABEN	230
2.4	BIBLIOGRAPHIE	232
2.4.1	LITERATURHINWEISE	232
2.4.2	ZUSÄTZLICHE LITERATUR	233
3.	EIN BLICK AUF DIE GEGENWART	234
3.1	HEUTIGE AUFFASSUNGEN ÜBER BENACHTEILIGUNG David Johnstone	234
3.1.1	EINFÜHRUNG	234
3.1.2	ZIELE	235
3.1.3	LERNERGEBNISSE	236
3.1.4	DIE INDIVIDUELLE TRAGÖDIE ODER DAS MEDIZINISCHE MODELL	236
3.1.5	DAS SOZIALE MODELL VON BEHINDERUNG	238
3.1.6	BEHINDERUNG UND LEBENSQUALITÄT	240
3.1.7	LEBENSQUALITÄT – EIN EWIGER WIDERSPRUCH	242
3.1.8	LEBENSQUALITÄT ALS EINE SUMME VON VARIABLEN	244
3.1.9	DER ZUSAMMENHANG ZWISCHEN BEHINDERUNG UND SONDERPÄDAGOGISCHEN ERFORDERNISSEN	248
3.1.10	VON DER INTEGRATION ZUR INCLUSION	251
3.1.11	AUFGABEN	255
3.1.12	BIBLIOGRAPHIE	255
3.1.12.1	LITERATURHINWEISE	255
3.1.12.2	ZUSÄTZLICHE LITERATUR	257

3.2	**POLITIK CONTRA PRAXIS** Bengt Eriksson	258
3.2.1	EINLEITUNG	258
3.2.2	ZIELE	261
3.2.3	LERNERGEBNISSE	262
3.2.4	WAS IST „SOZIALPOLITIK"?	262
3.2.4.1	DER KONSENS - EIN SCHLÜSSELKONZEPT IN DER DISKUSSION ÜBER SOZIALPOLITIK?	265
3.2.4.2	SOZIALPOLITIK UND SOZIALE FÜRSORGE IN DEUTSCHLAND, ENGLAND UND SCHWEDEN	267
3.2.4.3	GESETZESGRUNDLAGEN ZUR SOZIALPOLITIK UND SPEZIELLE REGELUNGEN UND VORSCHRIFTEN IN BEZUG AUF BEHINDERTE MENSCHEN IN DEN DREI BETEILIGTEN LÄNDERN	272
3.2.4.4	WIE SIEHT DIE REALITÄT AUS?	274
3.2.4.5	POLITIK CONTRA PRAXIS!	275
3.2.5	AUFGABEN	275
3.2.6	BIBLIOGRAPHIE	276
3.2.6.1	LITERATURHINWEISE	276
3.2.6.2	ZUSÄTZLICHE LITERATUR	276
3.3	**MACHT, POLITIK UND DIE EINBEZIEHUNG VON BETROFFENEN** Åse-Britt Falch	277
3.3.1	EINLEITUNG	277
3.3.2	ZIELE	280
3.3.3	LERNERGEBNISSE	281
3.3.4	FÜRSPRACHE, GRUPPENARBEIT UND EMPOWERMENT	281
3.3.4.1	VERSCHIEDENE KONZEPTE UND HINTERGRÜNDE VON FÜRSPRACHE UND EMPOWERMENT	281
3.3.4.2	GRUPPENARBEIT, GRUPPENPROZESSE, SELBSTHILFEGRUPPEN UND SELBSTBESTIMMTE GRUPPENARBEIT	286
3.3.4.3	PARTIZIPATIVE FORSCHUNG UND EMPOWERMENT	291
3.3.4.4	EINIGE BEISPIELE	292
3.3.5	AUFGABEN	294
3.3.6	BIBLIOGRAPHIE	295
3.3.6.1	LITERATURHINWEISE	295
3.3.6.2	ZUSÄTZLICHE LITERATUR	296

4.	**EIN BLICK NACH VORN – MANAGEMENT IM WANDEL** **Fritz-Helmut Wisch**	**297**
4.1	EINLEITUNG	297
4.1.1	ZIELE	297
4.1.2	LERNERGEBNISSE	297
4.1.3	ZUR KULTUR DER ORGANISATIONSTRUKTUREN UND DES ROLLENVERSTÄNDNISSES DER BETEILIGTEN	298
4.1.3.1	DAS HIRARCHISCHE, DIREKTIVE STUFENMODELL	298
4.1.3.2	DAS INTERAKTIVE KREISMODELL	301
4.1.3.3	KOMMUNIKATIONSFÄHIGKEITEN	304
4.1.3.4	KUNDENORIENTIERTE KOMMUNIKATION	304
4.1.3.5	DIE NOTWENDIGKEIT DES WANDELS IM UMGANG MIT UND ZWISCHEN DEN BETEILIGTEN	306
4.1.3.6	EINSCHÄTZUNG UND ANALYSE DES STRUKTUR- UND MANAGEMENTWANDELS EINER ORGANISATION FÜR BEHINDERTE MENSCHEN	309
4.1.3.7	ENTWURF EINER VISION DES MITEINANDERS	311
4.1.4	AUFGABEN	312
4.1.5	BIBLIOGRAPHIE	313
4.1.5.1	LITERATURHINWEISE	313
4.1.5.2	ZUSÄTZLICHE LITERATUR	314
5.	**EUROPÄISCHE IDENTITÄT!** **Wolf Bloemers**	**315**
5.1	ZUSAMMENFASSUNG UND AUSBLICK	315
5.2	AUFGABEN	318
5.3	BIBLIOGRAPHIE	318
5.3.1	LITERATURHINWEISE	318
5.3.2	ZUSÄTZLICHE LITERATUR	319
6.	**VORSCHLÄGE FÜR PORTFOLIO – AUFGABEN**	**320**
	SACHREGISTER	322
	ÜBER DIE AUTOREN	325
	ADRESSEN DER HOCHSCHULEN	326

VORWORT DER HERAUSGEBER

Das vorliegende Buch ist von den fünf beteiligten Autoren ursprünglich für Studierende von Heil-, Sonder- und Sozialpädagogik als Handbuch für ein „Euro-Modul" geschrieben worden, das an den drei Hochschulen

- Edge Hill University College, Ormskirk (England)
- Karlstad Universitet, Karlstad (Schweden)
- Fachhochschule Magdeburg
  University of Applied Sciences, (Deutschland)

in deren Studienprogrammen/Curricula seit 1998/99 regelmäßig gelehrt wird.

Es ist der erste Band von insgesamt drei Modul-Büchern, die in sich jeweils eigenständig und abgeschlossen sind, jedoch aufeinander aufbauen.

Module sind Lehrbausteine, in sich abgeschlossene Lehreinheiten/ Studieneinheiten, die mit einer Prüfung enden und für die „Kreditpunkte" vergeben werden; diese „Kreditpunkte" sind Rechnungseinheiten, die im Rahmen von nach vergleichbaren Maßstäben konstruierten, konsekutiv aufgebauten Studiengängen (Bachelor / Master) als „Guthaben" für das Gesamtsoll an Lehreinheiten eines Studienprogrammes angerechnet und von anderen Hochschulen als kompatibel anerkannt werden. Um zukünftig zu national und international vergleichbaren Strukturen, Maßstäben und Anrechnungsmöglichkeiten von bislang recht unterschiedlichen Studiengängen und Studienabschlüssen (z.B. akademischen Graden wie Bachelor, Master, Diplom, Staatsexamen, Lizenziat etc.) zu gelangen, ist eine Modularisierung und eine Einführung eines Kreditpunktesystems besonders förderlich, bzw. erforderlich.

Euro-Module sind Studieneinheiten, die von mindestens drei europäischen Hochschulen mit finanzieller Unterstützung der Europäischen Union im Rahmen des Sokrates-Programmes entwickelt werden. Die an der Entwicklung beteiligten Universitäten haben sich verpflichtet, diese Module in ihren Lehrkanon zu implementieren. Diese Lehrbausteine beinhalten eine europäische Dimension, das heißt, sie sind gekennzeichnet von einem plurinationalen und/oder supranationalen Fokus, der darauf abzielt, ein mehrperspektivisches, nationale Grenzen überwindendes Denken und ein gemeinsames, „europäisches" Handeln anzuregen.

Die Kapitel dieses Euro-Moduls verstehen sich als *einführende* Texte in verschiedene Problemfelder der historischen, gegenwärtigen und zukünftigen Lebensbedingungen behinderter und benachteiligter Menschen aus drei europäischen Blickwinkeln, bzw aus drei kulturell unterschiedlich geprägten gedanklichen Zugriffen. Das Buch dient – als Pflichtlektüre für die am Lehrmodul teilnehmenden Studierenden – als gemeinsamer Basistext, als Problemaufriß im europäischen Kontext und als Startgrundlage sowohl für das erweiternde und vertiefende Eigenstudium, als auch als Diskussionsplattform eines „active engagement" für die Seminarbeit und eines damit verbundenen vielgestaltigen Ideenaustauschens mit den Studierenden der Partnerhochschulen per e-mail, Video, Fax oder anderen Kommunikationsmedien.

Aus diesem Grund sind alle Kapitel trotz autorenspezifisch verschiedener Zugangsweisen nach demselben Konstruktionsprinzip aufgebaut: Einführung, Ziele, erwartete Lernergebnisse, Lehrtext, weiterführende Aufgaben und Literaturangaben. Die inhaltlichen Anforderungen sind in etwa ausgerichtet auf das zweite Studienjahr. Gelehrt und bearbeitet wird dieses Euro-Modul zweisprachig: sowohl in Englisch als auch in der jeweiligen Landessprache; deshalb erscheint es auch in diesem Band zum einen in der englischen Version, als auch in der Sprache der Herausgeber. Einige sprachliche Unebenheiten resultieren aus Schwierigkeiten beim Übersetzen - zum Teil von Studierenden vorgenommen -, als auch aus einem zuweilen verwendeten „European English", für das wir um Nachsicht bitten.

Über diese – auf Studierende abzielenden – hochschuldidaktischen Absichten und Konstruktionsmerkmale hinaus wollen die Autoren mit dem vorliegenden Buch auch andere, im pädagogischen, psychologischen und sozialpolitischen Feld Tätigen und an Fragen von Behinderung, Ausgrenzung und Integration interessierten Personen ansprechen, um für europäisch orientierte Sicht- und Denkweisen in der Arbeit mit und für behinderte und benachteiligte Menschen zu sensibilisieren sowie für eine Trennungslinien überwindende, diesbezügliche europäische Zusammenarbeit. Die kommunikative, zum reflexiven Dialog einladende Ausrichtung der Texte sowie die in etlichen Aufgaben enthaltenen Aktionsvorschläge wollen Impulse zum kritischen Weiterdenken und zum innovativen Handeln geben in Richtung eines zukünftigen Sozialraumes Europa.

Zur Fortführung dieser auf die europäische Dimension ausgerichteten Gedanken- und Aktionserweiterung von behindertenpolitischen und -pädagogischen Fragestellungen erscheinen - im Rahmen dieser Reihe - zwei weitere „Euro-Modul"- Bücher (Bände zwei und drei).

Euro-Modul Band 2 („Quality of Life Research and Disabled People – Ways to research in different European Settings") fokussiert Forschungsfragen und Zukunftsaufgaben hinsichtlich der Verbesserung von Lebensbedingungen von behinderten und benachteiligten Personen in unterschiedlichen europäischen

Gegebenheiten und will für diesbezügliche verantwortliche Handlungsforschungstätigkeit sensibilisieren und ein Stück weit qualifizieren.

Der abschließende Euro-Modul Band 3 („Voices of Europe – Comparative Studies of Disabled People") stellt ein beispielgebendes „Anwendungsprodukt" der Module 1 und 2 dar; es dokumentiert gemeinsam und partnerschaftlich von behinderten Menschen, Studenten und Dozenten durchgeführte Reflexions- und Forschungsprozesse sowie Forschungsergebnisse, eröffnet behinderten Personen aus drei Ländern ein „europäisches Forum" zur Darstellung eigener Lebensgeschichten und ermöglicht einen länderübergreifenden, öffentlichen Erfahrungsaustausch und Kommunikationsprozeß. Darüber hinaus versteht sich dieser Band als Anregung, Handlungsmuster und Lerninstrument / Werkzeugkoffer für partizipative, anwendungsorientierte Forschung.

Magdeburg, im Januar 2000　　　　　　　　Wolf Bloemers
　　　　　　　　　　　　　　　　　　　　Fritz-Helmut Wisch

0. VORBEMERKUNGEN

0.1 DIE BEWEGGRÜNDE – ÜBER DIE ANFÄNGE DES MODULS

Die Idee, dieses Modul zu entwickeln, entstand aus dem Sokrates-Programm für Europäische Kooperation und den gemeinsamen Überlegungen von Partnern in drei europäischen Staaten. Bereits im Jahre 1995 waren der Fachbereich Sozial- und Gesundheitswesen der Fachhochschule Magdeburg und das Zentrum für Öffentliche Gesundheitsforschung (Centre for Public Health Research) in Karlstad in Zusammenarbeit mit der Hochschule Värmland, Abteilung für Gesundheits- und Pflegedienste, gemeinsam in europäischen Initiativen involviert. Im Jahre 1996 wurde die Edge Hill Universität eingeladen, sich dieser Gruppe anzuschließen. Den Anlaß zu dieser Zusammenarbeit gab die gemeinsame Ansicht dieser drei Hochschulen, daß die sozialen Strukturen in Europa im Wandel begriffen sind. Diese Veränderungen resultieren aus politischen und wirtschaftlichen Überlegungen der Europäischen Gremien in Straßburg, Luxemburg und Brüssel, die alle „neuen" Europäer dazu bewegen sollen, die Vorstellung von „sozialer Gerechtigkeit" neu zu überdenken. Allerdings sind diese Veränderungen auch die Folge größerer Möglichkeiten der Mobilität, die durch die Öffnung der Grenzen, aber auch durch die Erweiterung des Horizonts der Menschen entstanden sind.

Von Beginn an wurde die Programmstruktur der Euro-Module in zwei Bereiche aufgeteilt:

Modul 1 "Behinderung - Beeinträchtigung, Lern- und Lebensschwierigkeiten: Politik und Praxis vor dem Hintergrund unterschiedlicher europäischer Gegebenheiten"

Modul 2 "Wissenschaftliche Forschungsmethoden auf dem Gebiet behinderter Menschen"

Beide Module sollen einen "gemeinsamen Wissensschatz" entwickeln, mit dem Ziel eines möglichen Wandels von nationalem zu europäischem Denken in Bezug zu Themen wie Behinderung und Benachteiligung.

Die Module sollen in die Lehrpläne jeder der beteiligten Universitäten aufgenommen werden. Sie sind in erster Linie nicht dazu gedacht, den Studenten eine größere Mobilität zu ermöglichen, sondern sollen dazu dienen, Möglichkeiten für den Austausch von Ideen, Unterrichtsmaterialien und Lehrpersonal zu schaffen. Diese Module sollen den Anfang für ein Studien- und Arbeitsprogramm bilden, das an unseren drei Hochschulen gemeinsam gelehrt und bewertet werden kann.

Die zentrale Koordination dieser Module liegt in den Händen von Prof. Dr. Wolf Bloemers an der Fachhochschule Magdeburg.

0.2 ZUR ENTSTEHUNG DES AUTORENTEAMS

Das Modul 1 wurde von einzelnen Wissenschaftlern aus Deutschland, Schweden und dem Vereinigten Königreich entwickelt. Alle Mitwirkenden sind in irgendeiner Weise in die Arbeit mit Menschen involviert, welche als „beeinträchtigt", „behindert" oder im weiteren Sinne als „benachteiligt" beschrieben werden. Dies war auch ein Aspekt der gemeinsamen Forschungsarbeit der drei beteiligten Hochschulen. Abgesehen von den engagierten Beiträgen der beteiligten Personen wäre dieses Projekt jedoch nicht ohne die finanzielle Hilfe und Unterstützung aus den Fonds des Sokrates-Programms möglich gewesen.

Während der Entwicklung des Moduls 1 hatten die Mitwirkenden die Möglichkeit zur Zusammenarbeit in jedem der Partnerländer. Diese Workshops waren sowohl vom akademischen als auch vom professionellen Ansatz her gesehen sehr fruchtbar und konnten dazu beitragen, entstandene Freundschaften zu festigen. Bei diesen Gelegenheiten wurden von den Autoren auch Vorlesungen und Seminare mit Studenten des Sozial- und Gesundheitswesens in Schweden und Deutschland durchgeführt.

0.3 ZIELSETZUNGEN

Das Modul sieht vor, sich mit einer großen Anzahl von wichtigen Zielen auseinanderzusetzen:

- das gemeinsame Bewußtsein, eine europäische Identität zu entwickeln und zu teilen;
- nationale Auffassungen von Benachteiligung in Frage zu stellen und zu überwinden;

- ein besseres Verstehen durch einen gemeinsamen Wissensschatz zu entwickeln;
- zu der fortschreitenden Entwicklung von beruflichen und professionellen Möglichkeiten im Bereich der „fürsorgenden Dienste" bzw. des „Sozialwesens" in Europa beizutragen;
- Fähigkeiten zu erwerben, um neue theoretische und praktische Erkenntnisse kritisch zu analysieren, zu reflektieren und weiterzuentwickeln.

0.4 ÜBERBLICK ÜBER DIE KAPITEL

Die fünf Kapitel, aus denen das Modul 1 besteht, sind bewußt interaktiv angelegt, so daß die Studenten ermutigt werden, sich auf den jeweiligen Autor einzulassen und die dargestellten Punkte kritisch zu betrachten.

Kapitel 1 - Europäische Identität? fordert die Studenten dazu auf, darüber nachzudenken, was es ausmacht, Europäer zu sein. Gibt es gemeinsame Visionen? Was sind die persönlichen Werte und Einstellungen bezüglich der europäischen Identität? Das Fragezeichen in der Kapitelüberschrift ist wohlüberlegt und soll bewußt dazu aufrufen, sich Fragen zu stellen.

Kapitel 2 - Ein Blick zurück – Geschichte der „Behinderungen" untersucht im europäischen Kontext einige historische Beziehungen zwischen Behinderung, Benachteiligung und der Marginalisierung beeinträchtigter Menschen.

Kapitel 3 - Ein Blick auf die Gegenwart ist in drei Unterpunkte unterteilt und stellt zugleich den zentralen Punkt des Moduls 1 dar; Kapitel 3.1 *Heutige Auffassungen über Benachteiligung* untersucht die aktuelle Situation europäischer Bürger mit Lern- und Lebensschwierigkeiten ; Kapitel 3.2 *Politik contra Praxis* beschäftigt sich mit den unterschiedlichen Formen der Gesetzgebung und Dienstleistungen, die zur Unterstützung der sozialen Bedürfnisse von benachteiligten Menschen entwickelt worden sind. Das Kapitel 3.3 *Macht, Politik und die Einbeziehung von Betroffenen* ist die Untersuchung von Empowerment und der Fürsprache (Advocacy) durch Betroffene.

Kapitel 4 - Ein Blick nach vorn – Management im Wandel betrachtet das Management im Wandel sowohl in der Kommunikation als auch bezogen auf Zukunftsmöglichkeiten. In diesem Zusammenhang wird auch die mögliche Bedeutung einer Kultur von Behinderung und Benachteiligung im europäischen Kontext dargestellt.

Kapitel 5 - Europäische Identität! faßt die zuvor dargelegten Ansätze zusammen und wirft neue Fragen auf. Dieses abschließende Kapitel fordert die Studenten auf, sich Gedanken darüber zu machen, was es bedeutet, in Europa benachteiligt und marginalisiert zu sein.

Alle Kapitel verfolgen die Absicht, die Studenten dazu zu ermutigen, über zukünftige Modelle der Dienstleistung für behinderte und benachteiligte Menschen nachzudenken.

Es ist zu hoffen, daß ihr Denken durch die Lektüre der Modulinhalte positiv beeinflußt wird!

0.5 STRUKTUREN IN DEN DREI BETEILIGTEN LÄNDERN

Die Autoren der vorliegenden Kapitel sind in Fachbereichen von Hochschulen tätig und bilden ihre Studenten in der Arbeit mit behinderten Menschen aus. Alle Autoren haben einen profunden, theoretischen und praktischen Hintergrund bezüglich der Problematik und haben ihr Wissen und ihre Fachkenntnisse in die Entwicklung der Module eingebracht. Es wurde darauf geachtet, daß das Niveau des Studiums vergleichbar ist mit dem eines Bachelor-Abschlusses in den beteiligten Ländern.

Englisch ist die gemeinsame Sprache, in der dieses Modul geschrieben wurde und gelehrt wird. Trotz der unterschiedlichen Aufnahmebedingungen in den beteiligten Ländern, ist es notwendig, zumindest ein Grundwissen der englischen Sprache zu besitzen. Das Einstiegsalter für dieses Modul liegt bei 19 Jahren, wobei die Mehrzahl wahrscheinlich älter sein wird. Denjenigen Studenten, die sich für Details bezüglich der Lehrpläne und das Kursangebot an den Hochschulen in Karlstad, Magdeburg und Ormskirk interessieren, wird empfohlen, sich an die jeweiligen Hochschulen zu wenden und die individuellen Studienführer und Lehrkataloge zu erfragen.

0.6 LEHR- UND LERNANSÄTZE

Der Ansatz in der Lehre, die für das Studium dieses europäischen Moduls vorgesehen ist, erfordert "aktives Engagement". Die Studenten sollen dazu ermutigt werden zu erkennen, daß ein Studium viele verschiedene Disziplinen einbeziehen kann, um die geschichtlichen und aktuellen Umstände der Situation behinderter Menschen zu verstehen.

Zahlreiche Punkte in jedem Kapitel fordern die Studenten zum Selbststudium auf, um ihre Denkstrukturen zu schärfen. Außerdem gibt es in jedem Kapitel auch "bildende" Bestandteile und eine Reihe von zusammenfassenden Aufgaben, welche die Arbeit eines jeden Einzelnen der Gruppe erfordert. Einzelheiten dazu können im Kapitel 6 nachgelesen werden. Begleitliteratur und Hinweise auf weiterführende Literatur werden am Ende eines jeden Kapitels aufgeführt. Eine breite Auswahl an englischen, schwedischen und deutschen Texten soll die Studenten zum Lesen anregen.

0.7 BEWERTUNGSMASSSTÄBE

Die Studenten werden auf verschiedene Art und Weise bewertet. Während des Modulstudiums werden den Studierenden Aufgaben gestellt, die entweder allein oder in Kleingruppen zu bearbeiten sind. Die Abschlußarbeit soll in Form eines Portfolios (d.h. Belegmappe) abgefaßt werden. Diese Regelungen eröffnen den Studenten eine Reihe von Möglichkeiten, wie z.B. Videoeinsatz, Aufsätze und szenische Gestaltungen, die ebenfalls als Prüfungsleistung anerkannt werden können. Zum Bestehen einer Prüfung, müssen die Studenten mindestens 60% der nachfolgend aufgelisteten Anforderungen erbringen.
Das Portfolio wird folgendermaßen bewertet:

Einleitung	5%
Literaturbearbeitung	20%
Theoretische Verbindungen	25%
Kritische Analyse	30%
Gliederung/Präsentation	5%
Schlußfolgerung	15%

Es wird davon ausgegangen, daß die Bearbeitungszeit eines Portfolios mindestens 25 Stunden beträgt.

Am Ende des Moduls können die Studenten die Effektivität des Moduls, die Vermittlung der Lerninhalte und die damit verbundenen Anforderungen auswerten.

0.8 WAS DIE STUDENTEN ZU DEM EUROPÄISCHEN MODUL BEITRAGEN KÖNNEN

Die Studenten werden aufgefordert, sich aktiv am Studium des Moduls zu beteiligen. Die geplante Studiendauer beträgt zwischen 150 und 200 Stunden. Darin enthalten sind sowohl Vorlesungen, Seminare und Workshops als auch das Selbststudium.

0.9 LITERATUR UND SCHLÜSSELTEXTE

Es ist schwierig, ein Buch zu finden, das die gesamte Bandbreite dieses Moduls abdeckt. Die folgenden englischen und deutschen Texte und Bücher sind daher als Anregung und Einführung gedacht. Wir denken, daß sie hilfreich und informativ sind.

Zeitschriften
Shakespeare T. and
Watson N. (1997)   Defending the Social Model of Disability, *Disability and Society* 12, 2, 293-298

Bücher

Kapitel 1
Daunt, P. (1991)   *Meeting Disability – A European Response*, London Cassell

Baumann, U./
Klesczewski, R. (Hrsg.) (1997)   *Penser l'Europe – Europa denken*, Tübingen und Basel, Francke Verlag

Kapitel 2
Hevey, D. (1992)   *The Creatures Time Forgot*, London, Routledge

Möckel, A. (1988)	*Geschichte der Heilpädagogik*, Stuttgart, Klett-Cotta
Oliver, M. (1990)	*The Politics of Disablement*, London, Macmillan
Kapitel 3.i	
Johnstone, D. (1998)	*An Introduction to Disability Studies*, London, Fulton
McKnight, J. (1995)	*The Careless Society*, New York,
Opp, G./ Peterander, F. (Hrsg.) (1996)	*Focus Heilpädagogik – Projekt Zukunft*, München, E. Reinhardt
Kapitel 3.ii	
Bundesministerium für Arbeit und Sozialordnung (1997)	*EURO-ATLAS. Soziale Sicherheit im Vergleich*, Bonn
Swain, J. Finkelstein V., French, S. et al (1996)	*Disabling Barriers – Enabling Environments*, London, Sage
Johnstone, D (1998)	*An Introduction to Disability Studies*, London, Fulton
Coleridge, P. (1994)	*Disability, Liberation and Development*, London, Oxfam
Kapitel 3.iii	
Campbell, J and Oliver, M. (1996)	*Disability Politics: understanding our past changing our future*, London, Routledge
Gooding, C. (1994)	*Disabling Laws, Enabling Acts*, London, Pluto
Theunissen, G./ Plaute, W. (1996)	*Empowerment und Heilpädagogik,* Freiburg im Breisgau, Lambertus
Kapitel 4	
Billis, D and Harris, M. (1996)	*Challenges of Organisation and Management,* London, Macmillan
Mullins, L. (1996)	*Management and Organisational Behaviour*, London, Pitman
Belz, H./ Siegrist, M. (1997)	*Kursbuch Schlüsselqualifikationen, Ein Trainingsprogramm*, Freiburg im Breisgau, Lambertus

Kapitel 5
Christensen, C and
Rizvi, R. (1996) *Disability and the Dilemmas of Education and Justice*, Buckingham, Open University Press

Schleicher, K./
Bos, W. (Hrsg.) (1994) *Realisierung der Bildung in Europa*, Darmstadt, Wissenschaftliche Buchgesellschaft

1. EUROPÄISCHE IDENTITÄT?

Wolf Bloemers

1.1 EINFÜHRUNG

Dieser Teilbaustein setzt sich mit dem Problemfeld der/einer europäischen Lebensgemeinschaft auseinander.

Gibt es eine solche, oft propagierte, gewünschte, beschworene, bezweifelte überhaupt? Ist sie Mythos, Tradition, Faktum oder Desiderat? Ist sie notwendig, und wenn ja, wozu? Welche Sozialisationseinflüsse hat ein mögliches "europäisches" Kulturerbe und welche Konsequenzen können für die zukünftige Entwicklung von humaneren Lebensformen aus den Antworten auf diese Fragen gezogen werden? Welchen spezifischen Beitrag für ein sozialeres Miteinander kann ein internalisiertes europäisches Bewußtsein leisten?

Diesen und weiteren Fragen will das Kapitel durch vertiefte Auseinandersetzungen mit der Geschichte, der Politik, der Kultur, der Sprache, den Künsten, der Literatur, den Glaubenssystemen, kurz, den Manifestationen menschlicher Lebensverständnisse in Europa nachgehen und Antworten nach einer "europäischen" Identität suchen.

Aufgrund der hohen Komplexität des Themas, seiner Verwobenheit mit den vielfältigsten wissenschaftlichen Disziplinen, diversen politischen Perspektiven und seiner Abhängigkeit von den jeweiligen nationalen und subjektiven Wahrnehmungsmustern kann dieses Kapitel im Rahmen des Moduls nur einen sehr ausschnitthaften, fokussierten Zugang eröffnen, der zu weiteren rationalen intensiven Auseinandersetzungen anregen soll.

Unter Verzicht auf Vollständigkeit und fachliche Systematik erfolgt hier deshalb eine didaktische Reduktion auf einige grundlegende Fragestellungen und Sachverhalte, die anhand der Bearbeitung von konkreten Ausschnitten, Details und Teilbereichen aus dem Thema "Europa" zu den Zielen:

- Wissenserwerb,
- Reflexion,
- kritische Einschätzung und zur Bewußtseinsbildung hinsichtlich der Frage nach der europäischen Identität führen sollen.

Dieses Kapitel thematisiert:

- Das Verständnis von Europa: *Was ist Europa? Wer (was) sind Europäer?*
- Das Problem von Zugehörigkeit: *Wie und wozu entsteht Identität?*
- Nationale und supranationale Wahrnehmungen und Einstellungen: *Wie sehen die "Europäer" Europa?*
- Den Europabedarf/Zukunftsentwürfe: *Wie soll Europa sein, werden? Gibt es "Europabedarf"?*
- Lern- und Vermittlungsprozesse: *(Wie) Werden wir Europäer?*

1.1.1 ZIELE

Die Bearbeitung der Fragen soll die Studierenden befähigen:

- Dimensionen europäischer Kultur und Geschichte zu identifizieren und kritisch einzuschätzen,
- Die Identität von Ort, Nation, Nachbarschaft und Gemeinschaft im europäischen Zusammenhang zu betrachten,
- Die Rolle von Sprache, Glaubenssystemen, Architektur, Kunst, Literatur im Identitätsprozess kritisch zu bewerten,
- Sinn und Bedeutung der europäischen Einigung kritisch zu reflektieren, eine eigene Position dazu zu entwickeln und evtl. eigene Beiträge dazu zu entwerfen,
- Die Entwicklung europäischer Bewußtseinselemente als pädagogische Bildungsaufgabe wahrzunehmen.

Als Arbeitsformen sind für diesen Studienteil vorgesehen:

- Sachinformationsblöcke (Texte hier und in Vorlesungen)
- Selbststudium angegebener Literatur
- Seminar (Haus) arbeiten mit Quellentextanalysen
- Seminardiskussionen auf der Basis von Thesenpapieren
- Herstellung von Dossiers/Themenmappen mit themenrelevanten aktuellen Materialien/Medien
- Referate
- Evtl. Exkursion zu relevanten Institutionen
- Produktion von Wandzeitungen
- Erstellung von Interviews und deren Auswertung
- Sprachanalysen politischer Texte

1.1.2 LERNERGEBNISSE

Am Ende des Kapitels werden die Studenten

- Kenntnisse über die vielfältigen Quellen europäischer Kultur und über ein europäisches Bewußtseins erworben haben,
- sich einen Überblick über die Prozesse von Identitätsbildung und über die Streitpunkte und Herausforderungen verschafft haben, die aus überlappenden Identitäten resultieren,
- ein kritisches Bewußtsein hinsichtlich des Fehlbedarfs an sozialer und kommunikativer Mitgestaltung bei der Schaffung eines vereinten Europas entwickelt haben,
- sich bewußt sein, daß bezüglich der Konzeptentwicklung zu einer Einheit Europas ein eigener, persönlicher Beitrag erforderlich ist.

Internationalisierung, Globalisierung, Europäisierung - internationale Tendenzen von Zusammenschlüssen und suprastaatlichen Kooperationen - sind weltweit zu verzeichnende Entwicklungen, die das soziale Zusammenleben, die Zugehörigkeit zu traditionellen Gemeinschaften in zunehmendem Maße verändern und zu erheblichen Verunsicherungen führen. Neue Ideen, Lebensformen, Politiken, Kommunikationsmöglichkeiten, Wirtschaftsverbünde und Verkehrssysteme stellen bisheriges in Frage und fordern zu neuen Bewältigungsansätzen heraus. Dies trifft in besonderer Weise gesellschaftliche Randgruppen, wozu auch die sogenannten "Behinderten" zählen.

Was bedeutet dies für die Heilpädagogik? Ist auch hier eine Europäisierung erforderlich, wünschenswert, notwendig, sinnvoll und was meint dies? Was kann man sich darunter vorstellen? Gibt es "europäische" Behinderte, ist Behinderung eine europäische Dimension, gibt es - soll es geben - eine europäische Heilpädagogik?

Bevor diesen mehr spezifischen Fragen nachgegangen werden kann, muß vorweg das Verständnis von "Europa" gründlich thematisiert werden, denn die Meinungen, die Auffassungen zu diesem Begriff, die Auslegungen dessen, was "Europa" ausmacht sind so vielfältig, so facettenreich und auch so kontrovers, daß ohne eine rationale Klärung zur Gewinnung einer gemeinsamen Verständigung - und Verstehensbasis über Europa dieses Artefakt "Europa" diffus und manipulierbar bleibt.

1.2 WAS IST EUROPA? WER (WAS) SIND EUROPÄER?

Was denken Sie über die folgenden Antworten?

1. *"Man ist Europäer, wenn man >civis romanis< geworden ist"* (CURTIUS 1969, 22).

2. *"Die Idee der universalen Einigung der Menschen ist die Idee der Menschheit Europas, ihr verdankt sie ihre Zivilisation, für sie allein lebt sie".* (DOSTOJEWSKI).

3. *"Jeder Europäer ist ein Schlachtfeld von Leidenschaften, von Willensrichtungen, von Charakteren. In jedem Europäer morden und vergewaltigen seine Vorfahren einander"* (COUDENHOVE-KALERGI 1949).

Drei Meinungen von vielen, unzähligen, die das Europäische, das Gemeinsame, das Proprium, das Typische zu erfassen und auf den Punkt zu bringen versuchen. (Kennen Sie aus anderen Bezügen ähnliche oder abweichende Definitionsversuche?)

Hinter diesen Auffassungen stehen Grundhaltungen und Kontexte (anthropologische/politische/nationale etc.) und individuelle Vorverständnisse, deren Kenntnis und Herkunft zum Verstehen unabdingbar sind; ansonsten verbleiben die Zitate im rhetorischen Nebel oder im plakativen Blendfeuer. (Zum Kennenlernen dieser entsprechenden Zusammenhänge schlagen Sie nach in Literaturlexika, bzw. lesen Sie die angegebenen Quellen).

Den beispielhaft vorangestellten Zitaten unterschiedlichster Herkunft und gedanklichen Zugriffs ist gemeinsam, daß sie ein Zusammengehörigkeitsbewußtsein und ein Wertbewußtsein widerspiegeln bzw. unterstellen, mit dem eine große, über nationale Begrenzungen hinweg gesehene, empfundene Lebensgemeinschaft charakterisiert wird.

Es sind Versuche der Identifizierung mit Wertvorstellungen von sozialen Gemeinschaften und der Entwicklung bzw. Vision eines Gemeinschaftsbewußtseins. (Auf die Motive und Strukturen solcher sozialer Selbstdefinitionstendenzen, kollektiver Selbstdeutungen und Bewußtseinsbildungsprinzipien geht das nächste Teilkapitel genauer ein).

Vor dem Hintergrund der weltpolitischen Umbrüche und der Organisationsversuche in wirtschaftlichen, politischen, sozialen Großstrukturen sind die Bewußtseinsbildungsprozesse für neue Gemeinschaften in vollem Gange. Bezogen auf Europa heißt dies, Anknüpfungspunkte an Bisheriges, Geschichtliches, Gewachsenes, Verbindendes zu suchen und diese auf ihre Tragfähigkeit und Verwertbarkeit, bzw. tatsächliche oder gewünschte Wertgemeinsamkeit und Ideenheimat für zukünftige gemeinsame Lebenformen hin zu überprüfen.

"Ohne ein Bewußtsein von Europa als einer geschichtlich begründeten, politisch sinnvollen und moralisch legitimierten Gemeinschaft dürfte ein europäisches Parlament jedenfalls stets nur ein Abbild der nationalen Machtverhältnisse auf diesem Kontinent sein: Der Wirtschaftskraft, der Bevölkerungszahl, der politischen Koalitionen der einzelnen Völker - und ständig vor einem europäischen Verfassungsgericht weitere Verwaltungsnormen einklagen müssen, weil es ein von allen erkennbares und anerkanntes europäisches Gemeinwohl nicht gibt" (HENTIG 1993, 73).

Rückbesinnungen auf europäisches Gemeinsames haben vielfältige Zugänge. Einzelpersonen, soziale Gruppierungen, Künstler, Wissenschaftler, Politiker erschließen und interpretieren solche tatsächlichen oder empfundenen Ordnungsgefüge aus historischen Konstellationen, geistigen Traditionen, Symbolbezügen, Sozialstrukturen und anderen Wurzeln, je nach interessensgeleiteter und sozialisationsbedingter Sichtweise.

Im folgenden hierzu stichwortartig eine Auswahl:

- *Länderübergreifendes, europäisch-verschränktes Kulturgut:*

    Antike Kultur verbreitet durch römische Kaiser/Christianisierung durch Klöster (Religion)/dynastisches Verständnis von "Ahnherren" (z.B. Karl der Große in Deutschland und Frankreich)/Hanse/Reformation und Gegenreformation/lateinische Sprache/Kreuzzüge/militärische Bündelung gegen Türken/Künstler und Gelehrte als Europäer/wissenschaftliches Denken und Universitäten/Ästhetik/Trias: Regnum, Sacerdotium, Studium (vgl. SCHLEICHER 1993, 4 ff).

- *Geistige Ordnungen:*

    Europäische Menschenrechte (Individualrechte) / Demokratieentwicklung / Geldwirtschaft / Herrschaft des Rechts / Aufklärung / Kapitalismus / universaleWissenschaft / Berechenbarkeit / Freiheitsrechte / Humanitätsidee (vgl. JASPERS 1947, 9).

- *Literarische Tradition:*

    "We need not remind ourselves that, as Europe is a whole (and still, in its progressive mutilation and disfigurement, the organism out of which any greater world harmony must develop), so European literature is a whole, the several numbers of which cannot flourish, if the same blood-stream does not

circulate throughout the whole body" (ELIOT, zit. nach ASSMANN 1993, 98).

- *Das Fundament der "Latinitas":*

    "Latinitas bedeutet ja mehr als nur sprachliche Zusammengehörigkeit, wie sie die romanischen Völker miteinander verbindet, Latinitas ist die knappste Formel für die Gesittung, die der europäische Geist, allen Rückschlägen und Rückfällen zum Trotz, seit mehr als zwei Jahrtausenden zu verwirklichen trachtet" (EBERLE 1966, 230).

- *Wertorientierungen:*

    "Zum Lebensstil und Verhaltens- wie Wertstandard, die nach Ansicht der Befragten spezifisch ...europäisch sind und denen die größte Zuneigung entgegengebracht wurde, gehörten 1990: Frieden (47%); Demokratie (38%); Kultur (33%) und Lebensqualität (28%)... "Auf ähnliche Akzentuierungen weist ein Resümee von Erhebungsdaten aus dem Jahr 1989 hin, und zwar gehörte danach die Achtung der Grund- und Menschenrechte ... zum gemeinsamen Erbe politischer Traditionen und Ideale in Europa. 78% der Europäer halten die Demokratie für die beste aller Regierungsformen. Für 60% ist die Achtung der Menschenrechte eines der Anliegen, für die "es der Mühe wert ist, einiges zu riskieren und auf manches zu verzichten" (Eurobarometer Juni 1990, S. 3; November 989, S. 4, 31 ff.).

Europäische Kultur und Identität beruhen entscheidend „auf der Entwicklung einer Gesellschaft, die auf Achtung der Menschenrechte beruht, auf Demokratie, Meinungs- und Redefreiheit, Pluralismus, ... auf dem Bewußtsein eines gemeinsamen kulturellen Erbes, dem Wunsch, gemeinsam die Zukunft aufzubauen ...". Auf dieser Grundlage soll zwischen den verschiedenen Kulturen ein Ausgleich gesucht und eine Kooperation angestrebt werden (MULCAHY 1992, 46).

Auch Nichteuropäer beschäftigen sich mit Vorstellungen über Europäisches:

- *"Typische Verbindungen":*

    Individualismus und kollektive Sicherheit, humanistische Tradition und wirtschaftliche Dynamik, Abgrenzung nach außen bei gleichzeitig begrenzter globaler Verantwortlichkeit (vgl. SCHLEICHER 1993, 2).

- *Aus amerikanischer Perspektive:*

    "Wenn ich beschreiben müßte, was Europa mir als Amerikanerin bedeutet, würde ich anfangen mit - Befreiung. Befreiung von dem, was in Amerika als

Kultur durchgeht. Die Vielfalt, Ernsthaftigkeit, der Anspruch, die Dichte der europäischen Kultur bilden einen archimedischen Punkt, von dem aus ich geistig, die Welt in Bewegung setzen kann" (SONTAG 1988, 131 f.).

Nicht nur Verbindendes, auch Trennendes scheint ein Spezifikum von Europa zu sein. Hierzu ebenfalls eine beschränkte Auswahl von Fakten, Entwicklungen und deren Interpretation, mit Hilfe derer die derzeit stark zentrifugalen wie diversifizierenden, sozialen und kulturellen Entwicklungstendenzen angedeutet werden sollen, die sich in offensichtlichem Gegensatz zu den auf Vereinheitlichung ausgerichteten wirtschaftlichen und politischen Anstrengungen befinden (vgl. McLEAN 1993, 264).

Zu nennen sind hier:

- Zunehmende Regionalismen wie z.B. in Spanien oder Belgien,
- neue nationale Abgrenzungen (Tschechien/Slowakei),
- ethnische Ausgrenzungen und Gewalttätigkeiten/Völkermord (Serben, Kroaten),
- religiöse Segregationen (Islam/Christentum),
- politisch-rechtliche Entzweiungen (Bio-Ethik-Konvention),
- Kluftvergrößerung zwischen Arm und Reich (Arbeitslosigkeit/Abwehr baltischer Kontakte).

All dies führt zu auch Euroskepsis, die die von der Europäischen Union zuweilen als "gegeben" unterstellte europäische Identität Lügen straft. Statt dessen zeigen letztgenannte Trends auch, daß der Aufbau einer europäischen Identität durch Erblasten von Nationalismus, Chauvinismus, Rassismus und Fremdenfeindlichkeit gefährdet ist (vgl. BÜRLI 1997, 18), die allesamt als Zeichen tiefsitzender Angst vor dem Fremden, dem Dunklen in jedem von uns zu verstehen sind und zu innerer Fremdheit führen und das Entstehen von Zusammengehörigkeitsgefühl blockieren.

So ist Europäisches auch:

"... unsere Lage - die geographische, die historische, die welt- und umweltpolitische. Was einst Barrieren waren: Weichsel und Rhein, Alpen und Pyrenäen, Nordsee und Adria, sind heute Nahtstellen geworden, Ziel von Reisen, Gelegenheiten für Austausch und Begegnung - aber auch tödliche Verbindungen: Die Flüsse tragen das Gift von einem Land ins andere; alle Anlieger eines Meeres erleiden dessen Verseuchung; die Windseite der Gebirge fängt den sauren Regen auf, der Hunderte von Kilometern entfernt entstanden ist; radioaktive Wolken kennen ohnedies keine Hindernisse. Kriege - die Erblast vergangener Jahrhunderte - und die Beschädigung der gemeinsamen Natur, die Flucht der Armen aus Regionen ohne Zukunft in Regionen ohne Raum - das alles wird

uns nötigen, kontinental zu denken, uns auf ein Kerncurriculum europäischer Überzeugung zu einigen, ohne die die Völker die Opfer und Kompromisse nicht aufbringen werden, die die Lage von ihnen fordert. Daß Europa kein oder nur ein schwaches Bewußtsein von einem ihm eigenen Gemeinwohl, einer es auszeichnenden und verbindenden Gesinnung hat, beweist der politische Alltag: Wenn Kernkraftabfall von einem Land ins andere verschoben wird; wenn Einheitsgesetze benutzt werden, um den Import zu regulieren; vollends wenn die Staatengemeinschaft so gut wie tatenlos dem jugoslawischen Völkermorden zusieht. Ich richte nicht; ich habe keine schlüssige Vorstellung, was hier hätte geschehen können; ich stelle nur den Mangel fest " (VON HENTIG 1993, 79 f).

Was ist Europa? Wer (was) sind Europäer? Resümierend können wir nach der Reflexion über die vorangegangenen Skizzierungen mit BÜRLI festhalten:

"Das Konsistente in der historischen Entwicklung der europäischen Zivilisation, Kultur und Politik ist, u.a. nach den Ausführungen von KÜNZLI (1992), das Widersprüchliche, das Ambivalente, die Skepsis. Europa war und ist in der Bestimmung der eigenen kulturellen Identität unsicher, hat sich sogar geweigert, eine vollständige Identifikation zuzulassen, so daß Unruhe und Ungewißheit bestehen bleiben. Europa hat, wenn es von außen bedroht war und sich deshalb seiner eigenen kulturellen Identität bewußt wurde, auch gleichzeitig die Überlegenheit seiner eigenen Werte in Frage gestellt und einen Prozeß der permanenten Selbstkritik in Gang gesetzt. Das gesamteuropäische Bildungserbe war bisher nicht in der Lage, ein gemeinsames europäisches Bewußtsein zu stiften. So läßt sich denn heute noch europäische Identität nicht in erster Linie durch Einheitlichkeit, sondern durch Vielfalt charakterisieren" (BÜRLI 1979, 15).

Dies bedeutet aber auch, "daß das Bewußtsein einer gemeinsamen europäischen Kultur, der gegenseitigen Bindungen und der gegenseitigen Abhängigkeit der Geschicke aller Länder des Kontinents sowie der Notwendigkeit der Zusammenarbeit noch nicht verlorengegangen ist" (GORBATSCHOW 1987, 258) und daß damit ein ethischer Imperativ zur Entwicklung gemeinsamer Perspektiven begründet ist.

WEITERFÜHRENDE, VERTIEFENDE AUFGABEN:

- Identifizieren Sie drei bildende Künstler von europäischer Bedeutung / Dimension / Format und begründen Sie Ihre Auswahl unter Verwendung konkreter Beispiele und deren Einordnungen in übergeordnete Werte- und Bewußtseinsvorstellungen.
- Identifizieren Sie drei Schriftsteller von europäischer Bedeutung / Dimension / Format und begründen Sie Ihre Auswahl unter Verwendung konkreter

Beispiele und deren Einordnungen in übergeordnete Werte- und Bewußtseinsvorstellungen.
- Identifizieren Sie drei Musiker von europäischer Bedeutung / Dimension / Format und begründen Sie Ihre Auswahl unter Verwendung konkreter Beispiele und deren Einordnungen in übergeordnete Werte- und Bewußtseinsvorstellungen.
- Identifizieren Sie zwei kunsthistorische Stilrichtungen von europäischer Bedeutung / Dimension / Format und begründen Sie Ihre Auswahl unter Verwendung konkreter Beispiele und deren Einordnungen in übergeordnete Werte- und Bewußtseinsvorstellungen.
- Identifizieren Sie weitere Beispiele für die Pluralität und für die Diversifizierung europäischer Gegebenheiten.
- Bewerten Sie die im Text aufgeführten Zitate kritisch und begründen Sie diese Kritik.

1.3   WIE UND WOZU ENTSTEHT IDENTITÄT?

In den vorangegangenen Abschnitten hat mehrfach der Begriff "Identität" Verwendung gefunden.

Identität wird verstanden als Gleichheit oder Übereinstimmung von mehreren Dingen oder Personen oder wenigstens des ihnen Gemeinsamen; außerdem als Echtheit in Ordnung zu sein, man selbst zu sein. Zu unterscheiden sind demnach:

- eine Ich-Identität (Ego-Identity), die den Innenaspekt von Identität meint; diese ist "das subjektive Empfinden seiner eigenen Situation und seiner eigenen Kontinuität und Eigenart, das ein Individuum allmählich als ein Resultat seiner verschiedenen sozialen Erfahrungen erwirbt" (GOFFMAN 1967,132). Ich-Identität basiert also auf subjektiven Empfindungen, auf dem Innenbild des Selbst,

- und eine soziale Identität (Social identity); hierbei ordnen sich Menschen routinemäßig typisierend in soziale Kategorien ein. Soziale Identität beschreibt die Zugehörigkeit zu einer solchen Kategorie (z.B. Student, Deutscher, Soldat etc.) (vgl. GOFFMAN ebd. 10) und verdeutlicht die Gruppenzugehörigkeit, die Teilhabe am Rollensystem, das Sosein wie andere.

Andere soziologische Identitätstheorien (KRAPPMANN, THIMM, FREY) betonen hinsichtlich der sozialen Identität den Anforderungscharakter der anderen, nämlich sich den allgemeinen Erwartungen unterzuordnen und so zu sein, wie alle, d.h. sich externen Zuschreibungsprozessen zu unterwerfen.

Alle Vertreter von Identitätstheorien stellen heraus, daß Identität stets einen Balanceakt zwischen dem Selbstbild, dem vermuteten und dem realen Fremdbild, zwischen Ich-Identität und sozialer Identität darstellt und daß Menschen stets danach streben, das einmal etablierte Selbst zu behalten, d.h. Veränderungen abzuwehren. Die gesicherte Verortung im sozialen Bezugssystem stellt einen besonders hohen Wert dar, so daß Kontinuität für den Erhalt von Identität besondere Priorität besitzt. Außerdem erfolgen nach entwicklungs- und sozialpsychologischen Forschungserkenntnissen die fundamentalen Identitätsbildungen und -prägungen weitgehend in den primären und sekundären Sozialisationsinstanzen (Familie, Schule) über Entkulturations- und Sozialisationsprozesse, vor allem im regionalen Kontext. Diese Merkmale der Identitätsprozesse:

- stärkere Prägung durch Zeit als durch Raumdimensionen (vgl. SCHLEICHER 1974, 113),
- Vermeidungstendenzen von Wandlungen mit Beharrungsstrategien,
- Ausbildung von Bewußtseins- und Wertstrukturen eher in frühkindlichen als in Erwachsenenjahren und eher in Lang- als in Kurzzeitprozessen,
- Identitätsbedürfnisse nach relativ stabilen Umwelt-, Kultur- und Kommunikationserfahrungen –

machen deutlich, daß aufgrund dieser psychologischen Gegebenheiten das Ringen um neue transnationale Gemeinsamkeiten, um eine (neue) europäische Identität mit erheblichen Konfliktpotentialen befrachtet ist (vgl. SCHLEICHER 1974, 7). Außerdem sind nach Aussagen der politischen Sozialisationsforschung grundlegende ethnische und national ausgerichtete Einstellungen bis zur Pubertät vorgeprägt (TORNEY-PURTA u.a. 1986) und ethnische Erfahrungen und gemeinsame Bewußtseinsprozesse meistens älter als nationalstaatliche, und sie wirken viel stärker auf die Bevölkerung ein, als neue europäische, von "anderen" konstruierte Konstellationen. Gleichermaßen sind langfristig gewachsene religiöse Zugehörigkeiten verbindender und identitätsstiftender als politisch ausgehandelte oder verordnete, nicht kommunizierte Lösungssetzungen.

Auch eingegrenzte soziale Räume wie Regionen und Kulturkreise dienen als "Identifikationsräume", mehr noch als die als Identitätsbedrohung empfundenen, anonymen, europäischen Großstrukturen. "Wie bedeutsam diese Identifikationsmöglichkeiten für die Bürger sind, zeigt ein *Vergleich ihrer lokalen, regionalen, nationalen und europäischen Identifikationsbereitschaft.* Nach Umfragedaten von 1991 empfinden wesentlich mehr Bürger (85% +) enge Bindungen zu lokalen, regionalen und nationalen Lebensformen als zur Europäischen Gemeinschaft bzw. zu Europa insgesamt (47% +) (vgl. Eurobarometer, Dezember 1991, S. 66).

Offensichtlich fühlen sich etwa nur halb so viele Bürger der Europäischen Gemeinschaft wie ihrem Land oder ihrer Region verbunden. Im Ländervergleich sind die *lokalen und regionalen Bindungen* am stärksten in Griechenland, Portugal und Spanien (lokal 73% +, regional 69% +), die *nationalen* daneben sehr ausgeprägt: ebenfalls in Griechenland, aber auch in Dänemark und Irland (72% +). Zur EG sind sie generell geringer, am höchsten noch in Spanien, Italien und Luxemburg (16% +) (ibid., S. 66 f)".

Abb.1: Lokale, regionale, nationale und europäische Identifikationen

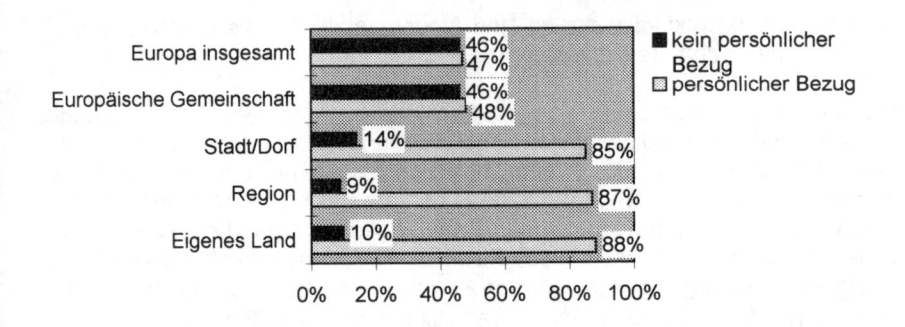

Europa insgesamt: 46% / 47%
Europäische Gemeinschaft: 46% / 48%
Stadt/Dorf: 14% / 85%
Region: 9% / 87%
Eigenes Land: 10% / 88%

■ kein persönlicher Bezug
☐ persönlicher Bezug

Quelle: SCHLEICHER 1994, 108

Tab.1: Länderspezifische Identifikationen (in %)
(jeweils 3 höchste und niedrigste Nationalwerte)

Identifikation (feeling attached)	EG 12 ∅	höchste				niedrigste		
Gemeinwesen	54	GR 81	P 75	E 73	...	UK 73	F 40	NL 28
Region	55	GR 87	E 71	P 69	...	B 41	F 41	NL 34
Nation	53	GR 86	DK 84	IRL 72	...	D(Ost) 45	NL 40	B 30
EG	12	E 18	I 18	L 16	...	D(Ost) 8	UK 6	NL 4
Europa insgesamt	12	I 19	E 18	GR 16	...	IRL 8	UK 8	NL 5

Quelle: SCHLEICHER 1994, 108

Resümiert nach: Eurobarometer, Dec. 1991, A67.

Anhand dieser empirischen Befunde des Eurobarometers wird neben der Tatsache der stärkeren Bindung und Identifizierung mit kleinräumigeren und überlappende, doppelte, partikulare Identitäten gibt, die nicht statisch sind, sondern durch dynamische Prozesse und durch Vielfalt gekennzeichnet sind.

Identitätsfindung und -bewahrung sind fundamentale, für die psychische Gesundheit unverzichtbare Prozesse.

Diese Prozesse eines zwischen den verschiedenen Anforderungen von außen ausbalancierten Selbstkonzeptes, eines Welt- und Menschenbildes, dem man sich verbunden, zugehörig, in dem man sich beheimatet und "behaust" und verwurzelt, also eins (vereint) fühlt, gedeihen am besten im nächsten = nahesten Lebenskontext, in bedeutsamen Erfahrungen mit Gruppen und Sozialgebilden, vor allem dann, wenn diese Bewußtseinbildungen durch starke eigene erfolgreiche Beteiligung und vielfältige Kommunikationsprozesse zu Identitätsklärungen = Sinnstiftungen führen. Selbstbestimmte Teilnahme und Teilhabe, aktives Mitgestalten an sozialen Lebensformen vermitteln die gefühlsmäßige Sicherheit in der Beziehung zu Partnern und Gruppenmitgliedern, das Gefühl "richtig" zu sein und die richtige Rolle in der Gesellschaft gefunden zu haben.

In Anlehnung an ERIKSON kann Identität abschließend als das Gefühl von Übereinstimmung der Vorstellungen über sich als Glied der Gesellschaft, als Mann oder Frau, als Angehöriger eines Berufsstandes, einer sozialen Gruppe mit den diesbezüglichen Erwartungen der Gesellschaft gekennzeichnet werden. Dieses Gefühl des Sichwohlfühlens auf dem eingeschlagenen eigenen Weg und des Glaubens, seine Sache auch in den Augen der anderen gut zu machen, verleiht dem Menschen Sicherheit und Zufriedenheit. Auch als Sozialpartner ist er verläßlich, denn er handelt im großen Rahmen gemäß der sozialen Rolle, mit der er sich identifiziert hat und die ihn in das tragende "Wir-Gefühl" einbindet (vgl. SCHRAML 1976[6], 197).

In einer pluralistischen und sich vor allem durch die derzeitigen gesamtgesellschaftlichen, europäischen Umbruchprozesse sehr fragil und changierend darstellenden Gesellschaft, die stets neue Erwartungen postuliert und neue Gruppierungen produziert, werden Identitätsfindungsprozesse ungeheuer erschwert und schon bestehende in Frage gestellt. Die daraus resultierenden sozialpsychischen Gefahren der Flucht in, bzw. Anklammerung an abschottende Identität von rassistischen, religiös-fanatischen und anderen vorurteilsgeprägten Gruppen sind derzeit in Europa allzu bekannt.

WEITERFÜHRENDE, VERTIEFENDE AUFGABEN:

- Identifizieren Sie mehrere Beispiele für aktuelle Tendenzen verstärkter ethnischer Identitätsprozesse/Separationsvorgänge und begründen Sie diese im politisch-historischen Kontext.
- Identifizieren Sie mehrere Beispiele für aktuelle Tendenzen verstärkter regionaler, kulturkreisorientierter Identitätsprozesse/Separationsvorgänge und begründen Sie diese im politisch/historischen Kontext.
- Reflektieren Sie über Ihre eigene(n) Identität(en), schreiben Sie die(se) als Substantiv(e) auf und begründen Sie, weshalb Sie sich damit wohl fühlen - oder auch nicht.

Diskutieren Sie das unten abgebildete Interaktionsmodell zum Identitätskonzept von FREY (entnommen aus: CLOERKES, G.: Soziologie der Behinderten 1997) mit Kommilitonen und versuchen Sie, sich selbst, Ihre eigenen Identitätsprozesse darin wiederzufinden; dies gelingt am besten, indem Sie die einzelnen Stichwörter mit ganz konkreten Beispielen unterlegen, bzw. sie mit ganz konkreten Beispielen ersetzen.

Beispiel:

- Interaktionspartner schreibt sozialen Status zu: Prof. X sieht mich als Student
- Interaktionspartner bewertet das Individuum: Prof. X schätzt mich als intelligent und distanziert/kommunikativ ein
- Interaktionspartner hat Erwartungen an das Individuum: Prof. X erwartet eine sehr gute Prüfung von mir.

Abb.2: Interaktionsmodell zum Identitätskonzept von FREY
(Cloerkes 1997, 163)

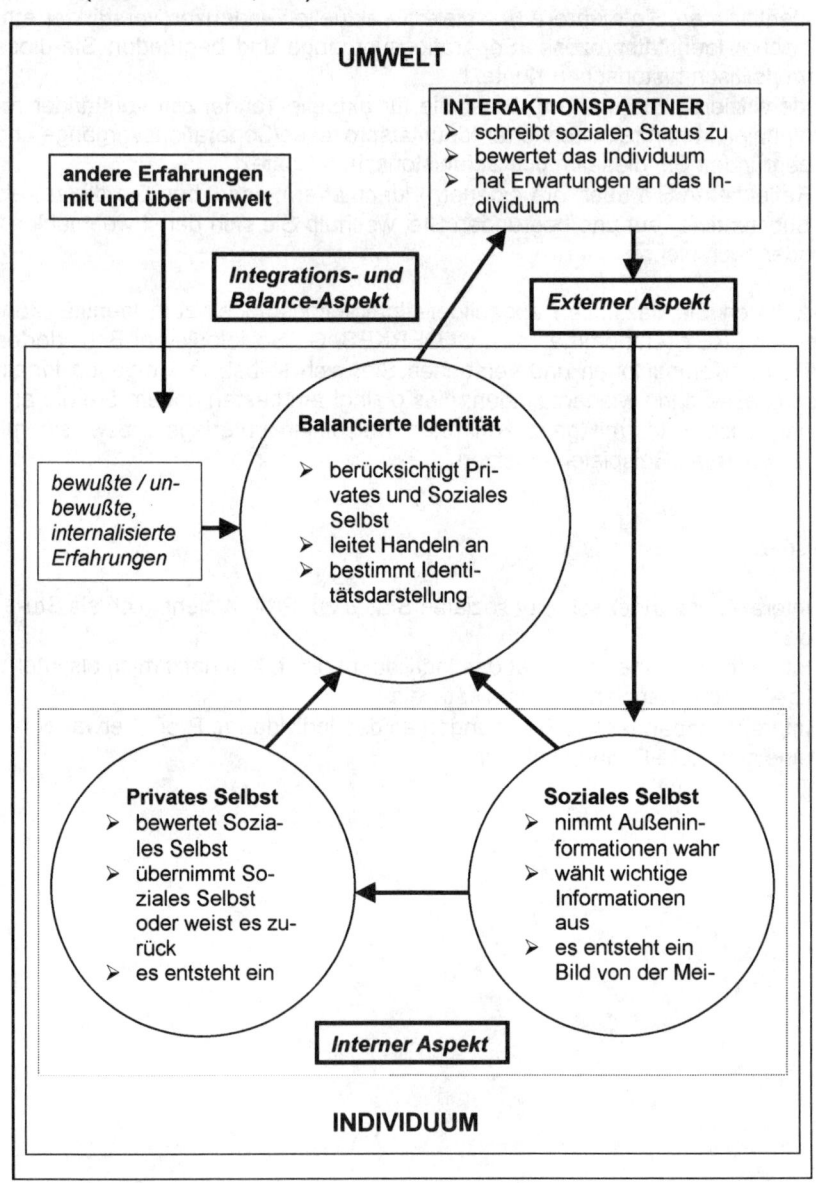

UMWELT

andere Erfahrungen mit und über Umwelt

INTERAKTIONSPARTNER
- schreibt sozialen Status zu
- bewertet das Individuum
- hat Erwartungen an das Individuum

Integrations- und Balance-Aspekt

Externer Aspekt

bewußte / unbewußte, internalisierte Erfahrungen

Balancierte Identität
- berücksichtigt Privates und Soziales Selbst
- leitet Handeln an
- bestimmt Identitätsdarstellung

Privates Selbst
- bewertet Soziales Selbst
- übernimmt Soziales Selbst oder weist es zurück
- es entsteht ein

Soziales Selbst
- nimmt Außeninformationen wahr
- wählt wichtige Informationen aus
- es entsteht ein Bild von der Mei-

Interner Aspekt

INDIVIDUUM

1.4 WIE SEHEN DIE "EUROPÄER" EUROPA?

Hartmut v. Hentig unterstellt - spöttisch? - in einem Kapitel über Europa: "Ein guter Deutscher ist ein guter Europäer" (1993, 73).

Wunschbild? Trugbild? Fehlsicht? Sind Identifizierungen mit Europa vor dem Hintergrund der zuvor dargelegten Identitätsprobleme und Identitätsfixierungen derzeit noch Desiderat oder gibt es bereits belegbare europäische Identitäten? Wie stark ist ein transnationales, eurokollektives Bewußtsein mittlerweile? Wie sehen die "Europäer" Europa?

Diesen Fragen gehen empirische Erhebungen der Commission of the European Communities mit dem Instrument des *Eurobarometer* nach, das die öffentliche Meinung zu europäischen Problemstellungen punktuell erkundet und zugleich die Entwicklungen des öffentlichen Meinungsbildungsprozesses erforscht.

Nachfolgende Tabellen geben Einblicke in Selbsteinschätzungen hinsichtlich nationaler und/oder europäischer Identität.

Tab 2: Europaeinstellungen der EG-Bürger

EG	"Inwieweit fühlen Sie sich nicht nur als Nationalbürger, sondern auch als Europäer?"		
	1988 (Herbst)	1989 (Frühjahr)	1990 (Frühjahr)
oftmals	16%	14%	15%
manchmal	37%	34%	31%

Quelle: SCHLEICHER 1994, 91

Tab.3: Einstellungsveränderungen in der EG (in %)
(10-Punkte-Skala von 'sehr stark' bis 'überhaupt nicht' allgemein in 4 Kategorien untergliedert, 2 positive referiert)

	EG (10)						EG (12)					
	sehr	ziemlich	sehr	ziemlich	sehr	ziemlich	sehr	ziemlich	sehr	ziemlich	sehr	ziemlich
	1975**		1985		1985		1989		1989		1991	1991
Allg. Lebenszufriedenheit*	19	56	18	57	18	56	24	59	23	58
Positive Einstellung zur europäische Einigung	31	38	28	47	29	45	37	41	33	46
Interesse an der EG-Politik	22	-	1976		1986							
			24	-	24	-	14	40	11	36
Zufriedenheit mit demokratischer Funktionsweise	7	42	1985		1985							
			8	42	10	42	10	47	7	43
Bedeutung des Europaparlaments für die EG	1977		1986		1986							
	10	27	13	40	11	38	15	44	13	43
Positive Einstellung zum Binnenmarkt	-	-	1988		1988							
			19	47	18	48	17	49	15	45

* Erhebungsmonate überwiegend: X und XI.   ** Nicht aus allen Jahren liegen Daten vor.
Eurobarometer 1974-91, S. 16ff., 34ff., 74ff., 151ff., 178, 203f.

Auffällig an Tabelle 2 ist die Verringerung der Identitätsbereitschaft mit Europa seit 1988 und an Tabelle 3 die durchgehende Verminderung an europaorientierten Einstellungen seit 1989. Diese negativen Trends haben eine Reihe von Ursachen, die insgesamt weitgehend in einer Diskrepanz zwischen den - hauptsächlich positiven - Vorstellungen und Erwartungen der Bürger bezüglich Europa und ihren - mehrheitlich negativen – Einschätzungen / Bewertungen hinsichtlich der Umsetzungen der europapolitischen Entscheidungen durch die Politiker zu finden ist.

Auch die nachfolgende Grafik (Abb.3) zeigt Veränderungsprozesse in der Einstellung zu einer europäischen und einer nationalen Identität; außer in Dänemark ist insgesamt ein positiver Trend auszumachen hinsichtlich der Sichtweise, daß die beiden Identitäten - europäische und nationale - als komplementär verstanden werden.

Abb.3: Europäische und nationale Identität. Als Gegensatz oder komplementäre Ergänzung? (EG 12).

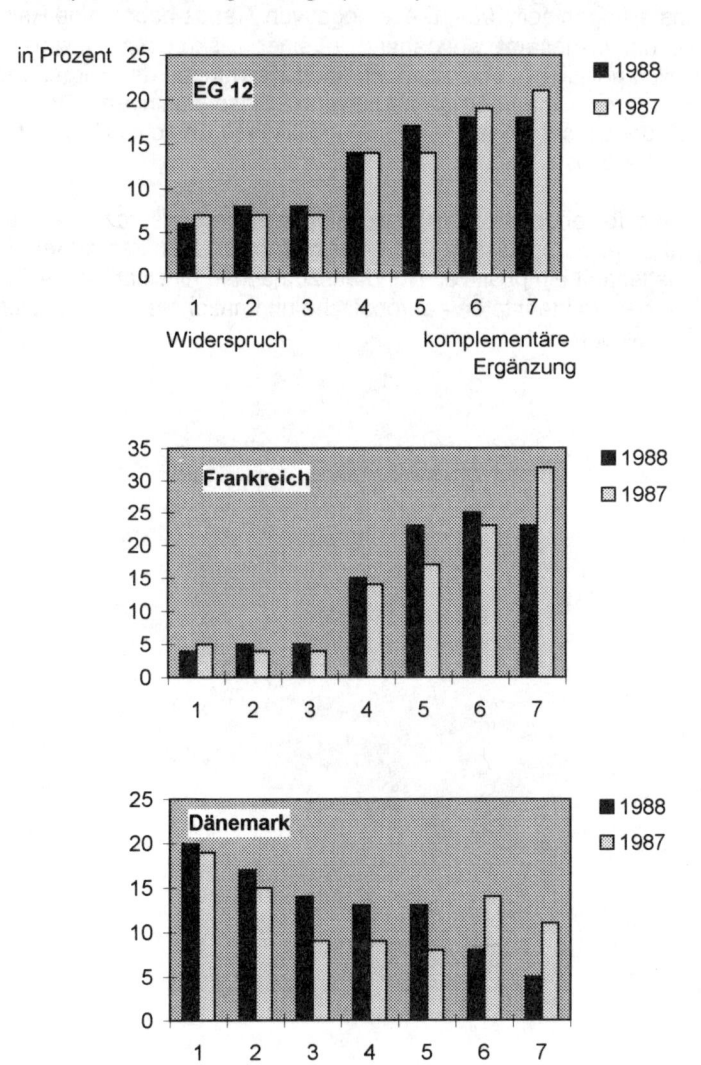

in Prozent

EG 12
■ 1988
□ 1987

1 2 3 4 5 6 7
Widerspruch   komplementäre
                Ergänzung

Frankreich
■ 1988
□ 1987

Dänemark
■ 1988
□ 1987

Quelle: SCHLEICHER 1994, 104

Aufschlußreich hinsichtlich der Zuerkennung unterschiedlicher Entscheidungskompetenzen in verschiedenen Politikbereichen (national/supranational) ist die Abb. 4 (Eurobarometer, June 1993, S. 42, A26);

Abb.4: Europäische oder nationale Entscheidungskompetenzen (EG 12). (Hier sind 10 von insgesamt 20 Entscheidungsbereichen resümiert.)

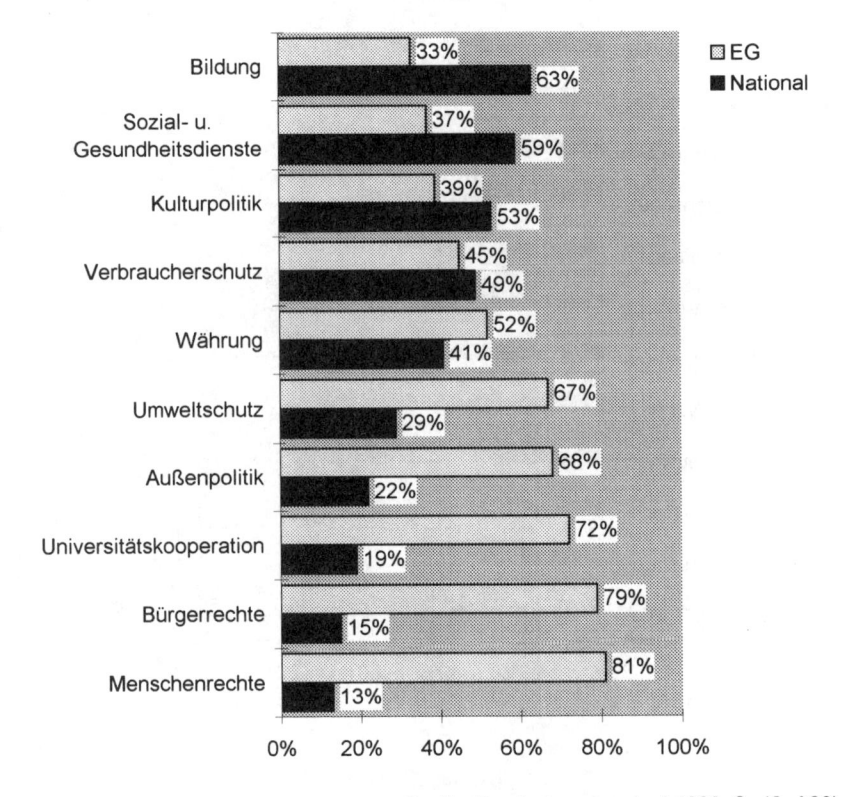

Bereich	EG	National
Bildung	33%	63%
Sozial- u. Gesundheitsdienste	37%	59%
Kulturpolitik	39%	53%
Verbraucherschutz	45%	49%
Währung	52%	41%
Umweltschutz	67%	29%
Außenpolitik	68%	22%
Universitätskooperation	72%	19%
Bürgerrechte	79%	15%
Menschenrechte	81%	13%

Quelle: Eurobarometer, Juni 1993, S. 42, A26)

Fragen der Menschenrechte, der Bürgerrechte, der Universitätskooperation, der Außenpolitik, des Umweltschutzes und auch des Geldes werden überwiegend als europäische Aufgaben und europäische Kompetenzen gesehen, wohingegen der Verbraucherschutz, die Kulturpolitik, die Sozial- und Gesundheitsdienste sowie die Bildungspolitik als nationale Entscheidungsbereiche erwünscht waren. Ähnlich plädierten die Bürger zwei Jahre früher (1991) für analoge Kompetenzzuordnungen (Abb.5)

Abb.5: Halten Sie europäische oder nationale Entscheidungen für besser?

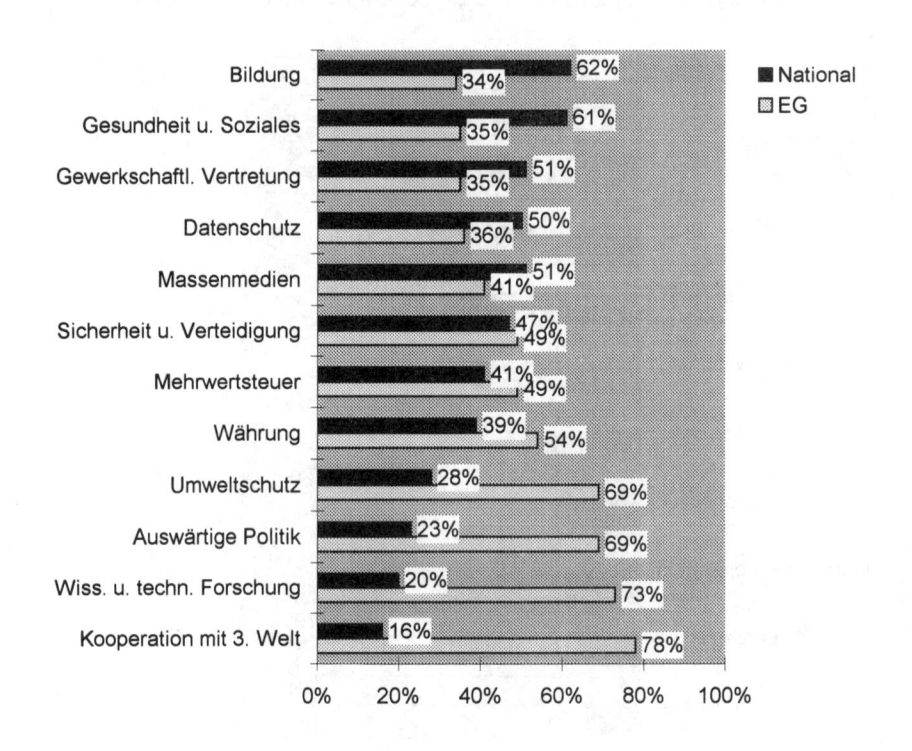

Bereich	National	EG
Bildung	34%	62%
Gesundheit u. Soziales	35%	61%
Gewerkschaftl. Vertretung	35%	51%
Datenschutz	36%	50%
Massenmedien	41%	51%
Sicherheit u. Verteidigung	47%	49%
Mehrwertsteuer	41%	49%
Währung	39%	54%
Umweltschutz	28%	69%
Auswärtige Politik	23%	69%
Wiss. u. techn. Forschung	20%	73%
Kooperation mit 3. Welt	16%	78%

Quelle: SCHLEICHER 1993,15

Quelle: Commission of the European Communities: Eurobarometer, No. 36. Brussels, Dec. 1991, p. 30. Illustration 5

Zusammenfassend kann festgehalten werden, daß die Einstellungen der "Europäer" zu Europa durchaus unterschiedlich sind: themenbezogen, nationalitätenbezogen (erinnert sei an das erste ablehnende Referendum in Dänemark zum Vertrag von Maastricht) ebenso wie altersbezogen (Jugendliche/ältere Bürger) und sozialstatusabhängig.

WEITERFÜHRENDE, VERTIEFENDE AUFGABEN:

- Gehen Sie den Gründen der Verringerung europaorientierter Einstellungen in den Tabellen 2 und 3 nach: Stellen Sie Hypothesen auf und überprüfen Sie diese an Hand von Literaturstudium (z.B. SCHLEICHER (Hrsg.): Realisierung der Bildung in Europa. Europäisches Bewußtsein trotz kultureller Identität? 1994, 91 bis 136).
- Befragen Sie Freunde, Bekannte, Kommilitonen, analog den Problemstellungen der zuvor abgelichteten Tabellen/Abbildungen und vergleichen Sie die Ergebnisse. Die Befragungsgruppen sollten etwa jeweils 20 Personen umfassen.
- Fragen Sie Freunde, Bekannte, Kommilitonen nach den Begründungen für die Einschätzungen/Bewertungen und schreiben Sie diese auf.
- Wie sehen Sie Europa? Stellen Sie Ihre Sichtweisen, Ihre Identitätsgefühle dar und begründen Sie diese.

1.5 WIE SOLL EUROPA SEIN, WERDEN? GIBT ES "EUROPABEDARF"?

Die zuvor mehrfach erwähnten ökonomischen, politischen und kommunikativen Herausforderungen mit nationalen, supranationalen, suprakontinentalen und globalen Dimensionen haben zu ebenso großdimensionierten Umstrukturierungsprozessen geführt, die jedoch - noch - weitgehend vornehmlich nur auf administrativem und wirtschaftlichem Gebiet sichtbar und spürbar sind und übergreifende humane Gestaltungs- und Bewältigungsprozesse vermissen lassen.

Wohin soll die Entwicklung gehen und wer bestimmt dies?

Ökonomisch und verwaltungsmäßig wächst Europa strukturell immer mehr zusammen und vernetzt sich auf diesen Feldern immer stärker, wohingegen die Trennungstendenzen, Konkurrenzen und Insuffizienzen auf dem Gebiet transnationalen Bewußtseins und gemeinsamer Identität immer klarer hervortreten. Die Wahrung nationaler Vorteile (Finanzierungsrabatte/Asyldebatte etc.) und die Hilflosigkeit, ja das Versagen bei außenpolitischen Krisen (Bosnien/Albanien/Kurdenflucht) machen deutlich, wie weit Europa noch von einer Gemeinschaft im Sinne von internationaler Solidarität, Loyalität und Effektivität entfernt ist.

Europa als Wirtschaftsraum und als Verwaltungsraum: Ja; aber Europa als Sozialraum? "Räume" verweisen assoziativ auf ein übergeordnetes Merkmal: auf ein Haus. In der Zeit der Perestroika entwarf der vormalige sowjetische Präsident Michail Gorbatschow 1987 das Bild vom "Gemeinsamen Haus Europa", wobei er ausdrücklich feststellte, daß diese Metapher kein Märchen, sondern das Ergebnis einer sorgfältigen Analyse der Lage auf dem Kontinent sei (1987, 254). Er verstand darunter vor mittlerweile über einem Jahrzehnt ein gemeinsames Haus, in dem jede Familie zwar ihre eigene Wohnung hat und es auch verschiedene Eingänge gibt, doch die Bewahrung des Hauses vor Feuerbrunst und anderen Katastrophen, die Sicherung und Erhaltung in einwandfreiem Zustand könne nur gemeinschaftlich erfolgen (vgl. 1987, 253). Dies impliziert einen moralischen Imperativ, der im Wort der gemeinsamen, gegenseitigen *Verantwortung* zentriert.

Elf Jahre später scheint die 1993 von SCHLEICHER gemachte Feststellung, daß derzeit für dieses "Europäische Haus" nur ein Architektenentwurf existiert, für das noch Bewohner gesucht werden (1993, 303) noch Gültigkeit zu besitzen. Liegt dies - um bei der Metapher zu bleiben -

a) am Entwurf/Design/der Konstruktion (= den Zielsetzungen) oder

b) an den Bauleuten, deren Ausbildung, Anleitung, und deren Arbeitsweisen (= den Methoden zum Bau und zum Bewohnen)?

Gehen wir in diesem Teilkapitel der Frage a) nach. Antworten auf Frage b) will das Folgekapitel aufsuchen.

Schon im vorigen Abschnitt wurde deutlich, daß die Mehrzahl der Bewohner Europas durchaus transnationale Ziele und Kompetenzen befürwortet, d.h. Nationalräume übersteigende Ziele und Aufgaben identifiziert. Gibt es ein von und für multikulturelle und multinationale Gruppierungen einverständlich//konsensual empfundenes, tragfähiges Wertepaket, das ein europäisches Gemeinschaftsbewußtsein konstituieren kann?

Eine aus unterschiedlichen Kulturen und Traditionen sich zusammensetzende Gesellschaft ist als Gemeinschaft mit realen, partnerschaftlichen Partizipationsmöglichkeiten für alle Mitglieder, mit voller Teilhabe aller an allen Gemeinschaftsgütern nur möglich, wenn sie sich auf einige gemeinsam anerkannte

Kern- und Grundwerte - SMOLICZ (1985) nennt sie *core values* - in einem übergreifenden Wertesystem, in einem zwei oder mehrere Kulturen verbindenden Überschneidungssegment - *overarching framework* - stützen kann. Die Bedeutsamkeit gemeinsamer Grundwerte und ideologischer Identifikationen haben ANWEILER/KUEBART (1987) beispielsweise für das ethnischpluralistische Kanada herausgearbeitet: das Integrationskonzept der "Canadian citizenship" als gesamtkanadisches Staatsbewußtsein. Je weniger gemeinsame Grundwerte als Stiftungen für Zusammengehörigkeitsgefühle in einer Vielvölkergemeinschaft vorhanden sind, desto mehr Gefahren der Destabilisierung sind vorhanden; die erschütternden Erfahrungen im ehemaligen "Zwangsstaat" Jugoslawien belegen dies schmerzlich.

Was heißt dies übersetzt auf unsere Frage nach den Zielen Europas, nach der Überwindung interethnischer Konflikte zugunsten des Aufbaus einer humanen europäischen Union, eines alle Bürger der Europäischen Gemeinschaft verbindenden, innerlich einenden Europabewußtseins?

Welche Kern- und Grundwerte können als *Europäische,* als alle europäischen Völker und mit und zwischen ihnen lebenden Minderheiten als verbindende ausgemacht werden? Das ethnisch hoch bewertete Kulturmerkmal Sprache scheitert auf Grund der politischen Festlegung zur europäischen Mehrsprachigkeit dafür aus. Was statt dessen? Der Euro als Währungseinheit und merkantiles Symbol? Umstritten, und für unsere Fragestellungen als Lösungsmittel kontraindiziert.

Der Frage nach den Zielen Europas, dem Gesicht Europas, der europäischen Dimension haben sich bereits zahlreiche Aktionsprogramme der EG-Kommission verschrieben - in erster Linie im Bildungssektor - die alle auf Austausch, Integration, Kooperation hin ausgelegt sind, z.B. *ERASMUS, KOMMETT, FORCE, LINGUA, TEMPUS, SOKRATES* und viele andere mehr. Sie alle haben durchaus hoffnungerzeugende Saaten zu einer Identitätsentwicklung eingebracht, doch ist die Saat an vielen Stellen nicht aufgegangen, wie aktuelle Ereignisse ängstlich - feindseliger Gespanntheit und irrationaler Entladungen in einigen Teilen Europas belegen.

Unter Zugrundelegung der sozialwissenschaftlich abgesicherten Erkenntnis, daß Identitätsbildungen und interne Orientierungen jeweils historischen Veränderungsprozessen unterworfen und damit prozeßhaft angelegt sind (vgl. u.a. LEONTJEW 1982) - erinnert sei hier an die sogenannte Migrantenkultur, die in der Regel zwei sozialen Welten angehört (vgl. STRAUBE 1987) - und daß Identität als Prozeß und als Leistung vom historischen Individuationsverlauf und von den aktuellen Lebensbedingungen abhängig ist (vgl. DECS/EGT

1986, 41), sind die *core values*, die Kern- und Grundwerte einer sich bildenden europäischen Identität aus eben diesen Bedingungen entwickelbar: Als anstehende aktuelle Deutungsversuche der Beziehungen zueinander und als gemeinschaftliche Sinnsuche.

Wie soll Europa sein? Wie soll Europa werden? Welche Kern- und Grundwerte scheinen entwickelbar im Sinne von "Synchronen Bewußtseinselementen" (SCHMIDT 1987, 116) von übergreifenden europäischen Wertprinzipien, etwa aus dem Bündel der spezifischen Probleme des italienischen Rechtsstaates, des britischen Sozialstaates, des irischen Glaubensstaates und des französischen Agrarstaates? (vgl. SCHLEICHER 1993, 302).

Ohne Hierarchisierung wären zu nennen:

- Schutz der Biosphäre
- Beseitigung der Armut
- Gemeinsame Kontrolle der gesellschaftlichen Entwicklung und Güter
- Einheit nicht als Einheitlichkeit, sondern als tolerierte, akzeptierte Vielfalt unterschiedlicher Identitäten und Identitätsbedürfnisse
- Komplementarität von Identitäten und föderale Strukturen
- Durchlässigkeit von Bildungssystemen
- Akzeptanz von kulturellem Pluralismus, Wahrung und Bejahung und Achtung von Fremdem
- Multikulturalität: Migranten und Minderheiten als Bereicherung und gesellschaftlicher Gewinn.

Diese gemeinsamen und verzahnten Ziele und Aufgaben könnten von unterschiedlichen Weltbildern, kulturellen Traditionen und Lebensstilen her angegangen werden.

Dies wären die Konstruktionspfeiler, tragenden Wände und das Dach des *"gemeinsamen europäischen Hauses"*, wobei das Fundamentum, die Basis ethischer Natur ist: eine *"Ethik der Verantwortung"* (WEBER 1958), ein *"Prinzip Verantwortung"* (JONAS 1984), eine *"gemeinsame Verantwortung in gegenseitigem Respekt"* (KÜNG 1991, 61) und eine *"Moral der einfühlenden Voraussicht"* (MITSCHERLICH 1977).

Aus diesem Blickwinkel richtet sich damit die Aufmerksamkeit von den bisherigen Grenzauflösungen quantitativer Steigerung und Erweiterung in Europa zu den *qualitativen* Entfaltungen des menschlichen, auf die Erforschung und Ausdehnung der inneren Grenzen und Erfahrungen der individuellen und der sozialen Bewußtheit, auf die Steigerung und Ausschöpfung der *"human res-*

sources ", des "human potentials", der Entdeckung, Aufarbeitung und Nutzung innerer Fülle, auf das im epistemologischen Menschenbild und Subjektmodell beschriebene Potential zur Rationalität, Reflexivität, Autonomie und Kommunikation (SCHLEE 1992).

Den Kerngedanken des darin zum Ausdruck kommenden grundlegenden neuen Paradigmas der humanistischen subjektiven und sozialen Bewußtheit (vgl. HARMAN 1978, 57) hat AURELIO PECCEI, der Präsident des Club of Rome 1981 auf den Punkt gebracht, in dem er sagte, daß das Problem, mit dem wir es individuell, europäisch und global zu tun haben *"in uns selbst und nicht in äußeren Umständen"* steckt (1981, 153).

Wie soll Europa werden?

Psychosoziale Unsicherheiten, strukturelle Umbrüche und Auflösungserscheinungen traditioneller Werte zeigen einen "Europabedarf" auf, bieten gerade auf Grund der derzeitigen Vertrauenskrise und Entfremdungen und der fundamentalen bildungspolitischen Lücken im Aufbau Europas die Chance einer Neubesinnung auf Ziele, die vor allem eine soziale, humane Neuorientierung und Sinnfindung eröffnen.

In diesem Geist wird gedanklich ein "neues Europa" entworfen, das *"auf den Menschenrechten und fundamentalen Freiheiten fußenden Demokratie, eine Gesellschaft, die auf Wohlstand durch ökonomische Freiheit und soziale Gerechtigkeit sowie auf gleicher Sicherheit für alle Länder "* beruht (EUROPARAT 1990).

Und daß damit keine Einheitsgesellschaft gemeint ist, zeigt der Artikel 128, 1 des Maastrichter Vertrages, der besagt:

"Die Gemeinschaft leistet einen Beitrag zur Entfaltung der Kulturen ihrer Mitgliedsstaaten unter Wahrung ihrer nationalen und regionalen Vielfalt sowie gleichzeitiger Hervorhebung des gemeinsamen kulturellen Erbes" (EUROPÄISCHE GEMEINSCHAFT/EUROPÄISCHE UNION 1992).

Es gibt "Europabedarf", doch wie weit ist eine, unsere "Europafähigkeit" (SCHLEICHER 1993, 306) gediehen? Dies ist eine Frage, die nicht mehr nur für die "Europäer" selbst von Bedeutung ist: das außereuropäische Ausland hat anläßlich der Golfkrise sowie der kriegerischen und völkermörderischen Auseinandersetzungen im ehemaligen Jugoslawien nach der Haltung "Europas", zumindest nach derjenigen der Europäischen Union, der "Gemeinschaft" gefragt, d.h. jenseits von Europa geht man bereits von einer gesamteuropäischen Verantwortung im Kräftespiel der Welt aus: politisch, wirtschaftlich, human-sozial (vgl. PINGEL 1994, 168 f.).

WEITERFÜHRENDE, VERTIEFENDE AUFGABEN:

- Stellen Sie eine Liste europäisch-politischer Institutionen und Gremien zusammen und geben Sie stichwortartig deren jeweilige Hauptaufgaben an.
- Erstellen Sie eine Übersicht über europäische Bildungsprogramme und geben Sie stichwortartig deren Zielsetzungen, Zielgruppen und Arbeitsformen an.
- Stellen Sie mit Kommilitoninnen/Kommilitonen eine Collage her zum Thema: "Wie soll Europa nach unseren Vorstellungen aussehen?"
- Stellen Sie mit Kommilitoninnen/Kommilitonen eine Wandzeitung her aus aktuellen Printmedien (Zeitungen/Magazine/Broschüren) zum Thema: "So soll Europa sein!".
- Lesen Sie die bildungs- und sozialpolitischen Passagen des Maastrichter Vertrages kritisch und stellen Sie daraus eine Soll-Ist-Tabelle her.

1.6   (WIE) WERDEN WIR EUROPÄER?

Die bisherigen Ausführungen haben gezeigt, daß - summarisch gesehen - einerseits die Notwendigkeit europäischen Zusammenwachsens, des Bedarfs an europäischer Identitätsentwicklung wahrgenommen wird und daß seitens der Bevölkerungen durchaus Zustimmung zu diesen Veränderungen vorhanden ist (wenn auch mit nationalen Unterschieden); andererseits wurde ebenso offenkundig, daß es zu erheblicher Euroskepsis, Euroabwehr, zu Euroängsten, ja in einigen Bereichen zunehmend auch zu einer "Euroregression" kommt.

Dieses Mißverhältnis, bzw. Spannungsfeld, diese Ambivalenz von gleichzeitiger Zustimmung und Ablehnung provoziert zwei Fragen:

1. Welche Gründe gibt es für diese Diskrepanz?
und
2. wie könnte/müßte sie behoben werden, d.h. wie soll es weitergehen?

Wenden wir uns zunächst der Suche nach Antworten auf die erste Frage zu.

Zwei Hauptursachen können für die gegenläufigen Tendenzen ausgemacht werden, wobei beide in wechselseitiger Abhängigkeit stehen:

a) psychosoziale Gegebenheiten von bestehenden, gewachsenen Sozialgruppen/Bürgern
b) politisch-administrative Setzungsvorgänge von Organisationen und politischen Gremien.

zu a)

Die Auflösungen und Veränderungen von identitätsstiftenden Schutz, Sicherheit und Zugehörigkeit vermittelnden Gemeinschafts- und Lebensformen, vor allem durch Eindringen, Durchdringen von "Fremden", "Nicht-Zugehörigen", "Anderen", verursachen Ängste. Dieses Phänomen läßt sich am besten am Beispiel von interethnischen Konfliktkonstellationen beleuchten.

Arbeitsmigranten, Asylbewerber, Flüchtlinge, Aussiedler oder autochthone Minderheiten in allen europäischen Ländern: Einwanderungswellen und vielfältige Lebensraumsuche von sich bedroht fühlenden Einzelpersonen und Gruppen haben zu gewaltigen Veränderungen geführt; die europapolitisch gewollte Mobilität, die berufliche und niederlassungsmäßige Freizügigkeit wird den Prozentsatz der ethnischen und kulturellen Durchmischung wahrscheinlich noch beträchtlich erhöhen. Dabei macht nicht die Tatsache der Anzahl das Problem, sondern das Bewußtsein davon, und zwar auf beiden Seiten; dieses Bewußtsein wird von mehreren Faktoren bestimmt, und zwar von der *Funktion* der Einwanderer, von ihrer *Verteilung*, ihrer *Dynamik*, ihrer *äußeren Erscheinung*, ihrem *ethnischen, kulturellen, religiösen, politischen Selbstbewußtsein* wie auch *dem des Aufnahmelandes* (vgl. HENTIG 1993, 82).

Entscheidend ist das gesellschaftliche Wertesystem, sind die Einschätzungen, Empfindungen, Gefühle zueinander, die sich an den kulturell gelernten und tradierten Wahrnehmungsmustern, an den dadurch gefilterten Erfahrungen des Unterschiedes entzünden, beunruhigen und Fremdheit bewirken. In seinem Aufsatz über Rassismus stellt der aus Tunesien stammende Soziologe MEMMI 1987 fest:

"Der Unterschied beunruhigt... Der Unterschied, das ist das Unbekannte, und das Unbekannte erscheint uns voller Gefahren. Der Unterschied beunruhigt uns sogar in jenen seltenen Fällen, in denen er uns zugleich verführt" (1987, 35). Das Gefühl des Bedrohtseins führt zu Reaktionen mit Erscheinungsformen wie Fremdenhaß und nationalem Eigensinn, Fundamentalismus und Okkultismus, autonomem Chaotentum und politischem Terror oder zu totaler

Apolitie, die als die irrationalen Ausdrucksformen dieser Ängste, seelischer, politischer, intellektueller und existenzieller Nöte mit körperlicher, seelischer, ökonomischer und struktureller Gewalt neue Grenzen ziehen; diese lassen zugleich die ganze Ratlosigkeit, Wut, Hilflosigkeit, die Lebenslügen deutlich werden, die aus Überforderung resultieren.

Dies sind nicht gerade günstige Bedingungen für den Einigungsprozeß Europas, wenn sich mit den wirtschaftlichen und mobilitätsorientierten Grenzaufhebungen, wenn sich mit der Entgrenzung und der Entfesselung der Wirtschaft zugleich unbearbeitete Emotionen gegeneinander entladen und sich Irrationales schrankenlos, unbegrenzt austobt, die Grenzen der Menschenrechte und Menschenwürde mißachtend. Balkankrieg ohne Ende, Attentate der ETA, der IRA, der RAF, egozentrische Ellenbogenmentalität und soziale Unbekümmertheit sind die häßlichen, äußeren Wirklichkeiten als Spiegelungen unserer inneren Grenzen, Spaltungen, Trennungen. Nach tiefenpsychologischer Auffassung verdrängen diese das Ungeliebte, die Schatten und die Unterschiede in sich, richten das abgespaltene "Böse" nach außen gegen hergestellte Feindbilder (Projektion) und brechen als Angstabwehr die Grenzen zum Du gewaltsam ein.

Unterschiede beunruhigen, Veränderung und Umwälzungen machen Angst. Individuen wie Gruppen leisten Widerstände und verdrängen gerade das Wissen, was man am meisten zur Problemlösung braucht. Die Tiefenpsychologie spricht von Neurotikern, die bedrohliches Wissen um sich selbst, gefährdende Nähe und echte offene Beziehungen zu anderen zum Schutz der eigenen Lebensordnung so lange abwehren und bekämpfen, bis sie psychisch zusammenbrechen, weil die Umwelt dies nicht mehr toleriert. Nach HARMAN (vgl. 1978, 25) kann es analog auch zu einem möglichen "gesellschaftlichen Nervenzusammenbruch" aufgrund nicht mehr zu beschwichtigender Beunruhigungen über drohende Entfremdungen, Vereinzelungen, Identitätsfragmentierungen, Perspektiv- und Sinnlosigkeit für einen steigenden Prozentsatz Arbeitsloser, Obdachloser, sozial Entwurzelter und durch aufgelöste Bindungen Orientierungsloser kommen; ein solcher Zusammenbruch wird aber nicht als ein weiterer Grund zu kulturpessimistischen Klagen begriffen, sondern als große Chance und Herausforderung jenseits aller bislang verfehlten Antworten, aller Lähmungen und Kaschierungen, den Dingen auf den Grund zu gehen, zu grundsätzlicheren Überlegungen zu kommen und zu konstruktiven Übergängen zu gelangen; denn tief im Inneren wissen wir, daß es so wie jetzt nicht sein sollte und daß die Brüche und Zusammenbrüche die "psychosozialen Kosten" (HURRELMANN) unserer derzeitigen Lebensweise sind.

Zu den zuvor angerissenen, komplexen Bedingungszusammenhängen und Problemfeldern psycho-sozialer Wirklichkeiten gruppenbezogenen Gegeneinanders von Mehrheiten gegen Minderheiten und von defizitärem Gemeinschaftsbewußtsein einer in multiethnischer und multikultureller Transformation befindlichen Gesellschaft und zu einem vereinten Europa gibt es eine Fülle von human- und sozialwissenschaftlichen Erklärungsansätzen, Deutungsmustern und Forschungsergebnissen. Hier sind u.a. stichwortartig zu nennen die recht jungen Forschungszweige der "Ausländerpädagogik", der "multicultural education", der "education interculturelle", der "Migrationsforschung", der "ethic heritage studies", der "vergleichenden Erziehungswissenschaft" mit jeweils anderem Bedeutungskontext.

Zur schlaglichtartigen Erhellung des vielschichtigen Problemfeldes interethnischer Konflikte in Europa im folgenden eine Übersicht von HEITMEYER (1993), die für das Verstehen der Fremdheitserfahrung als Voraussetzung für deren Bewältigung im Sinne europäischen Zusammenlebens hilfreich erscheint.

Tab.4: Interethnische Konflikte in Europa

Syndromvariante	Argumentationskern	Dominierende psychische Verankerung
Rassismus (Antisemitismus)	Abwertung anderer aufgrund der Bewertung biologischer Unterschiede ("natürliche Höherwertigkeit")	Glauben
Ethnozentrismus	Eigene Aufwertung durch Reklamation von kultureller und ökonomischer Leistung (Entwicklungsunterschiede)	Stolz/Überheblichkeit
Fremdenfeindlichkeit	Konkurrenz gegen ethnische andere (Ressourcen, kulturelle "Überfremdung")	Angst
Heterophobie	"Norm"-Abweichung (Nicht-Zulassen von "Anders-Sein" bei ethnisch Gleichen: Homosexuelle, Behinderte etc.)	Angst
Etablierten-Rechte	Raum-zeitliche Vorrangstellung und Ansprüche gegenüber "Außenseitern" (z.B. auch, wenn ansässige Ausländer gegen den Zuzug von "neuen" Ausländern votieren).	Egoismus/ Selbstdurchsetzung

Quelle: HEITMEYER, 1993

In diesem Spektrum ist allen Einstellungen gemeinsam, daß ihnen Phantasien und Ideologien der *Ungleichheit* aus unterschiedlichen Ursachen zugrunde liegen, die die Legitimationsbasis für Gewalt bilden. Wie zu sehen ist, sind in dieser Grobtabelle verschiedene Formen und Haltungen verzeichnet, die auch verschiedener pädagogischer Interventionen bedürfen. Ausschlaggebend sind die *negativen Wertungen* der Unterschiede aus verschiedenen Interessenslagen heraus.

Von entscheidender Bedeutung sind nun die sozialwissenschaftlich herausgearbeiteten Forschungsergebnisse, daß die Festschreibung der Differenzen und ihrer damit verbundenen Einstellungen vor allem durch sozialstrukturelle Unterschiede begünstigt werden, d.h., daß die Minderheitspositionen und Marginalisierungen durch soziale Randstellungen - Qualifikationen, Entlohnung, Wohnung, Bildung etc. - festgeschrieben werden. Anders gewendet: die Sozialstruktur, die soziale Realität der schlechten Lebensbedingungen sind die eigentlichen Ursachen für die soziale und psychosoziale Lage der Minderheiten (vgl. GRIESE 1980 und 1984). Sozioökonomische Benachteiligung kann mit GALTUNG auch als *strukturelle Gewalt* bezeichnet werden (1975), an der wir alle teilhaben, "indem wir durch unsere Tätigkeit dafür sorgen, daß der reiche Norden dieses Globus immer reicher wird und der Süden entsprechend ärmer. Das neutrale Kennzeichen dafür heißt: terms of trade, das Gesetz der Weltwirtschaft. Da alle in unterschiedlichem Maße an dieser Disproportion mitwirken, sind wir kaum interessiert, daß sich das alsbald ändere" (GAMM 1993, 56).

So ergibt sich ein circulus vitiosus von verschiedenen Gewaltformen, der unheilvolle Lernprozesse in Gang setzt: Ungleichheit der Menschen wird als naturgegeben aufgefaßt - und nicht als gesellschaftlich-historisch vermittelt - und führt zu Hegemoniestreben. Dadurch zu Unrecht festgeschriebene ethnische Unterschiede stellen sich demnach als verdrängte Schichtunterschiede dar und widerlegen kulturalistische Konfliktdeutungen.

Zur Konkretisierung des o.a. Syndroms "Ethnozentrismus" und zur Differenzierung von Deutungsmustern seien noch kurz Forschungsergebnisse von ADORNO skizziert, der in seinen "Studien über Autorität und Vorurteil" Ethnozentrismus als verhältnismäßig konstante mentale Struktur mit unelastisch abwertenden Reaktionen gegen alles Fremdartige beschreibt. Unter Rückgriff auf die psychoanalytische Theorie stellt er heraus, daß durch rigide Erziehung negativ bewertete Anteile des Selbst abgespalten und auf andere, auf Fremdgruppen projiziert werden. Die sogenannten Ich-Funktionen sind schwach und eine Identifikation kann nur mit der Eigengruppe erfolgen: der Ethnozentriker ist unfähig, individuierte Erfahrungen zu machen (vgl. ADORNO 1968).

Diese hier vorgestellten Ursachenskizzen deuten darauf hin, daß zum einen die gesellschaftlichen Voraussetzungen, die sozialstrukturellen Tatsachen und zum anderen die durch die soziale Erziehung erworbenen, psychosozialen Einstellungen des Einzelnen in erheblichem Maße ursächlich für die interethnischen Konflikte mitverantwortlich sind. Da soziale Fakten prinzipiell gesellschaftlich hergestellte sind, sind sie aber auch veränderbare Tatsachen.

Die Tatsache der Zunahme "struktureller Gewalt" und der gegenseitigen Abgrenzungen läßt darauf schließen, daß die zuvor referierten sozialwissenschaftlichen Erkenntnisse in politischen Weiterentwicklungsprozessen nicht/kaum Berücksichtigung gefunden haben; damit kommen wir

zu b)

Nahezu alle kritischen Analysen bisheriger offizieller Europapolitik stimmen darin überein, daß die europapolitischen Entwicklungen weitgehend durch Setzungen von oben, von den Regierungen und Organisationen ohne hinreichende Information und kommunikative Beteiligung der Bürger und ihrer sozialen Gruppierungen erfolgt sind; diese "top down policy", die die öffentliche Meinung als unverzichtbares Demokratie- und Identifizierungsinstrument sträflich vernachlässigt, vergessen und durchaus (auch aus Angst vor der Übermittlung unangenehmer Wahrheiten, und daraus resultierender Angst, nicht wiedergewählt zu werden) verdrängt hat, hat dazu geführt, daß die zuvor aufgezeigten Angstmechanismen vor Fremdem unaufgearbeitet blieben, ja verstärkt wurden, und die Bürger weitgehend unvorbereitet, unangeleitet von oben auf Europa hin „umprogrammiert" wurden.

Die nachfolgende Tabelle aus dem Eurobarometer vom Juni 1993 belegt den recht geringen Kenntnisstand bezüglich europäischer Institutionen. Wie die politische Sozialisationsforschung zeigt, gibt die öffentliche Informiertheit Hinweise darauf, wie wenig oder wieviel sich die Bürger mit europäischen Strukturen und Prozessen beschäftigen, bzw. wie hoch oder wie tief der damit in Zusammenhang stehende Interessens- und Identifikationsgrad ist.

Tabelle 5: Kenntnis nationaler und europäischer Institutionen

Index* Nationale Kenntnis	EG	B	DK	D(W)	GR	E	F	IRL	I	L	NL	P	GB **
recht gut	13	16	12	8	14	13	11	26	13	6	17	16	23
gut	65	66	57	63	64	61	70	62	72	48	67	77	57
begrenzt	19	15	22	25	21	26	18	12	13	43	14	5	17
recht begrenzt	3	0	5	4	1	1	1	1	2	3	2	2	3
Index* EG-Kenntnis													
recht gut	2	2	3	2	2	2	4	2	0	1	1	1	1
gut	36	49	58	30	47	32	55	39	29	58	34	40	30
begrenzt	49	45	37	55	34	49	36	46	58	36	57	40	52
recht begrenzt	4	3	13	15	18	18	6	13	14	5	9	19	18

* Index = die unterschiedliche Anzahl der nationalen und europäischen Fragen wurde je nach Anteil der richtigen Antworten in vier Gruppen zusammengefaßt, die hier der Übersichtlichkeit mit `recht gut` bis `recht begrenzt`umschrieben werden.
** GB ohne Nordirland

Quelle: Eurobarometer, June 1993 A36, Tab. 41a.   Quelle: SCHLEICHER 1994, 99

Nicht mehr verstehbare, eurokratische Auseinandersetzungen und Regelungen z.B. über die Länge und Krümmung von eurogerechten Bananen haben zusätzlich als abgehobene, bürgerfremde, erzwungene Merkmale von Vereinheitlichungen zu Europawut oder Europaresignation geführt.

Die *"psychischen Bedingungen für eine rationale und europäisch selektive Wahrnehmung"* (SCHLEICHER 1994, 95) sind viel zu wenig beachtet worden; eine öffentliche Abklärung von Gemeinschaftszielen hat nicht stattgefunden. ... *"Wie können Bürger europamündig werden und wie soll eine europäische Öffentlichkeit entstehen, wenn diese an ihrer Bildung und der Gestaltung Europas nicht mitbeteiligt werden?"(*SCHLEICHER 1994, 79).

Festzuhalten ist, daß neben der als herrschaftlich empfundenen top-down-policy vor allem eine fundamentale Lücke in bildungspolitischer Hinsicht bzgl. des Aufbaus von Europa besteht und daß diese Leerstelle der Bildungsdefizite als gravierendes politisches Versagen bezeichnet werden muß, vor allem vor dem Hintergrund der durch die Lücken mitverursachten, neuen psychosozialen Ängste und Abgrenzungsprozesse gewachsener, festgefügter sozialer Gruppierungen gegenüber dem neuen Europa.

Nach einigen hier gefundenen Antworten auf die Frage 1 nach dem Spannungsfeld zwischen Ablehnung und Zustimmung zu europaorientierten Veränderungen nun der Versuch, für den zweiten Fragenkomplex ("Wie kann sich ein bürgerorientierteres, ein mehrheitlich akzeptiertes und gelebtes Europabewußtsein entwickeln? ") einen Horizont für konstruktive Problemlösungen und Zukunftsorientierungen auszumachen.

Kritische Europaanalysen aus unterschiedlichen Betrachtungswinkeln kommen durchgängig zu dem Schluß, daß

- die im vorigen Teilkapitel (1.5) entworfenen "core values", diese visionären, real-utopischen Umwandlungsaufgaben, großen Ideen und Worte und inneren Bilder zur Entwicklung eines neues Bewußtseins zur sozialen Verantwortung und Respektierung der multikulturellen Vielfalt nur erreicht werden können, und
- daß die in diesem Teilkapitel skizzierten Trennungen und Ausgrenzungen und die angstmachenden Empfindungen des Unterschiedes nur überwunden werden können,

wenn wir uns auf große Umlernprozesse einlassen.

Mit diesem Lernen ist das gesamte bildungspolitische Feld angesprochen - das 1988 sogar als "Herzstück der europäischen Integration" erkannt (EG-KOMMISSION 1988) aber bislang leider nur sehr verkürzt auf den beruflichen Sektor ausgerichtet war - , dem für das Wachsen des Europabewußtseins, für das europäische Werden die Schlüsselaufgabe zukommt. Das Bildungswesen wird deshalb als Hauptfaktor für den sozialen und wirtschaftlichen Fortschritt sowie für die Erhaltung des Friedens gesehen (vgl. BÜRLI 1997, 189). Auf diesem Feld müssen vielgestaltige Vorbereitungen für Kenntniserweiterungen, für Überwindung von nationalen Wahrnehmungsverengungen, für interkulturelle Kommunikation, für Mobilisierung politischer Basiskräfte und andere Maßnahmen zur Aufhebung von Entfremdungen getroffen werden.

- **Konkret** gemeint sind damit Entwicklungslinien bzw. Handlungskonzepte, die möglichst alle Bevölkerungsgruppen und -schichten an sozialen Planungen und deren Ausführungen beteiligen und mitgestalten lassen und dies kontinuierlich, vor Ort, und damit gemeinsame Lernprozesse in Gang setzen.

- **Konkret** gemeint ist eine "bottom up policy ex post", eine Einbeziehung der Bevölkerung, um das Versäumte umgehend nachzuholen. "42 Jahre sind seit dem Montanvertrag, 36 Jahre seit den Römischen Verträgen vergan-

gen, ohne daß die Verantwortlichen in Straßburg oder in Brüssel sich viel
Gedanken darüber gemacht hätten, wie in den Gesellschaften der europäischen Staaten ein Bewußtsein davon erzeugt werden könnte, jeder sei ein
Europäer" (LENZEN 1994, 31).

- **Konkret** gemeint sind z.b. öffentliche Infomationsveranstaltungen, wie etwa auch die "Europawoche 1998" in Sachsen-Anhalt, die zur Mitgestaltung aufruft und die einem Anschreiben des Ministeriums für Wirtschaft, Technologie und Europaangelegenheiten u.a. als Zielvorstellungen angibt: "Wie auch in den letzten Jahren soll die Europawoche den Bürgerinnen und Bürgern unseres Landes vielfältige Möglichkeiten geben, sich über europarelevante Themen und europapolitische Aktivitäten Sachsen-Anhalts zu informieren. ..... Die Europawoche sollte über diese Sachfragen hinaus Gelegenheiten bieten, möglichst breite Kreise der Öffentlichkeit unseres Landes mit den verschiedenen Facetten des europäischen Integrationsprozesses und der gesamteuropäischen Einigung bekannt zu machen" (BEHRENDT 1997)

Die von SCHLEICHER (vgl. 1994, 120) getroffene Feststellung, daß europäische Identität nur in dem Maße entstehen wird, wie Bürger vor Ort Interesse an Europa entwickeln und sich zur Mitgestaltung aufgerufen sehen, trägt - wie letztgenannte Aktivität beispielhaft belegt - mittlerweile vielerlei Früchte.

- **Konkret** gemeint ist der vermehrte Wissenserwerb über die Vielfalt der Kultur, Geschichte, Politik, Wirtschaft europäischer Völker und Gruppen, um das Defizit an Europakenntnissen zu reduzieren (teaching about Europe).

- **Konkret** gemeint ist die Anwendung von Lernmethoden (multidisziplinäre, multiperspektivische, multinationale, problem-, situations- und handlungsorientierte, multisensorische Sichtweisen) zur rationalen und transparenten Auseinandersetzung mit verschiedenen kulturellen Sichtweisen, Wahrnehmungsmustern, Interpretationsformen und unterschiedlichen Interessen.

- **Konkret** gemeint sind vor allem Formen des Erfahrungslernens, regelmäßige supranationale, interkulturelle Austauschprozesse und -programme (Schüler, Lehrer, Studenten, Familien, Lehrlinge usw.), dauernde Patenschaften, gemeinsame, supranationale Projekte und Lernvorhaben unter Zugrundelegung von jeweils doppelter originaler Sichtweise und Wahrnehmungsstruktur.

- **Konkret** gemeint sind vielfältige, interkulturelle Kooperationen in kleinen überschaubaren Einheiten zwischen Familien, kirchlichen Einrichtungen, Sportvereinen, auch Straßenfesten mit Migrantenfamilien, Benachteiligten, sogenannten Behinderten, und anderen marginalisierten Gruppierungen.
- **Konkret** gemeint ist das verstärkte Lernen von Fremdsprachen. Konkret gemeint sind internationale Sozialdienste, Personalaustausch in Betrieben, Auslandspraktika, supranationale Umweltprojekte, Sportprojekte, medizinische Hilfsprojekte.
- **Konkret** gemeint ist nicht zuletzt die Forcierung der akademischen Mobilität, der Entwicklung europäischer Lehrbausteine und Lehrprogramme, des Ausbaus von Äquivalenzregelungen bei den Hochschuldiplomen sowie der Ausbau von Europastudien (Anmerkung: Die anvisierte Mobilitätsquote von 10% der Studierenden war bereits im 14. Jahrhundert an der Universität Ferrara erreicht; hier herrscht also ganz erheblicher Wiederaufholbedarf!).

Dies alles sind ganz konkrete Maßnahmen, Lernformen und Lernprozesse sozialer Erziehung, psycho-sozialer Wandlungen zur Verbesserung gegenseitigen Verstehens und zur Entwicklung gemeinsamer, verbindender Bewußtseinsbestände. Sind vor allem *gemeinsame Lernprozesse, die sich in ganz konkreten Vorhaben ereignen können und dies auch schon in einigen Teilen tun.*

Allerdings - und dies bedarf zur Psychohygiene eines ausdrücklichen Hinweises - sind diese skizzierten, konkreten Entwicklungsaktivitäten und -prozesse nicht von heute auf morgen machbar: mit nüchterner Realitätswahrnehmung der Geschichte muß festgestellt werden, daß Erziehung, Bildung, Pädagogik immer nur einen kleinen Beitrag, in kleinen Schritten und in langen Zeiträumen zu Veränderungen und Einstellungen beisteuern kann. Allerdings fordert dieses Wissen umsomehr dann dazu heraus, sich für eine Verstärkung und Vermehrung dieser konkreten Maßnahmen/Vorhaben einzusetzen und für eine europäische Dauerlerngemeinschaft in kleinschrittigen, aber stetigen Teilprozessen einzutreten unter Inrechnungstellung der Kompliziertheit und Zerbrechlichkeit zwischenmenschlicher, sozial vermittelter Beziehungen.

(Wie) Werden wir Europäer?

Unter anderem durch Versuche von und Einübungen in die vorgenannten konkreten Vorhaben.

Bleibt die Frage, wer sich verantwortlich dem widmet, wer diese Maßnahmen initiiert, organisiert, begleitet und evaluiert.

Hier sind die bildungspolitischen Programme der EU zu nennen: COMETT / ERASMUS / SOKRATES (aus dem heraus auch die Entwicklung dieses Europamoduls mitgefördert wird) / LINGUS / TEMPUS / PETRA / EUROTECNET u.a.m., der Europarat, die Unesco, europäische Netzwerke (Lehrervereinigungen, Elternvereinigungen, Europäische Rektorenkonferenz u.a.m.) Verlage, Wirtschaftsverbände und nicht zuletzt die Hochschulen, die ja *die* europäischen Institutionen par excellence waren, historisch, in ihren sozialen Rollen, und auch heute von ihrem Auftrag noch sind/sein sollten: durch Lehre und Forschung Einsicht in die komplexen, übernationalen Wirkzusammenhänge zu vermitteln, kritisch-klärende Funktion für das - ubiquitär anzutreffende - sozial-kulturelle Gefüge aus individuellen Bedürfnissen, wirtschaftlich-politischen Bedingungen sowie gesellschaftlichen Strukturen und Prozessen einzunehmen und gesellschaftliche Innovationen anzuregen, vor allem unter anthroprozentrischen Aspekten.

(Wie) Werden wir Europäer? Meint nicht zuletzt den einzelnen Bürger, das Individuum in der Gemeinschaft. "Europäer" werden heißt: sich international zu bewegen und einen eigenen Interaktions- und Integrationsbeitrag in anderen Ländern durch die eigene Person zu leisten.

(Wie) Werden wir Europäer? Auf einem langen Weg im Spannungsfeld von Vision und Traum:
"Wir dürfen angesichts der Träume vom anscheinend Unmöglichen nicht verzweifeln, wenn wir wollen, daß diese Träume Wirklichkeit werden. Ohne Traum vom besseren Europa werden wir niemals ein besseres Europa schaffen"
(HAVEL, zitiert nach STOBART 1994, 43)
sowie von Bemühung und Kompetenz:
"viel Arbeit, viel Behutsamkeit und viel Kenntnis sind vonnöten, um auf diesem Weg erfolgreich voranzukommen" (SCHAUMANN 1994, 20).

Fangen wir zum Schluß dieses Kapitels mit diesen letzten Aufgaben an, indem wir der Frage nachgehen, ob nicht auch unsere Alltagssprache als bewußtseinsschaffende Kraft bezüglich etlicher überkommener, Fremdheit und Distanz schaffender, ausgrenzender Begriffe und Kennzeichnungen sensibel Revision nötig hätte: was heißt, was bedeutet, wen meint in Europa das historisch beladene Wort "Ausländer"?

Vielleicht schärft unsere Beschäftigung mit dem Wandel der Bedeutung unsere Wahrnehmung von ihr und unsere Nachdenklichkeit über sie. Erweiterte und veränderte Wahrnehmung von uns selbst und von anderen und damit auch von den einengenden sprachlichen Verpackungen von Welt (vgl. BONO 1991, 156) könnte ein erster, konkreter eigener Baustein für den humansozialen Aufbau des gemeinsamen Hauses Europa sein, ein weiterer Schritt auf dem Weg, Europäer zu werden.

1.7 WEITERFÜHRENDE, VERTIEFENDE AUFGABEN:

- Legen Sie eine Themenmappe aus Printmedienerzeugnissen zur Problematik "Ausländerfeindlichkeit" an, suchen und begründen Sie Gliederungspunkte für die gefundenen Dokumente und stellen Sie Thesen zu Lösungsansätzen auf.

- Analysieren Sie kritisch Aussagen und Haltungen, die z.b. bekunden, daß "billige ausländische Arbeitskräfte aus dem Osten den Deutschen Arbeitsplätze und Wohnungen wegnehmen", beziehen Sie Position und begründen Sie diese, indem Sie auch Bezug auf die im Text eingefügte Tabelle von HEITMEYER nehmen können.

- Diskutieren Sie in der Gruppe das Zitat von GAMM in diesem Teilkapitel und stellen Sie Thesen zu Lösungsansätzen auf.

- Machen Sie Interviews mit fünf ausländischen Arbeitnehmerinnen/Arbeitnehmern aus verschiedenen Ländern und befragen Sie sie nach deren Gefühlen hinsichtlich Akzeptanz und Integration in ihren deutschen Lebenskreisen (Arbeit/Wohnung). Schreiben Sie auf, welchen Beitrag Sie persönlich zu einer Veränderung, Verbesserung solcher Gefühle leisten können.

- Machen Sie drei konkrete Vorschläge für eine öffentlichkeitsbewußte Bildungspolitik in Magdeburg (bzw. in Ihrer Wohnumgebung) hinsichtlich des europäischen Integrationsprozesses.

- Machen Sie sich und Ihren KommilitonInnen ein konkretes Angebot, wie Sie mit Ihrer Person einen Beitrag zur europäischen Integration leisten. Schreiben Sie dieses ganz detailliert auf. Falls Sie dies nicht können oder wollen, begründen Sie dies bitte.

1.8 BIBLIOGRAPHIE

1.8.1 LITERATURHINWEISE

ADORNO, T.:	Erziehung nach Auschwitz. In: Erziehung zur Mündigkeit. Frankfurt o.J., S. 88-104.
ANWEILER, O./KUEBART, E.:	"International 'ne vospitanie" und "multicultural education" - Aspekte eines Vergleichs zweier politisch-pädagogischer Konzepte. In: Erz.i.d. multikulturellen Gesellschaft. VE-Info. Nr. 17, 1987, S. 128 ff.
ASSMANN, A.:	Arbeit am nationalen Gedächtnis. Eine kurze Geschichte der deutschen Bildungsidee. Frankfurt/New York 1993.
BACHMANN, W. / MESTERH'AZI, Z.(Hrsg.):	Trends und Perspektiven der gegenwärtigen ungarischen Heilpädagogik. Giessen 1990.
BACHMANN, W../ECKERT, U./POZNANSKI, K. (Hrsg.):	Tradition und Tends der polnischen Sonderpädagogik. Giessen 1991.
BACHMANN, W.:	Das unselige Erbe des Christentums: die Wechselbälge. Giessen: 1985.
BACHMANN, W.:	Bausteine zu einer europäischen Geschichte der Heilpädagogik. In: Heilpädagogik 1992 (5), 290-298.
BEHRENDT, R.:	Europawoche 1998. Verfügung des Ministeriums für Wirtschaft, Technologie und Europaangelegenheiten des Landes Sachsen-Anhalt. 1997, 02.12.
BONO, E.:de:	I am right - you are wrong. London, Penguin Book 1991.
BONO, E.: de:	Der Klügere gibt nach. Düsseldorf, Wien, New York 1991.
BÜRLI, A.:	Sonderpädagogik international. Luzern 1997.
CLOERKES, G.:	Soziologie der Behinderten. Heidelberg 1997.
COUDENHOVE-KALERGI, R.:	Ein Leben für Europa. Kampf um Europa. Aus meinem Leben. Zürich 1948.
CURTIUS, E.R.:	Europäische Literatur und lateinisches Mittelalter. Bern 1969.
DECS/EGT, Directorate for Education, Culture and Sport:	The education and cultural development of migrants. Project No. 7. Final report of the project group. Council of Europe. Strasbourg 1986.

DEUTSCHE GESELLSCHAFT FÜR ERZIEHUNGSWISSENSCHAFT:	Bildung und Erziehung in Europa. Weinheim und Basel 1994.
EBERLE, I.:	Lateinische Nächte. Essays über die lateinische Welt. Stuttgart 1966.
EG-KOMMISSION der Europäischen Gemeinschaften:	Bildungspolitik - ein Herzstück der europäischen Integration. In: Perspektive '92 der Kommission 1 (1988).
ERIKSON, E.H.:	Kindheit und Gesellschaft. Stuttgart 1982[8].
EUROBAROMETER:	Public Opinion in the European Community. Commission of the European Communities, Brussels, 1987-1994.
EUROPÄISCHE GEMEINSCHAFT:	Die Vertragstexte von Maastricht. Bonn 1992.
EUROPARAT/COUNCIL OF EUROPE:	Recommendation No. R(90/5).
FERNAU, J.:	Wie es euch gefällt. Eine lächelnde Stilkunde. Donauwörth 1969.
FREY, H.P.:	Stigma und Identität. Eine empirische Untersuchung zur Genese und Änderung krimineller Identität bei Jugendlichen. Weinheim/Basel 1983.
GAMM, H.J.:	Fremdenfeindlichkeit und Erziehung. In: Pädagogik 10/1993, 55-57.
GALTUNG, J.:	Strukturelle Gewalt. Reinbek 1975.
GOFFMAN, E.:	Stigma. Über Techniken der Bewältigung beschädigter Identität. Frankfurt/Main 1967.
GORBATSCHOW, M.:	Perestroika. Die zweite russische Revolution. München 1987.
GRIESE, H.M.:	Wider die Pädagogisierung der Ausländerprobleme. In: Materialien zum Projektbereich "Ausländische Arbeiter". 1980, Nr. 30.; S. 41 ff.
GRIESE, H.M.:	Kritisch-exemplarische Überlegungen zur Situation und Funktion der Ausländerforschung und einer verstehenden Ausländerpolitik. In: ders. (Hrsg.): Der gläserne Fremde. Opladen 1984.
HARMAN, W.W.:	Gangbare Wege in die Zukunft? Darmstadt 1978.
HEITMEYER, W.:	Pädagogik und Fremdenfeindlichkeit. In: Landesinstitut für Schule und Weiterbildung (Hrsg.): Aktuelle Gewaltentwicklung in der Gesellschaft. SOEST 1993, 33-41.
HENTIG, H. von:	Die Schule neu denken. Eine Übung in praktischer Vernunft. München, Wien 1993.
HURRELMANN, K.:	Aggression und Gewalt in der Schule. In: Ursachen, Erscheinungsformen und Gegenmaßnahmen. In: Pädagogisches Forum 2/1992, 65-74.
JASPERS, K.:	Vom europäischen Geist. München 1947.

JONAS, H.: Das Prinzip Verantwortung. Versuch einer Ethik für die technologische Zivilisation. Frankfurt/Main 1984.
KLAUER, K.J./MITTER, W. (Hrsg.): Vergleichende Sonderpädagogik. Berlin, Marhold 1987.
KOCH, W.: Kleine Stilkunde der Baukunst. Gütersloh 1970.
KÜNG, H.: Projekt Weltethos. München, Zürich 1991.
KÜNZLI, R.: Herkunft und Zukunft oder inwiefern Europa ein vernünftiger Bezugspunkt für Bildungsprozesse sein kann. In: Bund-Länder-Kommission für Bildungsplanung (Hrsg.): Lernen für Europa. Köllen Verlag 1992, 8-20.
LENZEN, D.: Bildung und Erziehung für Europa? In: DGFE (Hrsg.): Bildung und Erziehung in Europa. Weinheim und Basel 1994, 31-48.
LEONTJEW, A.N.: Tätigkeit, Bewußtsein, Persönlichkeit. Köln 1982.
LISSNER, I.: Wir sind das Abendland. Gütersloh 1966.
McLEAN, M.: Das europäische Curriculum. In: Schleicher (Hrsg.) 1993, S. 261-276.
MEMMI, A.: Rassismus. Frankfurt/Main 1987.
MITSCHERLICH, A.u.M.: Die Unfähigkeit zu trauern. München 1977.
MULCAHY, D.G.: Auf der Suche nach der Europäischen Dimension im Bildungswesen. In: Pädagogik und Schule in Ost und West 1 (1992), S. 43 ff.
MÜLLER, K.E.: Der Krüppel. Ethnologia passionis humanae. München 1996.
PECCEI, A.: Die Zukunft in unserer Hand. Gedanken und Reflexionen des Präsidenten des Club of Rome. Wien 1981.
PINGEL, F.: Europa - Nation - Region: Historisch-politische Bildung in europäischen Schulbüchern. In: Schleicher/Bos (Hrsg.) 1194, 153-170.
SCHAUMANN, F.: Grußwort. In: DGFE (Hrsg.), Weinheim und Basel 1994, S. 20-22.
SCHLEE, J.: Förderung und Unterstützung von Reflexivität. In: Schulamt für die Stadt Aachen (Hrsg.): Beiträge zur Bedeutung des Forschungsprogramms "Subjektive Theorien" für Schule und Lehrerbildung. Aachen 1992.
SCHLEICHER, K.:(Hrsg.) Zukunft der Bildung in Europa. Darmstadt 1993.
SCHLEICHER, K./BOS, W.: (Hrsg.) Realisierung der Bildung in Europa. Darmstadt 1994.
SCHMIDT, U.: Interkulturelle Kommunikation und interkulturelles Lernen. In: Jahrbuch "Pädagogik: Dritte Welt" 1986. Kulturelle Identität und Universalität. Frankfurt/Main 1987.

SCHRAML, W.J.:	Einführung in die Tiefenpsychologie für Pädagogen und Sozialpädagogen. Stuttgart 1976[6].
SMOLICZ, J.J.:	Multiculturalism and an overarching framework of values: Educational responses to assimilation, interaction and separatism in ethically plural societies. In: Bildung und Erziehung, Beiheft 2, Mitter/Swift 1985.
SONTAG, S.:	Noch eine Elegie. In: Literaturmagazin 22.Sonderband. Ein Traum von Europa. Reinbek b. Hamburg 1988, S. 131-136.
STOBART, M.:	Der Europarat und die Bildungsanforderungen im "Neuen Europa". In: Schleicher/Bos, 1994, 19-45.
STRAUBE, H.:	Türkisches Leben in der Bundesrepublik. Frankfurt, New York 1987.
TORNEY-PURTA, J./SCHWILLE, J.:	Civic Values Learned in School: Policy and Practice in Industrialized Countries. In: Comparative Education/Review 1 (1986).
WEBER, M.:	Politik als Beruf. In: Gesammelte politische Schriften. Tübingen 1958, S. 505-560.

1.8.2 ZUSÄTZLICHE LITERATUR

DAUN, Å.:	Den europeiska identiteten: Sverige och Italien, EU och framtiden
FJORDBO, M.:	En europeisk coctail. 1993
KNUDSEN, A.:	Kulturelle världar: kultur och kulturkonflikter i Europa.1997
VIKLUND, D.:	Att första EU: Sverige och Europa
WEBER, M.:	Politik als Beruf. In: Gesammelte politische Schriften. Tübingen 1958, S. 505-560.

2. EIN BLICK ZURÜCK – GESCHICHTE DER "BEHINDERUNGEN"

David Johnstone

2.1 EINLEITUNG

Dieses Kapitel erforscht den geschichtlichen Hintergrund von Behinderung und die Entwicklung der Sonderpädagogik in Europa. Um dieses Kapitel zu verstehen, ist es nicht notwendig, über profundes Vorwissen zu verfügen. Dennoch können Studenten, die bereits direkte oder indirekte Erfahrungen mit Beeinträchtigung, Schädigung und Behinderung gemacht haben, viel zum Modul beitragen.

Dieses Kapitel will die Studenten dazu anregen, die Konzepte von Behinderung und Nichtbehinderung in ihrem Heimatland kritisch zu hinterfragen. Obgleich wir nicht voraussetzen, daß die Studenten ein großes Vorwissen über das Thema Behinderung mitbringen, wird erwartet, daß die Studenten Interesse an aktuellen Debatten, z.B. der Organisation von Unterstützung für und durch behinderte Menschen haben. Das Modul geht davon aus, daß das Konzept von Behinderung weder als endgültig noch als absolut anzusehen ist. Es wurde im Laufe der Geschichte und wird auch in Zukunft immer wieder neu definiert. Dieser Kurs setzt es sich zum Ziel, einige Sichtweisen anzusprechen und die große Anzahl an Fehlkonzeptionen und Stereotypen zu hinterfragen, die im Laufe der Zeit entstanden sind.

2.1.1 ZIELE

Von den Studenten wird erwartet, daß sie

- die Geschichte der Behinderung als „pathologisches" oder als persönliches Defizit kritisch bewerten;
- die sozialen Konstruktionen von Behinderung an zwei verschiedenen Punkten in der Geschichte vergleichen und gegenüberstellen

- kritisch den Zweck und die Philosophie der Eugenik-Bewegung zu Beginn des 20. Jahrhunderts beurteilen
- kritisch die Rolle von religiösen Einrichtungen in der Entwicklung der Versorgung behinderter Menschen untersuchen und beschreiben

Die Arbeiten, die zu diesen Themen gemacht werden, sollten in engem Zusammenhang mit den Lernzielen bestehen.

2.1.2 LERNERGEBNISSE

Am Ende dieses Abschnitts sollten die Studenten die folgenden Fähigkeiten erlangt haben:

- ein kritisches Bewußtsein der historischen Erklärungen für die Unterdrükkung und "Unsichtbarkeit" von behinderten Menschen
- Wissen über die historischen Grundlagen für Kontroversen und Auseinandersetzungen, denen behinderte Menschen in Großbritannien und auf dem Festland von Europa auch weiterhin gegenüberstehen.

Die Geschichte von behinderten Menschen und ihrem Leben kann mit Hilfe von drei großen und sich überschneidenden Phasen aufgezeichnet werden. Jede dieser Phasen ist mit verschiedenen Abschnitten der politischen, historischen und wirtschaftlichen Entwicklung Europas verbunden. Keinen dieser Abschnitte kann man getrennt von den anderen betrachten, und alle haben bis heute sichtbare Spuren hinterlassen. Jedoch kann man sie folgendermaßen in einer geschichtlichen Abfolge darstellen:

Medizinische Behandlung	Abgrenzung Isolation	Rechte und Soziale Gerechtigkeit

2.2 EIN CHRONOLOGISCHER ABRISS VON „BEHINDERUNG" IN EUROPA

Jahr	Person/Staat	Ereignis	Kategorie
597	Augustinus		allgemeine Pflege
1260	Louis IX/Frankreich	Hospice Nationale des Quinze-Vingts	Blindheit
1570	Pedro Ponce/ Spanien	Lippenablesen	Taubheit
1601	Vereinigtes Königreich		Arme/Bedürftige
1620	Juan Paulo Bonet/Spanien		Taubheit
1624	Schweden	Gesetz für die Armen Anfang der staatlichen Verantwortung für die Armen und Bedürftigen in jeder Gemeinde, bezahlt durch örtliche Steuer	
1651	Dr. Harsdorffer/ Deutschland	Zeichensprache	Blindheit
1745	Vereinigtes Königreich/London	Findlingskrankenhaus für Körperbehinderte	Körperbehinderung
1766	Thomas Braidwood/ Vereinigtes Königreich	Akademie für Taubstumme	Taubheit
1778	Pestalozzi/Schweiz	Heim für geistig Zurückgebliebene und geistig Behinderte	geistige Behinderung
1778	Samuel Heinicke/ Leipzig/Deutschland	mündliche Methoden	Taubheit
1785	Vereinigtes Königreich	Sonntagsschulen	Benachteiligung
1799	Itard/Frankreich Edouard Seguin	der wilde Junge von Aveyron	geistige Behinderung (Autismus)
1829	Louis Braille/ Frankreich	veröffentlicht zum ersten Mal seine Blindenschrift	Blindheit
1832	München/ Deutschland	Kurtz Foundation	Körperbehinderung
1841	Guggenbühl/ Abendburg/Deutschland	Institution für Kretinismus	geistige Behinderung
1842	Schweden	allgemeine Schulpflicht	

1850	Christiania, Göteborg/Schweden	Industrieschulen	Körperbehinderung
1865	J.D.Georgens M.Deinhardt/ Baden/Wien	Heilpflege- und Erziehungsanstalt "Levana"	geistige Behinderung
1866	John L. Down/ England	Forschung und Systematik/ Training von Trisomie 21/ Downsyndrom	geistige Behinderung
1867	Dresden/ Deutschland	Tageshilfsschule	geistige Behinderung
1904	Kerr und Eichholz/ Charlottenburg/ Deutschland	erste Freilichtschule	Schwächlichkeit
1908	Cambewell/ London/Vereinigtes Königreich	erste Sondereinrichtung	Sehbehinderung

2.2.1 ANFÄNGE DER HILFEN FÜR BEHINDERTE MENSCHEN

Der eigentliche Beginn der Fürsorge für behinderte Menschen im allgemeinen liegt im mystischen Dunkel. Er wird durch offizielle Aufzeichnungen, religiösen Aberglauben und Berichte karitativer Einrichtungen verschleiert. Vor dem 18. Jahrhundert waren die Diskussionen eng mit medizinischen Behandlungen und christlichen Prinzipien der Pflege verbunden. Paracelsus, ein Schweizer Arzt des frühen 16. Jahrhunderts, verursachte eine fundamentale Auseinandersetzung in der Kirche hinsichtlich der Pflege und Behandlung von Menschen mit geistigen Behinderungen:

"Die Weisheit des Menschen ist nichts vor Gott; und so sind wir in unserer Weisheit wie die Dummen. Und die Dummköpfe, unsere Brüder, stehen vor uns... Und der, der die Intelligenten erlöste, der erlöste auch die Dummen, so wie den Dummen, und damit auch den Intelligenten."

Paracelsus ging sogar so weit zu behaupten, daß Dummköpfe vor Gott nicht nur gleich wären, sondern von Gott sogar bevorzugt würden, Gott näher seien, *"denn der Tierkörper, in dem sie stecken, wurde beschädigt ... der Glaube aber, der auch in Dummköpfen ist – wie in einem Nebel – scheint viel klarer durch."*

Der Glaube, daß geistig behinderte Menschen weit weniger unter weltlicher Verdorbenheit leiden als andere und der wahren bzw. grundlegenden Konzeption vom Menschsein in gewisser Weise näher sind, hat sich bis in die heutige

Zeit gehalten. Auf der anderen Seite ist aber auch die Auffassung, daß Behinderte eine Folge des Bösen im Menschen sind, in der Frühgeschichte ein immer wiederkehrendes Thema. Augustinus stellt in aller Klarheit fest, daß Narren/Dummköpfe die Strafe für Adams Sündenfall darstellen. Und der Glaube, daß behinderte Kinder als „Wechselbälge" untergeschoben gelten und vom Teufel im Austausch gegen "menschlichere" Kinder weggenommen wurden, wurde hauptsächlich von Martin Luther verbreitet, "der Teufel sitzt in solchen Wechselbälgen an der Stelle, wo die Seele sitzen sollte". Auch die Ansicht, daß behinderte Kinder mehr eine Strafe für einzelne sündige Eltern als für die gesamte Menschheit darstellen, wurde eindeutig von Luther vertreten. Abnormale Kinder galten als das Ergebnis des Geschlechtsverkehrs zwischen einer Frau und dem Teufel, und lange Zeit wurden Frauen, die behinderte Kinder gebaren, als Hexen angesehen. Auch die Beziehungen zwischen Sinnlichkeit, Unmoral und der tierischen Natur behinderter Menschen wurde Frauen als Schuld in die Schuhe geschoben. Es gibt sogar noch im 19. und 20. Jahrhundert Fälle, in denen Frauen, die ein behindertes Kind zur Welt gebracht hatten, dafür die Schuld zugesprochen bekamen.

Dennoch kann man erkennen, daß die Geschichte der staatlichen Unterstützung von behinderten Menschen immer weiter weg von der Erforschung individueller Fälle hin zu mehr öffentlichem Interesse führte. Seit Anfang des 19. Jahrhunderts beeinflußte das Interesse an behinderten Menschen auch die Beziehung zwischen dem Arbeitsmarkt und den Kosten für soziale Fürsorgeleistungen. Darüber hinaus wurde es auch immer mehr eine Sache politischer Gruppierungen, die ihre wirtschaftlichen Interessen unter den Deckmantel der Menschenfreundlichkeit stellten. Die Geschichte der Schulbildung für behinderte Menschen bildet hier keine Ausnahme:

"... zu lange haben alle Bereiche der Bildung zusammen mit dem Arbeitsmarkt versucht, beeinträchtigte Menschen von der Arbeit fernzuhalten. Den meisten behinderten Kindern, die die Schule verlassen, wird das Gefühl vermittelt, für den Arbeitsmarkt nicht vermittelbar zu sein, und diese Meinung wird von den sozialen Fördereinrichtungen und weiterführenden Schulen mit ihren „Förderkursen" und "Unabhängigkeitstrainings" noch verstärkt" Oliver 1992 S. 6).

Die Beziehung zwischen behinderten Menschen und der Wirtschaft wird anhand der ursprünglichen Zielsetzung der "Philanthropie" erkennbar, die hinter der Entwicklung eines Struktursystems von Institutionen und "Kolonien" lag, die im 19. Jh. sowohl in Europa als auch in den USA entstanden. In einigen Gebieten wurde auf Grundlage der Heimpflege bis zum gegenwärtigen politischen Umschwung in Richtung häuslicher Pflege, weitergearbeitet. Einige halb-offizielle Bildungs- und Ausbildungsprogramme für Menschen mit Beeinträchtigungen und Lernschwierigkeiten waren Merkmale der Heime im 19.

Jahrhundert. Der Edinburgh-Review von 1885 bietet einen interessanten und unter dem Aspekt der Chancengleichheit voyeuristischen und gönnerhaft anmutenden Einblick in die Aktivitäten des Earlswood-Heims, das damals außerhalb von London ansässig war. Dort bekamen junge Männer und Frauen mit Lernschwierigkeiten und psychischen Störungen Unterricht in Tischler-, Näh- und Gartenbauarbeiten, sowie in Grundlagen des Schreibens, Lesens und Rechnens.

"...es ging darum, Wege zu finden, die Situation der "Idioten" zu verbessern. Das Hauptaugenmerk lag darauf, diejenigen, die den größtmöglichen Nutzen daraus ziehen können, in die Lage zu versetzen, den Einstieg in einen Industriezweig zu ermöglichen und damit ihre Arbeit profitabel zu gestalten. Dabei sollte ihre Untätigkeit und Einsamkeit in soziale, fleißige und produktive Beschäftigung umgewandelt werden" (Edinburgh Review 1865 S.56).

Dieser gute, wenn auch autoritäre Weg wurde bald von härteren und unter größerer Aufsicht stehenden Aktivitäten ersetzt, in Verbindung mit Heimen, die mehr als Schutzzone für die Gesellschaft fungierten, denn als Zufluchtsort für behinderte Menschen. In der "moralischen Panik", die um die Eugenik herum entstand, entwickelte sich seitens des Volkes der Wunsch, die Heime in Stätten der Aufsicht umzufunktionieren. Das bedeutete eine Verschiebung des Anspruchs, nämlich weg von der Ausbildung von Individuen, um sie vor der Bedrohung und Ausbeutung durch den Rest der Gesellschaft zu schützen, hin zum Schutz der Gesellschaft vor ihrer vermeintlichen Schwächung durch körperlich, intellektuell (jegliche im moralischen Sinne) unpassende Menschen. Dieses Führungsmodell des Umgangs mit behinderten Menschen kam dem alten Modell von medizinischer Behandlung durch einen mächtigen Arzt sehr nah, der eine Diagnose des „Problems" stellt, eine Behandlung verschreibt und als Ergebnis dieser „Expertenarbeit" ist der Patient geheilt. Im Falle der Diagnostik oder der Beurteilung von Behinderung lagen endgültigen Urteile damals noch fest in den Händen der Mediziner.

Behinderung wurde unter diesen Umständen als persönliches Schicksal und als eine Tragödie für die betroffene Person angesehen. Das hatte wiederum einen nachhaltigen Einfluß auf die Art und Weise der schulischen und beruflichen Förderung sowie auf deren Ausführung. Auch heutzutage geht das medizinische Ursachenmodell bei behinderten Menschen vom Eigenverschulden aus: „Es ist Deine eigene Schuld!" Wie Oliver im Jahre 1990 herausstellte, ist der beherrschende Einfluß der Medizin ein Hauptfaktor der Individualisierung von "Pflege"/Versorgung. Brisenden, selbst behindert, hat im Jahre 1986 das medizinische Modell sogar noch drastischer in den Blickwinkel gerückt:

"... das Problem aus unserer Sicht ist, daß Mediziner dazu tendieren, alle Patientenprobleme ausschließlich aus Sicht der vorgeschlagenen Behandlung zu sehen, ohne darauf zu achten, daß der Einzelne selbst abwägen muß, ob die Behandlung in die generellen Umstände seines Lebens paßt. Besonders in der Vergangenheit waren die Ärzte zu stark darauf aus, Medikamente zu verschreiben oder Einweisungen in Krankenhäuser zu veranlassen, auch wenn diese Maßnahmen die Lebensqualität der Betroffenen nicht entscheidend verbesserten. Tatsächlich wurden Fragen über die Lebensqualität manchmal als Einmischung in die Entscheidungskompetenz der Mediziner angesehen. Dieses geschah aufgrund der Fehlvorstellung, daß das Einbeziehen der Mediziner bei der Findung einer Definition für Behinderung behilflich sein könnte, was aber nur am Rande und sehr begrenzt der Fall war. Die Definition erklärte eine Behinderung fast ausschließlich als medizinisches Problem und führte zu einer Situation, in der Ärzte und andere Opfer ihrer eigenen Definitionen geworden sind."
(Brisenden 1986 S.8)

Es ist nicht schwer zu erkennen, daß das Phänomen Behinderung von Anfang an fast ausschließlich durch die traditionelle Medizin definiert wurde. Für Schüler mit Lernschwierigkeiten und Behinderungen die ein Schulsystem durchlaufen haben, das den Interpretationen und Wünschen der Medizin nach wie vor große Beachtung beimißt, gibt es die stillschweigende Übereinkunft, daß medizinische Interventionen und Interpretationen bezüglich ihrer „Verschiedenheit" zu ihrem Leben dazugehört. Im Jahre 1986 hat Oliver die Theorie vorgebracht, daß deren Bildung und Ausbildung wohl durch die therapeutischen Maßnahmen von einer großen Anzahl von Pseudo- oder Paramedizinern wie z.B. Physio- oder Sprachtherapeuten etc. unterbrochen wurde. Wenn Kinder nach der Schullaufbahn erwachsen werden und durch eine große Anzahl von medizinischen und paramedizinischen Interventionen daran glauben, krank zu sein, dann ist es keine Überraschung, daß sie ihre passive Rolle als Kranke und Abhängige akzeptieren, sozusagen als Empfänger von Hilfe und Pflege, von denen dafür auch noch Dankbarkeit erwartet wird.

Es gibt eine überwältigende Zahl an Beweisen, daß behinderten Personen das Recht auf volle Staatsbürgerschaft aufgrund des Bedarfs am Arbeitsmarkt verweigert wird. Es scheint offensichtlich, daß trotz politischer Rhetorik, die das Gegenteil behauptet, die soziale Benachteiligung in engem Zusammenhang mit Behinderung und Lernschwierigkeiten steht und daß junge Menschen mit Behinderungen noch immer eher „Fälle" sind, die behandelt werden müssen, anstatt Individuen mit staatsbürgerlichen Rechten.

Die Entwicklung der Psychologie als eine Disziplin der Medizin zu Beginn des 20. Jahrhunderts brachte den Glauben auf, daß Behinderung ein meßbares Phänomen sei und daß behinderte Menschen genauso betrachtet werden könnten wie Patienten im Krankenhaus. Heutzutage ist der Glaube, daß Behinderung eine Krankheit ist, immer noch sehr stark verbreitet. Während das menschliche Verhalten nicht allein von der Vererbung abhängen dürfte, wird das System der biologischen Bedürfnisse und Funktionen, die vom Genotypus transportiert werden, nach der Empfängnis weitergegeben und läßt uns daher in irgendeiner Weise mit allen anderen lebenden Kreaturen verwandt sein. Eine der ältesten Debatten auf dem Gebiet der Forschung über Behinderung ist allerdings, wieviele der menschlichen intellektuellen Fähigkeiten von Umweltfaktoren bestimmt werden und inwieweit dies möglicherweise schon durch die individuelle Genstruktur einer Person entschieden ist. Durch Vererbung können durchaus intellektuelle Möglichkeiten vorbestimmt sein, aber erst die Umwelt bestimmt, wie sehr jeder einzelne sein Potential ausschöpfen kann. Die Beziehung zwischen Genen und den äußeren Umständen, in denen Menschen mit einer Beeinträchtigung leben, führt uns zur Betrachtung der launischen Vorgänge der Mutationsgesetze und den Prinzipien der Vererbung, der Dominanz und rezessiver Gene.

2.2.2 DER SINN UND DIE PHILOSOPHIE DER EUGENIK

Das späte 19. Jahrhundert sah die Entstehung der Eugenik als eine Wissenschaft, aber das Konzept hat eine längere Geschichte. Jetzt am Ende unseres 20. Jahrhunderts, haben sich die Fragen der Eugenik von der sehr eingeschränkten Definition einer Vererbungslehre verschoben zu Themen wie Schwangerschaft, Abtreibung, Euthanasie und Genmanipulation. Ziel dieses Kapitels ist es, die Diskussion über die Auffassung von Genetik als gefährlicher Wissenschaft zu erweitern und statt dessen den Fokus auf die Gentechnologie als eine Dimension effektiver therapeutischer Strategien und persönlicher Wahl zu richten.

Vor nicht allzu langer Zeit ist das Thema der erzwungenen Sterilisation wieder aufgekommen. So stellten z.B. Hernstein und Murray im Jahre 1994 in ihrem provokativen Bericht über die Dispersion des IQ die rassistische Behauptung auf, daß Schwarze intellektuell gesehen Weißen unterlegen seien aufgrund der vererbten Charakteristika. Zu der Zeit, als dieser Bericht geschrieben wurde, wurde die nordische Politik von erzwungenen Sterilisationen bei Menschen mit Entwicklungsbeeinträchtigungen, wie sie in Skandinavien zwischen 1934 und 1976 praktiziert wurde, veröffentlicht (The Guardian 3. September 1997 S. 13). Es ist eine Erinnerung daran, daß der Wahn von Rassenreinheit sehr nah unter der dünnen Oberfläche der kollektiven menschlichen Psyche lauert.

2.2.3 DIE BEZIEHUNG ZWISCHEN EUGENISCHER THEORIE UND BEHINDERUNG

Eugenik als bewußte Antwort, ungewollte Beeinträchtigungen zu kontrollieren, gibt es geschichtlich gesehen bereits seit der Zeit der Griechen und ihrer Mythologie. Künstlerische Portraits der Fortpflanzung zwischen den Göttern und Normalsterblichen in einer Komposition körperlicher Perfektion, praktischer Vollendung und intellektueller Agilität sind in Kunstgalerien und in der Literatur ausgestellt. Die griechische Zivilisation, besessen von körperlicher Vollkommenheit, diente auch als Rechtfertigung für die Aussetzung und den Tod von Neugeborenen, die nicht als perfekt angesehen wurden. Diese äußerste Form der Unterordnung beeinträchtigter Menschen setzt sich auch heute noch in einer Vielzahl abgeschwächterer Formen von Vorurteilen fort.

Barker bot im Jahr 1983 eine gut argumentierende Analyse über die Glaubenssysteme, die die Eugenik-Theorie unterstrich. Zusammengefaßt zeigt er die drei folgenden Annahmen auf, die auf der Lehre gründen:

- menschliche Charakteristika könnten durch Vererbung entsprechend der bekannten Gesetze bestimmt sein;
- es wäre möglich, „erwünschte" und „unerwünschte" menschliche Charaktereigenschaften zu identifizieren;
- die Sozialpolitik sollte die erhöhte Fruchtbarkeit derer mit erwünschten Charaktereigenschaften fördern.

Wunschdenken, wie körperliche Perfektion, ist historisch gesehen immer noch mit Männlichkeit und männlicher Dominanz besetzt. Der körperlich starke, schlanke und aktive männliche Körper steht, traditionell und stereotyp, dem passiven weiblichen Körper gegenüber. Die Frau ist puppenartig, sie verhält sich so, bekleidet und unbekleidet. Femininsten behaupten, daß sich der Wunsch, seinen eigenen Körper zu manipulieren, in den institutionalisierten Motiven wie Mode, Gesundheit und der Pornoindustrie widerspiegelt (Marris 1996; Wilson 1985 S. 3).

Biologische Vorbestimmung setzt sich heute fort in den Lebensgeschichten Tausender behinderter Menschen, die die brutalen Realitäten der institutionalisierten Gleichförmigkeit und der Vorurteile durchlebt haben. Die neuen Bedrohungen des "Rechts auf Leben" behinderter Menschen sind ebenso wieder aufgetaucht, wie die Bedeutung eines menschlichen Gen-Projekts (Human Genome Project), welches weitreichender betrachtet und verstanden wird. Einige Kommentatoren sehen dieses Projekt als Durchbruch in der Gentherapie an, während andere im Umfeld von behinderten Menschen befürchten, daß "es den Forderungen nach biologischem Determinismus wieder neuen Schwung und ein neues rhetorisches Gewicht gegeben hat" (Shakespesare 1995, S. 23).

Die praktische Realität hinter jedem Diskurs über das Recht zu leben (und das Recht zu sterben) ist genau genommen das Töten von Menschen, entweder schon zu Beginn oder am Ende ihres Lebens. Behinderte Menschen und deren Eltern stehen im Zentrum dieses Problems. Befürwortern dieser Tötungsforderungen wird auf dieser Grundlage Recht gegeben, daß behinderte Menschen einen Überschuß/"ein „Zuviel" der gesellschaftlichen Bedürfnisse darstellen. Die Diskussion ist deshalb umso aktueller und dringender geworden, weil die wissenschaftlichen Erkenntnisse immer schneller unseren moralischen Interpretationen dieser Ergebnisse und den gesetzlichen Prozessen vorauseilen, die deren Lösungsansätze formen. Hinzu kommt, daß der Begriff "neue" Eugenik einige der ethischen Dilemmas hervorhebt, denen wir im Zuge der fortschreitenden Globalisierung gegenüberstehen.

Die Unterdrückung von behinderten Menschen tritt über die Grenzen verschiedener kultureller Gruppen hinweg auf und verfestigt sich auf unterschiedliche Weise. Rassismus ist wohl das offensichtlichste Phänomen von Stereotypen und Diskriminierung auf der Basis und in der Gestalt von Vorurteilen. Die pseudowissenschaftliche Ideologie von Rassismus, die als Rechtfertigung für institutionalisierte Unterdrückung von schwarzen Menschen herhalten mußte, hat ihre Parallelen in der Macht und in der Voreingenommenheit der Eugenik als Rechtfertigung für die verschleierten Ausbeutungserfahrungen von Menschen mit Behinderungen. Die Versuche, eine Meßmethode zu kreieren, die die genetische Basis für Intelligenz und menschliches Potential erfaßt, hat die Geschichte von behinderten Menschen im Laufe des 20. Jahrhunderts stark geprägt. Die Beziehung zwischen Statistik und Eugenik verbindet den Statistiker Sir Francis Galton mit seinem Cousin Charles Darwin, dessen Begriff des Evolutionsvorteils der Gesündesten die Basis für die Eugenik bildet. Die Möglichkeiten für eine wissenschaftliche Erklärung der Intelligenz - anstatt sie als göttliche Intervention zu sehen - verursachte eine Explosion des Interesses bei Versuchen, die Unterschiede meßtechnisch zu ermitteln. Francis Galton glaubte ernsthaft, daß "die Möglichkeiten eines Kindes, durch Vererbung berühmt zu werden, vierundzwanzigfach höher seien, wenn es einen berühmten Vater hat" (zitiert bei Malson and Itard 1972 S.16). Er ging auch davon aus, daß es möglich wäre, ein Gen als Intelligenzgen zu bestimmen und daß das „Überleben der Gesünderen" die Eliminierung von "defektem Potential" in der Gesellschaft erforderte.

Die Ablehnung von behinderten Menschen hatte ihren negativen Höhepunkt sicherlich in der Ideologie des Faschismus. Die faschistische Verherrlichung des "perfekten" Menschen führte in der Hitlerära dazu, daß behinderte Menschen mit größter "Akribie" ausgerottet und als mangelhafte Wesen, die den "genetischen Strom verunreinigten", angesehen wurden (Coleridge 1993, S. 45). Das Nazi-Euthanasieprogramm versuchte, die Eliminierung behinderter Menschen auf die Weise zu rechtfertigen, daß sie ja keinen Beitrag zum Wohl der Gesellschaft leisteten und daß sie lediglich eine Belastung der finanziellen Mittel darstellten; sie wurden als "unnütze Esser" angesehen, die keine eigenen Mittel hatten, um einen Beitrag zum Wohl der Gesellschaft zu leisten. Die Nazis und die Eugeniker mögen der Geschichte angehören, aber das Auftreten neuer Formen sozialen Darwinismus' setzt die Auffassung fort, daß lediglich die Gesunden und voll Funktionstüchtigen ein Recht zu leben haben (siehe Levine, 1985).

Die irreführende Logik von Eugenikern, die versuchen, den Verfall der sozialen Ordnung in der Gesellschaft mit der Größe der Familien und unkontrollierten Fortpflanzungspraktiken in Verbindung zu bringen, ist auf unbarmherzige Weise aufgedeckt worden (z.B. Gould 1996). Dennoch kann man ein neues Interesse an biologischem Determinismus erkennen, der versucht, reaktionäre Antworten auf die neue wahre und "Zurück-zu-den-Wurzeln"-Biologie zu geben. Unterstützt wird dies durch die Massenmedien und pseudowissenschaftliche Forschungsstudien, wie z.B. die von Hernstein und Murray (1994), die den Intelligenzquotienten mit Klasse, Rasse und genetischen Ursachen in Verbindung zu bringen versuchen.

2.3 AUFGABEN

Beeinträchtigung im Altertum

Von den Studenten wird erwartet:

- den Ursprung der westlichen Zivilisation, wie z.b. die der Griechen und Römer und deren Haltung gegenüber behinderten Menschen zu betrachten,
- über das Streben nach körperlicher und intellektueller Perfektion zu reflektieren, wie sie die griechische Besessenheit hinsichtlich des Körpers zum Ausdruck brachte, und zu überdenken, ob diese Haltung auch heute noch im jeweiligen eigenen Land anzutreffen ist,

- über Zeiten nachzudenken, in denen man sich selbst schwächer und weniger leistungsfähig fühlte als andere, und die Gefühle zu beschreiben, die dabei aufgetreten sind,
- die Ansichten in bezug auf das Leben von behinderten Menschen im eigenen Land zu betrachten.

Behinderung und christliche Tradition

Von den Studenten wird erwartet:

- das Neue Testament auf Hinweise über Ereignisse mit behinderten Menschen zu untersuchen und herauszufinden, ob es Anzeichen dahingehend gibt, daß falsches Verhalten als Folge/Konsequenz einer Schädigung gilt,
- die jüdischen/christlichen Ansätze der Sorge für Kranke und für vom „Glück Verlassene" mit denen des Islams zu vergleichen,
- die wirtschaftlichen Gegebenheiten des Christentums auf dem Hintergrund zu betrachten, daß es sich als die Religion der Unterprivilegierten definiert und deren Beziehung zu Nächstenliebe und Behinderung zu untersuchen
- kritisch die Machtausübung durch Angst vor dem Teufel zu betrachten und die Beziehung zwischen Schädigung, Unreinheit und Sünde darzustellen,
- die Unterwerfung von Frauen und die Darstellung von behinderten Menschen im Theater, in der Kinderliteratur und in der Volkskultur (wie z.B. Luther, Shakespeare, Ibsen und Wichtcraft) zu untersuchen,
- über die Beziehungen zwischen Religion, Behinderung und Eigentumsrechten in der europäischen Kultur nachzudenken,
- den Verbindungen zwischen Behinderung, Religion, Pflege und Nächstenliebe nachzugehen und die Ergebnisse in Form eines Posters darzustellen,
- den Konflikt zwischen Wissenschaft und Aberglaube in bezug auf Behinderung zu untersuchen.

2.4 BIBLIOGRAPHIE

2.4.1 LITERATURHINWEISE

Abberley P (1993) — Disabled People and Normality, in Swain J et al (eds), *Disabling Barriers – Enabling Environments*, London, Sage

Begum N (1994) — *Reflections*, IPPR, London

Brechin A & Walmsley J (1990) — *Making Connections*, Hodder and Stoughton, London

Casling D (1993) — Cobblers and Songbirds: the language and imagery of disability, *Disability and Society*, 8,2, 203-210

Davis L (1995) — *Enforcing Normalcy – Disability, Deafness and the Body*, London, Verso

Foucault M (1977) — *Discipline and Punish*, Harmondsworth, Allen Lane

Gould SJ (1981) — *The Mismeasue of Man*, New York, W.W. Norton

Haffter C (1968) — The Changeling: History and Psycholdynamics of Attitudes to Handicapped Children in European Folklore, *Journal of the History of Behavioural Sciences*, 4, 55-61

Hevey D (1992) — *Creatures Time Forgot*, Routledge, London

Hooks B (1990) — *Yearning: Race, Gender and/cultural Politics*, South End Press New York

MacFarlene I (1979) — *The Origins of English Individualism*, Oxford, Basil Blackwell

Oliver M (1991) — *The Politics of Disablement*, Macmillan, London

Ryan J & Thonas F (1987) — *The Politics of Mental Handicap (revised edition)*, London, Free Association Books

Soder M (1990) — Prejudice or ambivalence? Attitudes towards persons with disabilities, *Disability, Handicap and Society* 5, 3, (227-241)

Stone D (1984) — *The Disabled State*, London, Macmillan

Swain, J Finkelstein V et al

(1993) *Disabling Barriers – Enabling Environments*, Sage, London

2.4.2 ZUSÄTZLICHE LITERATUR

BACHMANN, W.:	Das unselige Erbe des Christentums: Die Wechselbälge. Giessen 1985
MÜLLER, K.E. :	Der Krüppel. Ethnologia passionis humanae. München 1996
MÖCKEL, A.:	Geschichte der Heilpädagogik. Stuttgart 1988
HOLGERSSON, L.:	Socialtjänst, Lagtexter med kommentarer i historisk beslysning . Stockholm 1995
HOLGERSSON, L.:	Socialpolitik och socialt arbete. Stockholm 1997
LAGERHJELM, B.:	Att utvecklas med handikapp. Stockholm 1988
STATENS HANDIKAPPRAD:	Handikapp vad är det? 9 uppl. Stockholm 1966

3. EIN BLICK AUF DIE GEGENWART

3.1 HEUTIGE AUFFASSUNGEN ÜBER BENACHTEILIGUNG

David Johnstone

3.1.1 EINFÜHRUNG

Erklärungen von Behinderung als persönliches Schicksal und persönliche Tragödie der Betroffenen haben sich über lange Zeit manifestiert. Rioux (1996) und Johnstone (1995) haben einige der soziologischen und psychologischen Anpassungsmechanismen aufgezeigt, zu denen Nichtbehinderte in ihrer Einstellung gegenüber behinderten Menschen in der Gesellschaft neigen. Das medizinische Modell entwirft einen Dualismus, der nicht behinderte Menschen gegenüber Menschen mit Behinderung als „besser" oder überlegen einstuft. Es hat viel gemein mit der früheren Taxonomie von Kurtz (1964), bei der er sich insbesondere auf Menschen mit Lernschwierigkeiten bezog. Das Bild von behinderten Menschen wird mit Mitleid, Angst und Nächstenliebe identifiziert, und es sind genau diese Ansichten, die die erklärende Macht einer solchen Hypothese ausmachen. Die theoretische Erklärung des Modells beruht eher auf der Legitimation primitiver Ängste in Verbindung mit Behinderung als einem Versuch der objektiven Darstellung:

Nichtbehinderte vs.	**Behinderte**
normal	abnormal
gut	schlecht
sauber	unsauber
fit/gesund	unfit/nicht gesund
fähig	unfähig
unabhängig	abhängig

Solche Attribute werden verwendet, um die Annahme zu rechtfertigen, daß es legitim sei, lieber Dinge *für* Menschen mit Behinderung zu tun, als zu versuchen, Dinge gemeinsam *mit* ihnen zu tun. Solche Erklärungen dienten als Grundlage für große Heime und zwingend erforderliche Kontrolle über behinderte Menschen unter dem Deckmantel der Philanthropie, die den Menschen mit Behinderung zu Beginn des 20. Jahrhunderts das Recht auf Fortpflanzung verweigerte.

Wie bereits ausgeführt, lassen sich behinderte Menschen nicht ohne weiteres einem bestimmten Typus zuordnen. Die Schaffung einer Taxonomie von Kategorien ist bei der Erfassung der Vielzahl von Behinderung wenig hilfreich. Oliver (1990 S. 4) sagt über das medizinische Modell: „Es erhält die Ansicht von *Schädigung* als einer Abnormalität in der Funktion aufrecht, von *Beeinträchtigung,* als nicht fähig zu sein, eine Aktivität wirklich in der Art eines menschlichen Wesens durchzuführen, und von *Behinderung* als der Unfähigkeit, eine normale soziale Rolle zu übernehmen."

Rioux (1996) argumentiert, daß eine solche Erklärung von Behinderung als Taxonomie medizinisch/biologischer Probleme heute gewachsen und erweitert ist, und Charakteristika von Behinderung auch als Probleme von Diensten und soziale Probleme umfaßt:

"Wenn man sich dieser Formulierung bedient, so lautet die Hypothese, daß das Defizit beim Individuum liegt, daß aber die medizinische Therapie ausgeweitet wird; somit eine Verbesserung der körperlichen Situation und die Suche nach Möglichkeiten einschließt, die es dem Menschen ermöglicht, sein Potential auszuschöpfen. Vor diesem Hintergrund hat es keine Versuche gegeben, die Einstellung zu überdenken, daß die Probleme behinderter Menschen das Ergebnis ihrer individuellen Schädigung sind (Rioux 1996, S.124).

3.1.2 ZIELE

Von den Studenten wird erwartet,

daß sie „Benachteiligung" als meßbare, „feststehende" oder relative Größe kritisch untersuchen:

a) psychologisch
b) wirtschaftlich
c) gesetzlich
d) medizinisch
e) soziologisch
f) pädagogisch

3.1.3 LERNERGEBNISSE

Am Ende dieses Abschnitts wird von den Studenten erwartet, daß sie:

- eine chronologische Zeitachse über die Entwicklung integrativer/inclusiver Erziehung im 20. Jahrhundert anfertigen,
- die Anfänge wissenschaftlicher Forschung in bezug auf behinderte Menschen untersuchen,
- ein Verstehen der zugrundeliegenden Eugenik-Theorie und ihrer utopischen Ideale im Laufe des 20. Jahrhunderts entwickeln,
- humanitäre Gesinnung und Unterdrückung durch Erziehung und Ausbildung in einer industriellen und wirtschaftlich geprägten Gesellschaft vergleichen,
- ein Verständnis von einerseits einem marxistischen und andererseits einem radikal - liberalen Erklärungsmodell von Behinderung in der Gesellschaft entwickeln.

3.1.4 DIE INDIVIDUELLE TRAGÖDIE ODER DAS MEDIZINISCHE MODELL

Was als medizinisches Modell beschrieben wird, resultiert aus der Neigung der meisten unter uns, die Medizin als Inbegriff einer mächtigen Berufsgruppe zu verstehen. Ärzte umgibt eine Gott ähnliche Aura mit der Verantwortung für Leben und Tod. Dies wiederum hatte einen nachhaltigen Einfluß auf die verschiedenen professionellen Dienste, wie z. B. auf die Bildungs- und Ausbildungsmaßnahmen und auch auf die Art und Weise, wie diese durchgeführt wurden. Dieser mächtige Einfluß suggeriert, daß bei einer Behinderung das medizinische Modell der Kausalität im Grunde von „eigenem Verschulden" ausgeht: „Es ist Dein eigener Fehler". Oliver (1990) und Johnstone (1995) haben herausgestellt, daß der weitverbreitete Einfluß der Medizin ein Hauptfaktor für die Individualisierung von „Pflege" darstellt.

Es ist offensichtlich, daß Dienstleister das „Problem" der Behinderung von Anfang an als persönliche Verantwortung behinderter Menschen definiert haben. So kommt zum Beispiel den Ärzten die traditionelle Rolle zu, die Leiden von Patienten zu beurteilen, eine Therapie einzuleiten und den Heilungsprozeß zu unterstützen. Darin wird die Neigung eines jeden von uns deutlich, sich als allmächtig zu sehen. Behinderte Menschen neigen dazu, sich in gleicher Weise wie jeder andere auch dieser „Allmacht" zu unterwerfen und sich von

Ärzten bestimmen zu lassen. Das „medizinische Modell" funktioniert denkbar einfach. Wenn es jedoch als Erklärung für die Reaktion der Gesellschaft auf körperliche Schädigung und Beeinträchtigung verwendet wird, kann es als problematisch angesehen werden. Das medizinische Modell ist tief in dem Prinzip der Normalisierung (Heilung/Wiederherstellung) verwurzelt, der Rückkehr zur „Vollkommenheit", was unmöglich zu erreichen ist (und auch nicht wünschenswert sein dürfte). Die drei Elemente medizinischer Heilung, die in dem Modell dargestellt werden, haben viel mit den Charakteristika anderer fachbezogener Berufsgruppen gemeinsam:

- medizinischer Zustand (Symptome)
- Diagnose/Verordnung
- Heilung bzw. Behandlung

Dieses Modell verfolgt den unmittelbaren Anspruch auf die Wiederherstellung körperlicher oder sensorischer „Vollkommenheit". Wie auch immer, es ist bedenklich, wenn es auf behinderte Menschen angewandt wird, die möglicherweise bereits von Geburt an geschädigt sind. Es betont außerdem den Patientenstatus und führt damit zu der Erwägung einer wünschenswerten Passivität behinderter Menschen. Das Ergebnis ist eine Betonung der Dinge, die behinderte Menschen nicht können und die sie brauchen werden, damit ihr Leben adäquat mit bestimmten medizinischen Bedingungen funktioniert. „Man geht davon aus, daß behinderte Menschen auf niedrigerer Stufe „funktionieren" als ein „unversehrter" Mensch und daß behinderte Personen in der Tat unangemessen sind" (Gillespie-Sells und Campbell 1991 S. 15). Dies wiederum verstärkt den Teufelskreis von Vorurteil und Diskriminierung, in dem sich „schwierige" Patienten so oft befinden, wenn sie auf eine bestimmte Behandlung der Mediziner nicht in der erhofften Weise ansprechen:

- Scheitern (Stigmatisierung)
- Schuld (geringe Selbstachtung und/oder Abhängigkeit von Hilfeleistung)
- wiederholtes Begutachten der Symptome durch weitere Spezialisten

Das Verständnis dieses Konzepts von Beeinträchtigung beruht auf einem allgemeinen Verständnis von Normalität. Es unterstreicht deutlich die Machtstellung der professionellen Helfer und verstärkt die Theorie der persönlichen Tragödie von Beeinträchtigung. Die subtile Botschaft des medizinischen Modells ist, daß Menschen mit Schädigungen und Funktionsbeeinträchtigungen dankbar für ihre Behandlung sein sollten und daß bei Problemen jeweils der Fehler und die Verantwortung bei dem Patienten liegt, der die empfohlene Therapie nicht eingehalten hat

3.1.5 DAS SOZIALE MODELL VON BEHINDERUNG

Das medizinische Modell vertritt die stark vereinfachende These, daß Behinderung die persönliche Tragödie der Betroffenen ist. Es sind die behinderten Menschen, die von anderen als hilfsbedürftig angesehen werden und sich letztendlich selbst als der Hilfe bedürftig empfinden.

Die Herausforderung und die Stärke des sozialen Modells von Behinderung liegt in seiner Fähigkeit, die Ursachenbetonung umzukehren; weg von der individuellen und persönlichen zu einer geteilten und kollektiven Verantwortung. Diese Theorie stützt sich auf die Prämisse, daß es die Gesellschaft ist, die die Unterdrückung und die Ausgrenzung von Menschen mit Behinderungen aufrechterhält. Damit ist die Last der Verantwortung vom Individuum mit der Schädigung oder Beeinträchtigung verschoben, hin zu den Beschränkungen, die behinderten Menschen durch die Umwelt mit behindertenfeindlicher Architektur sowie durch die Haltung von Institutionen und Organisationen auferlegt sind.

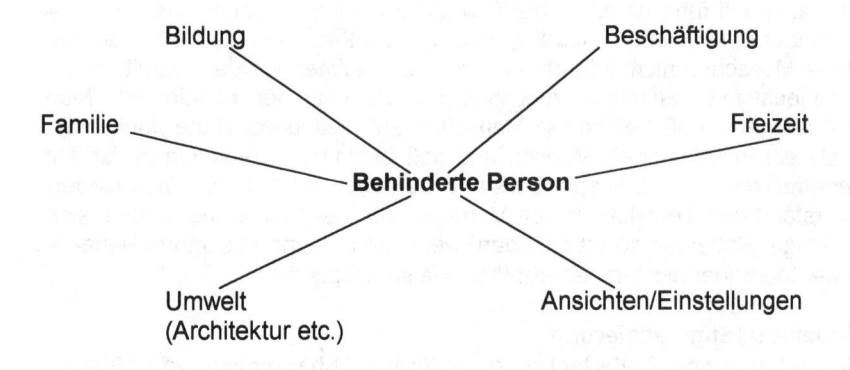

```
        Bildung                          Beschäftigung
              \                         /
   Familie ____                         ____ Freizeit
              ---- Behinderte Person ----
              /                         \
        Umwelt                           Ansichten/Einstellungen
        (Architektur etc.)
```

Der wesentliche Unterschied zwischen dem medizinischen und dem sozialen Modell von Behinderung liegt in der Verschiebung des Erklärungsansatzes. Das soziale Modell räumt im Gegensatz zum medizinischen ein, daß die Gesellschaft strukturelle und persönliche Hindernisse aufbaut. Es erkennt auch die Notwendigkeit, beeinträchtigte Menschen in Entscheidungsprozesse miteinzubeziehen und räumt ein, daß dem Fachwissen Grenzen gesetzt sind. Zusammengefaßt stellt sich das Modell wie folgt dar:

DAS SOZIALE MODELL

- erkennt die Wechselwirkung von strukturellen Variablen und Haltungen an, die Behinderung in der Gesellschaft hervorrufen,
- ist offen für die Ansichten/Meinungen behinderter Menschen,
- berücksichtigt die politischen Prozesse, die für die Unterdrückung und die Verweigerung staatsbürgerlicher Rechte für behinderte Menschen verantwortlich sind,
- beginnt, Macht und Information in die Hände von behinderten Menschen und deren Interessenvertretungen zu legen.

Seit Anfang der 90er Jahre wird aber auch Kritik an dem sozialen Modell laut. Dem sozialen Modell wird vorgeworfen, untheoretisch zu sein, ohne feste Grundlagen einer gesicherten, wissenschaftlichen „Wahrheit", an der es gemessen und getestet werden kann. Auch äußern behinderte Menschen ihre Befürchtungen. Diese haben nämlich die Tatsache in das Blickfeld der Öffentlichkeit gerückt, daß es manche Schädigungen gibt, die mit chronischen und bleibenden Schmerzen und Beschwerden einhergehen und die durch die Medizin gelindert werden können (Crow 1996). Diese Kritik ist wichtig, schwächt jedoch leider allzu oft den nützlichen und nachvollziehbaren Erklärungsansatz für die Verlagerung hin zu sowohl kollektivem und individuellem Denken über Fragen von Behinderung. Es ist außerdem äußerst anmaßend zu glauben, daß überhaupt irgendein Modell den sozialen Komponenten menschlichen Verhaltens vollständig Rechnung tragen könnte. Entstanden ist das Soziale Modell aus den gelebten Erfahrungen behinderter Menschen, dadurch konnte es seine Kräfte entfalten. Als Erklärungsmodell muß es auf irgendeine Weise das medizinische/defizitäre Modell von Behinderung berücksichtigen und nicht im Gegensatz dazu stehen. Mit anderen Worten: die Bürokratie und Einschränkungen des medizinischen Modells können als Teil institutioneller Beschränkungen angesehen werden, auf die sich das soziale Modell von Behinderung gründet.

Einige Menschen können mehrfach geschädigt sein, fühlen sich selbst aber nur durch eine dieser Schädigungen beeinträchtigt. So könnte z. B. eine Person, die unter Asthma, einer Hörschädigung und Arthritis leidet, der Ansicht sein, daß das Asthma durch entsprechende Medikation kontrolliert werden kann und daß mit einem Hörgerät das Hörvermögen soweit wieder hergestellt kann, um sich in den meisten Situationen weitgehend zurecht zu finden. Wenn diese Person jedoch durch ihre Arthritis keine Stufen und Treppen steigen kann, so besteht ihre Beeinträchtigung im Zusammenwirken von Arthritis und der vorhandenen Bebauung. Allgemeingültige Urteile über Behinderung sind des weiteren schwierig aufgrund der Vielzahl und der Variationsbreite, der Schwere der Auswirkungen und der Formen von Schädigungen. Wenn man die Fachliteratur zu dem Thema Behinderung konsultiert, wird deutlich, daß einige Menschen angeben, daß sich ihr Grad der Behinderung erhöht hat und wahrscheinlich noch steigen wird, während es bei anderen hingegen keinerlei Anzeichen für eine Verschlechterung gibt. In vielen Fällen geben die Betroffenen an, mal „gute" und mal „schlechte" Tage zu haben und dementsprechend zu leben.

Das soziale Modell scheint dennoch eher auf liberalen denn auf radikalen Ansichten von Chancengleichheit zu beruhen. Daher leidet es auch unter den Schwächen dieses Paradigmas (z.B. behindert zuviel Bürokratie die Entscheidungsprozesse, und der Begriff Fairneß wird eher als individuelle und nicht als kollektive Gerechtigkeit verstanden). Ein radikaler Ansatz für soziale Gerechtigkeit innerhalb der Politik für behinderte Menschen wird heute mit Gesetzgebung, Rechten und Lebensqualität in Verbindung gebracht.

3.1.6 BEHINDERUNG UND LEBENSQUALITÄT

Das soziale Modell von Behinderung betrachtet Behinderung als ein Phänomen, daß von der Gesellschaft mitbestimmt wird. In einer Welt, die von Nichtbehinderten und für Nichtbehinderte geschaffen wurde, besetzen behinderte Menschen weder Machtpositionen, noch tragen Institutionen und politische Gruppierungen, die unser Leben gestalten, den Bedürfnissen von behinderten Menschen Rechnung.

Historische Diskussionen über die Rechte und Ansprüche behinderter Menschen bilden den Hintergrund, vor dem die Schlüsselfragen zur Lebensqualität untersucht werden können:

Tab. 6: Objektive Einschätzung der Lebensqualität
Subjektive Einschätzung persönlicher Zufriedenheit

körperliches Wohlbefinden	materieller Wohlstand	soziales Wohlbefinden	Weiterentwicklung und Aktivität	Emotionale Zufriedenheit
• Gesundheit • persönliche Sicherheit • Fitneß • Mobilität	• Finanzen & Einkommen • Wohnqualität • Privatsphäre • Nachbarschaft • Eigentum • Essen • Auto • Sicherheit & Grundbesitz	• persönliche Beziehungen • Alltagsleben • Familie und Verwandte • Freunde & soziales Umfeld • Beteiligung an öffentlichen Leben • Aktivitäten • Akzeptanz & Unterstützung	• Kompetenz • Unabhängigkeit • Wahlmöglichkeit & Kontrolle • Produktivität & Aktivität • Arbeit • Alltag & Hausarbeit • Freizeit & Hobbys	• positive Einstellung • Erfüllung-Streß • geistige Gesundheit • Selbstachtung • Stellung und Respekt • Vertrauen & Glaube • Sexualität
		persönliche Werte | Lebensqualität		

Quelle: Felce D. und Perry J., 1996

Viele Determinanten, die Lebensqualität ausmachen, sind eindeutig subjektive und persönliche Einschätzungen der eigenen Stellung in der Umwelt und Reaktionen der Umwelt. Brown (et alii) haben 1992 über Forschungen in Kanada berichtet und sind dabei auf die Komplexität des Begriffes Lebensqualität eingegangen. Sie haben festgestellt, daß es dabei nicht nur um Glück und Zufriedenheit geht, sondern auch um Kampf und Unzufriedenheit (Brown et allii, 1992). Auch in Europa gab es einen ähnlichen Versuch, Lebensqualität anhand von Indikatoren zu messen (Moniga & Vianello, 1995). Die Zahl der Abhandlungen zeigt, daß es sowohl für die professionellen Dienstleister, den Pflegesektor als auch für die Auffassungen behinderter Menschen fundamentale Auswirkungen gibt. Die Forscher führen an, daß „Lebensqualität" ein komplexes Konzept darstellt, bei dem sich Zufriedenheit und Unzufriedenheit nicht nur die Waage halten. Es geht dabei in erster Linie darum, ein positives Selbstverständnis und ein Gefühl des „Empowerment" und der Kontrolle über die Mechanismen zu erlangen, die die Umwelt jedes einzelnen beeinflussen.

3.1.7 LEBENSQUALITÄT – EIN EWIGER WIDERSPRUCH ?

Johnstone (1995) hat für das Vereinigte Königreich, Banfelvy (1996) in einem breiteren europäischen Zusammenhang, festgestellt, daß das allgemeine Konzept von Lebensqualität in einer unterschwelligen Vertrauenskrise steckt. Es gibt diejenigen, die anprangern, daß das Fürsorgewesen die Arbeitsmoral und das moralische Empfinden der Beschäftigten einer Nation untergraben hat (Hernstein und Murray, 1994). Am Ende dieses Jahrhunderts werden neue Bedingungen für Sozialleistungen geschaffen und beeinflussen neue Gesetze und Maßnahmen, die eingeführt werden, um antisoziales Verhalten zu kontrollieren. Dieses Spannungsfeld an der Schwelle zum nächsten Jahrtausend spiegelt sich in der Suche nach moralischer Führung durch unsere Führungspersonen und unseren öffentlichen Dienst wider. Das offensichtliche Versagen menschlicher Beziehungen hat auch zu Benachteiligungen vieler Menschen geführt, die als sozial, sensorisch, kognitiv oder körperlich behindert angesehen werden. Behinderte Menschen führen Leben, in denen sie ambivalent behandelt werden. Dies manifestiert sich nicht selten in einer Form sozialer Unangemessenheit, in der sich behinderte Menschen selbst nicht nur als anders erfahren; sie werden auch als unvorbereitet oder unwillig angesehen, sich einer Reihe von sozialen Situationen anzupassen. Das kann dazu führen, daß funktionierende Beziehungen im Heim, am Arbeitsplatz und in der Gemeinschaft unterdrückt werden.

Die Fähigkeit, die Erwartungen der Menschen im Umfeld zu erfüllen, oder die Hoffnungen anderer wichtiger Menschen nicht zu enttäuschen, ist eine große Last, deren Folge Rückzug und Depression sein kann. Gleichzeitig haben behinderte Menschen oft auch enttäuschend wenig Kontakt untereinander. In einem Umfeld ständiger Kontrolle gibt es nur wenig Möglichkeiten, intime und auf gegenseitigem Respekt beruhende Freundschaften aufzubauen und zu pflegen. Gerade unter solchen Umständen und in solch zerbrechlichen Beziehungen brauchen behinderte Menschen mehr Kontakt zu Personen ihres Vertrauens, die ihnen sozialen Schutz der Unterstützung bieten können und sie ermutigen, ihr soziales Netzwerk zu erweitern und Freundschaften zu schließen. Ein solches Umfeld kann die Grenzen zwischen Generationen, sozialem Status und der Trennung der Geschlechter überwinden.

Fehlende Mittel oder leere Kassen wurden bereits als Grund für die schwierige Situation von Menschen ohne Ausbildung angeführt. Der Lohn von Menschen in niedrig bezahlten Arbeitsverhältnissen unterscheidet sich nur geringfügig von der Summe, die Menschen erhalten, die eine Ausbildung absolvieren oder Sozialhilfe empfangen. Für viele behinderte Menschen – unter ihnen sicherlich auch einige, die aufgrund ihrer Behinderung höhere Zuwendungen bekommen – können die Fürsorgeansprüche bei weitem das Einkommen übersteigen, das sie realistisch als Arbeitnehmer erzielen könnten. Da behinderten Menschen von der Gesellschaft staatsbürgerliche Rechte abgesprochen werden, bleiben sie aus den unterschiedlichsten Gründen weiterhin gezwungen, finanzielle Nachteile in Kauf zu nehmen. Unabhängigkeit wird für sie zur Illusion. Entweder leben sie weiterhin zu Hause bei ihren Familien, oder sie werden wirtschaftlich von anderen abhängig – sei es von ihrem Ehepartner, ihrem Lebensgefährten oder vom Staat. Wenn behinderte Menschen versuchen, allein oder in einer Gruppe zu leben, können sie schnell in finanzielle Schwierigkeiten kommen oder sehen sich mit behördlichen Bestimmungen konfrontiert. Unter diesen Umständen, in denen Menschen mit Behinderung erst beginnen, den Status eines unabhängigen Erwachsenen und die damit verbundenen bürokratischen Abläufe zu verstehen, sind kompetente Ansprechpartner wichtig.

Diejenigen, die nicht der Lage sind, sich in den immer unübersichtlicher werdenden behördlichen Bestimmungen zurechtzufinden, werden vielleicht versuchen, jeglichen Kontakt mit Behörden zu vermeiden, seien es Institutionen oder Ämter. Lebensqualität beginnt vielleicht schon damit, daß man Hilfe bei der Beantragung der Geburtsurkunde, dem Personalausweis, Reisepaß oder Meldenachweis und ähnlichen Dingen braucht. Vielleicht braucht man Rat und Hilfe beim Abschluß von Versicherungen oder der Kündigung überflüssiger oder zu teurer Versicherungen. Ebenfalls kann es vorkommen, daß man „technische" Hilfe bei der Korrespondenz mit öffentlichen Einrichtungen benötigt; z.B. wenn es darum geht, auf Schreiben oder Aufforderungen zu antworten oder Einspruch gegen behördliche Entscheidungen einzulegen, die das Leben in irgendeiner Weise negativ beeinflussen. Die Fähigkeit, entsprechend zu reagieren, kann dabei zum Schlüsselfaktor werden, wenn es darum geht, das eigene Selbstvertrauen und die Selbstachtung zu stärken.

3.1.8 LEBENSQUALITÄT ALS EINE SUMME VON VARIABLEN

Das Modell der Lebensqualität, wie es in Tabelle 6 aufgezeigt wird, bezieht sich oft auf den Lebensstil nichtbehinderter Menschen und die normalen sozialen Lebensrhythmen und -umstände, die gemeinhin als grundlegend angesehen werden. Daher ist es ein Modell, dem keine Theorie zugrunde liegt und das auf einfachen Grundsätzen beruht – ähnlich den „Five Accomplishments" nach O'Brien. Forschungsstudien im Vereinigten Königreich und in Europa (z.B. durch Moniga & Vianell oder Berrington et alii, 1996) über von behinderten Menschen definierten Determinaten von Lebensqualität haben gezeigt, daß das Modell als ein Produkt einer Vielzahl von miteinander verbundenen Variablen angesehen werden kann. Hieraus folgt, daß man das Modell der „Lebensqualität" sowohl nach subjektiven als auch nach objektiven Gesichtspunkten gliedern kann:

- **materieller Wohlstand**

Das ist ein sensibler Bereich: Neben Einkommensstufen kann er Einschätzungen und Urteile u. a. über die Wohnqualität, über Veränderungen der Lebenssituation im Hinblick auf die Wohnverhältnisse als auch finanzielle Gesichtspunkte und Verfügbarkeit von Transportmöglichkeiten beinhalten.

- **körperliches Wohlbefinden**

Dieser Punkt umfaßt alle zusätzlichen Schädigungen, die Notwendigkeit von Hilfsmitteln oder Prothesen. Es kann auch fachliche Betreuung wie Sprachtherapie, Fußpflege oder Diätberatung einschließen. Sicherlich gehört dazu auch das Bewußtsein für so wichtige Dinge wie Gesundheit und Fitneß, Gymnastik und Sicherheit.

- **soziales Wohlbefinden**

Soziales Wohlbefinden ist gekennzeichnet sowohl durch das Engagement in der Gemeinschaft als auch durch persönliche Beziehungen. Dieser Punkt umfaßt das Wissen, woher Unterstützung kommt, Aspekte des täglichen Lebens sowie Kenntnisse darüber, wer in der Gemeinschaft Hilfestellung leisten kann.

- **Weiterentwicklung und Aktivität**

Auch wenn diese Variable doch eigentlich mit meßbaren Zahlen von Beschäftigung verbunden ist, so hat sie doch subjektiv etwas mit dem Grad der Unabhängigkeit und den Wahl- und Kontrollmöglichkeiten im Leben der Menschen zu tun. Sie kann sich auf Bildungs- und Ausbildungsmöglichkeiten sowie auf die Nutzung von Tageszentren beziehen.

- **emotionales Wohlbefinden**

Dieser Punkt hat zu tun mit Selbstwertgefühl, dem von außen vermittelten und subjektiv empfundenen gesellschaftlichen Status und Respekt. Er ist aber auch mit dem Gefühl der Erfüllung verbunden, die Menschen ihrem Leben beimessen.

- **Mobilität**

Für die eindeutige Bestimmung von Lebensqualität muß die Mobilität behinderter Menschen berücksichtigt und gefördert werden. Das Erkennen und der Abbau baulicher Hindernisse (Treppen und Hauseingänge, Toiletten und öffentliche Gebäude) hat sich im Vereinigten Königreich und in Europa durch gesetzliche Regelungen verbessert. Diese Erkenntnisse, die Anpassung öffentlicher Verkehrsmittel (Busse, Züge, Flugzeuge, Taxis etc.), verbesserte Beschilderung und Information (z. B. akustische Ampelanlagen, Blindenschrift) sind grundlegende Erkenntnisse, die bei der Bewertung der Lebensqualität eine entscheidende Rolle spielen.

- **Haus/Wohnung**

Eine Reihe von Erwägungen sind bei der Betrachtung der Wohnbedingungen von behinderten Menschen zu berücksichtigen. Zum einen müssen Schwierigkeiten, die mit dem Grad der Autonomie der betreffenden Person zusammenhängen, berücksichtigt werden. Auf der anderen Seite stehen die ganz praktischen Überlegungen bei körperlich und in ihrer Sensorik geschädigten Menschen. Wir müssen aber auch zwischen den Bedürfnissen derer unterscheiden, die weiterhin in einer Einrichtung leben, sich für ein Leben in einer Wohngemeinschaft entscheiden, die ihr Haus oder ihre Wohnung mit jemandem teilen, oder denen, die eigenständig leben und wohnen.

- **Freizeit**

Lebensqualität hängt nicht nur von der Gesundheit und den Beschäftigungsperspektiven des Einzelnen ab, sondern auch von den Möglichkeiten der Freizeitgestaltung. Natürlich müssen auch Einrichtungen wie Ferienparks, Ferienhäuser, Campingplätze und Freizeit- und Sporteinrichtungen in die Überlegungen miteinbezogen werden und den Bedürfnissen entsprechend zugänglich und verfügbar gemacht werden. Im Freizeitbereich wird oft differenziert. Im Sport z.B. gibt es Sportarten, die speziell für behinderte Athleten und Sportler entwickelt wurden. Gleichzeitig werden jedoch Stimmen laut, daß Sport und Spiel im Grunde ideal sind, um eine Integration/Inclusion behinderter Menschen in das Gemeinschaftsleben zu fördern.

- **Berufsausbildung**

Viele Menschen mit Behinderung bleiben nach Jahren abgegrenzter Erziehung und Bildung für die breite Öffentlichkeit unsichtbar. Die Mehrzahl behinderter Schulabgänger, so wird argumentiert, verfügt nicht über die Voraussetzungen, um eine Anstellung auf dem Arbeitsmarkt zu finden. Sie bedürfen demnach besonderer Ausbildung, ungeachtet der Tatsache, ob ihre Defizite bereits während der Schulzeit erkannt wurden. Diese Meinung vertritt Freeman (1988). Er führt an, daß behinderte und „straffällig" gewordene Jugendliche, die aus der Schule entlassen werden, nicht nur als unbegabt, sondern sogar als sozial inkompetent hingestellt werden. Sie bedürfen daher expliziter Berufbildungsprogramme und weitergehender Schulung im Hinblick auf ihr Sozialverhalten.

In den letzten Jahren wurden in ganz Europa eine Reihe von Berufsbildungsprogrammen für behinderte Menschen geschaffen. Sie basieren auf dem Grundsatz erfolgreicher und zufriedenstellender Eingliederung in das Arbeitsleben und in die Gesellschaft. Die Programme fördern oft besondere Fähigkeiten, vermitteln aber auch soziale Verhaltensmuster, die am Arbeitsplatz gemeinhin als wünschenswert angesehen werden. Sie schulen weiterhin grundlegende Fähigkeiten und Fertigkeiten und betonen dabei Selbstbestimmung, Unabhängigkeit, Ungebundenheit und staatsbürgerliche Rechte. Es wird deutlich, daß Berufsausbildung allmählich die in der Schule geltenden inclusiven/integrativen Erziehungsprinzipien weiterführt. Daraus folgt, daß berufliche Bildung, die Selbstbestimmung und Unabhängigkeit fördert, auch die Bedeutung unterstreicht, daß sich die Haltung gegenüber behinderten Menschen ändern muß. Möglicherweise müssen die Beziehungen zwischen jungen Menschen, ihren Eltern, Lehrern und Sozialarbeitern überdacht und neu definiert werden.

- **Zugang zu Arbeit und Beschäftigung**

Die Kritik an der Bildung läßt sich auch auf andere Formen der Förderung behinderter Menschen übertragen. Die Ausbildungsförderung wird von der Ansicht bestimmt, daß behinderte Menschen der Fürsorge bedürfen. Professionelle neigen dazu, in Kategorien wie „Bedürfnisse" und „Pflege" zu denken und zu handeln. Man könnte daher schlußfolgern, daß behinderte Menschen Arbeitsplätze für (überwiegend nicht behindertes) Pflegepersonal schaffen. Behinderte Menschen sprechen eher von „persönlicher Unterstützung" und lehnen die Assoziation zwischen Pflege und Abhängigkeit ab. Das angenehme Gefühl der Sicherheit und die Rituale der Kindheit sollen auf das oftmals zwanglosere und planlosere Leben als Erwachsener vorbereiten. Bis in die 90er Jahre war eines des selbstverständlichsten und normalsten Dinge im Leben eines Erwachsenen die Arbeit. Es überrascht daher nicht, daß viele unserer prägenden Kindheitserlebnisse und „vorgegebenen" Erfahrungen sich auf die Arbeit beziehen. In ähnlicher Weise wird von Bildung und Ausbildung erwartet, bei der Vorbereitung junger Menschen auf den Arbeitsmarkt die Erwartungen der Arbeitgeber zu berücksichtigen. Dazu gehören die Entwicklung persönlicher und sozialer Verhaltensweisen, handwerkliche Fähigkeiten und Qualifikationen, die später den Arbeitsplatz sichern sollen.

Einige Vorteile bezahlter Arbeit sind offensichtlich. Wie bereits ausgeführt, haben sich die Menschen in diesem Jahrhundert über ihre Arbeit definiert.

"Sie waren Bergleute, Ingenieure, Drucker, Rollkutscher, Gerber. Und die meisten waren männlich. Als die produzierende Industrie zusammenbrach, wurden mehr Arbeitsplätze von Frauen besetzt, und Millionen schlecht ausgebildeter Männer konnten sich selbst nicht mehr über ihre Arbeit definieren. „Ich bin Drucker", konnte man früher mit Stolz über sich sagen. „Ich bin auf soziale Unterstützung angewiesen" bedeutet Ausgrenzung."
(Hugill, The Observer 1997, S. 29)

Die sozialen Kontakte und das Selbstwertgefühl, die sich durch Arbeit und die Einbindung in den Leistungsprozeß entwickeln, lassen sich so auch auf behinderte Menschen übertragen. Einige der Vorteile, Arbeit zu haben, können wie folgt zusammengefaßt werden:

i) Arbeit bedeutet wirtschaftliche Unabhängigkeit und ermöglicht einen höheren Lebensstandard.

ii) Arbeit kann Menschen Kraft verleihen, ihr Leben selbst zu bestimmen und sich nicht fremdbestimmen zu lassen.

iii) Arbeit bedeutet Status, der die Einstellung gegenüber behinderten Menschen positiv beeinflußt und sie in der Öffentlichkeit „sichtbar" werden läßt.

iv) Integrative Arbeitsplätze ermöglichen soziale Interaktion und fördern Freundschaften.

v) Arbeit ist für die Mehrheit der Menschen eine Möglichkeit, sich weiter zu bilden, Fertigkeiten, Kompetenzen und intellektuelle Fähigkeiten zu entwickeln.

vi) Arbeit verleiht unserem Leben eine gewisse Routine und Struktur. Erfolg bei der Arbeit und Zufriedenheit im Beruf vermitteln den Menschen ein Gefühl der Erfüllung, des Erfolges, des Selbstvertrauens und der Würde.

In der Diktion der traditionell geprägten Industriegesellschaft lautet die Theorie über den Wert eines Menschen in bezug auf seinen Arbeitsplatz wie folgt: das Arbeitspotential wird bestimmt durch die Leistungsfähigkeit und die Produktivität des Arbeitnehmers. Diejenigen, die nicht in der Lage sind, eine Ausbildung erfolgreich abzuschließen, sind wahrscheinlich weder wirtschaftlich effizient noch profitabel. Nach dieser Definition verfügen behinderte Menschen über weniger Fähigkeiten und sind abhängiger als nicht behinderte Menschen. Deshalb sind sie beides, benachteiligt und teurer. Diese Ansichten sind tief verwurzelt, und obwohl die Zahl der speziellen Ausbildungsprogramme für junge Menschen zugenommen hat, liefern diese Ansichten immer neue subtile Gründe für den Fortbestand von Vorurteilen, die die gesellschaftliche und wirtschaftliche Position einer steigenden Zahl desillusionierter und „entfremdeter" junger Menschen einschränkt. Gleichzeitig besteht die Gefahr, daß Arbeitsmöglichkeiten für beeinträchtigte Menschen neu definiert werden, um dadurch eine immer größer werdende Zahl von Menschen in die sogenannte Unterklasse einzuschließen – Menschen, die eher gesellschaftlich und wirtschaftlich unterprivilegiert als durch Schädigungen benachteiligt sind. Im gleichen Maße wie Arbeitsplätze verschwinden und besondere Dienste neu definiert werden, um diese Unterklasse einzubeziehen, entstehen immer mehr spezielle Fördermaßnahmen für diejenigen, die wirtschaftlich und beruflich versagt haben.

3.1.9 DER ZUSAMMENHANG ZWISCHEN BEEINTRÄCHTIGUNG UND SONDERPÄDAGOGISCHEN ERFORDERNISSEN

Das Konzept der „pädagogischen Erfordernisse" ist in Europa erstmals nach dem 2. Weltkrieg entstanden. Der wirtschaftliche Aufbau unterstrich die Notwendigkeit, größtmöglichen Nutzen aus dem Bildungssystem zu ziehen.

Im Vereinigten Königreich führten Vorschriften zur Gründung von Diensten und Schulen, die im Namen *von* anstatt gemeinsam *mit* behinderten Menschen agierten. Bis vor kurzem noch war das Ergebnis eine Art passive

Staatsbürgerschaft von behinderten Menschen, die auf Grundbedürfnisse abgestellt und von professionellen Diensten bestimmt war. Die Gesetze des Vereinigten Königreichs betrachten behinderte Menschen noch immer als Kostenfaktor für die Staatskasse und nicht als Individuen mit staatsbürgerlichen Rechten. Wir haben ein System installiert, daß behinderte Menschen weiterhin ausschließt und weit davon entfernt ist, sie in die Gesetzgebungsprozesse einzubinden, die die Rechte behinderter Menschen festlegen und es ihnen ermöglicht, ihre Bedürfnisse selbst zu definieren.

Ein Bestandteil des Gesetzes von 1944 war die Schaffung von Kategorien von Behinderung, die eher die Bedürfnisse der Gesellschaft als individuelle Erwägungen widerspiegelten. In den gesetzlichen Ausführungsbestimmungen zu dem Gesetz (Pamphlet 5) wurde tatsächlich festgelegt, daß einige Schüler möglicherweise einer sonderpädagogischen „Behandlung" bedürfen; eine Aussage, die sich sehr auf das bereits erwähnte medizinische Modell stützt. Für junge Schulabgänger mit Behinderungen und Beeinträchtigungen bedeutete dies möglicherweise eine Zukunft in der Arbeitswelt geschützter und geschlossener Einrichtungen. Noch im Jahre 1968 gingen Schätzungen von ca. 70.000 schwer geistig behinderten Erwachsenen in England und Wales aus, von denen ungefähr 24.500 Ausbildungszentren für Erwachsene besuchten (Whelan & Speake, 1977). Die Notwendigkeit, nach dem 2. Weltkrieg Arbeitsplätze für ehemalige Armeeangehörige zu schaffen, hatte zur Folge, daß behinderten Personen der Zugang zum offenen Arbeitsmarkt verweigert wurde, obwohl viele von ihnen während der Kriegsjahre wichtige Arbeiten verrichtet hatten.

Eine weitaus genauere Definition von Lernschwierigkeiten innerhalb des Konzepts der „sonderpädagogischen Erfordernisse" floß in die gesetzlichen Rahmenbedingungen des „Education Act" von 1981 ein und resultierte aus den Empfehlungen des „Warnock Committee of Enquiry (Warnock-Untersuchungsausschuß)" aus dem Jahre 1978. In seinen Empfehlungen für Schüler mit besonderen Bedürfnissen hinsichtlich höherer Bildung folgt das Gesetz der in Kapitel 10 des Berichts beschriebenen Vorstellung von Fortschritt und „Übergang ins Erwachsenenleben". Dabei lieferte es sowohl für die Unterscheidung zwischen Hochschul- und Schullehrplänen als auch für die gesetzliche Unterscheidung zwischen dem Status eines Studenten, eines jungen Menschen oder dem eines Kindes mit besonderen Bedürfnissen nur sehr wenige Anhaltspunkte. Der Definition zufolge sind Kinder Personen, die bis zum 19. Lebensjahr in die Schule gehen; jedoch fehlen Hinweise darauf, welchen Status „ein Kind" hat, das mit 16 Jahren die Schule verläßt, um dann auf das College zu gehen oder sich für ein anderes Ausbildungsprogramm entscheidet. Damit ließen die Prinzipien von Warnock in Hinblick auf eine Definition von Rechten und Ansprüchen, die den Status eines Erwachsenen ausmachen, und wie sie der Punkt „Übergang ins Erwachsenenleben" impliziert, einiges zu wünschen übrig. Auch andere Ungereimtheiten in den Definitionen von sonderpädagogischen Erfordernissen sind bis heute noch nicht vollständig beseitigt, obwohl diese Definitionen die eigentliche Kernaussage des Berichts des Warnock-Ausschusses sind und später die Grundlage für die „Education Acts" von 1981 und 1993 bildeten.

Laut Booth (1992) folgt aus diesen Definitionen, daß Kinder und Studenten nach zwei Methoden zu bewerten seien; erstens durch die Messung „individueller Fähigkeiten", wie z.B. Intelligenz- oder Leistungstests (die implizieren, daß in der Inkompetenz oder dem Versagen einer Person bereits der Grund für Lernschwierigkeiten liegt) und zweitens durch „Urteile der Umwelt" in Hinblick auf die Angemessenheit der vorhandenen Ressourcen, die das Lehren und Lernen erleichtern und unterstützen. Das gesamte Konzept von „Bedürfnis bzw. Erfordernis" ist problematisch und verwirrend. Für Schulkinder hat es zu einer Zunahme von Förderprogrammen geführt, die auf die individuellen Bedürfnisse zugeschnitten sind und Unterstützung bieten. Erst seit kurzem stellen Kommentatoren in Frage, ob diese Angebote zur Überwindung von Lernschwierigkeiten nicht womöglich erst zu den Problemen beitragen, die sie eigentlich lösen sollten (Booth, 1992. Corbett und Barton 1992).

Die grundlegenden, kindzentrierten Ideen des Warnock-Berichts versuchten, ein Staatsbürgerkonzept zu etablieren, das auf dem Begriff Bedürfnis beruht. Dieses Konzept sollte durch die Zusammenarbeit von „Experten" und die bessere Integration von Kindern aus sonderpädagogischen Einrichtungen in das Bildungswesen bestimmt sein. Tatsächlich hat es dieser Ansatz jedoch nicht geschafft, alte Vorurteile zu überwinden. Wären die Empfehlungen von Anfang an entsprechend finanziell ausgestattet worden, wären die gegenwärtigen Forderungen nach Veränderung nicht so massiv. Die Entwicklung hin zu integrativer/inklusiver Erziehung ist im Grunde die Feststellung, daß eine völlige Integration ein in naher Zukunft wahrscheinlich nicht zu erreichendes Idealziel ist und auch nicht allgemein erwünscht sein dürfte. Mehr als alles andere versäumte es das Konzept der sonderpädagogischen Erfordernisse, grundsätzlich sicherzustellen, daß jedes Kind ein Recht auf schulische Grundbildung hat. Wie Booth bemerkt, ist der Begriff „sonderpädagogische Erfordernisse" so sehr mißbraucht und mißverstanden worden, daß dadurch zwei an sich lobenswerte und wertvolle Konzepte in den Hintergrund gedrängt wurden; nämlich die von „Fürsorge" und „Bedürfnis". Diese haben eigentlich den Begriff zunächst stark geprägt. Das System, das die Bedürfnisse eines Kindes oder eines Studenten befriedigt, hat dazu geführt, daß einige der schlimmsten

„Mißbräuche" der alten medizinischen Pflegemodelle weiterhin bestehen; nämlich daß junge Menschen und ihre Familie bürokratische Bewertungsverfahren durchlaufen müssen und daß es immer noch isolierte Schulen und Heime gibt, die einigen Menschen das Recht nehmen, ihre Lebensumstände selbst zu bestimmen. Dies wiederum hat dazu geführt, daß ihnen verweigert wird, ein Gefühl der „Normalität" zu entwickeln. Kurz gesagt: das Konzept der „sonderpädagogischen Erfordernisse" stempelt junge Menschen mit Lernschwierigkeiten oder Behinderungen als Problemfälle ab, genauso wie es die früheren Kategorisierungen von Behinderung getan haben, dem System, das dieses Konzept eigentlich ablösen wollte (Fulcher 1989).

3.1.10 VON DER INTEGRATION ZUR INCLUSION

In einer Vielzahl von Ländern der westlichen Welt hat seit Ende der 70er, Anfang der 80er Jahre ein Zusammenspiel von Faktoren dazu geführt, daß die Separierung der Pädagogik für Menschen mit Behinderung zunehmend in Zweifel gezogen wird. Diese Faktoren traten im Zuge der Bestrebungen zu einer „Inclusive Education and Community" in Erscheinung, als man in den Einrichtungen der Sondererziehung begann, die Konzepte zur Chancengleichheit neu zu überdenken. Die Ironie der Geschichte: einige der Organisationen, die in ihren Anfängen an der Errichtung und Anerkennung von Sondereinrichtungen für junge Menschen mit Behinderungen und Lernschwierigkeiten beteiligt gewesen waren, gehörten nun zu den lautesten Verfechtern für den Abbau der Systeme, die das Ergebnis ihrer eigenen frühen Erfolge waren.

Die Unfähigkeit, den Bedürfnissen einer wachsenden Zahl junger Menschen gerecht zu werden, die aufgrund von Schwierigkeiten beim Lernen oder bei der Einhaltung von Verhaltensregeln ausgeschlossen wurden, führte zur Errichtung spezieller Versorgungssysteme, sowohl bezüglich des Ortes (spezielle Klassen, spezielle Schulen), als auch bezüglich der Lernhilfen (adaptierte Materialien, besondere Ausstattung, zusätzliche Unterstützung der Lehrenden). Diese bewußt eingeführte Handhabung aufzugeben und sie der Inclusion zu opfern, kommt für viele Lehrer der Aussage gleich, die in der Sonderpädagogik Tätigen haben sich selbst etwas vorgemacht; und vielleicht ist es so gewesen. Sie übernahmen Teile der Ausstattung der Kleinkindräume, Plastikgeld und Papp-Supermärkte, und simulierten damit in den Sonderschulen Lernfelder für viele behinderte Menschen. Diese Situationen tragen in keinster Weise zum Gedanken einer „Schulung für das Erwachsenenalter" bei, sondern verstärken vielmehr die Separierung und die Vorbereitung auf lange Jahre in der Tagesstätte.

Eines der wesentlichen Ziele in der Ausbildung von Menschen mit Lernschwierigkeiten und/oder Behinderungen ist die Übertragbarkeit auf das Erwachsenenalter anstatt einer Fortführung kindorientierter und geschützter Versorgung. In Abgrenzung zur Integration ist die Bewegung der „Inclusive Education" auf dem Grundsatz von Gerechtigkeit und den Rechten marginalisierter Gruppen aufgebaut worden, die traditionell von Bildungs- und Gemeindeangeboten ausgeschlossen waren. In einfachster Form sagt das Konzept aus, daß der Wert eines Individuums sich aus den Qualitäten ableitet, die es in eine Situation oder menschliche Begegnung einbringt, anstatt Bedingungen für deren Akzeptanz aufzustellen. Während also Integration mit der gleichen Akzeptanz aller in vielerlei Hinsicht das Endziel ist, ist die Inclusion ein Schritt auf diesem Weg, indem Menschen gerade wegen ihrer Unterschiede akzeptiert und wegen ihres Beitrages zur menschlichen Begegnung wertgeschätzt werden.

Es kann davon ausgegangen werden, daß die Mehrheit der auf irgendeiner Stufe am Erziehungssystem Beteiligten versucht, das Leben von Menschen zu verbessern. Diese Grundannahme ist sicherlich deutlich sichtbar bei denjenigen, die im landläufig als Sonderpädagogik (special education) bezeichneten Bereich arbeiten. Aus diesem Grund, falls nicht aus einem anderen, ist es schwierig, den Integrationsenthusiasmus mancher Lehrer, Eltern und Verantwortlichen zu deuten und einzuschätzen. Der anfänglichen und grundlegenden Reaktion „gut" sollte jeder zustimmen, der bekundet, daß ihm ein verbesserter Zugang zu sozialen- und Bildungsmöglichkeiten am Herzen liegt. Jedoch ist bei denjenigen, die in speziell für Menschen mit Behinderung und Lernschwierigkeiten entwickelten und ausgestatteten Verhältnissen arbeiten, die Verwirrung groß, wenn sie ihre Bemühungen jetzt dem Vorwurf ausgesetzt sehen, daß sie weiterhin Dienste schaffen, welche Menschen ausschließen und sie an einer vollen Beteiligung an sozialen Aktivitäten hindern. Für Lehrer, die über Jahre im getrennten System der Sondererziehung gearbeitet haben, kann es nur ein Schock sein, wenn sie feststellen, daß ihnen von ihren Kritikern vorgeworfen wird, sie hielten eine Art Bildungsapartheid aufrecht und hätten trotz bester Bemühungen zu helfen, Kinder und Schüler auf eine Zukunft im Abseits vorbereitet. In anderen Worten: die Erfahrungen, die das Bildungssystem für Kinder und junge Menschen mit Lernschwierigkeiten geschaffen hat, haben diese „systematisch ihrer natürlichen Beziehungen und der Gemeinschaft des Gemeindelebens entzogen" (Tyne 1993).

Die Bewegung der „Inclusive Education" ist aus der Debatte über die Effektivität des Mainstreaming und Fragen nach der Berechtigung von Sonderklassen entstanden. Als das Konzept der Integration Anfang der 80er Jahre an Bedeutung gewann, wurden ihm gemischte Reaktionen zuteil; es hatte wenige vollständige Befürworter. Was seitdem geschehen ist, spiegelt eine wachsende Bewußtheit der Normalisierungsprinzipien wider, die zunächst in Skandinavien und Kanada von Wolfensberger entwickelt worden waren. Der rapide wachsende Enthusiasmus in den letzten Jahren für die „Inclusive Education" in den anderen europäischen Ländern hingegen hat sich zeitgleich mit einem Anstieg der schönen Reden über die Rechte der Bürger abgespielt. Dies ist verständlich und unausweichlich, da die Befürworter der „Inclusive Education" angeführt haben, Bildung und Erziehung sei das angemessenste Vehikel für die vollständige Umsetzung dieser Gedanken. Fürsprecher des „Inclusive Education and Community Living" haben außerdem hervorgehoben, daß Bildung und Erziehung, will sie Teil einer Ausbildung für das „anbrechende Erwachsenenalter" sein, auf jeden Fall alle Schüler bestmöglich in die realistischen und allgemeinen Aktivitäten einbeziehen muß. (Whittaker 1989)

Wie schon in der Argumentation für die Integration in den 70er Jahren gibt es auch für die Inclusion moralischen Rückhalt. Und doch: trotz der augenscheinlichen „Richtigkeit" der Bewegung gibt es keine gesicherten Aussagen darüber, ob sie für die betroffenen jungen Menschen immer zu den besten Erfolgen im Bereich der Bildung und Erziehung oder in bezug auf soziale Beziehungen führen wird. Letztendlich gleicht das zentrale Thema der Inclusion dem anderer Bewegungen, die viele schöne Dinge sagen, aber auf wenig solider Basis in der Praxis stehen. Es geht um Empowerment und die Aufhebung von Einschränkungen, mit denen manche Menschen leben müssen; es geht um das Recht zu wählen.

Wie wir gesehen haben, ist die Sonderpädagogik als Antwort auf das Versagen der allgemeinen Pädagogik im Sinne einer Alternative zu dieser entstanden. Letztere hatte entweder den Bedürfnissen einer bestimmten Gruppe von Schülern nicht beggnen können oder andere Kinder aufgrund von bürokratischer oder administrativer Bequemlichkeit ausgeschlossen. In dem Versuch zu beschreiben, in welcher Art und Weise das Bildungs- und Wohlfahrtssystem für Menschen mit Behinderung weiterhin ausgrenzend wirkt, haben Befürworter der Inclusion erklärt:

„In bezug auf ,Ausgrenzung' spreche ich nicht von den Menschen, die eine klare Wahl zur ,Kultur der Behinderten' treffen, und auch nicht von den Gruppen behinderter und nichtbehinderter Menschen, die beschließen, gemeinsam ein mit Bedacht separiertes Leben in einer hierfür geschaffenen idealen Gemeinschaft zu führen. Auch meine ich mit ,systematisch' nicht, daß jemand bewußt vorhat, Menschen auszugrenzen. Ich spreche hingegen von einem System, das wenige oder keine Wahlmöglichkeiten für behinderte Kinder zu bieten hat und

das unausweichlich dazu führt, daß Kinder zu einem Erwachsenenleben in der Ausgegrenztheit heranwachsen." (Tyne 1994, S.151)

In den Diskussionen über Inclusion und Exclusion geht es nicht wirklich um das Versagen der Sonderpädagogik, sondern um das sichtbare Instrument der Ausgrenzung: die Sonderschule. Indem sie sich jedoch auf ein Ziel einschießen, das selbst ein Produkt des allgemeinen Erziehungssystems ist, reduzieren die Kritiker der Ausgrenzung eine komplexe Analyse von weitergefaßten sozialen, wirtschaftlichen und politischen Betrachtungen auf eine stark vereinfachte Formel: Regelschulen sind gut – Sonderschulen sind schlecht.

Auf der Basis dieses Argumentes erscheint das Konzept der Inclusion, gedacht als Wertschätzung der Unterschiede, als ein problematischeres Gebilde. Die erste Reaktion auf eine Bewegung, die Ideale von Integration und Chancengleichheit zu fördern scheint, ist eine positive; Inclusion ist ein Prozeß, mit dem man nur schwer nicht einverstanden sein kann. Die Erfahrung zeigt jedoch, daß der ursprüngliche Enthusiasmus nicht universell ist. Die Bewegung spiegelt die Wertesysteme verschiedener Lehrer und Erziehungsbereiche wieder, durch die ihre Bedeutung interpretiert werden wird. Inclusion kann kein statisches Wesen sein, das allein durch das Befolgen eingeführter Regeln und Verfahren erreicht wird.

Die Sonderpädagogik sieht sich in ganz Europa einer großen Zahl von Herausforderungen gegenüber, versucht man doch in den einzelnen Ländern, die Bestrebungen der Erklärung von Salamanca (1994) dahingehend zu interpretieren, derzufolge wir uns alle auf das Ziel der „Inclusive Education" hinbewegen sollen. Das Schließen von Sonderschulen und die Versetzung von Kindern in reguläre Klassen läßt darauf schließen, daß angemessene Unterstützungsmaßnahmen bereits vorhanden sind. Dies ist jedoch nicht immer der Fall:

„Sonderschulen in vielen Ländern (Europas) repräsentieren eine große Investition in Lehrkörper und Expertentum, in Gebäude und Ausstattung, in Software und andere Materialien – die ganze Palette der Dinge, die Regelschulen missen, an denen Schüler mit Schwierigkeiten beim Lernen betroffen sind." (Hegarty 1995, S.35)

Mit Hinblick auf das 21.Jahrhundert zwingt die Notwendigkeit der Einführung von Lernunterstützungssystemen in den Regelschulen alle Beteiligten, einen neuen Blick auf die Funktion und das Ziel des Lernens zu werfen, um die besten Anteile der Sonderschulversorgung übernehmen zu können.

3.1.11 AUFGABEN

- Untersuchen Sie kritisch, was die Soziologie zum Verständnis der staatsbürgerlichen Rechte von behinderten Menschen beiträgt.

- Entwickeln Sie eine chronologische Zeitachse über den Fortschritt der integrativen Erziehung im 20. Jahrhundert.

- Nehmen Sie kritisch zu der Aussage Stellung, daß Behinderung eher ein wirtschaftliches als ein medizinisches Problem ist.

- Erstellen Sie eine Belegmappe (Portfolio), die das Konzept der „Lebensqualität" in bezug auf behinderte Menschen darstellt.

- Erläutern Sie die miteinander konkurrierenden Erklärungen für die Unterdrückung und die „Unsichtbarkeit" von behinderten Menschen, die in diesem Abschnitt angesprochen wurden.

- Erstellen Sie eine Belegmappe (Portfolio), die ein soziales Modell von Behinderung nachweist.

- Untersuchen Sie die Gesetzgebung in zwei europäischen Ländern im Hinblick auf behinderte Menschen.

3.1.12 BIBLIOGRAPHIE

3.1.12.1 LITERATURHINWEISE

Alcock P (1993) *Understanding Poverty*, Macmillan, London
Barnes C (1994) *Disabled People in Britain and Discrimination*, Hurst, London
Barton L (1993) The Struggle for Citizenship: the case for disabled people, *Disability, Handicap and Society*, 8,3, (235-248)
Booth T (1992) *Making Connections*, Milton Keynes, Open University Press

Brechin A &
Walmsley J (1990) — *Making Connections*, Hodder and Stoughton, London

Brisenden A (1986) — Independent Living and the Medical Model, *Disability, Handicap and Society*, 1,2, 173-178

Corbett J &
Barton L (1992) — *The Struggle for Choice*, London, Routledge

Gould S J (1981 — *The Mismeasure of Man*, W W Norton, New York

Hernstein R &
Murray C (1994) — *The Bell Curve: Intelligence and Class Structure in American Live*, London, The Free Press

Hevey D (1992) — *The Creatures Time Forgot*, Routledge, London

Hernstein R &
Murray C (1994) — *The Bell Curve: Intelligence and Class Structure in American Life*, The Free Press, London

Hugill, B. (1997) — Britain's expansion zone, The Observer, 13th April, 29

Johnstone D (1995) — *Further Opportunities: Learning Difficulties and Disabilities in FE*, Cassell, London

Johnstone D (1998) — *An Introduction to Disability Studies*, London, Fulton

Morris J (1989) — *Able Lives*, Women's Press, London

Morris J (1991) — *Pride Against Prejudice: transforming attitudes towards disability*, The Women's Press, London

Oliver, M (1986) — Social Policy and Disability: Some Theoretical Issues, *Disability, Handicap and Society* 1, 1

Oliver M (1991) — *The Politics of Disablement*, Macmillan, London

Pritchard D (1960) — *Education and the Handicapped 1760-1960*, London, Routledge

Porter G &
Richler D (1991) — *Changing Canadian Schools*, Roher Institute, Toronto

Riesser R &
Mason M (1991) — *Disability in the Classroon*, ILEA, London

Ryan J &
Thomas F (1980) — *The politics of Mental Handicap*, Penguin, London

Swain J.
Finkelstein V et al (1993) — *Disabling Barriers – Enabling Environments*, Sage, London

Warnock M (Chair) (1978) *Report of the Committee of Enquiry into the Education of Handicapped Children and Young People*, London, HMSO

3.1.12.2 ZUSÄTZLICHE LITERATUR

Antor,G:/Bleidick, U.:	*Recht auf Leben - Recht auf Bildung.* Heidelberg 1995
Opp,G./ Peterander F. (Hrsg):	*Focus Heilpädagogik. Projekt Zukunft.* München/Basel 1996
Seligman, M.:	*Erlernte Hilflosigkeit.* Weinheim 1992
Theunissen,G.:	*Empowerment und Heilpädagogik.* Freiburg i.Br. 1995
Wolfensberger, W.:	*Der neue Genozid an den Benachteiligten, Alten und Behinderten.* Gütersloh 1996

http://bidok.uibk.ac.at/links/index.html
http://behinderung.org/all-info.htm
http://www.bbv.umweltdata.de/zeitung/zeitung.htm
http://selbsthilfe.seiten.de/laediert/

3.2 POLITIK CONTRA PRAXIS

Bengt Eriksson

3.2.1 EINLEITUNG

Eine große Mehrheit der europäischen Staaten betrachtet sich selbst mehr oder weniger als "Wohlfahrtsstaaten". Man könnte behaupten, daß es so etwas gibt wie das Bewußtsein einer "sozialen Dimension". In den meisten Staaten (in allen) gibt es Regelungen, um die Schwächsten zu unterstützen und mehr oder weniger lange Unterbrechungen des Wohlstandes – zumindest bezüglich materieller Grundlagen – zu überwinden. Dennoch unterscheiden sich die Wege, diese Ziele zu erreichen. Einige Länder legen die Hauptverantwortung in die Hand des Staates, indem sie sich selbst der Idee der "starken Gesellschaft" oder des "Wohlfahrtsstaates" verschreiben. In anderen hat sich eine mehr oder weniger ausgeglichene Zusammenarbeit zwischen dem Staat, einflußreichen Gewerkschaften und den Arbeitgebern herauskristallisiert, die manchmal als "Sozialpakt" beschrieben wird. Es gibt aber auch Staaten, die sich in großem Ausmaß auf die ehrenamtliche Arbeit von Organisationen wie Kirchen, Gewerkschaften oder Einzelpersonen, wie z.B. Verwandte oder Bekannte, verlassen. Trotz der Unterschiede im Aufbau scheint es in allen Ländern so zu sein, daß es eine Mischung aus staatlicher, arbeitsmarktpolitischer und freiwilliger Beteiligung gibt, die das "Wohlfahrtsgesicht" formen.

Dennoch stehen Wohlfahrtssysteme oft in der Kritik und Wohlfahrtsorganisationen nicht selten unter großem Druck. Die Kritik zielt dabei auf die Summe der zur Verfügung stehenden finanziellen Mittel und deren Verteilung unter den Bedürftigen. Auch gibt es kritische Stimmen in bezug auf die Organisation der Wohlfahrt und das Aufbringen finanzieller Mittel.

Ungeachtet der unterschiedlichen Systeme und Anwendungsbereiche bei Wohlfahrtsangelegenheiten in bezug auf den Bedarf scheint es jedoch eine Kluft zwischen Ideologie und Praxis zu geben. Es gibt Einzelpersonen und zuweilen auch große Gruppen, die nicht in dem Maße vom Wohlfahrtssystem profitieren, obwohl sie Anspruch darauf hätten. Dieser Punkt ist sehr problematisch, er kann aber von verschiedenen Standpunkten aus betrachtet werden: einmal als ein Problem der Vertrauenswürdigkeit eines demokratischen Systems, dann als Frage unausgeglichener Machtverhältnisse, weiterhin als ein Problem der Gerechtigkeit, als methodisches Versäumnis in bezug auf soziale Fürsorge und Sozialarbeit oder aber als individuelles Problem derer, die darunter leiden.

Im Blickfeld des Interesses in diesem Kurs stehen Personen mit einer Behinderung sowie deren Lebensbedingungen und wie diese Bedingungen durch soziale Fürsorge oder Sozialarbeit verbessert werden könnten. Den verschiedenen Herangehensweisen in Europa gilt das besondere Interesse. Um diesen Sachverhalt allerdings greifen zu können, scheint es notwendig, die Perspektive für einen Moment ein wenig zu erweitern, und zwar auf das Feld der Sozialpolitik als Ganzes. Soziale Fürsorge und Sozialarbeit zugunsten von behinderten Menschen und auch andere Bemühungen, die unternommen werden könnten, um deren Situation zu verbessern, sind nur ein Punkt auf dem weiten Aufgabengebiet der Sozialpolitik. Um diesen Abschnitt besser verstehen zu können, ist es vielleicht hilfreich, sich die Entstehung und die momentane Lage der Sozialpolitik in den verschiedenen europäischen Staaten genauer anzuschauen: was sind z.B. die eigentlichen Wurzeln der Sozialpolitik, welche Unterschiede und Ähnlichkeiten können beim Betrachten der geschichtlichen Hintergründe der Sozialpolitik in einigen europäischen Ländern entdeckt werden? Und wie sieht es mit den momentanen Gesetzen und Bestimmungen aus, die die Geschicke der Sozialpolitik regeln – im allgemeinen und speziell bezogen auf behinderte Menschen? Und schließlich, wie sieht es mit der Beziehung zwischen Regeln und Regelungen und den eigentlichen realen Bedingungen für behinderte Menschen aus? Gibt es einen Widerspruch, zwischen dem, was gesagt und letztendlich erreicht wird?

"Was ist Sozialpolitik?" Sozialpolitik wird im allgemeinen als unklares Konzept („fuzzy concept") angesehen, welches in unterschiedlichen Situationen verschiedene Bedeutungen haben kann. Dazu werden nun einige Definitionen genannt, und es wird darüber hinaus die Notwendigkeit diskutiert, diese Flut von Definitionen zu limitieren.

Wenn man sich die Sozialpolitik der demokratischen Staaten in Europa in der Nachkriegszeit ansieht, kommt man zu dem Schluß, daß dabei die Idee des Konsens' im Vordergrund zu stehen scheint. Strukturanalysen von Sozialpolitik sind nicht selten so angelegt, daß sie auf das Vorhandensein oder die Abwesenheit von Konsens abheben. Aus diesem Grund wird dieses Konzept besonders in den Vordergrund gerückt und diskutiert.

Anschließend richtet sich der Blick auf die historische Entwicklung der Sozialpolitik in den drei am Projekt beteiligten Ländern. Hierbei soll vornehmlich die Nachkriegszeit von besonderem Interesse sein. In allen drei Ländern gab es auf dem Wohlfahrtssektor offensichtlich große Zuwachsraten, wenn sie sich auch in vielen Punkten unterscheiden: in Deutschland wird ein Großteil der Verantwortung auf die Schultern der Arbeitgeber gelegt, um damit die Wohlfahrtsangelegenheiten durch den Arbeitsmarkt regeln zu lassen. Aber auch die Mitarbeit von Gewerkschaften und ehrenamtlichen Organisationen, wie z.B. den Kirchen, sind bei der Bereitstellung von sozialer Fürsorge eine große Unterstützung. In England wird dagegen bis zu einem bestimmten Grad auf einen Konsens zwischen dem Staat, den Gewerkschaften und den Arbeitgebern vertraut, um sich der sozialen Fürsorge anzunehmen. Dieser Konsens war allerdings unter rechtsgerichteten Regierungen immer wieder großen Bewährungsproben ausgesetzt. Auch in England spielt der ehrenamtliche Bereich eine wichtige Rolle. Im Vergleich dazu hat Schweden die ausgeprägteste Form eines Konsenses hinsichtlich der Notwendigkeiten eines Sozial- und Wohlfahrtsstaates bewiesen. Dieser Konsens hat sich in Zeiten wirtschaftlicher Probleme als relativ stabil erwiesen. Nun wenden wir den Blick weg von den historischen Aspekten und hin zum aktuellen Geschehen unserer Tage.

Wir werden uns dabei nun Dokumenten zuwenden, die die gegenwärtigen Absichten der drei Länder zum Thema „soziale Wohlfahrt" abstecken. Diese Dokumente bestehen in erster Linie aus grundlegenden Schriften der Gesetzgebung (Gesetze und Richtlinien) und aus gesetzlichen Schriften, die insbesondere die Bedingungen von Fürsorge für Behinderte festlegen. Diese Untersuchung verfolgt dabei zwei Aspekte: Erstens soll der öffentlich zugesagte Standard der Sozialfürsorge für behinderte Menschen definiert werden, um dann den tatsächlich erreichten Standard damit zu vergleichen. Zweitens sollen die politischen und ideologischen Absichten der drei beteiligten Länder untersucht werden.

Im nächsten Abschnitt wird es dann darum gehen, den politischen und ideologischen Anspruch mit den Fakten zu vergleichen. Durch das Heranziehen verschiedener Quellen werden die politischen Dokumente mit Hilfe von Fakten, die die Situation verschiedener Gruppen behinderter Menschen beschreiben, genau unter die Lupe genommen. Diese Quellen bestehen im Grunde genommen aus verfügbaren Statistiken über den sogenannten "Wohlfahrtskonsum", aber auch aus Berichten und Artikeln aus wissenschaftlichen Zeitschriften und der allgemeinen Presse. Auch Interviews werden eine Rolle spielen.

Dieser Abschnitt wird dann mit dem Versuch enden, die grundlegende Frage von Politik contra Praxis zu beantworten: gibt es Unterschiede zwischen Politik und Praxis? Wenn ja, welches sind die Widersprüche, die zu beobachten sind, zwischen dem, was dazu gesagt wird und dem, was dann letztlich getan und erreicht wird? Welchen Stellenwert haben behinderte Menschen als bedürftige Gruppe im Rahmen anderer Bedürftiger? Gibt es Muster von Ungleichheit innerhalb der Gruppe von behinderten Menschen? Können die Unterschiede zwischen den drei Staaten identifiziert (und erklärt) werden?

Die Arbeit zu diesem Abschnitt kann wie folgt untergliedert werden:

- Teilnahme an Vorlesungen,
- Arbeit mit empfohlener, aber auch selbstgewählter Literatur,
- Suche nach Statistiken und anderen Quellen, die die momentane Situation von behinderten Menschen beschreiben,
- Gruppenarbeit zum Vergleich von Politik und Praxis. Die Ergebnisse in Form von schriftlichen Arbeiten können auch Bestandteil der Prüfungen dieses Kursabschnittes sein,
- aktive Teilnahme an Diskussionen in den Seminaren über Ergebnisse und die Problematisierung der Widersprüche zwischen Politik und Praxis.

3.2.2 ZIELE

Von den Studenten wird erwartet:

- die politischen Schriftstücke über behinderte Menschen in den drei beteiligten europäischen Ländern zu vergleichen
- die Widersprüche zwischen der Gesetzgebung und der Praxis in Schweden, Großbritannien und Deutschland in bezug auf behinderte Menschen zu verstehen und zu bewerten
- in direkten Kontakt mit Kommilitonen in den Partnerländern zu treten und ein Portfolio über die Unterschiede und Ähnlichkeiten in dieser Politik zu erstellen.

3.2.3 LERNERGEBNISSE

Am Ende dieses Abschnitts sollten die Studenten die folgenden Fähigkeiten erlangt haben:

- die Vorgänge in der Sozialpolitik und deren Auswirkungen auf behinderte Menschen und auf Professionelle in den verschiedenen Ländern zu erkennen und verstehen

- die Gesetze und politischen Dokumente der verschiedenen Länder hinsichtlich behinderter Menschen zu kennen

3.2.4 WAS IST "SOZIALPOLITIK"?

In diesem Teil des Kurses geht es um das Problem von (sozialer) Politik contra Praxis. Aus diesem Grunde mag es hilfreich sein, sich zunächst Gedanken über das Konzept von Sozialpolitik zu machen. Es ist ein sehr weit gefaßtes Konzept, das in unterschiedlichen Situationen auch viele unterschiedliche Bedeutungen zuläßt. Titmuss hat dieses Konzept im Jahre 1974 sehr genau untersucht und ist dabei von den Begriffen "Politik" und "sozial" ausgegangen. Politik bedeutet eigentlich, daß gewisse Veränderungen zu erwarten sind, d.h., daß unerwünschte Bedingungen gegen gewünschte mit Hilfe geplanter Aktionen ausgetauscht werden können oder sollten. Selbstverständlich haben wir, wie Titmuss sagt, keine Politik, die sich um das Wetter kümmert, denn wir können nicht versuchen, es nach unseren Wünschen zu ändern. Der Begriff "sozial" wird in einer Vielzahl von Kontexten gebraucht (mißbraucht?) und in einer Reihe von Verbindungen sowie mit verschiedenen Bedeutungen verwendet. Titmuss argumentiert, daß sie alle betonen, „daß der Mensch ein soziales Wesen ist, nicht nur ein Wirtschaftswesen; und daß man Gesellschaft nicht in mechanisch-organischen oder physiologischen Modellen erfassen kann. (ibid. Seite 24)

Hinzu kommt, daß der Begriff Sozialpolitik unzweifelhaft auch Wertbedeutungen hat. Es gibt keine wertfreie Sozialpolitik. In den meisten Fällen wird Sozialpolitik als ein Weg gesehen, die Interessen Schwächerer, wie z.B. Arbeitsloser, Mittelloser und behinderter Menschen zu unterstützen. Obwohl es für gewöhnlich eine Menge berechtigter Bedürfnisse gibt, sind die Ressourcen zweifellos begrenzt. Das Problem, unter verschiedenen Bedürfnissen gerecht zu verteilen, ist letztlich eine Wertentscheidung. Daraus folgt, daß es grundsätzlich notwendig ist, seine jeweiligen eigenen Werte offen darzulegen, wenn man Sozialpolitik diskutiert.

Es gibt eine Vielzahl von Definitionen für Sozialpolitik, die z.T. sehr eng und begrenzt gefaßt sind oder aber sehr weit und umfassend. Ein Beispiel für das erstere könnte Hagenbuchs Definition sein, in der er sagt, daß "die treibende Kraft von Sozialpolitik als der Wunsch dargestellt werden könnte, jedem Teil der Gesellschaft ein Minimum an Standards und Möglichkeiten zu gewährleisten" (Titmuss, 1974). Das Gegenteil, eine weit gefaßte Definition, wird von Macbeath geliefert: "Sozialpolitik beschäftigt sich mit der gerechten Ordnung des Beziehungsnetzwerkes zwischen Männern und Frauen, die gemeinsam in der Gesellschaft leben, oder mit den Prinzipien, die die Tätigkeiten von Einzelpersonen und Gruppen regeln, wenn diese das Leben oder die Interessen anderer tangieren" (Titmuss, 1974). Schließlich gibt es noch ein drittes Beispiel, das aus der gleichen Quelle stammt und einen engeren und praktischeren Ansatz bietet; dieser wird von Marshall angeboten. Seiner Meinung nach hat das Konzept der Sozialpolitik keine wirklich exakte Bedeutung, "es nimmt jedoch Bezug auf die Regierungspolitik und ihre Aufgaben, die in direktem Bezug zum Wohl der Bürger stehen, diese nämlich mit Leistungen und Einkommen zu versorgen. Der Kern der Aussage bezieht sich daher auf Versicherungen, öffentliche (oder staatliche) Unterstützung, das Gesundheits- und Wohlfahrtssystem und auf die Wohnungspolitik" (ibid. Seite 30).

Aus der Untersuchung einer Reihe von Definitionen schließt Titmuss, daß es drei grundsätzlich unterschiedliche Perspektiven zur Sozialpolitik gibt. Die erste und zugleich am engsten gefaßte nennt er „Das Restwertwohlfahrtsmodell der Sozialpolitik" ("The Residual Welfare Model of Social Policy"). Entsprechend diesem Modell wird das Wohlergehen des Einzelnen normalerweise von der Familie (von der Privatsphäre) oder durch den freien Markt gewährleistet. Nur wenn diese beiden Möglichkeiten nicht greifen, sollte staatliche Fürsorge bereitgestellt werden, aber selbst in diesen Fällen nur bis in einem sehr begrenzten Maße. Dabei sollte vermieden werden, etwaige Strukturveränderungen, wie z.B. Nivellierungen von Lebensbedingungen vor allem großer Gruppen vorzunehmen.

Das zweite Modell ist „Das industrielle Leistungserfüllungsmodell der Sozialpolitik" ("The Industrial Achievement-Performance Model of Social Policy"). Bei diesem Modell spielt der Arbeitsmarkt eine bedeutende Rolle. Was man im Bedarfsfall an Unterstützung zu erwarten hat, hängt hauptsächlich davon ab, was man zuvor, vor allem im Arbeitsleben, eingebracht hat. Es ist ersichtlich, daß dieses Modell verbunden ist mit einer großen Benachteiligung der Menschen, die außerhalb des Arbeitsmarktes stehen und somit auf die meisten Sozialleistungen keinen Anspruch haben.

Als drittes Modell gibt es „Das institutionelle Neuverteilungsmodell der Sozialpolitik" ("The Institutional Redistributive Model of Social Policy"). Bei diesem Modell spielen Fürsorgeregelungen im weiteren Sinne eine sehr wichtige Rolle, wenn nicht sogar die entscheidende Rolle. Die Sozialpolitik muß nicht nur präsent sein, wenn alle anderen Möglichkeiten versagen, sondern es ist normal, bei zahlreichen Gelegenheiten von sozialer Fürsorge zu profitieren, von der Geburt an bis zum Tod. Sozialpolitik wird in diesem Fall auch als ein Weg angesehen, Ressourcen neu zu verteilen, und zwar von den Reichen zu den Armen. So wird der Einfluß der Sozialpolitik auch auf die Verteilung von Ressourcen und für den Ausgleich innerhalb der Gesellschaft ausgedehnt.

Auch wenn die Einteilung in diese drei Modelle schon vor 25 Jahren vorgenommen wurde, so hat sie doch noch immer ihre Gültigkeit. Spätere Autoren folgen zwar den Modellen von Titmuss (s. dazu Nygren 1994, Salonen 1994, Socialstyrelsen 1997), reduzieren sein Konzept aber auf zwei Modelle: das marginale Modell und das institutionelle Modell, die jeweils dem "Residual Welfare Model" und dem "Institutional Redistributive Model" entsprechen. Tatsächlich haben die meisten Staaten ein System, das eine Kombination aus allen drei Modellen darstellt.

Innerhalb der Europäischen Union gibt es Diskussionen über den Begriff "soziale Dimension". Grundsätzlich besteht die soziale Dimension aus zwei Teilen und zwar dem sozialen Dialog und der "öffentlichen Charta fundamentaler Rechte von Arbeitern". Allerdings sind diese Konzepte nur zu einem geringen Teil als das zu verstehen, was man gemeinhin als Sozialpolitik bezeichnen würde. Die soziale Dimension innerhalb der EU beschäftigt sich mit Arbeiter- und Arbeitsbedingungen, nicht mit sozialer Wohlfahrt im allgemeinen. Es geht um bestimmte Rechte für Arbeiter, wie z.B. das Recht auf den Aufbau und die Arbeit von Gewerkschaften, welche für die Allgemeinheit über Löhne und andere Bedingungen zu verhandeln; des weiteren geht es darum, Informationen und Einfluß zu erhalten, wenn innerhalb der Firma grundlegende Strukturveränderungen vorgenommem werden.

Diskussionsstoff für die Studenten:

- Denken Sie über die Einteilung nach Titmuss nach und überlegen Sie, ob es noch mehr mögliche Klassifikationsmodelle für Sozialpolitik gibt.

- Welches Modell dominiert in Ihrem Land? Ist es möglicherweise eine Mischung aus verschiedenen Modellen?
- Geben Sie praktische und konkrete Beispiele für dominierende sozialpolitische Modelle in Ihrem eigenen Land.

3.2.4.1 DER KONSENS – EIN SCHLÜSSELKONZEPT IN DER DISKUSSION ÜBER SOZIALPOLITIK?

Wie kommt es, daß sich Staaten zur Wohlfahrtsstaaten entwickeln? Diese grundlegende Frage ist von großem Interesse, sie führt uns allerdings etwas weg von der eigentlichen Fragestellung dieses Kurses. Augenscheinlich hat es etwas mit der Natur des Menschen zu tun und der fundamentalen Bestimmung von Männern und Frauen, soziale Wesen zu sein. Streng genommen haben wir eine uneingeschränkte Verantwortung, gegenseitig für uns zu sorgen. Einer kann nicht ohne den anderen überleben. Industriestaaten sind unter anderem gekennzeichnet durch ihre Komplexität, ihre Arbeitsteilung und ihren Bedarf an sozialen Regelungen, die die Grundbedürfnisse abdecken. Typische Beispiele für solche gesellschaftlichen Regelungen sind z.B. die Kommunikation, die Bildung, das Gesundheitssystem und die soziale Fürsorge, (daneben natürlich auch Dinge wie die Rechtsprechung, die Exekutive und die Verteidigung). Diese Angelegenheiten sind natürlich auch politische Fragen. Die Entwicklung der Sozialpolitik kann beispielsweise mit Hilfe von Konflikt- und Konsenskonzepten untersucht werden..

Unzweifelhaft hat eine bestimmte Art von Übereinstimmung die Debatten über Sozialpolitik und die dort getroffenen Entscheidungen in vielen westlichen Ländern mehr oder weniger lange geprägt. Gemeint ist damit der Konsens. Sullivan hat Konsens im Jahre 1992 als "wesentliche Übereinstimmung prinzipieller Art als Notwendigkeit für das Eingreifen einer Regierung zur Gewährleistung des Wirtschaftswachstums, der Vollbeschäftigung und eines möglichst umfassenden Fürsorgesystems" beschrieben (ibid. Seite 1).

Gemeint ist, daß der Staat, (die gesetzgebende Kraft), die Arbeitgeberorganisationen und die Gewerkschaften bei einer (mehr oder weniger formalen) Vereinbarung darüber, gegenseitig ihre Interessen zu unterstützen, alle Beteiligten davon profitieren: der Arbeitgeber erzielt ein wirtschaftliches Wachstum und politische Stabilität, die Arbeiter ziehen ihren Nutzen in Form von höheren Löhnen und anderen arbeitstechnischen Verbesserungen, und die Politiker können Sozialreformen in Gang setzen, die die Lebensbedingungen der Bevölkerung/ihrer Wähler verbessern (und dabei erhöhen sich ihre Chancen, an der Macht zu bleiben).

Schweden wird oftmals als das Land betrachtet, in dem Konsenspolitik am erfolgreichsten funktioniert. Die Kooperation zwischen der Regierung, den Gewerkschaften und den Arbeitgebern hatte sehr lange Bestand, von den Jahren zwischen den Kriegen bis in die 70er Jahre hinein (mit einigen Ausnahmen). Die formalisierte Kooperation zwischen den Arbeitgebern und den Gewerkschaften hatte sogar einen besonderen Namen: "Der Geist von Saltsjöbaden"; ein Name, der sich auf den Ort der Vereinbarung bezieht. Die notwendigen Voraussetzungen wurden durch die sozialdemokratische Führung, die lange Bestand hatte, und die engen Beziehungen zwischen der Regierung und den Gewerkschaften, die oft als zwei Äste am gleichen Baum bezeichnet wurden, geschaffen. Allerdings ist seit ungefähr 10 – 15 Jahren die Idee einer starken Gesellschaft sowohl in Schweden als auch in anderen westlichen Staaten sehr stark strapaziert worden. Laut Mishra (1990) hat Schweden entschieden, den Wohlfahrtsstaat weitgehend beizubehalten. Er nennt dies Erhaltungspolitik. Er deutet dies als ein Zeichen für die Stärke dieses Wohlfahrtsstaates.

In England hatte sich in den Jahren zwischen den Kriegen unter einer Minderheit von Parlamentariern die Meinung gebildet, daß eine Art Ausgleich zwischen Kapital und Arbeit (Sullivan 1992, S. 7) wünschenswert sei. Die Verfestigung solcher Ideen wurde durch die Theorie von Keynes erleichtert, die besagte, daß der Staat ausgleichend in das Auf und Ab im Wirtschaftskreislauf eingreifen sollte. Vom sozialen Gesichtspunkt aus gesehen vertritt der Beveridge-Bericht dieselben Ideen. Laut diesem Bericht trägt die Gesellschaft für ihre Mitglieder die Verantwortung, annehmbare Lebensbedingungen zu gewährleisten. Diese Meinung entstand gegen Ende des Krieges sowohl bei einer Mehrheit einflußreicher Politiker als auch unter der Bevölkerung und hatte die sogenannte "Einigung von 1945" zur Folge. Kurz gesagt war dies eine Vereinbarung zwischen Arbeitgebern und Gewerkschaften, zwischen dem Kapital und der Arbeit. Insgesamt war der Konsens, auf den man sich in England geeinigt hatte, bei weitem nicht so stark wie sein Äquivalent in Schweden. Und er wurde mit der Machtübernahme durch Frau Thatcher endgültig in Frage gestellt.

In Deutschland (gemeint ist im folgenden die Situation im ehemaligen Westdeutschland) geht die Entwicklung der Sozialpolitik bis in die Ära Bismarcks zurück. Gegen Ende des 19. Jahrhunderts begründete er Gesetze über Krankheits-, Unfall-, Alters- und Invaliditätsvorsorge. Das soziale Fürsorgesystem im heutigen Deutschland ist das Ergebnis einer schrittweisen gesellschaftlichen Entwicklung auf dieser Basis. (Socialstyrelsen 1991)

Eine der Grundfesten des deutschen Systems ist die Familie als Einheit und nicht die Einzelperson, wie es z.b. in Schweden der Fall ist. Die gegenseitige Verantwortung, die jedes Familienmitglied für das andere übernimmt, ist wesentlich ausgeprägter. Die Kinder sind zu einem großen Teil für das Wohlergehen ihrer Eltern verantwortlich. Die Verantwortung der Gesellschaft beginnt erst, wenn die Familie nicht mehr in der Lage ist, ihren Pflichten nachzukommen. Dieses System wird als „Subsidiaritätsprinzip" bezeichnet.

Ein weiterer wichtiger Eckpfeiler ist das Sozialversicherungsmodell. Genaugenommen beruht dieses System darauf, daß man das, was man eingezahlt hat, wieder zurück bekommt. Die Leistungen werden durch persönliche Beiträge des Arbeitnehmers und durch die Beteiligung des Arbeitgebers abgedeckt. Zusätzlich zur verpflichtenden Sozialversicherung kann auch noch private Vorsorge getroffen werden. Die Parteien des Arbeitsmarktes sind nach dem Gesetz von 1949 gemeinsam für die Sozialversicherung zuständig. Der Staat (die verschiedenen Bundesländer) steuert diesen Vorgang durch Gesetze und deren Kontrolle.

Man kann sehen, daß es auch in Deutschland in Hinblick auf den Bereich der Sozialfürsorge eine Art von Konsens gibt. Historisch gesehen ist dieser „Konsens" allerdings nicht durch erbitterte Kämpfe verschiedener gesellschaftlicher Klassen wie des "Kapitals und der Arbeit" entstanden, wie es in Schweden und besonders auch in England der Fall war. Die Familie fungiert als Basis für die soziale Absicherung. Verschiedene freiwillige Organisationen, die nicht selten mit den Kirchen oder mit Gewerkschaften in Verbindung stehen, spielen jedoch auch eine wichtige Rolle.

3.2.4.2 SOZIALPOLITIK UND SOZIALE FÜRSORGE IN DEUTSCHLAND, ENGLAND UND SCHWEDEN

Wie bereits erwähnt, gibt es prinzipiell und strukturell drei verschiedene Wege, Fürsorge zu gewähren. Zum einen kann der Staat das Sozialsystem regeln, garantieren und in die Tat umsetzen (state-run systems). Zweitens kann die Fürsorge auch dem Markt überantwortet werden, was zur Folge hat, daß man ein "kaufender Verbraucher" der Fürsorge sein muß. Das beinhaltet auch, daß Fürsorgeeinrichtungen dann verfügbar werden, wenn es sowohl einen klaren

Bedarf gibt als auch die Leute, die wohlhabend genug sind, für das zu bezahlen, was sie verlangen. Der dritte Weg, das Problem der sozialen Fürsorge anzupacken, besteht in der Fürsorge durch die Familie, freiwillige Organisationen und ein informelles soziales Netzwerk, das bisweilen als die "zivile Gesellschaft" bezeichnet wurde.

In Wirklichkeit betreiben alle Gesellschaftssysteme eine Mischung aus den drei Modellen, also einen Kompromiß zwischen dem informellen Sektor, dem Staat und dem Markt, wobei sie sich meist in ihrer Gewichtung unterscheiden. Die Abbildung 1 zeigt diese drei Systeme sozialer Fürsorge.

Abb.9: Übersicht über das Sozialfürsorgemodell von drei europäischen Ländern

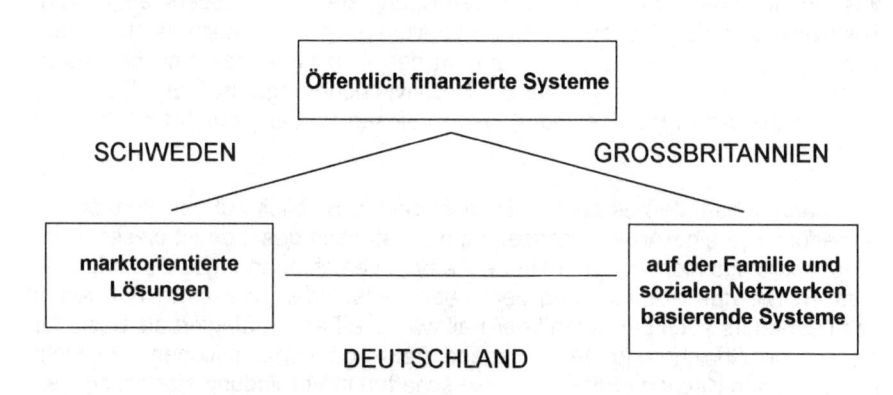

```
                    ┌─────────────────────────────┐
                    │ Öffentlich finanzierte Systeme │
                    └─────────────────────────────┘
         SCHWEDEN                               GROSSBRITANNIEN

┌──────────────────┐                          ┌──────────────────────┐
│  marktorientierte │                          │  auf der Familie und │
│     Lösungen      │                          │  sozialen Netzwerken │
└──────────────────┘                          │  basierende Systeme  │
                          DEUTSCHLAND          └──────────────────────┘
```

Quelle: Socialstyrelsen 1991, S. 10

Im folgenden Abschnitt soll jedes Land mit seinem System der Sozialfürsorge kurz beschrieben werden.

Deutschland

Die gegenseitige Verantwortung zwischen Einzelpersonen und Familienmitgliedern ist die Basis, auf der alles beruht. Dieses Prinzip wird besonders bei der Kinder-, Alten- und Behindertenfürsorge deutlich. Die Gesundheitsversorgung sowie die Renten- und Arbeitslosenvorsorge ist durch entsprechende Versicherungen gewährleistet, welche vom Staat (bis auf die Gesetzgebung) weitgehend unabhängig sind. Ca. 90% der Bevölkerung sind freiwillig oder verpflichtend in diese drei Basisversicherungsmodelle integriert. Ungefähr ein Viertel greift zusätzlich zu privater Vorsorge. Die finanzielle Deckung dieses Systems ist im allgemeinen gut.

Die Versicherungen werden in der Hauptsache von den Arbeitgebern und Arbeitnehmern mit je 50%iger Beteiligung auf Beitragsbasis finanziert. In Einzelfällen tritt auch der Staat ein. Es ist daher durchaus möglich, die Versicherungsleistungen in Anspruch zu nehmen, auch wenn keine berufliche Beschäftigung vorlag und man somit nicht fähig war, seine Beiträge zu leisten.

Was die Altersversorgung und die Fürsorge für behinderte Menschen betrifft, tritt in diesen Fällen zunächst die gegenseitige Verantwortung der Familienmitglieder ein. Es sind zudem Altersheime und Haushaltshilfen verfügbar, die gewöhnlich von ehrenamtlichen Organisationen angeboten werden, welche meistens mit der Kirche oder einer Gewerkschaft verbunden sind, jedoch von den Kommunen überwacht werden.

Aufgrund einer wachsenden Bedürfnislage und einer überstrapazierten Wirtschaft werden die Alters- und Behindertenfürsorge immer öfter diskutiert. Die Tradition, auf die Familie zu vertrauen, wird für eine große Gruppe von Frauen vielfach als Hindernis angesehen, in den Arbeitsmarkt einzutreten. Zudem ist die Integration zwischen Ost- und Westdeutschland noch immer ein Hauptproblem in Deutschland, die hauptsächlich auf die wirtschaftlichen Belastungen zurückzuführen ist.

England

In England basiert das Sozialfürsorgesystem auf der geteilten Verantwortung der Behörden auf der einen Seite und dem sozialen Umfeld mit den ehrenamtlich fungierenden Organisationen (dem informellen Sektor) auf der anderen Seite. Momentan gibt es Pläne, das System marktorientierter auszurichten (s. unten).

Zwei voneinander unabhängige Versicherungen bilden die fundamentalen Bestandteile dieses sozialen Fürsorgesystems. Beide werden in der Hauptsache durch den Staat reguliert, geleitet und finanziert. Da ist zum ersten die „Nationale Gesundheitsfürsorge" ("National Health Service" = NHS), die für die Gesundheits- und Zahnvorsorge zuständig ist. Das NHS beinhaltet zudem ein umfassendes System von Praktischen Ärzten, die sich um die grundlegenden Dinge der Gesundheitsfürsorge kümmern. Eingeschlossen sind zudem Krankenhäuser und Pflegeheime.

Zweitens gibt es ein Versicherungssystem für Renten-, Arbeitslosenvorsorge, etc. Obwohl der Staat den größten Anteil an diesem System finanziert, müssen auch die Einzelpersonen und Arbeitgeber ihren Teil über Beiträge beisteuern.

Was die Versorgung der alten und behinderten Menschen betrifft, so ist man zunächst bestrebt, dafür zu sorgen, daß diese in ihrer gewohnten Umgebung, d.h. zu Hause bleiben können. Daher konzentriert sich die Hilfe und Pflege auf diese Bemühungen. Die Behörden sind verantwortlich für diesen Service. Dennoch wird die meiste Arbeit von ehrenamtlichen Organisationen übernommen, die innerhalb der britischen Gesellschaft auf eine lange Tradition zurückschauen können. Es gibt annähernd 170.000 verschiedene ehrenamtliche Organisationen, die sich zum Teil durch die Kommunen und zu einem anderen Teil durch private Spenden finanzieren.

Von Familienmitgliedern, Verwandten und anderen, die in das soziale Umfeld integriert sind, wird erwartet, in Zusammenarbeit mit den Kommunen und ehrenamtlichen Organisationen zur Fürsorge beizutragen. Für Schwerbehinderte und gebrechliche Menschen sind Einrichtungen verfügbar, in denen z.Zt. ca. 5% der alten Menschen leben.

Schweden

Das schwedische Modell der sozialen Fürsorge basiert auf einem ausgesprochenen Konsens zwischen dem Kapital, der Arbeit und der Politik. Daher stehen der öffentlichen Sozialfürsorge immense finanzielle Mittel zur Verfügung. Daneben gibt es allerdings auch eine (ständig wachsende) Zahl von Fürsorgeleistungen, die von marktorientierten Gruppen geführt werden. Der schwedische Fürsorgesektor ist zum größten Teil dezentralisiert und wird von den Kommunen betrieben.

Die Systeme der Gesundheits- und Zahnpflege, der Renten, etc. umfaßt die gesamte Bevölkerung. Die Höhe der Erstattungsbeiträge ist grundsätzlich relativ hoch, obwohl sie in den letzten 10 Jahren aufgrund von Einschnitten in die Versicherungssysteme vielfach gesunken sind.

Genau wie in England besteht das Hauptanliegen der Hilfe und Fürsorge darin, es einem möglichst großen Teil der alten und behinderten Menschen zu ermöglichen, solange wie irgend möglich zu Hause zu bleiben. Daher gibt es auch ein gut ausgebautes und von den Kommunen geleitetes System der Hauspflege, des Transportservices und des Essens auf Rädern. Dennoch leisten Verwandte und andere Mitglieder des sozialen Umfelds einen bedeutenden Beitrag, der mindestens so groß ist wie der der Kommunen. Auch ehrenamtliche Organisationen spielen zunehmend eine wichtige Rolle.

Zukunftsmodelle

Die Modelle der Sozialpolitik in allen drei Ländern durchlaufen im Moment einen Prozeß der Veränderung. In Deutschland entwickelt sich ein größerer Einfluß seitens der politischen Bühne; der Staat übernimmt mehr Verantwortung. Auf die Zukunft hin gesehen könnte dies zu Entlastungen der Familie führen. Großbritannien geht in Richtung einer marktorientierteren und dezentralisierteren Organisation. Das Phänomen größerer Marktorientierung kann ebenfalls in Schweden beobachtet werden. Außerdem gibt es dort schon seit Jahren einen Prozeß der Dezentralisation. Wenn man diese Systeme nun in die vorherige Graphik einfügt, so ergibt sich folgendes Bild:

Abb.10: Übersicht über das soziale Fürsorgesystem von drei europäischen Ländern

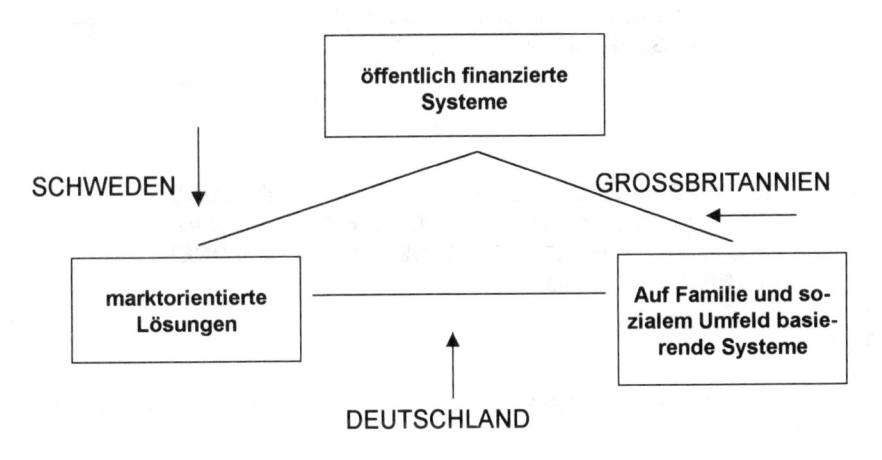

Quelle: Socialstyrelsen 1991, S. 10

Die drei Basismodelle sozialer Fürsorge stehen in den drei Ländern offensichtlich unter großem Druck. Bei einigen Aspekten bewegen sie sich aufeinander zu, bei anderen halten sie aufgrund kultureller und historischer Unterschiede an ihren Hauptmerkmalen fest. Dennoch war der Weg, der nach dem 2. Weltkrieg eingeschlagen wurde, grundsätzlich derselbe: nach einer recht langen Zeit des Aufbaus und der Expansion folgte eine Zeit der Stagnation, der Kürzungen und Neubewertungen (Lindberg 1998). Die Bedrohungen entstehen sowohl außerhalb als auch innerhalb der Sozialpolitiksysteme.

DISKUSSIONSSTOFF FÜR DIE STUDENTEN:

- Was sind die historischen und kulturellen Aspekte, die die Entwicklung der sozialpolitischen Systeme beeinflußt haben?

- Die Höhe der Leistungen und der Grad der Deckung sind zwei wichtige Aspekte bei den Sozialfürsorgevereinbarungen. Sie unterscheiden sich jedoch in den drei Ländern. Geben Sie Beispiele und diskutieren Sie diese Unterschiede.

- Sind die Sozialsysteme in den drei beteiligten Ländern dabei, sich aneinander anzunähern? Wenn ja, zeigen Sie, wie sich das äußert.

- Die europäische Zusammenarbeit intensiviert sich. Was bedeutet dies für die Systeme der Sozialpolitik?

3.2.4.3 GESETZESGRUNDLAGEN ZUR SOZIALPOLITIK UND SPEZIELLE REGELUNGEN UND VORSCHRIFTEN IN BEZUG AUF BEHINDERTE MENSCHEN IN DEN DREI BETEILIGTEN LÄNDERN

Deutschland

In Deutschland gibt es im besonderen vier Gesetze, die die soziale Fürsorgepolitik steuern.

1. Grundlegende Bedeutung hat der Artikel 3.1 des *„Grundgesetzes"*, in dem es heißt: "Niemand darf wegen seiner Behinderung benachteiligt werden."

2. Das *„Bundes-Sozial-Hilfe-Gesetz"*(BSHG) beinhaltet Paragraphen über unterschiedliche Fürsorgeleistungen in den unterschiedlichsten Lebenssituationen.

3. Das „Betreuungsgesetz" regelt Angelegenheiten, die in Zusammenhang mit der Pflege von beeinträchtigten und behinderten Menschen stehen. Es gewährt ihnen persönliche Hilfe und Unterstützung, wenn diese notwendig sind.

4. Im „Kinder-Jugend-Hilfe-Gesetz" (KJHG) sind Paragraphen über das Recht von Kindern und Jugendlichen auf Schutz und verschiedene Arten der Unterstützung verankert. Diese Leistungen werden von den Behörden und auch von anderen Organisationen übernommen.

England

In England bilden die folgenden vier Grundsätze die Basis für die Steuerung des sozialpolitischen Systems:

1. Das Behindertendiskriminierungsgesetz von 1995. Der erste Teil gibt Definitionen über Behinderungen, der zweite Teil widmet sich Beschäftigungsfragen, und der dritte Teil regelt Angelegenheiten von Gütern und Leistungen.

2. Das Gesetz für chronisch kranke und behinderte Personen von 1970

3. Das Bildungsgesetz von 1998

4. Der Tomlinson-Bericht von 1946

Schweden

In Schweden sind hauptsächlich die folgenden drei Gesetze von großer Bedeutung:

1. Das Sozialgesetz von 1982. Es beinhaltet die Grundrechte der Menschen, die Hilfe zu bekommen, die sie benötigen und die bedingungslose Verantwortung des Staates, Hilfe, Fürsorge und Unterstützung zu gewähren.

2. Das Gesetz zu Gesundheits- und Medizinaldiensten von 1981. Es regelt das Gesundheitsfürsorgesystem, das von Regional- und Kommunalkörperschaften geleitet wird.

3. Das Gesetz zur Unterstützung und Dienstleistung für Personen mit bestimmten funktionalen Schädigungen (1994) sichert behinderten und beeinträchtigten Menschen besondere Unterstützung zu.

Abgesehen von diesen nationalen Gesetzen in Deutschland, Großbritannien und Schweden sind aber auch die globalen Statements der Weltgesundheitsorganisation über Menschenrechte im allgemeinen und über behinderte und beeinträchtigte Menschen im besonderen maßgeblich. Die Salamanca-Erklärung der UNESCO ist auch eine grundlegende Quelle bezüglich der Menschenrechte gerade für diese Bevölkerungsgruppen.

3.2.4.4 WIE SIEHT DIE REALITÄT AUS?

In allen drei Staaten gibt es gut funktionierende Sozialfürsorgesysteme. Dennoch bedeutet das leider nicht, daß tatsächlich alle Menschen mit der Hilfe und Unterstützung rechnen können, die sie brauchen, um ihr Leben bestmöglich zu gestalten.

Es reicht nicht, sich nur auf politischem Parkett zu bewegen. Es ist wichtig, daß diese Ansätze auch mit empirischen Studien über die tatsächliche Fürsorge und deren Verteilung kombiniert werden. Die Studenten in den drei Ländern werden daher aufgefordert, Daten über Lebensbedingungen von bedürftigen Personen und Personengruppen zu sammeln und auszuwerten.

Das kann auf folgende Art und Weise geschehen:

1. durch Statistikstudien über die Wohlfahrt und die Verteilung von Fürsorgezuwendungen in der Bevölkerung

2. durch das Studium von Forschungsberichten über unterschiedliche Aspekte der Fürsorge oder der fehlenden Fürsorge für besondere Gruppen

3. durch das Studium von allgemeinen Presseartikeln

4. durch Interviews mit Vertretern von Organisationen oder mit Einzelpersonen, die Mitglieder hilfsbedürftiger Gruppen sind (wie z.B. Drogenabhängige, behinderte Menschen, notleidende Rentner und Familien in Not)

Jede Gruppe der Studenten kann allein entscheiden, welchen Weg der Informationsbeschaffung sie wählt und wie sie die gesammelten Informationen verarbeitet.

3.2.4.5 POLITIK CONTRA PRAXIS!

Dieser Teil dient dem Vergleich. Der Inhalt offizieller Dokumente soll mit den von den Studenten gesammelten realen Daten verglichen werden. Hier können auch Probleme der adäquaten Informationsbeschaffung besprochen werden.

DISKUSSIONSSTOFF FÜR DIE STUDENTEN:

- Repräsentiert das gesammelte Material wirklich die Situation der Pflege und Unterstützung bedürftiger Menschen?

- Inwieweit unterscheidet sich die Sozialpolitik unter den Gesichtspunkten, die verglichen wurden, von der tatsächlichen Praxis?

- Wenn man die verschiedenen Modelle der Sozialpolitik betrachtet: was kann über die unterschiedlichen Möglichkeiten ausgesagt werden, die jeweilige Bedürfnislage zu befriedigen?

3.2.5 AUFGABEN

- Ausgehend von dem Text in diesem Abschnitt sollten Sie Ihr Wissen über unterschiedliche Modelle der Sozialpolitik vertiefen.

- Untersuchen Sie allgemeine Aspekte der Sozialpolitik Ihres eigenen Landes in Kürze, und gehen Sie bei ausgewählten Aspekten etwas mehr ins Detail.

- Sammeln Sie empirisches Material über die Realität der Fürsorge von einigen ausgewählten bedürftigen Personengruppen.

- Vergleichen Sie kritisch die Sozialpolitik mit der tatsächlichen Situation dieser Gruppen.

- Betrachten Sie die negativen und positiven Konsequenzen der unterschiedlichen Sozialpolitikmodelle bezogen auf deren Fähigkeit, die Bedürfnislage zu befriedigen.

- Gestalten Sie ein Portfolio, das die Ergebnisse Ihres Vergleichs darstellt.

Die geleistete Arbeit der Studenten der drei beteiligten Hochschulen wird untereinander ausgetauscht, damit ein grenzüberschreitender Vergleich angestellt werden kann und jeder vom anderen etwas über die Unterschiede in der Sozialpolitik und die Widersprüche zwischen Politik und Praxis lernen kann.

3.2.6 BIBLIOGRAPHIE

3.2.6.1 LITERATURHINWEISE

Lindberg, I. (1998) Vägval i välfärdspolitik. LO Debatt
Mishra, R. (1990) The Welfare State in Capitalist Society. London: Harvester Wheatsheaf
Nygren, L. (1994) Trygghet under omprövning. Stockholm: Publica
Salonen, T. (1994) Välfärdens marginaler. Stockholm: Publica Social laws, from Germany, England and Sweden
Socialstyrelsen (1991) Vård och omsorg i sex europeiska länder. Rapport 1991:37. Stockholm: Allmänna förlaget.
Socialstyrelsen (1997) Social Rapport 1997. SoS-rapport 1997:14. Stockholm: Fritzes
Sullivan, M. (1992) The Politics of Social Policy. London: Harvester Wheatsheaf
Titmuss, M. (1974) Social policy - an introduction. London: George Allen & Unwin Ltd.
Trost, H. (1991) Sverige, EG-ismen och socialpolitiken. Stockholm: Verdandi Förlag

3.2.6.2 ZUSÄTZLICHE LITERATUR

Kaurmann, F.-X. (1997) Herausforderungen des Sozialstaats. Frankfurt/Main, edition Suhrkamp 2053.

Schmidt, M. G. (1988) Sozialpolitik. Historische und internationale Entwicklung im Vergleich. Opladen, Leske & Budrich

Schmid, J. (1996) Wohlfahrtsstaaten im Vergleich. Soziale Sicherungssysteme in Europa: Organisation, Finanzierung, Leistungen und Probleme. Opladen, Leske & Budrich.

Hughes B. and
Patterson K. (1997) The Social Model of Disability and the Disappearing Body; towards a sociology of impairment, *Disability and Society*, Vol 12,3,325-240

Shakespeare,T. and
Watson, N. (1997) Defending the Social Model of Disability, *Disability and Society*, 12,2,293

3.3 MACHT, POLITIK UND DIE EINBEZIEHUNG VON BETROFFENEN

Åse - Britt Falch

3.3.1 EINLEITUNG

Dieser Teil des 3. Kapitels beschäftigt sich mit den Fragen der Befürwortung der Einbeziehung von Betroffenen (in ihre eigenen Angelegenheiten) und des Empowerments. Während der letzten Jahre hat ein Umdenken stattgefunden, wie man Menschen mit Behinderung gegenübertritt. Von der Ansicht, daß es sich um eine Gruppe handelt, um die sich Fachkräfte zu kümmern haben - denn behinderte Menschen wurden bislang als eine Gruppe angesehen, die unfähig ist, Verantwortung für ihr eigenes Leben zu übernehmen - wandelte sich das Bild zu einer Gruppe von Individuen, die ihre eigene Macht haben.

Wenn man Menschen mit Behinderung als Individuen mit eigener Macht betrachtet, so verändert das auch die Fürsorge und die Sozialarbeit. Für professionelle Fachkräfte ist es wichtig zu lernen, wie Einzelpersonen und Gruppen mit sozialen, psychischen oder körperlichen Behinderungen zur Hilfe durch Selbsthilfe gebracht werden können und zu erkennen, welche Rolle und Aufgabe Gruppen/Organisationen „von" behinderten Menschen im Gegensatz zu Gruppen und Organisationen „für" behinderte Menschen zu erfüllen haben. Die Sozialarbeit von heute ist auch dazu da, Betroffenenprofile zu erstellen und umzusetzen.

Man muß Menschen mit Behinderung als Individuen und Experten ihres eigenen Lebens betrachten. Wenn man behinderten Menschen gegenübersteht, ist es wichtig zu erkennen, daß es sich dabei um Menschen mit eigenen Fähigkeiten handelt. Lebensqualität und eigener Antrieb sind wichtige Fragen, mit denen man sich auseinandersetzen muß, wenn man behinderte Menschen trifft. Jedes Individuum hat, wie es der alte emeritierte Professor der Sozialarbeit Harald Swedner definiert hat, ein Recht auf „eine gute Reise durch das Leben" (Swedner, 1983).

Auch wenn man behinderte Menschen als Individuen betrachtet, so muß man doch auch die Kraft der Gruppe dahinter sehen. Dabei spielt der Gedanke mit, daß sich Menschen mit gleichen Problemen organisieren könnten und Forderungen Kraft und Macht verleihen, wodurch sie in Arenen streiten könnten, in die ein Einzelner von ihnen keinen Zutritt hätte. Menschen mit ähnlichen Problemen können sich durch das Teilen und die aktive Anteilnahme an den Problemen auf eine Art und Weise gegenseitig helfen und unterstützen, wie es professionelle Helfer nicht imstande zu tun sind. Selbsthilfegruppen sind durch die Erfahrung des Teilens der gleichen Probleme auf der ganzen Welt entstanden. Eltern behinderter Kinder, Drogenabhängige, Menschen, die während ihrer Kindheit mißbraucht wurden und Menschen mit Zerebralparese stellen nur einige Beispiele für Gruppen dar, die sich zur Selbsthilfe zusammengeschlossen haben einander zu unterstützen und dadurch stärker geworden sind, ihre Rechte einzufordern.

Unterstützung finden behinderte Menschen auch in Wohlfahrtsorganisationen, die häufig einen religiösen Hintergrund haben. Diese Organisationen sind mit guten Absichten gegründet worden, nämlich Menschen mit Behinderung zu helfen. Heute kommen jedoch Stimmen auf, die besagen, daß man als Behinderter nicht um Wohlfahrt bitten sollte. Die Gesellschaft sollte verpflichtet werden, jedem Mitglied, ob behindert oder nicht, die gleichen gesetzlichen Rechte einzuräumen, was bedeutet, unter den gleichen Bedingungen leben zu können. Um diese Rechte zu bekommen, sind Organisationen *von* behinderten Menschen und nicht *für* behinderte Menschen ins Leben gerufen worden.

Es gibt Modelle mit dem Ziel, Gruppenprozesse in Gruppen mit behinderten Menschen in Gang zu setzen, um diesen Gruppen mehr Kräfte zu verleihen und sie dabei zu unterstützen, eigene Problemlösungen zu finden. Ein wichtiger Aspekt in der Praxis war, Selbsthilfegruppen bei deren Gründung unterstützend zur Seite zu stehen. Dabei haben Sozialarbeiter Gruppen unterstützt, die die gleiche Problemlage aufwiesen und sich gegenseitig helfen konnten. Aus diesen Gruppen erwachsen nicht selten Antworten und neue Ideen, wie Dienste noch verbessert werden könnten. Diese Ideen werden dann von den Gruppen entweder selbst in die Hand genommen oder die medizinischen und sozialen Dienste werden gedrängt, ihre Praktiken zu ändern. Für dieses Phänomen gibt es verschiedene Ausdrücke: selbstbestimmte Gruppenarbeit, Selbsthilfegruppen und teilhabendes Handeln sind nur einige der verwendeten Ausdrücke. In diesem Zusammenhang gibt es auch eine besondere Art von Forschungsprojekten, die partizipative Forschungen genannt werden.

In der Sozialarbeit gibt es eine lange Tradition, nach zwei unterschiedlichen Modellen zu arbeiten, eines zur Vermeidung der Individualisierung und eines zur Förderung der Gruppenarbeit. Diese beiden Modelle gehen auf Pioniere auf dem Gebiet der Sozialarbeit zurück, nämlich auf Mary Richmond und Jane Addams, die am Anfang des Jahrhunderts in den USA lebten. Mary Richmond, entwickelte ihr „Friendly Visitors"-Modell und ihre Einführung in die soziale Einzelarbeit, die „soziale Diagnose". Die andere Frau war Jane Addams.

Sie begründete die Settlementbewegung (Ausgleichsbewegung) und arbeitete fortwährend mitten in der Gesellschaft, um unterdrückten Gruppen Kraft zu geben. Sie betrachtete soziale Probleme im übrigen als Konsequenz der gesamten Gesellschaftsorganisation (Soydan, 1994).

Noch heute gibt es Diskussionen darüber, wie man Menschen mit besonderen Bedürfnissen helfen kann. Die Sozialarbeit und die Sozialfürsorge stehen auch heutzutage vor den Aufgaben, Einzelpersonen und Gruppen zu stärken und ihnen unterstützend zur Seite zu stehen. Erkennen kann man dies an Modellen von Gemeinwesenarbeit und psychosozialen Modellen auf dem Gebiet der Sozialarbeit. Gemeinwesenarbeit hat oft die Ambition, in der Gesellschaft in Erscheinung zu treten, d. h. nah beim „Klienten" zu sein und die Gruppen darin zu bestärken, ihr Leben selbst in die Hand zu nehmen.

In dem Kontext der Unterstützung von Einzelpersonen und Gruppen ist auf dem Feld der Sozialfürsorge und der Sozialarbeit ist es weit verbreitet, von Empowerment und Vertretung zu sprechen. Malcom Payne definiert Empowerment und Vertretung folgendermaßen (1997, Seite 266):

"Durch Empowerment versucht man den Klienten Kraft zur Entscheidung und Handlung über ihr eigenes Leben zu geben. Dabei sollen die Einflüsse sozialer Fürsorge und persönlicher Blockaden reduziert und das Vertrauen in eigenes Vermögen und Selbstbewußtsein geschult werden. Um das zu erreichen, wird versucht, die Kraft aus der Umwelt der Klienten zu schöpfen. Die Vertretung versucht, die Interessen kraft- und machtloser Klienten gegenüber mächtigen Personen und sozialen Strukturen geltend zu machen."

Die Definition von Payne ist eine gute Einführung in den folgenden Teil dieses Kapitels, bei dem es um Macht, Politik und Einbeziehung der Betroffenen geht.

3.3.2 ZIELE

Von den Studenten wird erwartet:

- verschiedene Arten der Vertretung in bezug auf Behinderung, Lern- und Lebensschwierigkeiten und Benachteiligung zu identifizieren,
- die Begriffe „Macht" und „Empowerment" in bezug auf Behinderung und Benachteiligung kritisch zu bewerten,

- die Rolle und Funktion von Gruppen/Organisationen „für" beeinträchtigte Menschen und „von" beeinträchtigten Menschen kritisch zu untersuchen.

Die Arbeiten können folgendermaßen strukturiert werden:

- Präsentation von Fakten in der Form von Literatur (wird hier bereitgestellt) und Vorlesungen
- Selbststudium empfohlener Literatur
- Feldstudien, Besuche von entsprechenden Organisationen und Interviews mit Betroffenen
- Seminare über die Feldstudien in Verbindung mit theoretischen Grundlagen aus der Literatur

3.3.3 LERNERGEBNISSE

Am Ende dieses Abschnitts werden von den Studenten folgende Fähigkeiten erwartet:

- die Konzepte „Vertretung" und „Empowerment" und deren Bedeutung in bezug auf benachteiligte Gruppen zu verstehen

- auf der Ebene von Gemeinwesenarbeit Selbsthilfegruppen gründen und organisieren zu können

3.3.4 FÜRSPRACHE, GRUPPENARBEIT UND EMPOWERMENT

3.3.4.1 VERSCHIEDENE KONZEPTE UND HINTERGRÜNDE VON FÜRSPRACHE UND EMPOWERMENT

Das Konzept des Empowerments entstand in den 70er Jahren in den USA und galt ursprünglich der lokalen Entwicklung und Mobilisierung von Gruppen benachteiligter Menschen. Die Sozialarbeit versuchte so strategisch neue Wege in der Arbeit mit benachteiligten Gruppen zu gehen. Voher hatte es die sogenannten Top-Down-Strategie gegeben, die nun in eine Bottom-Up-Strategie umgekehrt werden sollte. Das heißt, daß den Gruppierungen mehr Einfluß gewährt wurde. Großen Wert legte man zudem auf das Betroffenenprofil (Forsberg, Starrin, 1997).

Am Anfang hatte es einen radikalen politischen Anflug, wenn man über Empowerment sprach. Heutzutage gibt es diesen radikalen und politischen Touch nicht mehr in der damaligen Intensität. Der Begriff Empowerment wird in vielerlei Bedeutungen verwendet, aber grundsätzlich hat er immer eine positive Einfärbung. Das äußert sich in der Weise, daß es etwas damit zu tun hat, Menschen mit besonderen Bedürfnissen, die aus Benachteiligung entstanden sind, Kraft zu geben. Das können Gruppen mit unterschiedlichen Behinderungen sein. Sie können wirtschaftlicher, gesetzlicher, medizinischer oder soziologischer Natur sein. Die Gemeinsamkeit liegt darin, daß alle durch eine Bottom-Up-Strategie bestärkt werden müssen. Diese Strategie wird auch häufig als „Empowerment to groups" bezeichnet.

Wie man sehen kann, ist Empowerment eine gesellschaftliche Bewegung, die behinderten Menschen ihre Entscheidungsfreiheit zurückgeben möchte. Während der letzten 50 Jahre haben professionelle Fachkräfte und die Gesellschaft mehr und mehr die Verantwortung übernommen, die zuvor bei den Familien und Einzelnen lag. Man könnte durchaus behaupten, daß dies ein negativer Effekt der Sozialreformen während dieser Zeit war. Empowerment kann in gewisser Weise als eine Bewegung in Richtung sozialen Planens angesehen werden, die jedoch erst während der letzten Phase der Sozialreformen gesellschaftlich relevant wurde.

Soziale Reformen und ausgeprägte soziale Strategien sind durchaus positiv zu bewerten, jedoch können sie auch den Effekt haben, den Bürgern ein Stück weit die Macht nehmen. Der Staat kann seinerseits agieren und wirkt somit fast paternalistisch (bevormundend). Dies bedeutet, daß der Staat zwar die Sorge über den Einzelnen übernimmt, ihn jedoch zugleich auch beschränkt. Das könnte dazu führen, daß man sich von den professionellen Fachkräften der Sozialfürsorge und Sozialarbeit wie ein Kind behandelt fühlt und auch so behandelt wird. Das wiederum könnte dazu führen, daß behinderte Menschen ihr Selbstbewußtsein verlieren und Schwierigkeiten damit haben, ihre eigene Stärke zu erkennen. Dies ist ein Grund dafür, warum das Prinzip des Empowerments 1998 so populär ist.

Das Prinzip des Empowerments kann ebenfalls mit Gemeinwesenarbeit und Entwicklung auf lokaler Ebene in Verbindung gebracht werden. Es ist ebenfalls verbunden mit dem Prinzip der Hilfe zur Selbsthilfe. Man kann den Begriff

Empowerment ebenfalls verwenden, um lokale Autonomie und Selbstverwaltung im Bezug auf Prävention und Intervention zu beginnen und zu unterstützen.

Eine der ersten, die den Begriff Empowerment beschrieben haben, waren Barbara Solomon (1976) und Stephanie Riger (1981). Solomon beschrieb die Mobilisierung der Schwarzen (black people), und Riger widmete sich der Emanzipation der Frau. Ein oft zitierter Artikel ist der von Rappaport (1981). Dieser Artikel kritisiert das klassische Präventionsmodell und versucht, Alternativen zu diesem Modell zu liefern. Etwas später (1987), veröffentlichten Swift und Lewin einen Artikel über Empowerment und geistige Gesundheit (Forsberg, Starrin 1997).

Heutzutage kann man sagen, daß Empowerment ein in vielen verschiedenen Kontexten verwendetes Schlagwort ist, das verschiedene Bedeutungen in sich vereint. Es ist ein sehr populäres Wort, jedoch ist es schwer zu definieren. Allgemein kann man sicherlich sagen, daß Empowerment etwas durchweg Positives darstellt und daß es sich lohnt, danach zu streben. Wenn man amerikanische Wörterbücher zu Rate zieht, wird man zwei verschiedene Bedeutungen vorfinden:

1. jemandem Macht oder Autorität verleihen
2. jemandem Möglichkeiten bieten oder Erlaubnis erteilen

Das Wort „Empowerment" hat seine Wurzeln in dem lateinischen und in dem Wort „potere", was soviel bedeutet wie fähig sein, etwas zu tun. Man kann erkennen, daß es sich um ein aktives Wort handelt und daß es nichts damit zu tun hat, um etwas zu bitten. Man kann sagen, daß es die Bedeutung von „Macht übernehmen" beinhaltet. Es ist jedoch eigentlich viel leichter zu sagen, was „empower" nicht bedeutet, als zu sagen, was es ist. Es hat absolut nichts zu tun mit Entfremdung, Hilflosigkeit, Hoffnungslosigkeit und Machtlosigkeit. Es steht im Grunde genommen für soziale Unterstützung, Selbstvertrauen, Kompetenz, Autonomie, Selbstkontrolle, Staatsbürgerschaft und Stolz (Forsberg, Starrin 1997).

Wenn man von Empowerment spricht, hinterfragt man allgemein auch die Rolle der professionellen Helfer. Diese machen häufig den Eindruck, daß sie über ein Wissens- und Kompetenzmonopol verfügen, behinderten Menschen in ihrem täglichen Leben zu helfen. Wenn es um Empowerment geht, geht es jedoch primär darum, Menschen mit Behinderung die Macht zurückzugeben. Es geht darum zu verstehen, daß sie die Experten für ihr Leben sind, ob sie nun behindert sind oder nicht.

Oft hört man von Diskussionen, daß Professionelle die Lebensplanung von behinderten Menschen übernehmen. Als ein behinderter Mensch bekommt man das Gefühl, keine Macht über das eigene Leben zu haben. Viele behinderte Personen haben Worte dafür gefunden und auch erklärt, daß das Resultat dieser Behandlung ist, daß sie kein gutes Leben haben und sich abhängig fühlen.

Wenn man aktiv in einer Organisation mitwirkt und dem Prinzip des Empowerments folgt, dann kann das bewirken, daß die gesamte Organisation von Hierarchien befreit wird. Man beachtet, daß jeder Mensch die gleichen Rechte hat und man erfährt, welche Kraft man hat, wenn man Seite an Seite arbeitet. Man hat plötzlich ein gemeinsames Ziel, nämlich den Kampf um Menschenrechte und den Respekt für sich selbst und für die Gruppe, in der man wirkt. Autoritätsgedanken, Vormundschaft und Einflüsse seitens der Professionellen spielen keine Rolle und die Bottom-Up-Perspektive setzt sich durch. Man glaubt fest daran, daß es Möglichkeiten der Mobilisierung gibt, danach zu streben, wonach man, behindert oder nicht, zu streben berechtigt ist (Forsberg, Starrin 1997).

Um bei sozialen Handlungen und der Mobilisierung von Gruppen für behinderte Menschen erfolgreich zu sein, ist es notwendig, ein Gefühl der gemeinsamen Identifikation und des Stolzes zu schaffen. Viele behinderte Menschen haben ein Gefühl der Stigmatisierung und der Scham, was dazu führen kann, daß man sich hinter seiner eigenen Fassade versteckt. Bei Empowerment ist festzustellen, daß die Gefühle der Stigmatisierung und der Scham verschwinden. Man gewinnt die Stärke zurück, sich offen in der Gesellschaft zu zeigen. Wenn die Klienten nicht auf ihre Kraft aufmerksam gemacht werden, werden sie sie nie zu nutzen wissen. Gruppen, die unterdrückt werden, können dann sehr stark werden, wenn alle Gruppenkräfte mobilisiert werden können. Das kann allerdings auch dazu führen, daß Gruppen soziale Aktionen durchführen, um ihre Rechte einzufordern, die illegal sind. Die Loyalität und Solidarität der Gruppe wird stärker als das Gesetz der Gesellschaft.

Der Begriff „Vertretung" (Fürsprache) kann als ein Aspekt von Empowerment angesehen werden und zwar in der Hinsicht, daß er dazu verwandt werden kann, für die Hilfe für unterdrückte Bevölkerungsgruppen zu kämpfen. Historisch gesehen ist es wohl eher ein Aspekt der Arbeit für Wohlfahrtsgerechtigkeit. Die Vertretung (Fürsprache) hat sich als der starke Teil der Bewegung entwickelt, der die Entlassung vieler Leute aus der Dauerpflege in Heimen bewirkte. Dies ist eine Arbeit für Rechte und Gerechtigkeit in der Fürsorge (Payne, 1997).

Professionelle Helfer, Sozialarbeiter und „Vertreter" haben im Auftrag behinderter Personen mit ihren eigenen und anderen Institutionen gerungen, um für benachteiligte Gruppen soziale und gesetzliche Gerechtigkeit zu bekommen. Es gab jedoch auch kritische Stimmen zu diesen Vorgehensweisen von Personen, die meinten, daß solche Dinge wohl besser von den Betroffenen durchgefochten werden sollten – in einer Art Selbst- oder Gruppenvertretung. Wie auch immer, ebenso wie es die traditionelle Rolle des professionellen Helfers ist, im Auftrag des Klienten zu arbeiten, können Helfer als formelle Vertreter handeln, indem sie den Instruktionen der Klienten folgen. (Payne, 1997).

Macht, die von einem Sozialarbeiter gegeben wird, überträgt sich in der Regel auch auf die Klienten, die diese Macht übernehmen müssen, und es ist die Rolle der Sozialarbeit, die Antworten der Institutionen zu organisieren, was diese Machtübernahme erst möglich macht. Wenn es dann geschieht, soll es die Sozialarbeit akzeptieren. Ideen wie die Normalisierung und die „Selbstvertretung" sind oft mit Perspektiven bürgerlicher Freiheiten im Hinblick auf die Bedürfnisse freier Klienten in Verbindung gebracht worden. Man nahm an, daß diese Rechte unterdrückt würden, da die Klienten von der Fürsorge abhängig seien (Payne, 1997).

In den Universitäten, die Sozialpfleger und Sozialarbeiter ausbilden, wird oftmals verbreitet, daß man zu „Anwälten der Armen" ausgebildete werde. Das heißt, daß eine gute Wissensgrundlage in Rechtsfragen und in bezug auf das Sozialsystem von großer Bedeutung sind, wenn man unterdrückten Bevölkerungsgruppen zu ihren Rechten verhelfen möchte. Das Arbeiten als „Anwalt" sollte zum alltäglichen Arbeitstag eines heutigen Sozialarbeiters dazugehören.

Ein weiterer wichtiger Punkt ist, daß man immer den Klienten in den Mittelpunkt stellen sollte. Nur so kann man die Klienten verstehen und sie in den Arbeitsprozeß einbeziehen. Diese Frage ist heute von besonders großer Bedeutung, da sich die wirtschaftlichen Situationen verschlechtern und daher die Professionellen aufgefordert sind, so wenig wie möglich das Geld der Kommunen in den Organisationen für Sozialfürsorge auszugeben. Daher ist es möglich, daß behinderte Menschen aus diesen Gründen Schwierigkeiten haben können, ihre Rechte und die Möglichkeit auf ein normales Leben in der Gesellschaft zu bekommen. Im Moment sieht es so aus, als wenn die Professionellen in Zukunft immer mehr als „Anwälte" arbeiten werden müssen, um behinderten Menschen zu helfen, ihre Rechte zu bekommen.

3.3.4.2 GRUPPENARBEIT, GRUPPENPROZESSE, SELBSTHILFEGRUPPEN UND SELBSTBESTIMMTE GRUPPENARBEIT

Eine sehr wichtige Praxis auf dem Gebiet der Sozialarbeit und der Sozialfürsorge stellt die Gründung und die Unterstützung von Gruppen von und für behinderte Menschen dar. Als Arbeiter für die Gemeinschaft wird vom Sozialarbeiter erwartet, daß er Klientengruppen mit ähnlichen Problemen unterstützt, damit diese sich gegenseitige Unterstützung geben können. Aus diesen Gruppen erwachsen nicht selten Antworten und neue Ideen, wie die Dienste verbessert werden können. Diese Ideen werden dann entweder selbst in die Hand genommen, oder die medizinischen und sozialen Dienste werden gedrängt, ihre Praktiken zu ändern (Payne, 1997).

Gruppenarbeit kann auf unterschiedliche Art und Weisen beschrieben und zu unterschiedlichen Zwecken entwickelt werden. Das Prinzip der Gruppenarbeit ist auf allen Gebieten der Pädagogik sehr verbreitet. Es ist bekannt, daß es ein guter Weg ist, Denkweisen zu verändern, ein soziales Gefühl der Gemeinschaft zu entwickeln, Verständnis zu gewinnen und das Lernen zu vereinfachen. Sie kann aber ebenso auf politischer Ebene eingesetzt werden, um beispielsweise Druck auf die Gesellschaft auszuüben, damit diese sich ändert. Selbsthilfegruppen sind eine fortgeschrittene Form der Gruppenarbeit. Dort kommt der Gruppenarbeit ein sozialer Aspekt zu.

Was passiert in den Gruppen? Sobald mehrere Menschen in einer Gruppe zusammen sind, entwickelt sich ein Prozeß, der Gruppenprozeß genannt wird. Es ist jedoch etwas kompliziert zu beschreiben, was einen Gruppenprozeß ausmacht. Es ist ein für jedes Gruppenmitglied spürbares Gefühl, wenn die Gruppe die Möglichkeit hatte, gemeinsam zu arbeiten. Man kann sagen, daß ein Gruppenprozeß das ist, was in der Gruppe passiert; dazu gehören auch verschiedene Beziehungen, die sich zwischen den Gruppenmitgliedern ergeben. Der Gruppenprozeß ist so etwas wie eine Kooperation; er macht verschiedene Bedeutungen und Aspekte, neues Wissen, Unterstützung, Identifikation, Gefühle, Gemeinschaft und ein Gefühl von Teilen sichtbar. Oft ist es nicht einfach, einen positiven Gruppenprozeß zu erreichen, es ist also möglich, daß Gruppenarbeit auch negative Ergebnisse zutage bringt. Die Mitglieder werden verunsichert, die Arbeit in der Gruppe erzeugt schlechte und unbefriedigende Gefühle. Daher ist es wichtig, sich dieser negativen Seite von Gruppenarbeit und Gruppenprozessen bewußt zu sein. Hilfreich in diesen Situationen kann eine sogenannte Supervision sein, die die Probleme der Gruppe offen auf den Tisch bringt und dabei hilft, wieder in einen positiven Gruppenprozeß zu kommen.

Wenn man über Gruppen und Gruppenprozesse für unterdrückte Gruppen spricht, geht der Gedanke fast automatisch über zu Selbsthilfegruppen. Es wird in diesem Zusammenhang auch oft von „selbstbestimmter Gruppenarbeit" gesprochen. Bei Selbsthilfegruppen können die Ziele der Gruppenarbeit in sechs Punkten zusammengefaßt werden:

1. Sich aus der Isolation befreien
2. Soziale Anpassung fördern
3. Auf Lebensveränderungen oder Krisen vorbereiten
4. Persönliche oder familiäre Probleme lösen
5. Probleme im Umfeld aufspüren und lösen
6. Einblick, Verständnis und Wissen über Probleme gewinnen

(Heap, 1987)

Bei der Gründung einer Selbsthilfegruppe ist es wichtig, Techniken zu beachten, um den Start so gut wie möglich zu gestalten. Um eine gute Kommunikation und Interaktion zu erreichen, sollte die Gruppenstärke 6 bis 10 Mitglieder nicht übersteigen, sie sollte also nicht zu groß sein. Von einer Selbsthilfegruppe sollten nicht zwangsläufig Ergebnisse erwartet werden (Heap, 1987). Wichtig ist nur, was in der Gruppe passiert, daß sich die Gruppe gegenseitig unterstützt und auffängt. Daher ist es das Beste, wenn die Gruppenmitglieder die gleichen Probleme haben. Für behinderte Menschen kann es sehr wichtig sein, daß über Stigmatisierung und Scham gesprochen wird. Diskussionen in der Gruppe lassen ein Gefühl der Geborgenheit aufkommen und lassen den Einzelnen gestärkt heraustreten, um Verantwortung in der Gesellschaft zu übernehmen. Elterngruppen behinderter Kinder finden in Selbsthilfegruppen sehr viel Hilfe und Verständnis für die eigene Situation, da über ähnliche Probleme gesprochen wird.

Wenn man einer Selbsthilfegruppe beitritt, sollte das aus einer eigenen Motivation heraus geschehen. Bei der Gründung von Selbsthilfegruppen sind professionelle Fachkräfte oft eine gute Hilfe, da sie mit ihren Erfahrungen dabei helfen können, die Gruppenarbeit in Gang zu bringen und Mittel und Wege aufzuzeigen, den Gruppenprozeß zu fördern. Dies sollte in der Rolle des „Supervisors" geschehen, wobei darauf zu achten ist, daß nicht zu sehr in den Gruppenprozeß eingegriffen wird.

Mullender und Wards bieten 1991 in ihrem Buch über „selbstbestimmte Gruppenarbeit: Betroffene unternehmen Schritte in Richtung des Empowerments" einen klaren Einblick in die Empowermenttheorie bei Gruppenarbeit und Gruppenprozessen. Sie schlagen Empowerment auch als Basis für ausgedehntere Formen sozialer Handlungen vor. Sie argumentieren, daß „empowernde" Handlungen selbstbestimmt geschehen sollten und vor allem Unterdrückung abgelehnt werden muß. Solch eine Definition bringt mit sich, daß Empowermentarbeit dem Wesen von Macht entgegensteht. Viele Ideen aus der Arbeit von Feministinnen und des Anti-Rassismus sind für die selbstbestimmte Gruppenarbeit von Relevanz. In den Dankesworten ihres Buches schreiben sie: „Dieses Buch ist aus den Anstrengungen vieler Gruppenarbeiter und Gruppenmitglieder geboren, die versucht haben, Wege der Zusammenarbeit zu finden, die frei sind von Unterdrückung."

Mullender und Wards sagen, daß der Prozeß des Empowerments unterdrückter Menschen am besten in Gruppen vonstatten geht, da bei individueller und auf der Familie basierender Arbeit zu sehr der private Ärger mit hineinspielt, der zu machtvoll ist, gemeinsame, soziale Antworten zu befördern. Gruppen erlauben es den Menschen, Ressourcen zu teilen und gemeinsam die Initiative zu ergreifen. Dies heißt auch gemeinsames Handeln zu erproben. Mullender und Wards zeigen dies anhand eines praxisnahen Modells des Empowerments in fünf Schritten:

1. *Vorplanung*: ein kompatibles, zusammenarbeitendes Team, eine beratende Unterstützung zu finden und eine Einigung über die „Empowermentprinzipien" herbeizuführen.
2. *Start*: sich mit Betroffenen auf partnerschaftlicher Basis zusammenschließen und die Gruppe offen planen.
3. *Aktionsvorbereitung der Gruppe*: der Gruppe helfen, ihre Themen zu entwickeln und die Frage aufzuwerfen, warum diese Probleme behandelt werden und wie Veränderungen herbeigeführt werden können.
4. *Aufnahme der Aktion*: Die Gruppe führt abgesprochene Aktionen aus.
5. *Übernahme*: Sozialarbeiter beginnen, sich zurückzuziehen, und die Gruppe betrachtet ihre Ergebnisse in Zusammenhang von Fragen nach dem Was, Warum und Wie. Dann werden neue Themen aufgebracht, man betrachtet die Gemeinsamkeiten und entscheidet sich für die eine oder andere Aktion. Dieser Prozeß setzt sich im Gruppenleben immer weiter fort.

(Payne 1997, S. 281)

Mullenders und Wards (1991) sprechen auch über fünf sogenannte Prinzipien der Empowermentpraxis:

1. Alle Personen haben Fertigkeiten, Verstand und Fähigkeiten. Man sollte eher diese zu erkennen versuchen als negative Eigenschaften zu beachten.

2. Menschen haben Rechte: insbesondere gehört zu werden, ihr eigenes Leben zu kontrollieren, selbst zu wählen, sich zu beteiligen oder nicht, Probleme aufzuwerfen und zu handeln.
3. Die Probleme der Personen repräsentieren immer Probleme von Unterdrückung, Politik, Wirtschaft, Macht ebenso wie persönliche Unzulänglichkeiten
4. Gemeinsame Aktionen können machtvoll sein, und die Praxis sollte darauf aufbauen.
5. Tatsächlich durchführen, was man propagiert anstatt zu „führen" und Unterdrückung herauszufordern.
(Payne, 1997, S. 281)

Selbsthilfegruppen und selbstbestimmte Gruppen haben gemeinsam, daß beide über die Einbeziehung der Betroffenen sprechen und daß Macht und Kraft entwickelt werden, wenn Menschen zusammenarbeiten, die die gleichen Erfahrungen teilen. Der Unterschied liegt darin, daß Selbsthilfegruppen mehr mit dem Ziel arbeiten, dem einzelnen Kraft zu geben, um mit dem eigenen Leben fertig zu werden. Selbstbestimmte Gruppen sind eher Aktionsgruppen, die gegen politische Unterdrückung angehen. Damit stärken sie Gruppen, um mehr Einfluß in der Gesellschaft zu bekommen und stärker zu sozialen Aktionsformen befähigt zu sein.

Wenn man Empowerment als eine Bewegung betrachtet, die die Unterdrückung behinderter und benachteiligter Gruppen bekämpft, kann man die Bedeutung von Gruppenarbeit, Gruppenprozessen, Selbsthilfegruppen und selbstbestimmten Gruppen verstehen. Als professioneller Helfer ist es nötig, Respekt walten zu lassen und den unterdrückten Gruppen die Möglichkeit einzuräumen, selbst die Verantwortung über ihr eigenes Leben zu übernehmen und zu verstehen, was es heißt, eine gute Lebensqualität zu erhalten.

ROISIN MULDOON

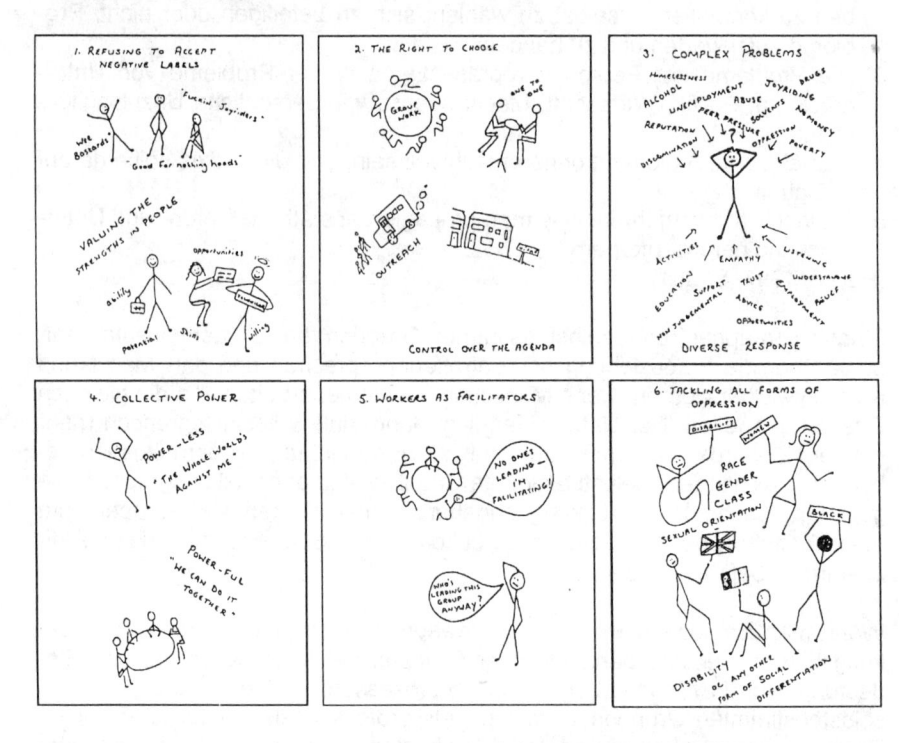

3.3.4.3 PARTIZIPATIVE FORSCHUNG UND EMPOWERMENT

Die Forschung hat auf die benachteiligten Gruppen aufmerksam gemacht. Den Wissenschaftlern zufolge resultiert die soziale Unterprivilegierung daraus, daß die Benachteiligungen und Defizite in der Fürsorge in Verbindung mit ungleichen Möglichkeiten und Chancen stehen. Die Weltgesundheitsorganisation (WHO) ist der Meinung, daß bessere Kooperation zwischen Wissenschaft und Praxis grundlegend wichtig ist. Wie oft werden diejenigen, die das Objekt von Forschung sind, über die Ergebnisse informiert? Wie oft erfahren die Gruppen überhaupt etwas über die Forschungen, die ihnen helfen könnten, etwas an ihrer Situation zu verändern? (Svensson, Starrin, 1992)

Wenn man mit Hilfe des Empowerments und unterschiedlichen Methoden arbeitet, um zu erreichen, daß unterdrückte Gruppen eigene Macht erhalten, dann ist partizipative Forschung eine hilfreiche Möglichkeit. Schon Lewin hat diese im Jahre 1946 als Aktionsforschung beschrieben, die es ermöglicht, praktische Probleme zu lösen und die soziale Veränderung in ihren Mittelpunkt zu rücken. Heutzutage ist die partizipative Forschung in Europa sehr verbreitet, jedoch wurde sie zuerst in der Dritten Welt angewendet. Aber auch wenn die Tradition der partizipativen Forschung in der Dritten Welt liegt, so gilt die partizipative Forschung in erster Linie den Nöten aller Menschen, die zu kämpfen haben und unterdrückt werden, ganz gleich, ob sie nun in Afrika oder in Europa leben.

Partizipative Forschung kann als Forschung, Ausbildung und handlungsorientierte Aktivität betrachtet werden. Eine der Hauptannahmen der partizipativen Forschung ist, daß sie sowohl für die Forschenden als auch für die Betroffenen, über die geforscht wird, zu Veränderungen führen wird. Partizipative Forschung ist hauptsächlich ein Projekt für diejenigen Menschen, deren Existenz gefährdet ist, die unterdrückt werden und in Armut leben. Das Ziel der partizipativen Forschung liegt darin, Strategien und Wege des Empowerment zu entwickeln. Kritik kam von seiten der konventionellen Wissenschaft. Sie behauptete, daß bei der partizipativen Forschung die Datenbeschaffung und – analyse nicht ausreichend systematisch vonstatten gehe. Dabei ist jedoch zu beachten, daß die wissenschaftliche Gesellschaft für gewöhnliche Menschen schnell irrelevant werden kann (Svensson, Starrin, 1992).

Anwender der partizipatorischen Forschungsmethode haben durch ihre Arbeit einige Grundprinzipien entwickelt. Sie sind als konzeptionelle und praktische Werkzeuge gedacht, jedoch sollte bemerkt werden, daß es kein absolutes Modell der partizipativen Forschung gibt. Die Prinzipien, auf die man sich allgemein geeinigt hat, sind von Hall im Jahre 1984 folgendermaßen formuliert worden:

1. Die Forschung sollte die Menschen von Beginn an in den gesamten Prozeß der Problemstellung, der Diskussion, der Informationsbeschaffung, der Analyse und der Verwendung der Ergebnisse im Kontext der Handlungen einbeziehen.
2. Die Forschung sollte in direkter und positiver Weise den beteiligten Personen zugute kommen.
3. Forschung ist ein systematischer Prozeß der Wissensbildung, der sowohl Personen mit oder ohne wissenschaftliche Ausbildung einbeziehen kann.
4. Wissen ist konkreter, ergiebiger und für die Gesellschaft nützlicher, wenn es gemeinschaftlich produziert wird.
5. Forschung vereint eine Kombination von Methoden, die geschaffen wurden, um einen sozialen, kooperativen und kollektiven Wissensaufbau zu erleichtern.
6. Forschung, Lernen und Wissensaufbau sind oftmals Aspekte desselben intellektuellen Prozesses im Kontext von Handlung (Hall, 1984, S. 291-292).

Wenn man die Hallschen Prinzipien betrachtet, kann man die Verbindung zwischen partizipativer Forschung und Empowerment nachvollziehen. Es handelt sich um eine Bottom-Up-Strategie, die es ermöglicht, Machtkonzepte unterdrückter Gruppen zu evaluieren. Beide weisen ein Profil der Betroffenen auf.

3.3.4.4 EINIGE BEISPIELE

In Dissertationen, Artikeln und Büchern kann man schnell Beispiele über Macht, Politik und die Einbeziehung der Betroffenen ausmachen. Es ist ein Bereich, der für Wissenschaftler, Sozialarbeiter und Betroffenenorganisationen mehr und mehr an Bedeutung gewonnen hat.

In „Disability, Handicap and Society" aus dem Jahre 1989 kann man einen Artikel von Brown und Ringma lesen, der mit „New disability services: the critical role of staff in a consumer-directed empowerment model for service for physically disabled people" überschrieben ist. Dieser Artikel berichtet über ein nicht institutionelles Dienstleistungsmodell und bewertet dieses. Es handelt sich um ein Wohngemeinschaftsmodell für körperbehinderte Menschen, bei dem versucht wird, Empowerment der Betroffenen zu erreichen.

Brown und Ringma beschreiben (1989) ein Projekt des Katholischen Fürsorgereferats in Brisbane, einer nicht staatlichen, freien Wohlfahrtsorganisation. Das Projekt beschreibt die Zusammenarbeit mit vier zuvor in Heimen lebenden, körperlich schwerbehinderten Erwachsenen, die nun gemeinsam in einer Wohngemeinschaft leben. Die Personen waren 18 bis 42 Jahre alt. Das Projekt hatte den Zweck, den Prozeß der Deinstitutionalisierung zu erleichtern und ein Wohngruppenmodell zu entwickeln, in dem die Bewohner die volle Kontrolle innehaben, neue Lebensfertigkeiten entwickeln und eine Integration in die Gemeinde erreichen können.

Das Projekt lief so ab, daß die vier Bewohner in alle Aspekte der Organisation und Verwaltung ihrer Wohngemeinschaft involviert waren. Sie bekamen die Verantwortung für die Führung des Haushalts und für die Anstellung von Personal übertragen. Durch das Projekt kann man sehen, daß Empowerment in allen Phasen verwandt wurde, um die Betroffenen einzubeziehen. Die gleichen Ansätze kann man in den USA und in Europa erkennen, wo auch Projekte von unterschiedlichen „unabhängigen Wohngemeinschaften" aufgebaut wurden. In diesen Gruppen übernehmen behinderte Personen die volle Verantwortung für ihr Leben und sehen sich selbst als Arbeitgeber für die Angestellten, die sie zum Leben in der Gesellschaft benötigen.

In Schweden hatte man 1994 das Gesetz zur Unterstützung und Fürsorge für Personen mit bestimmten funktionalen Schädigungen geschaffen (LSS). Dieses Gesetz gibt Menschen mit schweren körperlichen oder geistigen Behinderungen die Möglichkeit, ihre persönlichen „Assistenten" anzustellen. Dieses Gesetz wurde aufgrund starker Forderungen seitens verschiedener Behindertenorganisationen entworfen. Man kann sagen, daß das schwedische Gesetz (LSS) das Ergebnis von Empowerment und Mitwirkung von Betroffenen darstellt. Pressure - groups organisierten sich, formulierten das Gesetz und fochten es durch (Allmänna råd, Socialstyrelsen 1994:1).

Es sind mittlerweile auf der ganzen Welt Projekte ins Leben gerufen worden, die auf dem Konzept der Gemeinde getragenen Rehabilitation (Community Based Rehabilitation – CBR) beruhen. Das CBR schließt Rehabilitationsmaßnahmen auf Gemeindebasis ein. Es nutzt die Ressourcen der Gemeinschaft, baut auf diesen auf und schließt die geschädigten, beeinträchtigten und behinderten Menschen selbst, ihre Familien und Nachbarschaft mit ein. Behinderung wird als soziales Phänomen gesehen, das entsteht, wenn eine Person mit einer Schädigung oder Beeinträchtigung nicht die von der Gesellschaft vorgegebene Rolle erfüllen kann. Bei dieser Sichtweise sind Einstellungen, psychologische und körperliche Barrieren die ausschlaggebenden Faktoren.

Eine beeinträchtigte Person kann in einer Umgebung behindert sein, in einer anderen aber nicht.

CBR-Projekte sind mit einem starken Betroffenenprofil und mit Gruppen von behinderten Menschen begonnen worden. Die Rolle der professionellen Helfer liegt darin, sich im Hintergrund zu halten, Prozesse zu initiieren und nicht allzu sehr in die Geschehnisse einzugreifen. Das Projekt arbeitet auf der Basis von Empowerment, das oft vom Modell der partizipativen Forschung unterstützt wird. Damit wird die Kraft mobilisiert, die nötig ist, um Chancengleichheit und volle Teilnahme an der Gesellschaft zu erreichen.

In Värmland, Schweden, sind im Jahre 1994 zwei CBR-Projekte gestartet worden. Eines zielt auf die individuelle Planung der Hilfeleistung (ISP). Dort wird mit den Eltern geschädigter Kindern ein Netzwerk von Konsultationen aufgebaut. Die Initiativen und die Entscheidungen, wer in diesem Netzwerk ist und darüber, welche Unterstützungen erforderlich sind, werden von den Eltern und nicht von den professionellen Helfern getroffen. Das andere CBR-Projekt arbeitet darauf hin, Eltern mit beeinträchtigten Kindern in dünn besiedelten Gebieten mit Hilfe des partizipativen Forschungsmodells zu unterstützen. Ziel dieses Projekts ist es, die Perspektiven zu wechseln, nämlich weg von professionellen Organisationen und hin zu den Kindern und deren Eltern, um soziale Bindung vor Ort zu schaffen. Die Gruppe erfüllt außerdem den Anspruch auf Selbstversorgung und Selbsthilfe (Svensson, Starrin, 1997).

Die partizipative Forschung wurde in verschiedenen Ländern von und für Menschen mit Lernschwierigkeiten gestartet. Berith Cech hat (1997) damit begonnen, Gruppen zu gründen, und der Prozeß des Empowerments in diesen Gruppen hat sich als stark erwiesen. Menschen mit geistigen Behinderungen sind eine Gruppe, die Schwierigkeiten hat, Macht zu erlangen. Deren Leben wurde gewöhnlich von den professionellen Helfern oder den Eltern organisiert, und nur wenige Betroffene wurden nach ihrer Meinung gefragt. Die Forschung zeigt, daß partizipative Forschung ein Modell sein kann, um auch in diesen Gruppen Empowerment zu erreichen.

3.3.5 AUFGABEN

1. Beschreiben Sie verschiedene Formen von Empowerment und Anwaltschaft im Hinblick auf Behinderung, Lern- und Lebensschwierigkeiten und Benachteiligungen in Ihrem Land.

2. Einbeziehung von Betroffenen? Existiert das heutzutage?
3. Worin liegt der Unterschied der Rolle und der Funktionen von Gruppen/Organisationen „von" behinderten Menschen gegenüber Gruppen und Organisationen „für" behinderte Menschen?
4. Geben Sie eigene Beispiele über Ihre Erfahrungen mit Gruppenarbeit und Gruppenprozessen.
5. Geben Sie Beispiele, wie behinderte Menschen „ermächtigt"/empowered werden können.
6. Hatten Experten und professionelle Helfer zu großen Einfluß auf das Leben von behinderten Menschen?
7. Gibt es Gefahren mit Empowerment und sozialen Handlungen? Kann es auch als Entschuldigung für die Politiker verwendet werden, keine Mittel für die Ausbildung und Einstellung von Professionellen bereitzustellen?

3.3.6 BIBLIOGRAPHIE

3.3.6.1 LITERATURHINWEISE

Brown, C & Ringma C. (1989) *New Disability Services: the critical role of staff in a consumer-directed empowerment model of service for physically disabled persons.* Disability Handicap & Society. Vol, NO 3.

Cech, B. (1997). *Vardagsverklighet och livskvalitet för personer med utvecklingsstörning.* Vårdhögskolan i Göteborg, Institutionen för social omsorg.

Forsberg, E & Starrin, B. (1997) *Frigörande kraft, empowerment som modell i skola, omsorg och arbetsliv.* Göteborg.

Hall, B. (1984) *Research, commitment and action: The role of participatory research.* International Review of Education, 30.

Heap, K. (1987) *Gruppmetod för socialarbetare och personal inom hälso och sjukvård.* Helsingborg.

Levin, K. (1946) *Action research and minority problems.* Journal of Social Problems, 2.

LSS. (1994)	Socialstyrelsens Almänna Råd 1994:4
Muldoon, R. (1994/95)	The demystfication of social action groupwork principles.
SOCIAL ACTION, Volume Two, Number Three 1994/95.	
Mullender, A & Ward, D. (1991)	Self-directed Groupwork: Users Take Action for Empowerment. London.
Payne, M. (1997)	Modern social work theory. London.
Rappaport, J. (1981)	In Praise of Paradox: a social policy of Empowerment over Prevention. American Journal of Community Psychology.
Riger, S. (1981)	Towards A Community. Psychology Newsletter
Solomon, B. (1976)	Black Empowerment: Social work in Oppressed communities. New York.
Soydan, H. (1993)	Det sociala arbets ide´historia. Lund.
Svensson, P-G & Starrin, B. (1992)	Health Policy. Development for disadvantaged groups. Kristinasand.
Swedner, H. (1983)	Socialt arbete en tankeram. Lund.
Swift, C. & Lewin G. (1987)	Empowerment: An Emerging Mental Health Technology. Journal of Primary Prevention.

3.3.6.2 ZUSÄTZLICHE LITERATUR

Theunissen, G. & Plaute, W. (1996)	Empowerment und Heilpädagogik. Freiburg im Breisgau.

4. EIN BLICK NACH VORN - MANAGEMENT IM WANDEL

Fritz-Helmut Wisch

4.1 EINLEITUNG

Sozialformen sind nach bestimmten Organisationsstrukturen aufgebaut. Familien, Gruppen, Vereine, Betriebe u.ä. ordnen und organisieren sich nach vereinbarten (tradierten) Regeln. Heute unterscheiden wir vor allem *autoritär* geführte von *demokratisch* organisierten Sozialformen.

Anhand einer fiktiven Einrichtung für behinderte Kinder, wir nennen sie EUROHAND, werden unterschiedliche Sozialformen diskutiert, wobei deutlich wird: Autoritär strukturierte Systeme folgen *hierarchischen* Prinzipien, *demokratisch* organisierten Sozialformen sind *interaktiven* Prinzipien verpflichtet, unterliegen gegenseitiger Kontrolle bzw. Einflußnahme. Vorgestellt werden Aufgaben und Ziele solcher demokratisch organisierter Sozialformen, zudem findet eine Auseinandersetzung mit innovativen Führungstechniken, das sind aus unserer Sicht vor allem Kommunikationstechniken, statt. Ausführlicher setzen wir uns weiter auseinander mit der Notwendigkeit des Wandels (im Umgang) mit und zwischen den Menschen (Individuen), um abschließend eine Vision des Miteinanders zu entwerfen.

4.1.1 ZIELE

Die Studierenden werden

- die Kultur unterschiedlicher Organisationsstrukturen und das Rollenverständnis der Beteiligten untersuchen,
- Kommunikationsfähigkeiten einschätzen und vertiefen,
- die Notwendigkeit des Wandels im Umgang mit und zwischen den Beteiligten nachvollziehen und verstehen,
- veränderte Strukturformen und den Wandel des Managements in einer Behindertenorganisation/-Einrichtung kennenlernen und analysieren,
- Visionen des Miteinanders zwischen behinderten und nichtbehinderten Menschen entwerfen.

4.1.2 LERNERGEBNISSE

Am Ende dieses Kapitels sollen die Studierenden in der Lage sein

- die Organisations- und Management-Strukturen einer Einrichtung für behinderte Menschen zu verstehen und einzuschätzen,
- Visionen des Miteinanders kritisch einzuschätzen.

4.1.3 ZUR KULTUR DER ORGANISATIONSSTRUKTUREN UND DES ROLLENVERSTÄNDNISSES DER BETEILIGTEN

4.1.3.1 DAS HIERARCHISCHE, DIREKTIVE STUFENMODELL

Werfen wir einen Blick in eine fiktive Einrichtung für behinderte Kinder und Jugendliche. Wir wollen sie **EUROHAND** nennen. Wir sehen Gruppen, die nach familienähnlichen Strukturen aufgebaut sind, sich im Sinne *Bronfenbrenners* darstellen als *Mikrosysteme*. Erzieherinnen und Erzieher (Betreuer) arbeiten im Schichtdienst, es gibt eine Gruppenleitung, vielleicht eine Abteilungsleitung, bestimmt eine Leitung der Einrichtung. Weitere (kooperative) Fachleute arbeiten als Therapeuten wie Mediziner, Psychologen, Heil- und Sonderpädagogen, Logopäden, Ergotherapeuten usw. Hausmeister, Wirtschaftspersonal, Praktikanten (*Mesosysteme*) ... ergänzen den Mitarbeiterstab, der sich versteht als Dienstleistungsunternehmen zum Wohle der Betreuten.

Als wohlorganisierte Einrichtung arbeitet EUROHAND natürlich nicht autonom, sondern ist eingebunden in den *kommunalen* bzw. lokalen Heimverbund von EUROHAND*KOM*, der EUROHAND behindertenspezifisch, betriebswirtschaftlich und organisatorisch berät und unterstützt. Auch EUROHANDKOM agiert nicht nur auf der lokalen Ebene, sondern ist ebenso wie die weiteren EUROHANDKOMS der *Region* vereint unter dem Dach von EUROHAND*REG*. Alle EUROHANDREGS schließlich sind ihrerseits Mitglieder der *Landesvertretung* bzw. des Spitzenverbandes EUROHAND*LAND* ...

Wir sehen: Unsere Beispieleinrichtung EUROHAND steht nicht allein, Unterstützung, Informationen, Anweisungen erhält sie von allen Seiten, ist eingebettet in das hierarchische System der EUROHAND-ORGANISATION.

EUROHANDLAND
EUROHANDREG   EUROHANDREG
Eurohandkom   Eurohandkom   Eurohandkom   Eurohandkom
Eurohand   Eurohand   Eurohand   Eurohand   Eurohand   Eurohand   Eurohand

Ein Spiegel dieses Makrosystems EUROHAND-ORGANISATION, in der auf unterschiedlichen Ebenen Vorstände, Mitarbeiter das gleiche Ziel verfolgen, dem Wohle der Betreuten zu dienen, ist das Mikrosystem unserer Beispieleinrichtung EUROHAND, das sich dementsprechend wie folgt darstellt:

LEITUNG							
THERAPEUTEN ABTEILUNGSLEITUNG							
Betreuer	Betreuer	Betreuer	Betreuer	Hausmeister	Wirtschaftskräfte		Praktikanten
Betreute	Betreute	Betreute	Betreute	Betreute	Betreute	Betreute	Betreute

hierarchisches Stufenmodell

Es ist augenscheinlich, daß in diesem hierarchischen (Mikro-)System - ebenso wie in dem vergleichbaren Makrosystem - eine Reihe von Angst-, Konfliktbzw. Aggressionspotentialen steckt. Der *Führungsstil* des hier vorgestellten Modells ist aus naheliegenden Gründen *direktiv*, Attribute wie autoritär, patriarchalisch veranschaulichen das Modell der direktiven Führung (*Gregor-Rauschtenberger/Hansel* 1993, *Denger* 1997). Dieses "Modell von gestern" ist uns nur zu geläufig: die Führung eines Handwerksbetriebes wurde durch den Meister übernommen, ein Bauernhof vom Bauern geführt, ein Gründer zu Beginn des Industriezeitalters übernahm die Führung einer Fabrik. Beim Militär wurde nie das klare Verständnis von Führung *Befehl und Gehorsam* in Frage gestellt. In diesen Traditionen wurden wohl die meisten von uns erzogen, im persönlichen Bereich von den primären Bezugspersonen (den Eltern), in der Schule und in der Ausbildung von Lehrern, Ausbildern und Vorgesetzten. In diesem klar strukturierten Stufenmodell weiß jeder, wo er hingehört: nach unten, in die Mitte oder nach oben!

Schauen wir in unser EUROHAND-Musterhaus:

Betreute, die auf der untersten Stufe stehen, erleben einander als Rivalen und die Betreuer sowie alle übrigen *Höherrangigen* als Vorgesetzte, sie können Frustrationen nur untereinander an Gleichrangigen oder noch weiter unten stehenden Schwächeren auslassen ...

Betreuer erleben einander und die übrigen auf gleicher (d.h. auch auf unterer) Ebene Tätigen als Rivalen, alle übrigen *Höherrangigen* als Vorgesetzte, sie können Frustrationen nur an Schwächeren (Betreuten) auslassen ...

Therapeuten/Abteilungsleiter erleben einander und die übrigen auf gleicher Ebene Tätigen als Rivalen, nur die Leitung als Vorgesetzte, sie können Frustrationen nur an Schwächeren (Betreuern, Wirtschaftskräften,... Betreuten) auslassen ...

Die *Leitung* hat (in der Einrichtung) keine Vorgesetzten, kann Frustrationen nur an Schwächeren (Therapeuten, Abteilungslern, Betreuern, ..., Betreuten) auslassen ...

Diese lückenhaften Beispiele - auf die Rolle bzw. die System- oder Berufsbedingungen der Eltern und weiterer im System involvierter Personen (*Exosysteme*) ist bewußt nicht eingegangen worden - vielmehr sollen die Hinweise genügen, um deutlich zu machen, welches Konfliktpotential in unserer Mustereinrichtung EUROHAND steckt, welches hochexplosive Gebilde jede vergleichbare Einrichtung tatsächlich ist. Sehr groß ist das Potential möglicher Brennpunkte, und es ist naheliegend, daß ein solches Gebilde nur mit einer genügenden Anzahl Feuer verhütender Maßnahmen sich nicht entzündet, daß Schwelbrände laufend kontrolliert werden müssen...

Angst macht sich breit, die Mitarbeiter verbergen ihre Beobachtungen, achten peinlich genau darauf, daß nichts Brennbares herumliegt, ersticken sofort jedes Fünkchen (Kreativität), lassen keinen Sauerstoff, keinen frischen Wind durch die Einrichtung wehen, der rasch vorhandene Schwelbrände unkontrolliert entfachen könnte. So zeigt sich unser Musterhaus EUROHAND als typische, wohlorganisierte, klar durchstrukturierte Einrichtung, in der alles nach bewährtem Muster abläuft, jeder jeden einschätzen kann, jede Aktivität ge(maß)regelt, kontrolliert und damit überschaubar ist. Nichts wird dem Zufall überlassen, jeder kann sich jederzeit auf jeden verlassen. ...

Dieses auch heute noch vielerorts anzutreffende Organisationsstrukturmodell sollte eigentlich der Vergangenheit angehören, durch modernes, auf Qualität (der Betreuung) setzendes Betriebsmanagement ersetzt worden sein. Leider erleben wir immer wieder, bzw. immer noch Gebilde, Lebensgemeinschaften, Heime für behinderte Menschen, die exakt nach diesen o.g. Negativstrukturen organisiert, dem direktiven Stufenmodell verhaftet sind. *Unten*, wir müssen es noch einmal wiederholen, sind in diesem Modell die *Schwachen*, *oben* die Starken angesiedelt. Zwischen den Etagen herrscht die Hackordnung, lassen sich Machtspielchen beliebig oft reproduzieren. Wer sich außerhalb dieser Hackordnung positionieren möchte, wer aus der Reihe tanzen will, verliert den Halt in diesem Treppenhaus, kann sich, wenn er Glück hat, aus dem Ausgang retten, verletzt sich, wenn er unglücklich abrutscht oder die Treppe hinunterfällt. Den übrigen Hausbewohnern fällt es verständlicherweise schwer, einem Außenseiter, der die klare, bewährte Gliederung durcheinanderbringt, zu helfen.

Das hier beschriebene Stufenmodell des Miteinanders setzt, es wurde schon gesagt, auf Befehl, Disziplin und Gehorsam, auf *law and order*, wie wir es vom Militär kennen, bringt Duckmäusertum mit all seinen bekannten negativen Auswüchsen hervor. Nein, das Stufenmodell taugt aus den o. g. Gründen als Strukturmodell für eine moderne, zukunftsorientierte Lebensgemeinschaft überhaupt nicht. Deshalb sind auch alle Versuche, ein solches Modell zu konservieren, zu restaurieren oder gar zu konsolidieren nicht nur zu verwerfen, sie sind zu bekämpfen. Das Stufenmodell hat seine Wurzeln in der Vergangenheit, und die Geschichte hat gezeigt, daß blinder Gehorsam, daß rigides Vertrauen auf law and order ins Unglück, ins Chaos, in den Krieg führen.

4.1.3.2 DAS INTERAKTIVE KREISMODELL

Auf der Schwelle zum Dritten Jahrtausend, auf dem Weg in die Zukunft deuten sich ganz andere Modelle an, gewinnen an Konturen, und werden sich durchsetzen, denn menschliches Handeln, humanes Miteinander, freiheitlich demokratische Grundordnungen gilt es zu manifestieren, Menschenrechte durchzusetzen und zu zementieren.

Wie sieht unser Zukunftsmdell des friedlichen Miteinanders aus?

Dieses Zukunftsmodell verzichtet auf hierarchische Strukturen, es geht vorrangig nicht um Betreute und Betreuer, vielmehr verstehen sich alle Heimbewohner und -Mitarbeiter als ein Team, in dem es kein Oben und kein Unten gibt, sondern nur ein Wir. Ziel unseres Zukunftsmodells ist z.B. nicht ausschließlich die Verbesserung der Situation der Heimbewohner, das Ziel ist weiter gefaßt, durch ein demokratisches Miteinander gilt es, die Lebenssituation aller in der Einrichtung Seienden zu verbessern, ihr Wohlbefinden zu steigern. Wie das? Uns schwebt ein Kreismodell vor, welches zum Anecken keine Angriffsflächen bietet, wo es kein Unten und kein Oben, nur ein friedliches und demokratisches Miteinander gibt.

interaktives Kreismodell

Es liegt nahe, daß in dem hier vorgestellten (Kreis-)Modell ein be*fried*etes (*Begemann* 1994) Miteinander-Umgehen eher möglich ist als in dem traditionellen, dem Obrigkeitsprinzip verhafteten und hierarchischen Strukturen gehorchenden Treppen- bzw. Stufenmodell, zu dem konsekutiv ein Oben und ein Unten gehört. Im Kreismodell befinden sich alle Mitglieder des Teams auf der gleichen Ebene, verstehen sich Betreuer und Betreute als Lebensgemeinschaft, in der *Normalisierung und Integration als innovative Forderungen zu einer humaneren Ausgestaltung der Lebenswelt behinderter Menschen in einer demokratischen Gesellschaft* keine leeren Worthülsen sind (*Jacobs* 1995).

Obwohl die demokratischen Ziele *Normalisierung und Integration* bereits seit Jahrzehnten von unseren skandinavischen Nachbarn praktiziert bzw. vorgelebt werden (*Bank-Mikkelsen, DK/Nirje; SVE*), haben sich diese humanitären Ideologien bzw. Prinzipien europa- oder gar weltweit noch lange nicht durchgesetzt. Es liegt auf der Hand, daß sich diesen anthroposophischen Maximen nur dort genähert werden kann, wo die Organisationsstrukturen verändert werden (können), wo Bereitschaft und Wille herrscht zu interaktiven (nondirektiven) Umgangsformen.

Immerhin scheinen sich jedoch immer mehr Eirichtungen und Lebensgemeinschaften den demokratischen Zielen *Normalisierung und Integration* im Zusammenleben mit behinderten Menschen - wir werden sie in diesem Zusammenhang weiterhin Betreute nennen - zu verpflichten. Wir bleiben zuversichtlich, daß das Prinzip *Hoffnung* (*Bloch*) erweitert um das Prinzip der *Verantwortung* (*Jonas*) uns weiterhin auf dem Wege des Demokratisierungsprozesses im Umgang miteinander nicht nur tragen, sondern voranbringen wird, wir im *dialogischen* Umgang (*Buber*) uns den Sozialformen nähern, die ein humanes Miteinander uns abverlangen.

Auch im interaktiven Kreismodell gibt es eine Führung oder eine Leitung, sie ist jedoch nicht abgehoben, sie findet lediglich anders statt. Entscheidungs- und Lösungsprozesse werden nicht vorgegeben, sie werden gemeinsam, interaktiv, also in gegenseitiger Einflußnahme gesucht und gefunden. Die Integration aller Beteiligten ist nicht nur gewünscht, sondern erforderlich und bewirkt:

- jeder Einzelne wird gesehen und gefördert;
- Steigerung der Identifikation mit der Arbeit, den Zielen der Einrichtung;
- Handlungsspielräume des Einzelnen weiten sich aus;
- Entscheidungen werden transparent (akzeptiert);
- Team ist motiviert;
- Team entwickelt sich zur selbstgesteuerten Gruppe (selbst-coaching);
- Kooperation zwischen Leitung, Mitarbeitern und Betreuten.

Ein solches demokratisches Miteinander verlangt innovative Führungstechniken, künftig wird sich Führung mehr als Koordination von Kommunikations- und Konsensfindungsprozessen verstehen, d.h., sie beherrscht die Kunst der Rede (Rhetorik), oder wie wir heute besser sagen, Kommunikationstechniken und -strategien.

4.1.3.3 KOMMUNIKATIONSFÄHIGKEITEN

Ein interaktives Miteinander verlangt rücksichtsvolles, akzeptierendes aufeinander Zugehen und Eingehen. Von *Tausch und Tausch* haben wir gelernt, daß drei Haltungen von einer Person gegenüber Gesprächspartnern gelebt bzw. erkennbar werden müssen, will man Gespräche als einfühlsam und hilfreichen bezeichnen:

- den Gesprächspartner *verstehen* und ihm dies mitteilen,
- das Gespräch *achtungsvoll-warm* führen,
- die *Echtheit* des Gespräches spüren lassen.

Diese Grundeinstellungen bzw. -Haltungen gegenüber Gesprächen gelten sowohl für Einzel- als auch für Gruppengespräche, sie sind zudem "auch in anderen zwischenmenschlichen Beziehungen im allgemeinen weitgehend notwendige und hinreichende Bedingungen für die Förderung der persönlichen Weiterentwicklung und des persönlichen Lernens von Partnern. Dies gilt für Eltern und Kinder ebenso wie für Lebenspartner, Ärzte und Patienten, Hochschullehrer und Studenten und natürlich auch für Betriebsangehörige, Helfer und Klienten usw" (Tausch und Tausch, 1990, 300f.).

4.1.3.4 KUNDENORIENTIERTE KOMMUNIKATION

Wir kommen zurück auf unsere Mustereinrichtung EUROHAND:

Herrscht zwischen Leitung und Klienten bzw. Kunden, oder zwischen Betreuern und Betreuten ein Klima, welches die 3 Haltungen *Verstehen, Achtung-Wärme* und *Echtheit* spiegelt, so dürfen wir von einem guten Kommunikationsklima ausgehen.

In diesem Zusammenhang sprechen wir heute von *Kundenorientierter Kommunikation*, seltener von Klientenorientierter Kommunikation. *Kundenorientierte Kommunikation* will Klarheit schaffen einerseits für den Gesprächspartner, also den Empfänger, andererseits für den Sender:

- Was erwartet der Kunde von EUROHAND?
- Was bietet EUROHAND?

- Gibt es Grenzen bezüglich der Kundenwünsche?
- Lassen sich diese Grenzen verschieben?

Durch diese Klarheit wird der Gesprächspartner ernstgenommen, der Kunde erfährt, woran er ist, der Sender lernt die Kundenwünsche kennen. Die Gesprächsklarheit betrifft hauptsächlich drei Aspekte:

- Die *Beziehung* der Kommunikationspartner zueinander,
- Die Ziele und Themen des Gesprächs,
- Die Vorgehensweise.

Solche klar strukturierte Vorgehensweise, die Offenlegung von Absichten und die Transparenz der Ziele schaffen Orientierung und Sicherheit für die Kunden, die ja unterschiedlicher Herkunft sein können, sich aus ganz verschiedenen Kundenkreisen rekrutieren:

- Hilfsbedürftige als Bedarfsträger (Betreute),
- Kollegium,
- Bedarfsbestimmer (Ärzte, Angehörige, Betreuer),
- Finanzierungsträger (Sozial,- Jugendämter),
- Öffentlichkeit (Presse, Politik, Freunde, Mitbewerber),
- Gremien (Vorstände, Arbeitsgemeinschaften).

Insgesamt versteht sich *Kundenorientierte Kommunikation* als:

- zielorientierte Kommunikation,
- Kommunikation zwischen gleichberechtigten, bzw. integrierten Partnern,
- partnerschaftliche Kommunikation,
- individuelles Eingehen auf die ICH-Zustände des Gesprächspartners.

Kundenorientierte Kommunikation richtet sich, das sagt schon der Name, nach dem Bedarf des Kunden, geht also auf dessen Wünsche und Vorstellungen ein.

In einer Zeit der leeren Kassen wird es zunehmend schwerer, auch die im Bereich der sozialen Dienstleistungen errungenen Standards zu halten oder gar zu verbessern. Der gesamte Dienstleistungssektor und - vor dem Hintergrund unserer Betrachtungen besonders der Bereich der Rehabilitation - befindet sich im Umbruch, wird mit marktwirtschaftlichen Entwicklungen und finanziellen Begrenzungen konfrontiert.

4.1.3.5 DIE NOTWENDIGKEIT DES WANDELS IM UMGANG MIT UND ZWISCHEN DEN BETEILIGTEN

In dieser Umbruchphase, in dieser Zeit des Wandels, sind rasche und dabei intelligente Lösungen gefragt. Einerseits darf die bestehende Qualität auf keinen Fall verloren gehen, andererseits quälen Fragen, wie diese in Zeiten knappen Geldes zu erhalten oder gar noch zu verbessern ist.

Orientierungshilfen bieten Entwicklungen, die sich an markt- bzw. betriebswirtschaftlichen Erkenntnissen ausrichten.

Seit einigen Jahren zeichnet sich z.B. auch auf der Leitungsebene im Rehabereich eine zunehmende Professionalisierung ab. Ehrenamtliche Helfer werden allerorten unterstützt (oder abgelöst) von hauptamtlichen Mitarbeitern, die, um an unser Musterbeispiel EUROHAND anzuknüpfen, ein (Reha-) Unternehmen nach marktwirtschaftlichen Gesichtspunkten neu ordnen bzw. umgestalten.

Der Wandel findet auf zwei Ebenen statt, einerseits geht es um die Individuen (in Leitungsfunktion), andererseits um das Miteinander, die zwischenmenschlichen Beziehungen.

Warum dieser Wandel im Selbstverständnis der (ehrenamtlichen) Helfer? Überall ist zu hören, daß die Zeiten der sich aufopfernden "Ehrenamtlichen" zu Ende gingen. Die Gründe für diese Veränderungen auf der Leitungsebene sind in den vergangenen Jahren unter den Schlagwörtern "Helfer-Syndrom" und "Burnout-Syndrom" (nicht nur unter den Betroffenen) vielfach diskutiert worden. Die aufgrund ihrer eigenen Vita "Berufenen", der Ära der Selbsthilfgruppen entwachsenen ehrenamtlichen Helfer, taten und tun sich äußerst schwer damit, ihr zwar hoch motiviertes Tun als das der "hilflosen Helfer" (Schmidbauer 1977) einschätzen zu können. *Historische und inhaltliche Gründe* sind vor anderen zu nennen, die das Konfliktpotential zwischen Ehrenamtlichen und Hauptamtlichen verdeutlichen.

Wenden wir uns zunächst kurz der *historischen Dimension* zu:
Selbsthilfegruppen wurden und werden so lange von Ehrenamtlichen geleitet, bis diese so groß werden, daß es ohne Hauptamtliche nicht mehr geht, da die

Ehrenamtlichen irgendwann einsehen (müssen), daß sie zeitlich und inhaltlich überfordert sind. Bei Institutionen mit Selbsthilfe- und Betroffenencharakter kommt hinzu, daß die Gründer (Eltern- und Freundesgruppen) nicht loslassen können, auch weiterhin "das Sagen haben" wollen, bzw. sich als die Erfahrenen, Besserwissenden gegenüber den Hauptamtlichen verstehen.

Auf der *inhaltlichen Seite* ist vor allem die in der eigenen Betroffenheit begründete erhöhte Motivation zu nennen, die einerseits die Arbeit ungeheuer befördern, andererseits zu extrem komplizierten Beziehungen und überdurchschnittlichem Konfliktpotential führen kann. Sowohl *Vater-Sohn-Konflikte* als auch die Problematik von *Nähe und Distanz* machen beiden Seiten das Leben oft unerträglich schwer. Die Gründergeneration durfte im "blinden Vertrauen" aufeinander agieren. Diese unkontrollierte *Nähe* wird dann gefährlich, wenn sich auf der Ebene der Kumpanei Emotionalität anstatt Rationalität breit macht. Vetrauen aber allein genügt nicht, um nüchtern, sachbezogen, strukturiert, m.a.W. professionell *distanziert* Institutionen bzw. Mitarbeiter und Klienten zu führen.

Die anwachsende Professionalisierung ist also in hohem Maße konfliktträchtig, sie verlangt von den Beteiligten (Teamangehörigen) ein behutsames Miteinander-Umgehen im Sinne einer kundenorientierten Kommunikation. Traditionelles, an staatlicher Alimentierung orientiertes Denken und Handeln wird überführt in selbstbewußtes, marktorientiertes Verhalten, stellt sich somit den Herausforderungen und Chancen marktwirtschaftlicher Entwicklungen. Ökonomische Orientierung, das Bemühen um Strukturwandel läßt sich klar nachweisen anhand einer Reihe neuer Terminologien bzw. Schlagwörter, die in letzter Zeit auch in den Sozialbereichen Reha, Pflege und Gesundheit Einkehr gehalten haben. Dabei handelt es sich u.a. um Begriffe wie

- Lean Management
- Sozialmanagement
- Qualitätsmanagement, -sicherung
- Personalmanagement
- Fundraising
- Social Sponsering,

neue Strategien, die alle unter dem Zwang und damit der Notwendigkeit der (monetären) Veränderungen im sozialen Netz, des Strukturwandels im sozialen Feld entstanden. Das Sozial-*Management des Wandels* (*Holzamer 1996*) adaptiert somit markt- und betriebswirtschaftliche Strategien, um sich den anstehenden Fragen und Problemen auf dem Weg ins nächste Jahrtausend kompetent zu nähern.

Nicht nur in unserer Mustereinrichtung EUROHAND wird sich in diesem Zusammenhang vieles bewegen müssen. Im Sinne von *Lean Management*, (die übrigen Managementstrategien bleiben im folgenden unberücksichtigt), werden sich die Mitarbeiter (Leiter, Therapeuten, Betreuer, Wirtschaftspersonal ...) den Zielen dieser neuen Managementstrategie verpflichten.
Zu diesen zählen:

- Absolute Kundenorientierung
- Qualitätserhöhung
- Fehlervermeidung
- Verbesserung von Abläufen und Dienstleistungen
- Vermeidung von Verschwendung (Kostenmanagement)
- Flexibilität und schnelle Reaktion gegenüber sich verändernden Umfeldbedingungen
- Geringe Einführungszeiten
- Konzentration auf Kernaktivitäten
- Erhaltung und Sicherung der Wettbewerbsfähigkeit

Um diese Ziele zu erreichen, wird sich das Mitarbeiterteam von EUROHAND u.U. von liebgewonnenen Gepflogen- und Gewohnheiten verabschieden müssen, denn Lean Management kennt wenig Respekt vor tradierten Verhaltensweisen, vor eingeschliffenen Arbeitsabläufen und liebgewordenen Machtstrukturen. Die Mitarbeiter sind vor hohe Anforderungen gestellt, denn Lean Managemnet versteht sich nicht als einmaliger (kurzer) Prozeß, sondern als Daueraufgabe. Läßt sich eine Rehaeinrichtung wie EUROHAND aber auf dieses innovative Vorgehen ein, darf sie eine Reihe von Vorteilen erwarten:

- Neuorientierung statt Erstarren in Traditionen
- Flexibilität statt Verkrustung
- Transparenz statt Verschleierung
- Interaktion statt Hierarchie
- Dynamik statt Statik

Wer z.B. auf Lean Management setzt, nimmt selbstverantwortlich eine Reihe von Methoden in Kauf, die für die Beteiligten zunächst angstbesetzt, da unbekannt sein können, und von deren Effektivität alle Mitarbeiter behutsam zu überzeugen sind. Um diese zu motivieren, um das angestrebte günstigere Betriebsklima zu schaffen, bietet sich, eine engagierte Heimleitung vorausgesetzt, eine Auswahl von Verfahren an:

- Supervision
- Selbst Coaching

- Teambildung
- Fort- und Weiterbildung
- Fachausbildung Nachqualifikation
- Austausch von Fachkräften
- offene (Team-)Gespräche
- Übertragen von Freiraum und Verantwortlichkeit.

Mitarbeitermotivation scheint (nicht nur vor dem Hintergrund leerer Staatskassen, die sich schmerzlich gerade im sozialen Sektor bemerkbar machen,) besonders erschwert, ist aber unter Berücksichtigung der o.g. Herausforderungen ein zentrales Instrument zur Verbesserung des Arbeitsklimas, welches seinerseits Voraussetzung ist, um z.B. notwendige Qualitätssicherung bzw. -Verbesserung zu erreichen.

4.1.3.6 EINSCHÄTZUNG UND ANALYSE DES STRUKTUR- UND MANAGEMENTWANDELS EINER ORGANISATION FÜR BEHINDERTE MENSCHEN

Motivation der Mitarbeiter ist ein wichtiger - wenn nicht der wichtigste - Baustein, um den veränderten und sich verändernden Bedingungen in der Behindertenarbeit gerecht zu werden. Die bereits genannten zukunftsorientierten Strategien *Lean Management, Socialmanagement, Qualitätsmanagement, Qualitätssicherung, Personalmanagement, Fundraising und Social Sponsering* sind Ausdruck der vielfältigen Bemühungen, sich um marktgerechte Antworten auf die veränderten Marktsituationen zu bemühen.

Angenommen, unsere Mustereinrichtung EUROHAND hat dank konsequenter Anwendung zukunftsorientierter Strategien wie

- *kundenorientierter Kommunikation*
- *Lean Management*

den Strukturwandel von einem *hierarchisch* geführten zu einem *interaktiven* Unternehmen vollzogen.

Wie stellt sich die neue EUROHAND nach dem Wandel dar? Sehen wir uns das EUROHAND-Team ein wenig näher an:

Leitung	Auch die neue EUROHAND hat eine Leitung. Diese entscheidet jedoch nicht (wie im hierarchischen System) abgehoben selbstherrlich, sondern in stetigem Austausch mit dem Mitarbeiterteam. Beratung und Kritik erfährt und erteilt die Leitung ebenso wie die übrigen Mitarbeiter. Da sich EUROHAND kundenorientiert verhält, zielt auch die Leitung permanent auf Verbesserung des Angebotes für die Betreuten (Qualitätssicherung). Eigentlich unterscheidet sich das Verhalten der Leitung überhaupt nicht von dem der übrigen Mitarbeiter.
Mitarbeiter	Auf das gemeinsame Ziel eingeschworen, denken und handeln alle in die gleiche Richtung. Das erklärte, kundenorientierte Ziel heißt eben: Erhalt bzw. Steigerung des Wohlbefindens aller Betreuten (Kunden) in der Einrichtung EUROHAND. Im demokratischen, friedlichen Umgang sind alle bemüht, die (Dienst-)Leistungen zu verbessern. Wie die Leitung so betrachten auch die Betreuer, Therapeuten sowie die übrigen Mitarbeiter die Betreuten als gleichberechtigte Partner. Schwachpunkte in allen Bereichen werden offen angesprochen, benannt und nach Möglichkeit schnell ausgemerzt (Fehlervermeidung).
Betreute	Die Kunden als die eigentlichen Hauptpersonen im Musterhaus EUROHAND erleben sich in besonderer Weise als angenommen. Über Akzeptanz wird nicht gesprochen, Akzeptanz wird gelebt. In diesem Haus weht der Geist der HUMANITAS.

Von der Verwaltung zur Verantwortung, vom Herrschen zum Teilen darf der Wandel vom hierarchischen zum interaktiven Miteinander zusammenfassend genannt werden. Dieser Wandel, dieser Aufbruch zu neuen (Umgangs-) Formen vollzieht sich in vielen sozialen Bereichen. Längst sind noch nicht alle von diesem neuen Geist, dem WIND OF CHANGE erfaßt, und allenthalben spürt man Widerstände und Ängste vor dem Neuen. Diese zu überwinden ist *die Herausforderung* auf der Schwelle ins neue Jahrtausend, der wir uns entschlossen annehmen müssen, wollen wir nicht zum Gespött der Geschichte werden.

4.1.3.7 ENTWURF EINER VISION DES MITEINANDERS

I HAVE A DREAM (M. Luther-King)
WE SHALL OVERCOME (P. Seager)
ICH BIN EIN BERLINER (J.F.Kennedy)

Drei Sätze, die in der zweiten Hälfte des 20. Jahrhunderts, die Jugend, ja große Teile der Menschheit dieser Welt, bewegten, zu Tränen rührten und gleichzeitig in Aufbruchstimmung versetzten.

Martin Luther-King beschwor die Vision eines geeinten Amerikas, in dem die Unterschiede zwischen den Rassen aufgehoben werden. In unserem Kontext erkennen wir die Hoffnung auf INTEGRATION.

Pete Seager drückte mit seinem unvergessenen Lied unsere Sehnsucht nach FRIEDEN und NORMALITÄT aus. In unserem Zusammenhang (dem Miteinander behinderter und nicht behinderter Menschen) denken wir an die Überwindung von Benachteiligung unterdrückter, schwacher, behinderter Menschen.

John F. Kennedy's unvergessener Satz in Berlin vor dem Brandenburger Tor klang allen im Ohr, die unter der inhumanen Trennung und Teilung eines Volkes litten und die die Sehnsucht nach VEREINIGUNG in FRIEDEN und FREIHEIT nicht aufgegeben hatten. Darüber hinaus spürte die Menschheit etwas von Beethovens ALLE MENSCHEN WERDEN BRÜDER, der Sehnsucht, die auch für Heil- und Sonderpädagogen Weg und Ziel zugleich sein kann, ahnen wir doch in diesen Aussagen etwas von der Einmaligkeit, die Menschsein auch und gerade ausmacht: - RELIGIO (Bindung) eingehen zu können - und sich damit dem (christlichen) Gebot der Nächstenliebe zu nähern bzw. zu verpflichten.

Welche Visionen haben angehende Heilpädagogen heute?

Eine Befragung von Erst-Semester-Studenten der Heilpädagogik an der Fachhochschule Magdeburg im Frühjahr 1998 ergab u.a. folgende Antworten:

Visionen für die Heilpädagogik

- Heilpädagogik macht sich überflüssig (Heilpädagogik ist nicht mehr nötig)
- Kein Ausschließen von Menschen (Integration ist nicht mehr nötig)

- Die Wünsche aller behinderten Menschen erfüllen (eigene Wohnung etc.)
- Eine behindertenbereite Gesellschaft
- Keine Ausgrenzung beim Zugang zur Kultur, Bildung, Medizin, ...
- Internationale Zusammenarbeit (multikulturelles Zusammenleben)
- Andere Wichtung zwischen sozialen und wirtschaftlichen Interessen
- Werteänderung
- Keine Anhänger für den Utilitarismus (Singer)
- Keine Zwangssterilisation
- Freie Entwicklung aller Menschen (Erfüllung des Grundgesetzes)
- Nächstenliebe praktizieren

Die meisten der genannten Antworten überraschen nicht und würden vermutlich in ähnlicher Weise in anderen Regionen Deutschlands oder Europas ausfallen, denn sie sind Ausdruck der christlich-abendländischen Tradition, in die wir als Europäer hineingeboren werden. Sie spiegeln das kulturelle Erbe Europas, dem auch die jungen Europäer - gewollt oder ungewollt - verpflichtet sind.

Darüber hinaus spiegeln sie aber auch den Geist des Universellen, den die Jugend der Welt in zunehmenden Maße eindrucksvoll vorlebt.

4.1.4 AUFGABEN

1. Besuchen Sie eine Behinderten-Organisation/Einrichtung und untersuchen Sie Aufbau und Strukturen dieser Organisation!
2. Gestalten Sie ein Bild (Poster, ...), um die Strukturen dieser Organisation zu visualisieren!
3. Schreiben Sie ein Stück zum Thema "Kundenorientierte Kommunikation", finden Sie Spieler und bringen Sie diese Inszenierung zur Aufführung! Dokumentieren Sie diese Aufführung durch eine Videoaufnahme!
4. Schreiben Sie ein Stück zum Thema "Vision(en) des Miteinander", finden Sie Spieler und bringen Sie diese Inszenierung zur Aufführung! Dokumentieren Sie diese Aufführung durch eine Videoaufnahme!

4.1.5 BIBLIOGRAPHIE

4.1.5.1 LITERATURVERZEICHNIS

Beck, M.(Hrsg.): Handbuch Sozialmanagement. Stuttgart 1995
Begemann, E.: Frieden als (ethisches) Ziel der (Sonderschul-) Erziehung. Anregungen zu einem Verständnis, das nicht mehr trennt zwischen Unterricht und Erziehung. In: Schmetz, D./Wachtel, P. (Hrsg.): Erschwerte Lebenssituationen: Erziehung und pädagogische Begleitung. Würzburg 1994
Bloch, E.: Das Prinzip Hoffnung. Frankfurt 1959
Bronfenbrenner, U.: Die Ökologie der menschlichen Entwicklung. Stuttgart 1981
Buber, M.(Hrsg.): Das dialogische Prinzip. Frankfurt 1979
Bundesvereinigung Lebenshilfe für Geistig Behinderte (Hrsg.): Normalisierung - eine Chance für Menschen mit geistiger Behinderung. Marburg/Lahn 1986
Decker, F.: Das große Handbuch; Management für soziale Institutionen. Landsberg/Lech 1997
Denger, J. (Hrsg.): Lebensformen in der sozialtherapeutischen Arbeit. Stuttgart 1995
Gehm, T.: Kommunikation im Beruf. Weinheim; Basel 1994
Gregor-Rauschtenberger, B. & Hansel, J.: Innovative Projektführung. Berlin Heidelberg 1993
Holzamer, H.-H. (Hrsg.): Management des Wandels. München; Landsberg am Lech 1996
Jacobs, K.: Die Dorfgemeinschaft auf anthroposophischer Grundlage im Blickwinkel von Normalisierung und Integration. In: Denger, J. (Hrsg.): Lebensformen in der sozialtherapeutischen Arbeit. Stuttgart 1995
Jonas, H.: Technik, Medizin und Ethik. Zur Praxis des Prinzips Verantwortung. Frankfurt 1987
Owens, R.G.: Organizational Behaviour in Education. Boston, London, Toronto, Sydney, Tokyo, Singapore 1995

Rogers. C.:	Therapeut und Klient. Frankfurt am Main 1991
Schmetz, D./ Wachtel, P. (Hrsg.):	Erschwerte Lebenssituationen: Erziehung und pädagogische Begleitung. Würzburg 1994
Schmidbauer, W.:	Die hilflosen Helfer. Über die seelische Problematik der helfenden Berufe. Reinbek 1977
Schulz von Thun, F.:	Miteinander Reden. Bd.1 und 2. Reinbek 1989
Singer, P.:	Practical Ethics. Cambridge University Press 1993
Speck, O.:	System Heilpädagogik. Eine ökologisch reflexive Grundlegung. München, Basel 1991
Tausch, R./Tausch, A.-M.:	Gesprächs-Psychotherapie. 9. Aufl.; Göttingen 1990
Ysseldyke, J./Algozzine, B.:	Critical Issues in Special and Remedial Education. Boston 1992
Weiß, J (Hrsg.).:	Selbstcoaching. Paderborn 1990

4.1.5.2 ZUSÄTZLICHE LITERATUR

Andersson, C.:	Organisationsteorie. Lund 1994
Campbell, J. and Oliver, M.:	Disability Politics: understanding our past, changing our future. London, Routledge 1996
Thylefors, I.:	Ledarskap i vard, omsorg och utbildning. Stockholm 1991

5. EUROPÄISCHE IDENTITÄT!

Wolf Bloemers

5.1 ZUSAMMENFASSUNG UND AUSBLICK

Am Ende des Lehrbausteines, in der Überschrift des abschließenden Modulkapitels, setzt das Ausrufezeichen noch einmal einen deutlichen Akzent, gibt ein klares Signal:

a) zum einen bekräftigt es ausdrücklich die davor stehenden Worte in ihrer Bedeutsamkeit, gleichsam als komprimierte Antwort auf das (die) Fragezeichen des einleitenden Kapitels und auf die anschließenden Fragen und Inhalte der folgenden Modulteile,

b) zum anderen macht es auch optisch sichtbar, daß mit diesem Aus-Ruf - als einem Heraus-Rufen in die Öffentlichkeit - zugleich ein Stück Aufgabe und Verpflichtung für die Zukunft besteht, bzw. gleichsam ein professioneller Auftrag erteilt wird.

zu a)

Wie die historischen, gesellschafts- und sozialpolitischen sowie kulturellen Analysen gezeigt haben, ist Europa mehr als eine Ansammlung individueller Staaten und verschiedener Völker. Es gibt ein aus vielen einzelnen Fäden im Laufe langer Zeit gesponnenes Netz von supranationale Identität stiftenden Gemeinsamkeiten, deren Existenz- und Wirksamkeitserfordernis angesichts der aktuellen Umbrüche und Herausforderungen heute mehr denn je offenkundig ist; dies schließt zugleich die Beibehaltung kleinräumiger, anderer Identitäten ein. Die Fäden des Netzes, gesponnen aus gemeinsamen Quellen und Erbe von gleicher Kultur, Politik und Wirtschaft - negativer wie positiver Ausformungen! - haben ein gemeinsames Verständnis und Verstehen hervorgebracht, das die pluralen Beiträge zu einem Gemeinsamen verwebt.

Als besonders bedeutsam, ja konstitutiv für das europäische Identitätsnetz erweisen sich - um in der "Netz"-Metapher zu bleiben - die sozialen "Knoten", die festen, das Netz tragfähig machenden Verbindungsstellen.

Die Tatsache, daß wir alle heute durch die grenzüberschreitenden Verknüpfungen kommerzieller, finanzieller, ökologischer Lebensadern und funktionalen Wechselwirkungen in gegenseitiger Abhängigkeit leben (vgl. BIDDISS 1997, 8) zwingt geradezu zu dem, was MITTERAND einmal "une théorie des ensembles" genannt hat, um für die soziale Wirklichkeit der gegenseitigen Abhängigkeit einen gemeinsamen, einen kommunikativ entwickelten sozialen Wertekanon zu entwerfen und die darauf aufbauenden konkreten, übergreifenden ("crossborder") praktischen Entscheidungen, eben die "Knoten" zu knüpfen. Davon gibt es - so hat das Modul gezeigt - noch zu wenige, so daß das derzeitige Netz hinsichtlich der Auffangfähigkeit vor allem für die Marginalisierten, für die Benachteiligten, für die Menschen an den Rändern noch viel zu grobmaschig ist.

Das Ausrufezeichen europäischer Identität als ein ethischer Imperativ zur Entwicklung transnationaler, sozialer und demokratischer "Miteinanderknoten" verstärkt und unterstreicht das entscheidende humansoziale Thema der "Anerkennung des Anderen" (CACCIATORE 1997, 93) und des radikaldemokratischen Rechtes des anderen Menschen auf eine Neubesinnung hin, theoretisch wie praktisch.

Dies schließt alle ein, besonders die bislang an den Rand gedrängten, die benachteiligten und sogenannten behinderten Menschen.

Hier lädt das Modul am Ende noch einmal zur kritischen Reflexion ein mit den Fragen, ob eine in der Entwicklung befindliche europäische Identität Behinderung (schon) einschließt und welche Anstrengungen vor allem auf sogenannte heilpädagogische und sozialpädagogische "Profis" zukommt, entsprechende theoretische und praktische Neubesinnungsschritte als berufliche Aufgabe wahrzunehmen und zu unternehmen. Das Ausrufezeichen gibt die Richtung vor, entsprechende Konsequenzen zu ziehen, zumal sich Heilpädagogik als Handlungswissenschaft begreift.

zu b)

Als Erklärung und Detaillierung professioneller Aufträge und Anregungen als Ergebnis des Moduls - überleitend zu b) - soll ein Philosoph zu Wort kommen, der das Thema "Europäische Identität" von der Rechtsseite der Andersheit her beleuchtet und nahe an LEVINAS Gedanken zur Akzeptanz der Asymmetrie des Anderen ist:

"Mit dem anderen leben, mit dem anderen des anderen leben, ist eine universelle und im Kleinen wie im Großen gültige Aufgabe. Wie wir im Heranwachsen und, wie man sagt, im Eintreten in das Leben lernen, mit dem anderen zu leben lernen, so ist es auch für die anderen Menschengruppen, Völker und Staaten. Und wahr-scheinlich ist es das Privileg Europas, daß es mehr als andere Länder lernen konnte und mußte, mit der Andersheit zusammenzuleben" (GADAMER 1989, 21 f, zitiert nach CACCIATORE 1997, 97).

Privileg und Verpflichtung, Chance und Aufgabe als zweite Ableitung/Interpretation aus dem Ausrufezeichen: Hier gibt es professionell etwas zu tun!

Wenn Sie bis jetzt den Gedankengängen gefolgt sind und sich Ihr Denken und Fühlen über Europa und seinen Menschen, vor allem denjenigen mit Lern- und Lebenser-schwernissen darin aufgrund der Bearbeitung der Modulmaterialien und -aufgaben geändert hat, ist hier nun die Gelegenheit, innezuhalten, die für Sie wesentlichen Veränderungsmerkmale im Wissen und Empfinden stichwortartig noch einmal zu skizzieren sowie konkrete Ideen, Vorschläge, Wünsche etc. für Ihre persönlichen Konsequenzen aus diesem Lernprozeß aufzuschreiben.

Dies können ganz verschiedene Handlungselemente sein, für sich selbst, für und mit anderen, Reflexionen, Diskussionen und vielerlei Aktionen: auf jeden Fall aber sollte es dabei um die Teilhabe, um das Einbezogensein bzw. um die Mitwirkung von Menschen mit Benachteiligungen und Behinderungen gehen, damit sie als gleichberechtigte Europäer ihre jeweiligen Beiträge zum Prozeß der europäischen Identität mit einbringen können.

Das sozial zusammenwachsende Europa bietet die - auch historische - große Chance, daß Menschen mit Benachteiligungen und Behinderungen in diesem Identitätsprozeß aus der bisherigen Randposition herauskommen und zu Mitgewinnern eines neuen humaneren sozialen Zusammengehörigkeitsgefühls, einer bisherigen - auch innere - Grenzen überschreitenden Lebensgemeinschaft zu werden.

Abschließend wünschen sich die Autorin und die Autoren dieses Moduls, daß nach seiner Bearbeitung Sensibilisierung, Neugier und vielleicht ein Stück sozialpolitisch orientierte Engagementbereitschaft für mehr europäische Verständigung über und eine schrittweise Realisierung von Normalisierung, Integration, Inklusion und Empowerment entstanden ist: dies sind - gemäß dem professionellen Fokus und dem fachlichen Theoriekanon von Heil- und SozialpädagogInnen - entscheidende Wertkonstituenten einer europäischen Identität für benachteiligte und behinderte Mitbürgerinnen und Mitbürger.

Europäische Identität muß - wie das Modul gezeigt hat - vermittelt und von allen *gelernt* werden. Hier bietet sich als ein gemeinsames Lern- und Gestaltungsfeld u.a. internationale Zusammenarbeit in Organisationen, Partnerschaften und Netzwerken an, in denen die gemeinsamen Perspektiven und Programme erarbeitet werden; deren Herstellungsprozeß und deren Produkte und Anwendungen können zum Wachstum der Identität sehr konkrete Beiträge liefern.

5.2 AUFGABEN

- Finden Sie heraus, wie sich Ihr individuelles Denken über Europa durch die Bearbeitung dieses Moduls verändert hat; dokumentieren Sie diesen Veränderungsprozeß mit einer Video- oder Tonbandaufnahme einer Diskussion zu diesem Thema oder mit einer persönlichen (schriftlichen) Reflexion.

5.3 BIBLIOGRAPHIE

5.3.1 LITERATURHINWEISE

BÜRLI, A.: Sonderpädagogik international. Luzern 1997

BAUMANN, U.:/KLESZEWSKI, R.: (Hrsg.) Penser l' Europe - Europa denken. Tübingen und Basel 1997

CLOERKES, G.: Soziologie der Behinderten. Heidelberg 1997

COUDENHOVE-KALERGI, R.: Ein Leben für Europa. Kampf um Europa. Aus meinem Leben. Zürich 1948

DEUTSCHE GESELLSCHAFT FÜR ERZIEHUNGSWISSENSCHAFT: Bildung und Erziehung in Europa. Beiträge zum 14. Kongreß des DFG. Weinheim und Basel 1994

EUROPÄISCHE GEMEINSCHAFT: Die Vertragstexte von Maastricht. Bonn 1992

FERNAU, J.:	Wie es euch gefällt. Eine lächelnde Stilkunde. Donauwörth 1969
JASPERS, K.:	Vom europäischen Geist. München 1947
KÜNG, H.:	Projekt Weltethos. München/Zürich 1991
LISSNER, I.:	Wir sind das Abendland. Gütersloh 1966
SCHLEICHER, K./BOS, W.: (Hrsg.):	Realisierung der Bildung in Europa. Darmstadt 1994
SCHLEICHER, K. (Hrsg.):	Zukunft der Bildung in Europa. Darmstadt 1993

5.3.2 ZUSÄTZLICHE LITERATUR

BAUMANN, U./ KLESZEWSKI, R.(Hrsg.)	Penser L´ Europe - Europa denken. Tübingen/Basel 1997

6. VORSCHLÄGE FÜR PORTFOLIO - AUFGABEN

- Verfolgen Sie die Medien, führen Sie Interviews und Umfragen durch und stellen Sie fest, ob es in Ihrem Land eine Kluft zwischen den Gesetzesgrundlagen und ihrer Umsetzung in der Praxis gibt.

- Erstellen Sie ein Portfolio über die Gesetzesgrundlagen, Richtlinien und Anordnungen, die es in Ihrem Land bezüglich des sozialen Bereiches für Menschen mit Behinderung gibt.

- Wie sehen Sie Europa? Stellen Sie Ihre Sichtweisen und Ihre Identitätsgefühle dar und begründen Sie diese.

- Legen Sie eine Themenmappe aus Printmedienerzeugnissen zur Problematik „Ausländerfeindlichkeit" an, suchen und begründen Sie Gliederungspunkte für die gefundenen Dokumente und stellen Sie Thesen zu Lösungsansätzen auf.

- Überlegen Sie, wie Sie persönlich einen Beitrag zur europäischen Integration leisten können. Schreiben Sie diese ganz detailliert auf. Falls Sie dies nicht können oder wollen, begründen Sie dies bitte.

- Machen Sie drei konkrete Vorschläge für eine öffentlichkeitsbewußte Bildungspolitik hinsichtlich des europäischen Integrationsprozesses in Ihrem Land.

- Identifizieren Sie bitte drei bildende Künstler von europäischer Bedeutung/Dimension/Format und begründen Sie Ihre Auswahl unter Verwendung konkreter Beispiele und deren Einordnungen in übergeordnete Werte- und Bewußtseinsvorstellungen.

- Besuchen Sie eine Organisation von / für Menschen mit Behinderung und legen Sie ihre Organisationsstruktur dar. Malen Sie ein Bild / Schreiben Sie ein Gedicht zur Verdeutlichung dieser Organisationsstruktur.

- Entwickeln Sie ein Portfolio, das die Aspekte einschätzt, die bei der Umgestaltung der räumlichen oder sozialen Infrastruktur eines bestimmten Lebensumfeldes von Bedeutung sind.

Es sollte beinhalten:
Veränderungsvorschläge
Finanzierungsgrundlagen
Relevante Gesetzesgrundlagen
Technische Anforderungen
Architektonische Entwürfe
Die Art des Planungsverlaufes
Interviews mit / Kontakt zu Benutzern dieser Umgebung

- Beschreiben Sie verschiedene Formen von Empowerment und Anwaltschaft (Advocacy) in Hinblick auf Behinderung, Lern- und Lebensschwierigkeiten und Benachteiligung in Ihrem Land.

SACHREGISTER

A
Abgrenzung 183 ff, 209 ff, 221, 252
Aktionsforschung 291
Akzeptanz 202, 215, 241, 252, 310, 316
Altersversorgung 269
Aktivität 212, 225, 235 ff, 252 ff, 291, 300 ff

B
Beeinträchtigung 224 ff, 235 ff, 248 ff, 293
Behandlung 221 ff, 237, 249, 284
Berufsausbildung 246
Betroffene 225 ff, 234 ff, 253, 278 ff, 306
Betroffenenprofil 278, 282, 294
Bewegung 184, 221, 252 ff, 282 ff
Bewußtsein, kritisches 180, 221
Bibliographie 232, 255, 276, 295, 313, 319
Bottom-Up-Strategie 282, 292

C
Chancengleichheit 225, 240, 251 ff, 294

D
Deutschland 182, 222 ff, 260 ff, 312
Diagnose 225, 237, 279

E
Ehrenamtlich 258 ff, 269 ff, 306
Einbeziehung von Betroffenen 172, 278, 295
Empowerment 242, 253, 278 ff, 317 ff
England 223, 249, 260, 266 ff
Entscheidungsfreiheit 282
Ethik 202
Eugenik 221 ff, 236
Eurobarometer 183, 188 ff, 209 ff
EG / Europäische Gemeinschaft 178, 203
Europäische Identität 184 ff, 193, 212, 318 ff
Europabedarf 199, 203, 322
Europäische Kultur 183
Europäisches Bewußtsein 178, 185, 199

Euroskepsis 184, 204
Experten 225, 250, 254, 278, 283, 295

F
Fähigkeit 203, 227, 238, 242 ff
Fertigkeit 246, 288, 293
Finanzierung 199, 305, 321
Fort- und Weiterbildung 309
Freizeit 238
Fremd 184, 202, 205 ff, 214
Führung 225, 242, 297 ff, 303

G
Gemeinschaft 179 ff, 200 ff, 242 ff, 292 ff
Gemeinsamkeit 187, 282, 288, 315
Genetik 227
Genmanipulation 227
Genstruktur 227
Gentechnologie 227
Gesetzesgrundlagen 272, 321
Gesundheitsversorgung 268
Gewalt 184, 206, 209
Großbritannien 221, 261, 271 ff
Grundwerte 201 ff
Gruppenarbeit 261, 279 ff, 286 ff, 295
Gruppenprozeß 286 ff

H
Heilpädagogik 180, 311
Heilung 236 ff
Heim 222 ff, 293 ff
Hilfsmittel 244
Hilfe zur Selbsthilfe 282

I
Identität 179 ff, 183 ff, 199 ff, 315 ff
Identität, soziale 186
Ich-Identität 186 ff

Identitätskonzept 191
Identitätstheorien 186 ff
Inclusion 246, 251 ff
Interaktion 191, 214, 247, 287, 308
Intervention 208, 226 ff, 283
Isolation 221, 287

K
Kategorien von Behinderung 249
Körperliche Perfektion 228
Körperliches Wohlbefinden 244
Kommunikation 168 ff, 187 ff, 303 ff
Kommunikationsfähigkeit 297, 304
Konflikt 205 ff, 299 ff, 306 ff
Konsens 259 ff, 265 ff, 303
Kontrolle 202, 234, 241 ff, 267, 293 ff
Konzept der päd. Erfordernisse 248 ff
Kooperation 180 ff, 197 ff, 201, 266, 291
Krise 199, 203, 242, 287
Kundenorientierung 308

L
Lean Management 307 ff
Lebensqualität 183, 226, 240 ff, 278, 289
Lebensstil 183, 202, 244
Lebensveränderung 287
Lernhilfen 251
Lernschwierigkeiten 224 ff. 234, 249 ff, 294

M
Management im Wandel 297
Marktorientierung 271
Materieller Wohlstand 244
Medizin 225 ff, 235 ff, 312
Medizinische Behandlung 213, 221 ff, 279
Medizinischer Zustand 237
Menschenbild 190, 203
Menschenrechte 182 ff, 203 ff, 284, 301
Mesosystem 298
Migranten 201 ff, 213
Mikrosystem 298 ff
Mitarbeitermotivation 309
Mitgestaltung 180, 212

Mobilität 170, 205, 213, 241 ff
Modelle
- Hierarchisch-direktives Stufenmodell 298 ff
- Interaktionsmodell 191
- Interaktives Kreismodell 301 ff
- Medizinisches Modell 236
- Soziales Modell 255

Modul 167 ff, 315 ff
Moral 182, 200 ff, 224, ff, 242, 253

N
Nachqualifikation 309
Netzwerk 214, 242, 268, 294, 318
Normalisierung 237, 253, 285, 302 ff, 317

O
Organisationsstrukturen 297 ff, 320

P
Partizipative Forschung 279, 291 ff
Personalmanagement 307 ff
Pflege 222 ff, 241 ff, 269 ff, 284 ff, 307
Portfolio 174, 255, 261, 275, 320
Prävention 283
Professionalisierung 306 ff

Q
Qualitätsmanagement 307 ff
Qualitätssicherung 309 ff

R
Rehabilitation 293, 305
Rollenverständnis 297 ff

S
Schädigung 220, 231 ff, 244 ff, 273, 293
Schweden 222, 260 ff, 266 ff, 293 ff
Selbstachtung 237, 241 ff
Selbstbestimmung 246

Selbshilfegruppe 279 ff, 286 ff, 306
Selbstkonzept 190
Selbstvertrauen 243, 248, 280 ff
Selbstwertgefühl 245 ff
Sozialformen 297, 303
Soziale Anpassung 287
Soziale Einzelarbeit 279
Soziale Gerechtigkeit 203, 221, 240, 323
Soziales Wohlbefinden 244
Sozialarbeiter 246, 279, 285 ff, 292
Sozialpolitik 228, 262 ff, 272 ff
Sozialsystem 267, 272, 285
Sponsoring 140 ff
Staatsbürgerkonzept 250
Stigmatisierung 237, 284, 287

T
Teilhabe 186, 190, 200, 208, 279, 317
Top-Down-Strategie 282

U
Umweltfaktoren 227

Unterdrückung 221, 229, 236 ff, 255, 288 ff
Unterordnung 228
Unterprivilegierung 291

V
Vererbung 227 ff
Versicherung 243, 263, 267 ff
Vision 181, 214, 286, 297 ff, 311 ff
Vorschrift 248, 272
Vorurteile 228 ff, 248 ff

W
Werte 185 ff, 200 ff, 241, 254, 262 ff, 320
Wertesystem 201, 205, 254
Wirksamkeit 315

Z
Zugang zu Arbeit und Beschäftigung 246
Zukunftsmodelle 271

AUTOREN

Prof. Dr. Wolf Bloemers, Fachhochschule Magdeburg, Deutschland
Dr. Bengt Eriksson, Universität Karlstad, Schweden
Åse-Britt Falch, MA, Universität Karlstad, Schweden
David Johnstone, B.Phil., M.Ed., M.Sc., Cert. Ed., Edge Hill University College, Ormskirk, England
Prof. Dr. Fritz-Helmut Wisch, Fachhochschule Magdeburg, Deutschland

WOLF BLOEMERS
Professor für Heil- und Sonderpädagogik an der Fachhochschule Magdeburg. Er ist der Koordinator des Studienganges "Heilpädagogik und Rehabilitation", Vorsitzender der Auslandskommission der Fachhochschule Magdeburg und verantwortlicher Koordinator des Europäischen Sokratesprogrammes zur Entwicklung europäischer Module. Hauptschwerpunkte seiner Arbeit sind die Internationalisierung von Studiengängen und das interdisziplinäre Denken, Forschen und Handeln.

BENGT ERIKSSON
Ph D in Sozialpädagogik, Hochschullehrer für Sozialwesen im Fachbereich Sozialwissenschaft der Universität Karlstad, Schweden. Berufserfahrung als Sozialarbeiter, danach Promotionsstudium. Besondere Forschungsinteressen: Evaluierung, Bewertung und Qualitätsverbesserung in den Bereichen Sozialwesen/Sozialarbeit; Forschung zu Lebensbedingungen alter und behinderter Menschen.

ÅSE-BRITT FALCH
MA in Sozialpädagogik; Seit 1990 Hochschullehrerin im Fachbereich Sozialwissenschaft der Universität Karlstad, Schweden. Nach vorheriger 10-jähriger Tätigkeit als Sozialarbeiterin in verschiedenen Bereichen -.zuletzt Arbeit mit geistig behinderten Menschen - wirkte sie mit an Forschungen zu Menschen mit Lernschwierigkeiten und an einer Studie im Bereich kommunaler Projekte für Eltern mit behinderten Kindern.

DAVID JOHNSTONE
Hochschullehrer am Edge Hill University College, Ormskirk, Lancashire, England. Er ist verantwortlicher Kursleiter des modularen Studiengangs "Disability and Community Studies". Er hat akademische Grade der Universität Birmingham und der Universität von Virginia und war Leiter einer Abteilung Sonderpädagogik für Studenten mit Lernschwierigkeiten. Johnstone kann zu dem Thema "Nachschulische Ausbildung von Jugendlichen und behinderten Menschen" eine Vielzahl von Veröffentlichungen vorweisen.

FRITZ-HELMUT WISCH
Professor für Heil- und Sonderpädagogik an der Fachhochschule Magdeburg. Als Gehörlosenlehrer war er u.a als Elternberater, in der Frühförderung, der Lehrer- und Gebärdensprachdolmetscherausbildung tätig. Fritz-Helmut Wisch ist Mitautor des deutschen Gebärdenlexikons, einem vierbändigen Nachschlagewerk mit 20.000 Zeichen. Interessenschwerpunkte: Kommunikation, Ethik, Integration behinderter Menschen.

ADRESSEN DER HOCHSCHULEN

EDGE HILL UNIVERSITY COLLEGE
St. Helens Road
Ormskirk/Lancashire L39 4QP
England

KARLSTAD UNIVERSITET
Universitätsgatan
S 650 09 Karlstad
Sweden

UNIVERSITY OF APPLIED SCIENCES, MAGDEBURG
FACHHOCHSCHULE MAGDEBURG
Breitscheidstr. 2
39114 Magdeburg
Germany

**European Social Inclusion
Sozialgemeinschaft Europa**

Edited by Wolf Bloemers and Fritz-Helmut Wisch

Band 1 Wolf Bloemers / Fritz-Helmut Wisch (eds.): Handicap-Disability-Learning and Living Difficulties: Policy and Practice in Different European Settings. European Module. EU-Socrates Programme. 2000.

Band 2 Wolf Bloemers / Fritz-Helmut Wisch (eds.): Quality of Life Research and Disabled People: Ways to Research in Different European Settings. European Module. EU-Socrates Programme. 2000.

Dušan M. Saviçeviç

Adult Education:
From Practice to Theory Building

Frankfurt/M., Berlin, Bern, New York, Paris, Wien, 1999. 272 pp.
Studien zur Pädagogik, Andragogik und Gerontagogik.
Edited by Franz Pöggeler. Vol. 37
ISBN 3-631-32730-7 · pb. DM 79.–*
US-ISBN 0-8204-3553-8

The Book presents the problems of adult education as a worldwide movement. It includes literacy of adults, the connections between work and adult education, current problems of universities, training and research of adult education, philosophy of lifelong education and conceptions of andragogy in different countries. All the problems are based on comparative considerations.

Contents: Literacy as a factor of social and individual development and basic human right · The relationship between work and education · University and adult education · Training and research in the field of adult education · Lifelong education as a humanistic philosophy of man · Roots and roard in evolution of andragogy

Frankfurt/M · Berlin · Bern · New York · Paris · Wien
Distribution: Verlag Peter Lang AG
Jupiterstr. 15, CH-3000 Bern 15
Fax (004131) 9402131
*incl. value added tax
Prices are subject to change without notice.